Beyond
the Wall

ELIZABETH POND

Beyond the Wall

Germany's Road to Unification

A TWENTIETH CENTURY FUND BOOK

The Brookings Institution
Washington, D.C.

About Brookings

The Brookings Institution is a private nonprofit organization devoted to research, education, and publication on important issues of domestic and foreign policy. Its principal purpose is to bring knowledge to bear on current and emerging policy problems. The Institution was founded on December 8, 1927, to merge the activities of the Institute for Government Research, founded in 1916, the Institute of Economics, founded in 1922, and the Robert Brookings Graduate School of Economics, founded in 1924.

The Institution maintains a position of neutrality on issues of public policy. Interpretations or conclusions in Brookings publications should be understood to be solely those of the authors.

Library of Congress Cataloging-in-Publication data
Pond, Elizabeth.
    Beyond the wall : Germany's road to unification /
Elizabeth Pond.
        p.   cm.
    "A Twentieth Century Fund book."
    Includes bibliographical references and index.
    ISBN 0-8157-7154-1 (cl)—ISBN 0-8157-7155-X (pa)
    1. United States—Foreign relations—Germany. 2.
Germany—Foreign relations—United States. 3.
Germany—History—Unification, 1990. 4. United States—
Foreign relations—1989– 5. Germany—Strategic aspects.
I. Title.
    E183.8.G3P67   1993   92-42273
    327.73043—dc20   CIP

9 8 7 6 5 4

The paper used in this publication meets the minimum requirements of the American National Standard for Information Sciences—Permanence of paper for Printed Library
Materials, ANSI Z39.48-1984

To Doris and Robert Peel

Foreword

The foresight of the American foreign policy community has been severely tested over the past five years. Only a handful of scholars—and virtually no important office holders—predicted the possibility of a quick exit of Soviet communism from the world stage. There is ample evidence, as well, that our government perceived Iraq, in terms of U.S. interests, quite specifically as an awkward but useful counterweight to Iranian power in the Middle East. If anyone foresaw the deployment of American troops in Somalia, they were very quiet about the prospect. And, while ethnic tensions in the Balkans are anything but new, there was little consideration of U.S. policy options in the event of hostilities among Serbs, Croats, and Bosnians.

All of us, then, are especially indebted to those journalists, academics, and international specialists who have been willing to set forth their immediate reactions to these events. The risk in doing so, of course, is that events are moving so fast that even tentative conclusions may be out of date before they appear in print. On the other hand, there probably has been no time in the past several decades when fresh insights were more important to the shaping of national security policy and foreign relations.

Nearly three years ago, already at work on this book project for the Twentieth Century Fund, Elizabeth Pond found herself an eyewitness to the unexpected and breathtakingly swift redrawing of the political map of Europe. Most authors would have been paralyzed by these mighty events. Instead, Pond readily answered our request to produce a paper—a combination of reporting and analysis—on the reuniting of the two Germanys. Now, as was the case with the groundbreaking *After the Wall* published in 1990, this new book-length account is likely to become part of the critical raw material for histories of this remarkable period in world affairs. From the perspective of U.S. foreign policy, particularly, we are seeing a significant flow of works searching for an understanding and road map for the post–cold war world. This volume, in fact, represents an important early step in that process.

Pond, a journalist based in Germany, is accustomed to putting her views on the line. In this work, as in her last, she writes with boldness, acknowledging that others working later may see things differently. Her efforts continue to be of value in the important debate about the meaning of the changes in Europe.

The Fund has several other books on U.S. foreign policy slated for publication over the next few years, including an examination of Europe's search for peace and security in the aftermath of the cold war by Jonathan Dean, an analysis of America's grand strategy after the cold war by Robert Art, a look at American interest in a new world order by Joseph S. Nye, Jr., and an exploration of future American foreign policy by Henry Nau.

The world of foreign affairs surely is not "normal" yet. There must be moments of uncertainty for policymakers that almost invite a nostalgia for the conventional understanding of the national interests that existed before the collapse of the Soviet empire—almost, but, of course, not quite. For only a fool would trade even the most serious threats of today for the "end of the world" character of yesterday's nuclear confrontation between the West and the Soviet bloc. The task now is to provide new form and substance to our discussions about the present and the foreseeable future.

The Foreword to Pond's paper noted that "now, at the beginning of the 1990s, we are all a bit like travelers on a suddenly frozen lake, delighted and uncertain about the prospect before us. The way forward seems freshly clear and easy, but we are hesitant, nonetheless, for who can tell if the bright new surface is firm enough to support a new direction." In 1993, it is already quite clear that the risks posed by the "new world" are varied and serious enough to deter reckless optimism. We need the help of many thinkers and much debate to find the best direction to take.

Therefore, on behalf of the Fund's Trustees, I want to thank Elizabeth Pond for her continued willingness to assess the events of the recent past and to argue her case concerning their implications for American policy in the 1990s.

Richard C. Leone, *President*
THE TWENTIETH CENTURY FUND
March 1993

Preface

An author must answer two questions: Why write this book? Why write it now? The easy answers to the first question would be: because I was there, an eyewitness to the first successful German revolution in history, and because this is the epic story of the half-century. I cannot resist writing an account of the tumultuous end of the cold war from its epicenter. The answer to the second question would be: because events of this magnitude and turmoil need a second draft of history while memories are still fresh.

To address the second point, first, that history buff and key shaper of U.S. European policy in the year of transformation, Robert Zoellick, argues that "the only reason writing history gets easier with time is the complexity gets reduced." That is music to the ears of a journalist awash in complexity, and a scandalous point of view in Germany, where contemporary history tends to cover what has happened since World War I, but in all decency to end in 1945. In the proper German view, historians should take a vow of silence about the twentieth century's revenge on the failed revolution of 1848 until perhaps 2025.

Yet I think a good case can be made for attempting a reckoning in the wake of whirlwind events. It is in the nature of revolutions like the one in Germany in 1989–90 that a host of individual actors are thrust onto the stage for a brief, intense experience, and are then cast back to their more habitual worlds. On the one hand, if their exceptional involvement is not captured at the instant, the recollection of it fades or plays tricks. On the other hand, the sheer speed and turbulence of events militate against any comprehension of their overall flow as they occur. An evaluation in the immediate aftermath can offer some balance.

To return to the first question, there is particular reason to write this account for an American audience, since there is so much misinformation abroad about the tectonic change that continues to rumble in Europe. At issue here is not simply the fact that war is more newsworthy than peace, and that the Iraqi conquest of Kuwait two weeks after Mikhail Gorbachev gave his nod to German unification on the West's terms crowded further news about Germany off front pages in the United States. Nor is the main point that events moved so fast that everything but the dancing on top of the Berlin Wall has blurred by now.

The issue goes much deeper than that. Curiously, every politically literate American assumes that he or she knows Germany. Yet Germany has for years been considered a boring, far-off land that fluctuates on the attention scale between indifference and irritation, and impinges on American awareness only when neo-Nazis hurl gasoline bombs, or peace activists brandish caricatures of U.S. presidents. Americans have far more innate understanding of the British, or even of the French, than they do of the Germans, and they do not realize it. Perhaps the portrayal of basic facts and dynamics given here can serve as a reality check on some of the wilder notions extant.

Certainly the lack of American public attention to Germany led in 1989–90, perhaps providentially, to Washington's German policy being conducted in a vacuum. The United States backed unification from before the opening of the Berlin Wall—and swift unification after the breach—and few Americans realized just how vigorous this support was. Washington twisted British and French arms ruthlessly to get full Western support for German unity. And in what the former German Foreign Minister Hans-Dietrich Genscher calls "seamless" coordination with the Federal Republic, the United States massaged the Russians into realizing that acquiescence to unification, with Germany remaining in NATO, was in their best interests too.

At a crucial point, then, American policymakers rejected the residual suspicion of Germans and trusted German democracy. The wealth of good will this reaped for the United States in Bonn and Berlin is phenomenal. Throw a question about the American role to German officials absorbed in domestic issues, with little international contact, and they still respond immediately, "Fantastic! Fabulous!"

Yet when other German officials—those whose work takes them continuously across the Atlantic—open a talk to an American audience with heartfelt thanks for U.S. help in unification, they meet with polite puzzlement. American policy toward Germany was conducted at a remove not only from the public, it seems, but even from the usual elites. It was not secretive, but somehow it went unnoticed. Apart from the very few players in the game, even the Bush administration itself never realized just how good its own policy actually was.

Nor is this just a question of ephemeral gratitude. In the process of close German-American cooperation in the twelve months from fall 1989 to fall 1990, a recognition of common interests was forged that continues. Bonn still needs America's weight and world outlook to counterbalance its more parochial European partners (and they certainly need the United States to counterbalance Germany). For its part, the United States needs Germany—as it needs Japan—to help lift an interdependent world out of a slump.

Politically, then, there is reason enough to write this book. However, there is also another, moral reason. That is, there is a tendency in hindsight to reinterpret the astonishing events of 1989–90 as inevitable. A kind of sociological determinism has set in. Yet that approach forgets the vertiginous, split-second choices that had to be made time and again, by both governments and individuals. The minute-by-minute decisions not to use violence by 70,000 demonstrators and perhaps 8,000 security forces in Leipzig on October 9, 1989, were far from predestined. It required civil courage for the marchers to go out that evening and maintain nonviolent discipline. A significant number of them really feared that they might be killed.

That civil courage—a quality that has been rare in German history—has now been largely forgotten. It should be remembered. It was not the Russians who brought the East Germans their liberation (despite the hazy assumption of many Americans that this must have been the process). It was the East Germans themselves who seized the opportunity Gorbachev offered them. This book is written in part in tribute to the lathe operators and hairdressers and teachers of Leipzig who were suddenly fed up with the *Bevormundung* (guardianship) of being ordered about like kindergartners, and rebelled.

Yet another reason for writing this book would be Germany's role as a fulcrum in Eastern as in Western Europe. More than any other capital, Bonn and Berlin will decide what becomes of Jean Monnet's dream of a united (Western) Europe. More than any other capital, Bonn and Berlin will ease the difficult reception of Eastern Europe back into Europe proper.

These are both historic involvements the United States can only welcome as being in its own interests. We may not be leaving an American century, but we are surely entering, again, a European century. A real transatlantic community already exists. It behooves American citizens of that community to know what its eastern compatriots are doing, and especially what the most energetic of them, the Germans, are doing.

On a more personal note, there is one final reason to write this book. I lived in Czechoslovakia during the Prague Spring and Soviet invasion of 1968. I wish to record here that in the end, the Prague Spring did not fail.

Elizabeth Pond

Acknowledgments

My thanks go to Robert Gerald Livingston for prodding me to write this book; to the Twentieth Century Fund for financing it and waiting patiently for the manuscript; to the 100-plus actors in the events of 1989–92 whom I interviewed; to the Institute for the History of the Workers' Movement in Berlin for access to the Central Party Archives; to New Forum Leipzig for permission to quote interviews from *Jetzt oder nie-Demokratie!*; and to Donald Bandler, Jeffrey Boutwell, Frank Elbe, Hartmut Jäckel, Wolfgang Schlör, Elisabeth Wendt, Philip Zelikow, and participants in a seminar at the American Institute for Contemporary German Studies in Washington for commenting on various portions or versions of this book. In particular, I am grateful to Catherine Kelleher and David Schoenbaum for their generous professional and personal friendship in the course of writing this book.

Any questionable historical analogies I nonetheless insisted on drawing are not the fault of any of these readers.

I also thank Alice S. Dowsett for wrestling with my prose and Nancy D. Davidson of Brookings for shepherding the book there.

Portions of this book appeared previously in my monograph, *After the Wall: American Policy toward Germany* (Twentieth Century Fund, 1990). An excerpt appeared in "Germany in the New Europe," *Foreign Affairs*, vol. 71 (Spring 1992), pp. 114–30.

E. P.

Contents

1	November 1989	1
2	Prologue West	13
3	Prologue East	20
4	Nuclear Angst and Reassurance	33
5	Meanwhile, Europe	56
6	Meanwhile, Eastern Europe	69
7	Annus Mirabilis	85
8	The October Revolution: Dresden and Berlin	100
9	The October Revolution: Leipzig and Berlin	111
10	The Wall Falls	130
11	Taming the *Stasi*	140
12	Accleration	153
13	Two Plus Four Equals One Germany	173
14	Meanwhile, Domestic Politics	192
15	Denouement	210
16	Hangover	225
17	Agenda for America	249
Bibliographical Essay		271
Notes		289
References		330
Index		359

Chapter 1

November 1989

When the Berlin Wall fell, the crash obliterated a country, an empire, and an era. The fall redeemed the failed revolution of 1848, Europe's cavalier slide into war in 1914, and Hitler's rise to power in 1933. It lifted the specter of nuclear holocaust, yet expanded the paradoxical long peace the balance of terror had bestowed on a quarrelsome Europe.[1] For the first time since romantic demons were loosed among the Germans, it sealed their Western identity and began to heal their right-left schism. It united them once more, this time benignly, and demystified their existential questions into the more tolerable politics of everyday bickering. Mischievously, it let the United States drop its fixation on its superpower twin, hold up a mirror to its domestic self, and recoil. More malignly, the wall's disappearance dissolved the old pax sovietica into ancient blood feuds.

The Wall Comes Down

The upheaval began with an announcement that East German Politburo member Günter Schabowski made one Thursday, just in time for the evening television news. Henceforth, he let drop at the end of an hour's rambling press conference, East Germans could cross the border into West Germany.

There was utter confusion as to what he actually meant. Many East Germans thought that the thousands of emigrants who were deserting the German Democratic Republic (GDR) via the hole that had recently opened in Czechoslovakia could now go directly to the Federal Republic of Germany. Others surmised that the East-West German border proper—excluding the infamous wall sealing the enclave of West Berlin off from

1

surrounding East Germany—was now open. Still others tentatively took his words to mean that at last East Germans, who had been cooped up in the bleak Soviet bloc for four decades, could all travel freely.

The Politburo itself—or, more precisely, Schabowski and fledgling party General Secretary Egon Krenz, the Politburo's only two functioning members after the GDR's paralyzed old guard had been dumped the day before—apparently did intend to open all border crossings, but only in coming days and only in a bureaucratic fashion, with stamped visas for most, but continued rejection for some.

Within minutes of the proclamation, however, intent was irrelevant. A popular "explosion," as one East German official described it, occurred.[2] East Berliners rushed to the exits to West Berlin that had been barred to them for twenty-eight years—and found them still barred. This time, though, they did not just abandon the attempt and docilely go home. Instead, they planted themselves in place. They were used to standing in line, and they were patient, but they insisted with growing vehemence— and with swelling reinforcements and ever more Western television crews recording each gesture—that the armed, but vastly outnumbered, border guards let them pass. "Open the gate! Open the gate!" chanted the throng at Bornholmer Strasse, then added, as a good-humored promise, that if they were allowed this taste of the West they would still return to the GDR: "We'll come back! We'll come back!"

The date was November 9, 1989, the fifty-first anniversary of Hitler's Kristallnacht rampage against the synagogues, and the seventy-first anniversary of imperial Germany's collapse in World War I.

The rollercoaster of emotions that night went from a collective leap of joy, to deep-seated dread, to stubborn determination, then back to ecstasy. Even as the East Berliners began their vigil, the West German Bundestag heard the news and spontaneously broke into singing the national anthem. For whatever reason—awe, premonition, or perhaps a yearning for a new life for their Eastern brothers and sisters—this time the Green members of parliament did not walk out at such a display of national sentiment. The moment of truth had come, when the Westerners could only wait and watch and sing.

For more than three hours the crowds and the tension mounted as the standoff dragged on at the checkpoints between East and West Berlin. Then some taunts rang out, and some pushing and shoving erupted between East Berliners at the front of the pack and the border guards they confronted nose to nose.

The city's Soviet and Western military commanders—the four victorious powers of World War II were still legally responsible for the security of Berlin and of "Germany as a whole"—worried about the volatile situation. They contacted one another and stayed in constant touch throughout that night and the next few days to avoid dangerous misunderstandings. At any moment, they feared, tempers might flare or someone might panic as the irresistible force met the immovable object. No one was sure how the GDR border troops, the National People's Army (NVA), the *Stasi* (East Germany's secret police), or even the Soviet KGB might react. Ultimately, "the choice was either to let them through or shoot," explained a senior allied officer in West Berlin.[3]

By 10:30 P.M., the ranking East German border guards at Bornholmer Strasse and three other crossing points in the center of the city—still facing the crowds and still lacking instructions—made their unthinkable choice.[4] These servants of the most rigidly Prussian code of obedience and hierarchy in the entire Soviet bloc took authority into their own hands and opened the gates.[5]

The dike was breached. The flood could no longer be held back. By 11 P.M. East German Interior Minister Friedrich Dickel acknowledged the fait accompli and confirmed the local commanders' desperate decision with an official order.[6]

The multitude spilled through the openings. Suspense exploded into revelry. Western hosts, joining the fairy tale come true, dashed to the spots where East Berliners were pouring in, showered chocolate and carnations and gummibears on their guests, thumped their two-stroke Trabant cars in welcome, and even called the Trabis' nitrous plumes the perfume of freedom. Eyes shone. Tears flowed unashamedly. Total strangers embraced. New friends deluged each other with champagne. They shouted, sang, danced, ran, skipped, played, effervesced. Then, as one, they exorcised the wall forever by transforming it from a prison to a stage. In front of the Brandenburg Gate they clambered on top of it, and kept finding room to haul up yet another person, as in some gigantic circus trick. "The wall must fall," they chanted. "We shall overcome," they sang.

Even the GDR border guards and NVA troops were swept up in the jubilation, metamorphosing instantly from jailers to fellow celebrants. Here one officer accepted flowers tucked into his rifle. There another sheepishly gave away his hat to a girl who asked for it and won a kiss in return. At the Brandenburg Gate a third initially held fast to the cordon blocking public access, then succumbed to the anguish and tears of a grandmother who wanted just once in her life to walk to this symbol of Berlin, and escorted her there himself. Transfixed, the entire world watched the drama.

Early on, a few people standing on the "antifascist defense wall" started hammering at it as if they really meant to demolish it. At that point the East German police finally intervened with water cannon. Yet even this display of force was half-hearted: the law enforcers elevated the trajectory so that the jet would not blast all the roustabouts off the wall with full impact and possible injury, and left one grinning Berliner perched on the crest with his umbrella raised as a shield against the torrent.

The British, who administered the sector in the heart of the city, took no chances. They dispatched a military band to play at the wall, not only to help ease the atmosphere, but also to keep an inconspicuous eye on things. To avert any risky buildup of idle crowds in the formerly deserted Reichstag grounds that were now the focus of the events, they provided unmarked buses to shuttle passengers to and fro. To avoid the need for British riot control operations that might set off an international incident, they authorized the West Berlin police to enter the no-man's strip of East German territory west of the wall for the first time in twenty-eight years. Thus it was German police who prevented West Berliners fired by a generation's cumulative rage—or perhaps only the adrenaline of the moment—from tearing down their own segment of wall and bursting through to challenge the police on the other side.

The improvisation worked. In the end, the British band did not have to drop its trombones to contain violence, there were no *Stasi* provocations, and Berliners' suppressed wrath was engulfed by the new exuberance. In the next few days the wall avengers mellowed into wall woodpeckers, chiseling souvenirs out of the ugliest and now most superfluous piece of architecture in Berlin. One cyclist even rode atop the wall. His feat lay less in keeping his balance on the straight and narrow than in finding that rare moment when his way was not totally blocked by bodies.

As the novel relaxation spread throughout the GDR, one eleven-year-old in Karl Marx Stadt rushed home from school to tell his parents the fantastic news that his teacher had said "good morning" when she entered the classroom, and the class too had responded with "good morning" (instead of the rote exchange of "be prepared," "always prepared"). A nine-year-old Leipziger, asked to write about the most exciting experience in his life, described the adventure as his family drove into West Germany and the border guard actually smiled at them. And in fulfillment of every child's dream, the government canceled Saturday classes for the rest of the year, as so many pupils and teachers would otherwise be playing hooky in the Federal Republic.

On November 10, in front of his city hall, West Berlin Mayor Walter Momper told the first joint gathering of East and West Berliners in decades that Germans were now the happiest people on earth. Willy Brandt, the city's mayor when the wall sprang up in 1961, the West German chancellor who began *Ostpolitik* (Eastern policy) détente in 1969, and now, after a lifetime of partisan battles, the avuncular elder statesman, seconded the view of his fellow Social Democrat. "What belongs together is now growing together," he proclaimed.[7] Only conservative foes were churlish enough to remind him that shortly before the eruption in the GDR, Brandt himself had dismissed the Christian Democrats' striving for one Germany as a "life-long delusion."

Chancellor Helmut Kohl, who over the years had promoted that life-long delusion more doggedly than any other politician, was also on the podium, having interrupted a visit to Poland to be present at the making of history. He expected no immediate reward from his lightning trip. On the contrary, he anticipated the heckling he had to suffer from a group of West Berlin leftists. With an eye on the general election a year away, however, he was determined to avoid Konrad Adenauer's mistake of 1961. Then the first West German chancellor, deferring to the Western allies' request for restraint, had decided not to visit the beleaguered city after the Berlin Wall went up overnight. In consequence, he had taken a drubbing in the next election.[8]

In the course of the rally, Kohl at least had the mixed satisfaction of receiving an urgent message from Soviet President Mikhail Gorbachev asking the chancellor to try to calm down public passions in East as well as in West Berlin. Kohl welcomed Gorbachev's acknowledgment of a certain West German authority in East Berlin and implicit recognition that unification would be the central issue.[9] He worried, however, that the KGB or *Stasi* might be inciting Gorbachev to let the tanks roll by feeding him disinformation portraying the peaceful crowds as unruly. Kohl therefore stressed to Gorbachev that everything was under control and that a happy festival spirit prevailed.[10] The West Germans' concern that Gorbachev's message held a veiled warning was allayed only by the friendly phone conversation between Gorbachev and Kohl on November 11.[11]

Oblivious to this or any other threat for the first time in half a century, ordinary Germans continued their festival over the weekend. Easterners ate free pea soup; drank free beer; attended West German soccer games, rock concerts, and the Berlin Philharmonic for free; picked up their DM 100 "welcome gifts" from West German banks that had stayed open on Saturday and Sunday; and then bought Walkmans and jeans jackets at shops that had also been excused from adhering to the strict legal closing hours. They rode without tickets on West Berlin subways in densities approaching Tokyo levels. They collected free city maps and coffee, and that ultimate symbol of unattainability, bananas. A few had the good fortune to hear Mstislav Rostropovich, who sped to Checkpoint Charlie to play his beloved Bach cello suites there alfresco. Many more would later hear Leonard Bernstein conduct Beethoven's Ninth Symphony, and in artistic license that no German would dare take, change *Freude* (joy) to *Freiheit* (freedom) in the sacred Schiller text.

"We found we weren't so different after all," mused one East Berlin communist who lived two minutes away from the wall, but had never before set foot in West Berlin.

Soon he would change his mind, and so would disgruntled Western taxpayers. Yet he uttered a truth for those few extraordinary days of personal unification. In those magical hours Germans discovered not only that they could be as spontaneous as Latins, but also that they really were one people. West Germans, who had tended to support reunification in the abstract while finding their poor relations something of a burden in the flesh, realized that they really did care a great deal about their brothers and sisters. East Germans, who had half feared the West's chaos and violence, were dazzled instead by the casual opulence and generosity they encountered.

Three Weeks That Shook Off the Party

Afterward, the East German communists tried to patch Humpty Dumpty together again. Many different metaphors occurred to the various embarrassed observers of the disintegration, who for years had agreed that the GDR regime was entrenched and formidable. Some now called it a house of cards; others said it had been a grand building with an imposing facade that was suddenly found to be rotten at the core. "We created ruins without weapons," any number of East Germans began saying, not only a sardonic reference to the collapse of institutions and the physical decay of buildings unrepaired for half a century, but also a pun on the peace movement's slogan: "Create peace without weapons."

Civil society now reasserted itself against politics, then came to determine politics. Inside and outside the ruling party, pluralism burgeoned and political actors proliferated. To begin with, cracks appeared between rivals—in this case, Krenz and Schabowski—as is typical of an unstable succession period in a one-party system. Then institutionally, responsibility devolved from the incapacitated party to the government under reforming Prime Minister Hans Modrow. The somnolent parliament and nominally noncommunist "bloc parties" were revitalized. And in a conflict of generations, younger communists revolted and took to the new political fashion in their own mass demonstrations for the acceleration of Socialist Unity (Communist) party reforms.[12]

On Friday, the day after the wall opened, Krenz continued his earlier strategy of limited reforms from above just as if his whole world had not fractured. From the Central Committee he got formal approval for his action program proposing economic liberalization, freedom of assembly and association, and free, secret elections with multiple candidates. Under the program, discussion within the Socialist Unity party (SED) was to be broadened, but once decisions had been made, the discipline of democratic centralism from above would still prevail.

As so often since Krenz had been propelled into office three weeks before, it was too little too late. Four full or candidate members of his new Politburo had to give up their posts immediately because they were voted down in an unprecedented revolt by their local party organizations. Some 150,000 Communist party members again gathered outside the Central Committee building to protest the SED's slow evolution and to demand a full party congress in December with powers to dismiss the old Central Committee. Krenz's royal gesture in coming out to talk to them and assure them that the leadership understood the problems, instead of mollifying them, only infuriated them.

By Sunday the reshuffled Politburo gave in and approved a party congress. The West and East Berlin mayors shook hands at the new crossing point hacked out at Potsdamer Platz, the most egregious example of the wall's ruthless slicing through the heart of a neighborhood, separating two generations of children from their local park. The Interior Ministry announced that in the past three days it had already issued 4.3 million passports for travel to the West.

On Monday campaigns for the first ever open elections of delegates began in local party units. In Leipzig 200,000 people, unpacified and undiverted by the new lure of the golden West, turned up at the regular Monday prayers and demonstration.[13] Docent Christoph Kähler, preaching in the Nikolai Church, could not resist the clear parallel of Biblical Jericho: "When the trumpets sounded on the seventh day, the walls fell, of their own accord. A miracle!" he exclaimed. "On seven Mondays the Leipzigers encircled the city and called, 'Wir sind das Volk' [We are the people]. Then the wall fell, of its own accord, but, thank God, without violence. That is our peaceful revolution, a miracle. . . .

"But still [another wall] has fallen, the wall in our heads. That is the division between our own real opinion and what we dared say. That is the caution that we learned as children, then transmitted further to our children, in order to protect them. That is the game of hiding our thoughts, a game that relegated our most important political thinking to the arts and the church rather than the marketplace or city hall, where it actually belonged."[14]

Some activists had worried that the heady bread and circuses of bananas and free travel would sap political discontent and allow the old regime to reconsolidate. Instead, the maxim that the worst time for tyrants is when they improve things held true. Far from satisfying people who had felt victimized by the regime, reforms only raised their expectations and inspired the beneficiaries to ask for more. On November 13, just as on

November 6, the Leipzig crowds poured out of the Nikolai Church to make the next set of radicalized demands that Krenz would never catch up with.

Parliament Rejuvenated

Yet as the East Germans now turned from the elemental yearning for travel, free elections, and throwing the bums out and progressed to more complex choices about how to structure their new polity, the Leipzig Mondays in the Nikolai Church could no longer function adequately as the national town meeting. The first substitute consisted of the legislature and bloc parties that for forty years had been the SED's puppets. Gingerly at first, and then in a rush, these began shedding their obeisance to the SED's leading role, as enshrined in article 1 of the constitution.

The Liberals and the Democratic Farmers party sounded out the dissidents' New Forum and other fledgling political clubs with proposals of cooperation, and were scorned. The Christian Democrats ejected Gerald Götting, the communist clone who had run the party for decades, and selected as its less malleable new chairman Lothar de Maizière, an erstwhile professional violist, a lawyer who had defended dissenters, a vice president of the Protestant Synod, and the GDR's unlikely future prime minister. He wrestled with his decision all night before accepting, he said, but in the end agreed to do his part to ensure that the next generation of children would no longer have to lie, to be "Janus-headed and double-tongued."[15]

As the bloc parties quickened in mid-November, the SED decayed. Many local communist officials resigned, were kicked out, or, in at least three cases, committed suicide. The old communist leaders of the Free German Trade Union, the Free German Youth, and all the other mass organizations were deposed, along with the old editors of the party newspapers.[16] Hundreds of thousands of members quit the party; within months the rolls would shrink from 2.3 million to some 700,000.[17] The rolls of the Free German Youth also dropped, from close to 2 million to some 1 million. Not even the abruptly begun party expulsions and prosecution of old Politburo members, nor the equally abrupt rehabilitation of victims of Stalinism, could restore the party's reputation.

Parliament, which had met for only a few days every year, and until November had unanimously passed every resolution but one presented to it by the SED, now began to flex some muscle. After four weeks of ignored demands for its convening from individual Volkskammer delegates and the new grass-roots organizations, parliament finally met on Monday, November 13, and staged one unprecedented scene after another. Horst Sindermann, speaker for thirteen years, resigned. The Volkskammer promptly elected a new presidium, voting for the first time with secret ballots, and held the first real debate in its history. The just-deposed strongman of eighteen years, Erich Honecker, his wife Margot, and twenty-five other SED deputies gave up their seats. The remaining deputies suddenly began grilling various officials, including Sindermann and the outgoing prime minister of twenty-two years, Willi Stoph. They extracted from Finance Minister Ernst Höfner the previously classified information that firms in the GDR had 130 billion ost marks of internal debts (though at this point they could not yet extract the crucial figure of external debt, later revealed as $20.6 billion, double previous official figures).[18]

The Volkskammer even insisted on questioning the dreaded Erich Mielke, minister for state security for the past thirty-two years. Never before had the eighty-two-year-old felt obliged to report to parliament. Now the man who had administered the whole poisonous system of internal spying automatically addressed his listeners as comrades, and could not grasp why the noncommunist delegates bridled at this appellation. Grotesquely he justified himself with the explanation, "But I love you all!" Derisive laughter filled the chamber and the living rooms of those watching on television.

Many Germans watching Mielke's stumbling performance even concluded that he was senile. West German intelligence officers who interviewed him a year later did not share this view, and saw in his Volkskammer presentation a deliberate, spirited defense of the *Stasi*. In his parliamentary remarks, Mielke complained bitterly that party and government leaders had ignored all the excellent information his ministry had given them about unrest in the country in 1989. "We presented it. Believe me! Believe me! We did present it to them," he protested. "The only problem is that much of what we reported was not taken into consideration, was not appreciated."[19]

On Tuesday, November 14, censorship was lifted in the GDR.

On Wednesday, November 15, the GDR's general prosecutor applied to the courts to rehabilitate Walter Janka, an old communist intellectual and editor of the leading East German publishing house, Aufbau, in the 1940s and 1950s. He had been imprisoned in Hitler's Germany, had been wounded three times in the Spanish Civil War, had lived in exile in Mexico, and had returned to Germany's Soviet zone in 1947. In 1957, in an anachronistic show trial four years after Stalin's death, he was convicted of crimes against the state (in reality for conspiring to get Marxist philosopher György Lukacs out of Budapest after the suppression of the Hungarian revolt the previous year). Janka served four years in an isolation cell, was released from prison, then, three decades later in May 1989, was awarded a Service to the Fatherland medal. True to his Marxist-Leninist faith, he kept to himself his memories of abandonment by party comrades and leading East German writers. Only when Honecker sent Schabowski and Krenz to China in summer and fall 1989 to sanction the Tienanmen massacre of prodemocracy students did Janka finally break his silence and submit his manuscript, *Difficulties with the Truth*, to a Hamburg publisher for publication in West Germany.[20]

His case was perhaps nothing special, only one of hundreds of drearily similar tragedies of European communists in a grim twentieth century. It was the first such detailed account, however, in an East Germany that had skipped the kind of de-Stalinization that the rest of Central Europe had undergone. It still came as a shock to many, and ended their last attachment to the SED. "I hadn't known about Janka," explained one docent at East Berlin's Humboldt University in answer to the question of why she had remained loyal to the party until the end of 1989. She had heard about Janka's manuscript, and of the old man's appearance at a special reading in his honor at the German Theater in East Berlin on October 28. She was among the rank-and-file communist demonstrators who besieged the Central Committee plenum in November. Disgusted with Krenz's response, she would become one of the few women on the SED's emergency steering committee in December, then give up and campaign for the feminist party.

On Friday, November 17, in his maiden speech, Prime Minister Modrow promised that his government would institute even more far-reaching political, legal, economic, environmental, educational, and administrative reforms than Krenz had already done, with greater transparency and accountability. He wanted to do everything possible, Modrow said, "so that the democratic renewal of the whole of public life just begun will get and maintain deep roots."

The energized Volkskammer welcomed the government declaration and established its own committees to probe past corruption and misuse of office. On Saturday, November 18, it heard an initial report from the state prosecutor on brutality against demonstrators in East Berlin and elsewhere the previous October 7 and 8. Some seventy-six investigations were under way, it was told, that might lead to indictments of police officers and secret police officers. The same day New Forum, the group that had spearheaded those protests, held its first officially permitted meeting; 50,000 people attended.

That weekend, the second after the breaching of the wall, the East German news service ADN reported that more than 3 million East Germans had visited West Germany and West Berlin. A total of 10.3 million visas had been issued for travel to the West, and fifty new border crossings had been knocked out of the wall in Berlin and along the East-West German border. That Sunday Krenz moved out of the elite ghetto of suburban Wandlitz to a more humble Berlin apartment under the glare of television cameras. Hundreds of thousands demonstrated in various cities for an end to the communist monopoly on power and for punishment of those responsible for the country's crisis. In less than a month Mielke and two-thirds of the old Politburo would be the subjects of prosecutors' investigations.

By Tuesday, November 21, the Planning Commission had scrapped half of its compulsory production targets for firms. East Berlin lawyer Götz Berger, who had had his legal license revoked in 1976 after he had defended communist dissident Robert Havemann and criticized the stripping of GDR citizenship from balladeer Wolf Biermann, was rehabilitated. The same day Culture Minister Dietmar Keller personally received Walter Janka and admitted that the ministry had "left him in the lurch." Two days later Janka's party card was restored.

On Thursday, November 23, the SED expelled Honecker's confidant and economic czar Günter Mittag from the party and began to investigate abuse of office by Honecker himself. The GDR's Writers' Union readmitted Stefan Heym and eight other members it had expelled for nonconformity in 1979. The film *Trail of the Stones*, banned in 1966, was given its premier showing after a twenty-three-year delay. Yet that same day the Dresden *Stasi* issued a new command ordering surveillance of New Forum members.

On December 1 the Volkskammer, after deliberations that lasted all of fifteen minutes, voted to strike from the constitution article 1 guaranteeing the leading role of "the working class and its Marxist-Leninist party."

As breathtaking as they were, the political changes could not reverse the GDR's tailspin. In November industrial production dropped 2.5 percent below that of the previous year. Also in November 130,000 more East Germans moved to the Federal Republic, for an interim 1989 total of 305,000. West German athletic halls, pressed into use as temporary dormitories after the regular refugee camps and Bundeswehr barracks overflowed, themselves began to spill over. Disgruntled West Germans complained about a coming unification by evacuation. Old jokes revived about instructing the penultimate person to quit the GDR to leave a note to Erich (Honecker) asking him to turn out the lights when he too left.

By now the note would also have to be addressed to Todor, Milos, and Nicolae. Within ten days of the wall's fall, the East German revolution had leapt to Bulgaria and Czechoslovakia.[21] Soon it would consume the Romanian despots in the one country where it turned bloody. More slowly, it would catalyze a coup in Moscow that would fail, but would accelerate the final implosion of the three-century-old Russian empire. Within ten months Germans would be united and squabbling like any old married couple. Within a year and a half Yugoslavia would be a caldron.

This was not the way the cold war was supposed to end in anybody's book.[22] Peace activists had hoped for a preliminary improvement in human nature and a rejection of those Mephistophelian nuclear weapons, and had feared that a nuclear catastrophe might first have to sober mankind into giving up stereotypes of enemies. The left had bet on Western acceptance of Communist party rule in Eastern Europe based on a humane "third way" between Stalinist and capitalist exploitation that would be egalitarian, ecologically sound, and socialist.

Western conservatives were much closer to the mark in anticipating the rout of Marxism in Eastern Europe once the guns were removed and people discovered that democracy and a (relatively) free market constrain the human spirit far less than any other system. But in its heart of hearts, the right had not believed that the West's policy of containment of Soviet ambitions abroad really would turn the Kremlin inward to domestic reform. Even the diplomatic practitioners of containment, studiously avoiding its inflation into "rollback" after 1956, had worried that uncontrolled East European surges for freedom might upset stability and risk war. Gradualism was the order of the day. German division was deemed necessary for stability and peace. Reunification would be possible only, if at all, at the end of a long process of East-West rapprochement, after the opposing blocs had vanished. Everyone knew that the GDR would be the last to free itself from Soviet tutelage.

Chapter 2

Prologue West

How did the unthinkable happen? Surely the answer has to start with the political as well as the economic miracle of postwar West Germany.

Few dared hope in 1945 that the rigid, authoritarian, and obeisant Germans could shed the curse of history and re-create themselves as democrats in one generation. Countess Marion Dönhoff, for one, an ardent opponent of Hitler since the 1930s and a key contributor to the subsequent metamorphosis of the Federal Republic as editor and publisher of the weekly *Die Zeit*, thought her countrymen stood no chance. "I had experienced the Weimar Republic [established in Germany after World War I] as a young adult. . . . I had never experienced [real] democracy. I was quite typical. I said to myself: this democracy of Weimar produced Hitler. It's obvious—a society is an organism. How can you break up an organism into pure atoms and then bring them together again?" She conducted vehement arguments with British occupation officials who insisted that a democracy of individuals was possible, and she would only gradually conclude in retrospect that "we must be very thankful to the occupation powers for not leaving us to our own devices."[1]

The opportunity for such fundamental transformation arose in large part from the very totality of Hitler's debacle, and the obliteration of the old structures and dogmas that would otherwise have blocked change. There was a "caesura" in 1945, explains Count Wolf von Baudissin, designer of the training program to inculcate democratic conduct among soldiers in the armed forces that were reconstituted in the 1950s.[2] Whatever the subsequent left-right polemics about the authenticity of the *Stunde Null* (zero hour), as that period was popularly called, it was one of those rare fluid moments in history, and it permitted the invention of such notions as the concept of "inner leadership" that Baudissin tried to instill.

To be sure, it was no French Revolution. There was no euphoria that suddenly everything might be created anew. There was, however, the tabula rasa of a shattered, demoralized society, with concrete tasks of reconstruction facing the "rubble ladies" whose husbands, brothers, and sons had perished in the war. Alongside the shame of barbarity, disaster, and occupation, there was the possibility of evolution and growth. Thousands of young adults were going abroad for an intensely formative year of study at Harvard, Oxford, or the Sorbonne and returning home determined to build a more decent and open community.

Incorporation of the Right

Chancellor Konrad Adenauer's autocratic tutelage of his West German countrymen in the ways of democracy—a chancellor-democracy as people derisively called it—is easy to fault. Himself a Catholic with an impeccable record of opposition to Hitler, Adenauer nevertheless appointed as his aide one of the drafters of the infamous Nuremberg race laws, Hans-Maria Globke. Eschewing punishment, Adenauer sought instead to integrate back into society those who had supported Hitler. Early on, he called for an end to the witch hunt for Nazis, and after the cold war started, the Western powers also abandoned their de-Nazification program prematurely in their perceived need to recruit German allies—with no questions asked—against Europe's remaining totalitarian and would-be hegemonic power. Ex-Nazi judges, teachers, doctors, and industrialists flourished.

Yet the utterly self-confident Adenauer led his country out of trauma and demoralization. He brought the feuding Catholic and Protestant parties together and presided over a general consolidation and maturation of political parties that would have astounded the splintered factions that made up the Weimar Republic's National Assembly. To a remarkable degree he overcame the Germans' intellectual contempt for politics and abdication from it that had so sapped the republic's resistance to Hitler. He helped build the new institution of party government—with almost corporate representation by employees' and trade union lobbies—that would endure and adapt on the basis of macro stability and constant micro adjustment.[3]

In hindsight, Adenauer's incorporation of ex-Nazis and their supporters into the new system was shrewd. It neutralized their resentment over the loss of a quarter of prewar German territory to Poland and averted the rise of any new stab-in-the-back myth of the sort that festered after far lesser losses of land in World War I.[4] The fledgling Federal Republic assimilated 12 million German expellees from the East—a sixth of the country's total population—and assuaged their grievances by giving them food, shelter, and work. "First comes grub, and then morals," as Bertolt Brecht once smirked. And this time the tactic worked.

Adenauer may have used the bourgeois prosperity the left intelligentsia so despised to buy off the far right, but his ploy succeeded. The National Democratic party of Germany and its variously named successors might make subliminal racist appeals to Nazi sympathizers, but they would never prove able to muster the 5 percent of votes needed to get into the Bundestag. Elections would always be won in the boring center.

Moreover, Adenauer made one great final contribution to German democracy: an involuntary service not unlike the gift of General Douglas MacArthur to Japanese democracy. When his rigidity no longer kept pace with the shifting world around him, Adenauer was deposed—in this case with the consent of his own party—and thus learned, and taught, the salutary lesson that no leader's authority is absolute.

Channeling of the Left

Only slightly less noteworthy than the incorporation of the right in the decades following Adenauer's departure was the Federal Republic of Germany's channeling of youthful leftist energies of protest into the political system. The generation that conducted West Germany's "cultural revolution" in 1968 counterposed its sometimes intimidating street democracy to the chancellor-democracy, to the deafening silence of its parents about Hitler's murder of the Jews, to the materialistic consumer miracle, and to Defense Minister Franz Josef Strauss's intimidation of *Der Spiegel* magazine, as well as to America's Vietnam War and the shah of Iran. The protesters demanded perfection of the young German democracy, and when they did not find it, many accused their government of being neofascist.

Critics argued that Germans had proved in the abortive revolution of 1848 that they were too conformist to sustain self-rule; they had never wrested democracy for themselves, but had been handed it by their Western occupiers, and it remained an alien import. Philosopher Karl Jaspers warned of the danger of a restored dictatorship in Bonn and a resort to war. Psychiatrists Alexander and Margarete Mitscherlich, in a left Freudian dissection of society, found a fatal flaw in the West Germans' inability to mourn.[5] Many others derided the West's concern about a Soviet military threat as an unjustified excuse for extending American imperialism and militarism.

The government's initial response was to use its own greater force against the hippies, but after a plainclothesman shot and killed West Berlin student Benno Ohnesorg in a demonstration against the shah of Iran, the authorities reconsidered, and in most cases took live ammunition away from the riot police. Then, when the left anarchist fringe degenerated into kidnapping and murder, West Germany contained this threat and built an effective antiterrorist commando force—despite the fears of trendy movie directors in the late 1970s—without ever reverting to a Hitlerian police state. Ironically, its civil rights record remained far better than that of its neighbor, France, even as the French deplored the West Germans' "radical ban" on communists in the civil service, lionized a few glamorous associates of the Baader-Meinhof gang, and for years refused their extradition to the Federal Republic.

Along the way, of course, excesses and miscarriages of justice occurred. One jailed terrorist was denied adequate medical care and subsequently died. Overzealous police cut corners in procuring search warrants. The ban against extremists in government service was abused to blackball various kindergarten teachers, train drivers, and municipal gardening apprentices for real or imagined sympathies with the tiny West German Communist party (and even with the utterly respectable Social Democratic party on at least one occasion in Bavaria). Telephone bugs were planted with little accountability. And in a contrast of metaphors that speaks worlds, whistleblowers were regularly denounced as nest soilers.

Self-Correction

In the lurching way of democracies, the system somehow learned to be self-correcting. It kept producing those uncomfortable whistleblowers, including the smug gadfly *Der Spiegel* in Hamburg and maverick data-protection ombudsman Ruth Leuze in staid Swabia in the southwest. It resumed prosecuting Nazi war criminals after the trial of Adolf Eichmann in Israel, and paid substantial restitution to Israel and to Jews, in the name of all Germans, in penance for the Third Reich. It achieved reconciliation with Germany's ancient enemy, France, and began reconciliation with the erstwhile enemies, Russia and Poland. It produced a Willy Brandt to lead the first sustained Social Democratic government in German history, sign the Nuclear Non-Proliferation Treaty, and fall on his knees at the monument to the Jewish ghetto in Warsaw. And the new Germany showed itself when voters honored this accomplishment, ignored Adenauer's brutal mocking of Brandt for his illegitimate birth and active resistance abroad to Nazi Germany, and decisively reelected the Nobel Peace Prize laureate in 1972.

Along the way, conservative governments in Bonn, with some prodding, also honored the Federal Republic's unique constitutional guarantee of the right of conscientious objection to military service, and reaped a steady corps of alternative service workers for hospitals and old people's homes. In addition, the conservative state carried on the noblesse oblige mission of patronizing the arts, often subsidizing satires of itself, as in a post-Hitler rebound the intellectual fashion eschewed the right and embraced the left. The government might rebel at propagating such criticism of itself at Goethe institutes abroad, but press mockery of attempted censorship would keep the state from interfering too crudely, and West German subventions would continue to be the great hope of young American opera singers and the great bane of the involuntary conservative sponsors of establishment bashing.

Perhaps more than in any other Western nation, the baby-boomers did not outgrow their 1968 student protests and jump onto the corporate escalator. Nor did they share the conversion experience of the French intelligentsia in flipping overnight from Marxism to the new right (and from a phobia about German neo-Nazism to a phobia about German neutralism). To an impressive degree the "'68ers" conducted their announced "march through the institutions," especially high schools, the media, and the Social Democratic party, without losing faith. By the time the distinctive German nuclear angst and aversion to any use of force in the world combined to produce the million-strong antinuclear demonstrations of the early 1980s, the weekly magazines, a number of leading television programs, and some of the most vocal Social Democrats were cheerleading the protests. The postmaterialists of the successor generation, they preached, even if they could no longer avert the growth of the West German economic giant could at least ensure that their country would abjure squalid power and remain a political dwarf.[6]

Yet somehow the generation of artists and filmmakers like Joseph Beuys and Rainer Werner Fassbinder was succeeded by that of the far less political Anselm Kiefer and Wim Wenders. The chic of the angry urban guerrilla, though more enduring than in any other Western country apart from Italy, faded over time. Eventually the emerging West German system even allowed the alternative Green party to rise, carry its triumphal pots of flowers into parliamentary offices in the 1980s, put the environment firmly on the agenda of every major party, and blow some of the fustian out of the Bundestag. Despite the fears of the right, the Greens never made Bonn ungovernable or blocked NATO's military response to Soviet SS-20 deployments.

These may all have been solutions that were less than satisfying intellectually and morally. Often enough they let biology rather than justice retire Nazi collaborators from positions of responsibility. They evaded any catharsis that might have purged that "inability to mourn." They perpetuated an edgy ideological antagonism between left and right. Until 1989 they left Germany, as they left Europe, divided. They also left the sometimes morbidly idealistic Germans—once the vision of European union had faded in the 1950s—with no overarching political goal other than the dull virtues of due process and slow formation of majorities. However, they also gave the Germans a pragmatic Western normality for the first time in centuries.

Sonderweg

In the 1980s, after NATO decided it needed to respond to new medium-range Soviet missiles with new Euromissiles of its own, this legacy raised various American and allied doubts about the steadfastness of the West Germans. The Germans had a chronic identity crisis, the doubters hypothesized. They were unpredictable, afflicted with, as the French worried, *les incertitudes allemandes*. They might not be able to bear their unaccustomed normality. If there were a depression, or if they lost their nerve in standing up to the Soviet threat, they might revert to political romanticism, to the detriment of Europe.

Much of the fear of German malaise arose from the memory of Hitler and from the conventional wisdom that Germany, the belated nation, was a deviant in Europe and had followed its own special path, or *Sonderweg*. This thesis of uniqueness stressed that the German tribes had never united in the Middle Ages as had the English, French, and Poles, that Germany had then lost a third of its total population in the Thirty Years War in the seventeenth century, and then again lost the most energetic Germans to the American emigration after the abortive 1848 revolution. All these events or failed events left scars; romanticism strangled rationality and the Enlightenment; nationalism swamped liberalism. The Germans trailed behind France and the United Kingdom and envied their industrialization, navies, colonization of Africa, and all the other accoutrements of greatpower status. Pre-industrial structures and mentalities survived in disjunction with economic modernization. Various German elites saw this singularity as positive: they viewed full-blooded German *Kultur* as superior to effete Western (and especially American) *Zivilisation*. The *Sonderweg* became a point of pride.[7]

After World War II the concept of the *Sonderweg* endured, but took on negative connotations. The victorious powers banned the very name of Prussia, seeing in Prussia, the Junkers, and Nietzsche (along with the punitive Versailles Treaty, world depression, and rampant inflation) the inexorable path to Hitler.

By the 1980s the notion of German peculiarity ran thus: the romantic Germans will never be satisfied with Western normality. They are too competent, too big for the rest of Europe, too dynamic. Germans are not natural pluralists or democrats. They yearn for reunification and might sell

their freedom for the pottage of neutrality in order to gain it. At worst—
this was the dread scenario of the early 1980s—the Germans will bow to
Soviet nuclear blackmail, refuse to host necessary new missiles, and cut
another "Rapallo" deal of cooperation with Moscow as in 1922. At best—
the scenario after 1985—the diminished Soviet threat and "Gorbymania"
will cause the West Germans to neglect their defense and their American
alliance and leave themselves vulnerable when Mikhail Gorbachev gets
dumped and a hardliner inherits the Kremlin. Typically, one American
analysis in 1985 summed up its concern about the Germans and about the
alliance as a whole:

> After 1988, the United States will probably not be led by a figure in
> the charismatic mode of Ronald Reagan; and the manifold pressures
> toward dissensus in the Western alliance may surface at such a time,
> particularly if the new Soviet leadership succeeds in some measure in
> psychologically disarming Western leaderships and publics via almost
> inevitable "peace" offensives. Thus, in superpower politics, the years
> from 1988 to 1995 may be a period of maximum danger for the West.[8]

With the hindsight of the 1990s, those fears look exaggerated. The
foxy Adenauer left far too much conservative ballast behind in middle-
class appreciation of stability and consistency. "The old man" read his
constituents' propensities aright in gaining a landslide victory in 1957 on
the very conservative motto of "no experiments." And abroad, that arch
Rhinelander who himself mistrusted Prussians and Saxons—and once insisted that the Asian steppes start in Braunschweig—anchored his Germans firmly to the West for the first time in history. By the late 1980s any
departure from this orientation would be seen as constituting unwelcome
experiments, no matter how high the 80 percent of West Germans who in
the abstract wanted a nuclear-free Europe and the 44 percent who declared
a preference for neutrality between East and West.

Chapter 3

Prologue East

W est Germany's eastern twin entered the 1980s with no inkling of its impending demise. Strongman Erich Honecker, erector of the Berlin Wall in 1961 and unchallenged party leader since 1971, exuded self-satisfaction with his stewardship of the GDR. Even in private (some of his cronies would complain after everything fell apart), he was oblivious to the bitter end to the mounting troubles.

Indeed, on the surface, things looked relatively good. Economically, East Germany still appeared to be performing adequately. As late as 1988, the *Encyclopaedia Britannica* was pleased to describe it as "the most developed and prosperous of the Communist countries of eastern Europe and one of the major industrial nations of the world."[1] The GDR's own descriptions of itself were even more flattering.

Politically, unrest was so negligible that the servile East Germans became the butt of jokes throughout the Soviet bloc. The East Berlin workers, the first East Europeans to rebel after Stalin's death, had protested draconian work norms in June 1953, but once they were put down by Soviet tanks, they learned the lesson of docility for the next three and a half decades.[2] More positively, the East Germans increasingly had something to be proud of, their leaders believed: their country's growing prestige. Already the GDR was Moscow's most important partner, not only in its geographical position on the front line with the West and its exports of machine tools to the Soviet Union, but also in its contribution to Soviet influence abroad, sending troops to discipline heretical Czechoslovakia in 1968 and training indigenous secret police and security forces in Africa and the Middle East.[3] After Brezhnev died in 1981, Honecker even felt that his service and seniority—and his superior knowledge of the increasingly powerful Federal Republic—entitled him to special Russian deference. Indeed, he claimed some credit for the West German antinuclear movement that the Soviets had placed their hopes on in the early 1980s.[4]

In the West too the GDR could boast a stable and beneficial relationship with the Federal Republic. Even if it did not yet enjoy the full diplomatic recognition it craved, it received important financial and economic gains from West Germany's pragmatic *Ostpolitik* of détente.

All this constituted achievement, especially when cast against catastrophe in Romania, huge foreign indebtedness in Hungary and Poland, and even the growing economic and social crisis in the Soviet Union of Leonid Brezhnev and Konstantin Chernenko. Honecker was a success by the measure of orthodox Marxism-Leninism.

The Honecker Era

Erich Honecker grew up in the 1920s in the western corner of Germany, the Saarland, in a family and working-class milieu that took as a given the righteousness of the communist cause. As a young adult he seemed never to have questioned Stalin's shifts between opposition to and alliance with Hitler, but to have followed each zigzag of the party line faithfully. His decade in prison in Nazi Germany saved him from the purge that crept down the corridors of the Hotel Lux in Moscow where the exiled German communists lived and then, in many cases, vanished from. He came into his own as World War II ended, when he was freed from jail, and the communists crushed the Social Democratic plurality in the Soviet zone of occupied Germany and the Soviet sector of Berlin.

Honecker began his rise up the hierarchy as a popular and relatively cant-free leader of the party's youth wing between 1946 and 1955. He attended the KGB school for security police in the Soviet Union in 1956–57, then graduated to become a member of the Politburo and Central Committee secretary in charge of security in 1958. In the latter capacity he supervised the overnight building of the infamous Berlin Wall in 1961 to stanch East German emigration (and, as it turned out, end the second East-West crisis over Berlin).[5] Yet when Brezhnev subsequently moved toward détente with the West and East German founding father Walter Ulbricht did not, Honecker easily replaced his mentor as party first secretary in 1971 to implement the new line of the decade.

When Honecker took over, he was widely viewed as a liberalizer in social and cultural affairs. He was no longer the spellbinder of earlier years—by now he sounded as wooden as all the other apparatchiks—but hope still lingered that he would humanize the system once he came to power. Indeed, as party secretary he quickly replaced the parsimonious achievement principle for determining workers' pay and benefits with a more humane social principle. He introduced an ambitious plan for sorely needed housing construction. He provided loans for young married couples and increased grants to mothers. He further made consumer goods more widely available, lengthened vacation time, and expanded benefits for apprentices, the elderly, the handicapped, and other disadvantaged groups.[6]

Honecker was also more permissive intellectually. Free German Youth vigilantes no longer policed their neighborhoods to tear down antennae erected to receive West German broadcasts; anecdotes mocking communism no longer subjected the jokesters to arrest; and Honecker's promise of "no taboos in the field of art and literature," while a gross exaggeration, did come to mean that if East Germans gave lip service to the party at work and in public, they could say what they pleased in private. So long as they did not try to flee, they could live relatively unmolested in their niche society, conforming on the job, but retreating at home to their niche of family, friends, and West German television.[7]

Most significantly, perhaps, Honecker further reached a wobbly modus vivendi with the Protestant church in 1978. Educational and professional discrimination against practicing Christians would end, he promised. New churches could be built and the church would be given access to the airwaves. The church was already the real moral authority in the land, and with this new toleration it evolved into the main seedbed for the grass-roots antinuclear, environmental, and human rights movements that would swell to open the Berlin Wall in 1989.

To be sure, no one could criticize the system openly, as even Honecker's prisonmate of the 1940s, the physicist and Marxist idealist (and therefore dissident) Robert Havemann, discovered. Havemann suffered house arrest. Wolf Biermann, singer of satirical ballads, also found the limits. He was stripped of his citizenship while on tour in West Germany in the mid-1970s and was not allowed to return. Well-known authors who protested Biermann's treatment were expelled from the Writers' Union; lesser-known dissenters were jailed, expelled to the Federal Republic, or both.

Ultimately, of course, East German society was still based on coercion; on rule by a single party that jealously guarded its monopoly on authority, finances, appointments, and truth; on a vast secret police network; on a government, bureaucracy, and court system subservient to the Socialist Unity party (SED); on an East German officer corps loyal to the Soviet Union through its own direct ties to the Soviet command; and, finally, on the Soviet heavy-armored divisions that outnumbered East German troops by more than two to one in the GDR. Yet East Germans appreciated—for a time—the gentler glove on coercion.

In economics, the party general secretary, as Honecker retitled himself in 1976, was less liberal than in social policies. He choked off the disruptive experimentation with reform that Ulbricht, in common with some other East European leaders, had dabbled with in the 1960s. Indeed, Honecker even nationalized many private firms that had somehow managed to survive. He tried to make the command economy efficient, not by liberalizing it, but by centralizing it still more.

In agriculture he introduced huge, specialized collective farms, and in industry he created huge, vertically integrated *Kombinate* (conglomerates). The former failed, East German economists would admit in the 1980s, but the latter seemed to work much better than their sloppier counterparts elsewhere in the Soviet bloc. In 1985 Gorbachev would first look to the *Kombinate* as a model for economic change in the Soviet Union before discarding them for more decentralized reform.[8]

Outside analysts offered various explanations for the GDR's economic mini-miracle. Some contended sardonically that German discipline could make any system work, even one so contrary to human nature. Others believed that Bonn's help was the decisive factor.

Certainly the Federal Republic insisted that the European Community treat the two German states as one nation and waive tariffs on any imports from East into West Germany, thus making the GDR a tacit member of the EC. At the same time Bonn poured DM 2.0 billion (about $1.2 billion) annually into East German coffers, for example, to maintain transit routes and to ransom political prisoners. West German banks also helped out with loans of close to DM 2 billion in the mid-1980s.[9]

Swedish economist Anders Aslund suggests in an alternative interpretation that the key reason for the GDR's relative success was the short time that orthodox Stalinism prevailed in the East German economy. In the early 1950s, when national unification was still Stalin's declared policy, in an effort to make the East German model as attractive as possible to all Germans, Stalin did not regiment the GDR as completely as its East European neighbors. Only in 1952, shortly before his death, did Stalin finally resign himself to separate German development and conform the East German economy to the Stalinist system. The GDR thus endured only nine months of intense persecution of private entrepreneurs. Some survived, and despite the private sector's small size, Aslund argues, its competition kept the state sector more honest than in the more fully nationalized state economies.[10]

The Unification Minuet

Honecker's relaxed foreign policy, the whole raison d'être for his ascent to the SED's leadership, was more in line with his social liberalization than his economic restrictions. At first he was simply the passive recipient of Brezhnev's détente and of the curious Quadripartite Agreement of 1971 hammered out between the two superpowers and the other two occupiers of Berlin, the United Kingdom and France. That document, one of history's vaguest treaties (it promised to preserve the status quo while never defining the status quo), guaranteed Western access to West Berlin and the Federal Republic's political ties to the enclave city for two decades. Its signing ended Berlin crises.

On this foundation Honecker and Willy Brandt, chancellor of the center-left government that replaced Bonn's grand coalition in 1969, quickly became movers of détente in their own right. Brandt's hallmark was an *Ostpolitik* of small steps aimed at easing the life of ordinary East Germans; winning some private East-West German contact; and, coincidentally, neutralizing any lingering nationalist resentments about Germany's division by minimizing its everyday consequences.

Honecker accepted the gamble implicit in Bonn's outstretched hand. He perceived the risk of subversion by Western ideas—indeed, Bonn's announced aim was East German *Wandel durch Annäherung* (change through rapprochement or accommodation)—but he thought he could contain the risk by *Abgrenzung* (setting firm limits to the new relationship).

By 1972 the negotiations led to the inter-German treaty, which along with the flurry of the Quadripartite Agreement and the Soviet-West German, Polish-West German, Czechoslovak-West German, and superpower Strategic Arms Limitation treaties, constituted the framework for East-West détente. The two Germanys entered the United Nations, and also the thirty-five-nation Conference on Security and Cooperation in Europe in Helsinki, in tandem. The GDR pulled back further into its shell of *Abgrenzung*, renouncing even more vigorously than heretofore its earlier concept of a single German nation, and instead stressed the existence of two separate German nations, a socialist one and a capitalist one. The GDR emphasized that reunification could occur in the future only if West Germany first embraced socialism.

The new détente thus completed a reversal in the GDR's initial stance on reunification. In the beginning it was East rather than West Germany that championed unification. The GDR's 1949 constitution asserted flatly that "Germany is an indivisible democratic republic." This appeal was useful in competing for hearts and minds, and it cost the GDR nothing, as West German patriarch Konrad Adenauer consistently refused to have any dealings with the GDR. East Berlin could champion unity and reap the propaganda benefit without risking negotiations with and concessions to the more populous and democratically legitimized West German government.

The GDR quickly lost the popularity contest as the Russians stripped East German industry, mounted the Berlin blockade, and suppressed the East Berlin uprising. Yet the GDR still beat the drum of unification—with conditions that would ensure Eastern dominance. In 1950 East Berlin proposed a constituent council based on proportional party representation that would have magnified the communist voice in any joint government. In 1952, apparently in a bid to derail imminent German admission to NATO, Stalin sent an ambiguous note to the Western powers offering German unification in return for German neutrality; some Western observers believed that at that point Stalin might even have sacrificed his East German regime to thwart German incorporation into the West. Then in the uncertainty of the three months following Stalin's death, Soviet secret police chief Lavrenti Beria also flirted with sacrificing the GDR to obtain a neutral, united Germany. However, by 1956 Ulbricht returned to the proposal that West Germany nationalize its major industries as a prelude to confederation and eventual elections for a joint national assembly.

Bonn spurned the East's various overtures, seeing neither economic nor political incentives in them. Primed by Marshall Plan reconstruction, Economics Minister Ludwig Erhard's radical free market recovery, the demand for German machine tools as a result of the Korean War, and the labor pool of 12 million refugees from the east, the Federal Republic was enjoying an economic miracle that far outclassed the GDR's performance. And politically Adenauer rejected any intercourse with an East German government that had not been freely elected. He insisted that freedom must take priority over unity, West European integration over German nationalism, and alliance with the West over neutrality.

The Federal Republic's policy was therefore the Hallstein Doctrine of withholding diplomatic recognition from any state (except the Soviet Union) that recognized the GDR. The policy was effective. For almost two decades the GDR was isolated. Only communist and a few third world countries preferred to have diplomatic relations with the East German rump rather than with the dynamic Western core of Germany.

Moreover, the East German public shared this preference. Until the Berlin Wall locked them up in 1961, some 3.5 million of them, or more than one-sixth of the population, fled the workers' paradise.

In the 1960s, as Adenauer passed from the scene and Ulbricht reasserted control after the shocks that followed Stalin's death, the *pas de deux* began to shift. Both West and East Germany became less rigid, and East Germany grew less convinced of its advantage in any genuine East-West contact. Thus in the early 1960s the GDR replaced its old theory of two states in one nation by the more defensive concept of two distinct nations. Simultaneously, it issued more bluntly than ever the clearly unacceptable demand that the Federal Republic first turn socialist (that is, communist) before any unification.

In 1965 the West German Social Democrats—who in the post–World War II years were refuting a century-old accusation that they were unpatriotic by advocating pan-German policies ranging from dialogue with East Berlin to neutral unification—tested East German sincerity. They opened correspondence with the Socialist Unity party about exchanging speakers, and got as far as scheduling dates. Even such innocuous relations, it turned out, alarmed East Berlin. At the last minute the SED got cold feet and pulled out. When the grand coalition of conservatives and Social Democrats took office in Bonn in 1966 and put out its own feelers to East Germany, the SED backed off even more. In 1967, as the Federal Republic finally dropped the Hallstein Doctrine, the GDR declared itself to be a separate state and retracted its concept of an all-German citizenship. (For its part, West Germany continued its own version of this legal interpretation, giving instant citizenship in the Federal Republic to any East German who reached the West and applied for it.)

In 1968 the concept of the GDR as a socialist state within the German nation was written into the new East German constitution. The next year the SED forced East German Protestants to quit the umbrella church organization, which was the only remaining all-German institution.

In 1969 the Federal Republic also reformulated its position to postulate a single German nation comprising two separate states. In 1970, even before Honecker replaced Ulbricht, official negotiations on normalization opened between East and West Germany.[11]

The Nuclear Controversy and the Duel for German Identity

In the 1980s German nuclear angst first lent some new legitimacy to the SED regime, then contributed to the winds of change that swept it away. Honecker basked in the former, but never understood the latter.

The problem was that East Germany, even more than West Germany, lacked a clear identity. Even though after the 1968 student revolt young West Germans complained regularly that the Federal Republic was a soulless money machine, that it was rigid and crushingly conformist, and that it had never weeded old Nazis out of influential positions, at least it was a real entity that these West German rebels were railing against. There was no comparable challenge by young East Germans asking what their fathers (or some of their communist officials) did during the Hitler era.

This dearth of protest in the East reflected not only visceral knowledge of the coercive power of a would-be totalitarian regime—and therefore failure even to understand the Western moral question of how Germans might have behaved differently under Hitler—but also reflected a failure to take the East German regime seriously enough to bother arguing with it. Malcontents simply fled, in daring and sometimes tragic defiance of the automatic shooting machines at the wall, in a hot air balloon, perhaps, or on a vacation to Budapest that let determined hikers slip through the barbed wire into Austria.

Among most East German critics the assumption was that the Federal Republic was the real Germany and had, whatever the West Germans' own doubts, a vibrant identity. It was the total alternative next door, the much more successful and freer Germany, the one repository of a national identity.

For a long time the assumption therefore was that the GDR's leadership, unlike its Hungarian, Czech, or Polish counterparts, could not seek legitimation in a national appeal to its citizens. Any such bid would simply raise East Germans' desire to join that real Germany.

Indeed, in the 1980s, under the twin pressures of worsening East-West relations and the unnerving example of the Solidarity free trade union in Poland, party, and by now state, chief Honecker strengthened *Abgrenzung*. His action did not go as far as his campaign inside the Soviet bloc to send the Soviet, East German, and other fraternal armies into Poland to restore order at the point of a gun.[12] It was grim enough in the context of previous East-West German relations, however. Honecker raised the amount of hard currency that West German visitors had to pay for each trip to East Germany and East Berlin, thereby cutting their numbers. In addition, he stiffened his preconditions for good East-West German relations. In a speech in Gera in October 1980 he repackaged several old demands into new insistence that Bonn recognize East German citizenship (that is, no longer grant East Germans instant West German citizenship); upgrade relations to full ambassadorial level; accept mid-river rather than the eastern bank as the East-West German boundary on the Elbe; and close the Salzgitter archive, which recorded the names and dates of shootings of would-be East German escapees by East German border guards.[13]

Yet as East-West German relations settled into a stable pattern, Honecker did build up enough confidence to make his own claim to the common German heritage. Under his leadership the GDR reconstructed Frederick the Great's palace, Sans Souci, in Potsdam and the Zwinger museum in Dresden. In the early 1980s he rehabilitated more bits of aristocratic and bourgeois German history that the communists had previously denounced.

Frederick the Great, Martin Luther, and to a lesser extent Otto von Bismarck were the most sensational heroes the GDR reclaimed for its pantheon. The famous equestrian statue of Frederick by Christian Rauch was restored to its place of pride on Unter den Linden. Both state and church celebrated the 500th anniversary of Martin Luther's birth, and for the first time, Luther's city of Wittenberg was allocated the budget and workers to lift itself out of the 1920s. The Great Reformer himself was promoted from counterrevolutionary to "one of the greatest sons of the German people." Bismarck, while getting none of his monuments back, at least earned publication of a serious new biography by an East German historian. Finally, East Berlin's treasures of classical architecture were now lovingly restored if they had not, like Karl Friedrich Schinkel's royal palace, already been razed.[14]

West German conservatives watched the East German campaign with consternation; lamented the displacement of historical sensibilities by rootless sociological constructs at West German universities; and worried that the GDR might now become, by default, the guardian of German history. Many non-German conservatives expressed even more concern that history might yet return to West as well as East Germans in the form of an anti-Western *Sonderweg*. In West Germany's case foreign critics viewed the striking dearth of flag-waving patriotism not as reassuring, but as deceptive. They saw a dangerous vacuum of identity waiting to be filled by a demagogue. An impossible negative burden of proof was placed on the Germans—especially by their French neighbors—to demonstrate that they were not cryptonationalists in either a militarist or a neutralist manifestation.[15] The French, British, and Americans worried that Moscow might play its German card and offer unification for the price of West German aloofness from NATO. Foreign Minister Hans-Dietrich Genscher's regular counter that the Soviets had no German card to play, unless Bonn's allies gave them one by reneging on their previous commitments to unification, failed to allay the doubts.[16]

Both West German and non-German conservatives therefore fretted as Honecker began laying claim to a second sphere of pan-German sentiment: the yearning for peace and the sometimes subliminal suspicion that Germany was falling victim to morbid superpower confrontation. They feared that the East German leader would be able to touch a responsive chord, exploit the asymmetries between the open West German and the closed East German society, and turn Western public opinion against NATO's Euromissiles, while stifling any real debate in the regimented East.[17]

In the early stages of the intermediate-range nuclear forces (INF) controversy of the 1980s, Moscow and East Berlin certainly tried this tack. They appealed to the West German masses over the head of the Bonn government, to the Bonn government over the head of Washington, and to the Bonn government in an effort to influence Washington. They assiduously fanned the flames of West Germany's grass-roots antinuclear movement and cultivated West German interlocutors both before and after Social Democratic Chancellor Helmut Schmidt fell in October 1982 in a shift of allegiance by the coalition's junior Liberal party (over economic, not security, policy).

Like Schmidt, the new Christian Democratic Chancellor Helmut Kohl refused to yield to the combination of Soviet blandishments and threats and drop the Western shield in return for a dubious Soviet embrace. Also like Schmidt, he pressed Washington to pursue negotiations, arguing repeatedly that West German public opinion would support the stationing of missiles only if the West first exhausted the possibilities of arms control.

Kohl also continued *Ostpolitik*, just as if the conservatives' ten-year vilification of it had never existed. "*Pacta sunt servanda*," proclaimed the Bavarian potentate Franz Josef Strauss, and he promptly fulfilled the existing treaties by ignoring his own previous anticommunist rhetoric and negotiating a DM 1 billion loan to the GDR by Bavarian banks. With the ice thus broken, Christian Democratic politicians, like their Social Democratic colleagues, flocked to the Leipzig East-West Industrial Fair twice a year to see and be seen with Erich Honecker.

Unlike Schmidt, Kohl was sympathetic to Reagan, and the Reagan right was not as suspicious of him as it had been of Schmidt. Washington still remembered its recent clash with Europe in general and Bonn in particular as superpower détente broke down, the Soviets invaded Afghanistan, and the United States asserted that détente was not divisible, while Europeans sought to avert any import of out-of-area tensions to their part of the world and tried to duck the targeted 3 percent annual increases in NATO funding. However, Kohl's Christian Democrats did not rub salt in America's wounds by preaching their own peaceful moral superiority to the United States as Schmidt's Social Democrats did, and Kohl's party rank and file, unlike Schmidt's, did not alarm the United States by constantly threatening to use their nuclear pacifist pressures to topple their chancellor.

In the general election at the beginning of 1983 the Social Democrats experimented with an antimissile and partially anti-American campaign under the slogan: "In the German interest." They lost. The following November the Social Democrats, arguing that Washington had not explored all the arms control options, voted overwhelmingly against the Euromissiles and repudiated Schmidt, both in their convention in Cologne and in the final Bundestag INF session.

Left-wing Social Democrats further called for an undefined security partnership between Bonn and Moscow that at its most bland would mean only the truism that all must avoid mutual suicide in the nuclear age, and at its most suggestive would imply loosening of U.S. ties in return for some kind of Soviet promise of nonaggression. Many left-wing intellectuals in West Germany also tended to equate cooperative American hegemony in Western Europe with coercive Soviet hegemony in Eastern Europe, see the two Germanies as comparably victimized, and seek a "Europeanization" that would shuck off undue influence by both superpowers.[18]

Despite the fierce row, Kohl persisted in according top priority to solidarity with the United States, and therefore to stationing NATO's new Pershing II and cruise missiles in the Federal Republic if Moscow did not remove its SS-20s. His public argument was not that the missiles were essential for defense, but rather—echoing Adenauer—that West Germany must maintain a firm Western identity. His reasoning persuaded voters keen on preserving the order and predictability of the Western alliance that for forty years had given them peace and prosperity. Kohl's majority held. As the end of 1983 deadline approached, the conservatives and Liberals (Free Democrats) turned in a majority vote for deployment.

Western conservatives braced themselves for a Soviet stick and carrot reaction, however, and again feared the worst for the Federal Republic. The stick was the Soviet and East German threat to bring an ice age in East-West relations down on Bonn and reduce East-West German contact below the tolerance level of the West German public. The potential carrot, equally dreaded by Western conservatives, was a repetition of Stalin's offer of German reunification in exchange for neutrality that might wrest West Germany away from its postwar Western identity and unite the Soviet Union and Germany against the American presence in Europe. To a number of these observers Gorbachev's advocacy of a common European house looked like the first move in this direction.

This case had sounded plausible so long as it was Chancellor Schmidt whom Honecker was courting, and so long as there appeared to be a chance that Schmidt's party might reject the NATO missile deployment. Improved humanitarian East-West German contacts might lure Bonn, while Soviet threats of deterioration in East-West relations and military countermeasures might intimidate Bonn. Schmidt's humiliation as Poland declared martial law during his long-delayed visit to the GDR in December 1981—Schmidt nonetheless finished his tour in Güstrow before a rent-a-crowd composed entirely of security service supernumeraries—fit this view.

The context changed radically, however, once Kohl became chancellor. When the Christian Democratic–led government committed itself to stationing the Euromissiles, the ongoing dialogue and deals between East and West Germany took on an entirely new meaning: they helped make deployment palatable in the Federal Republic. The West German public was reassured that deployment would not, after all, exact a cost in diminished East-West German ties.

The East German–Soviet Wedge

Instead of an East-West German split or a transatlantic wedge, what developed—to everyone's astonishment—was an incipient wedge between East Berlin and its Soviet patron for the first time in thirty-five years. East Berlin accepted Kohl's firm stance on deployment, while Moscow did not.

Honecker continued to cultivate a good working relationship with the chancellor, with whom he shared a similar southwestern dialect, and ensured that East-West German détente would continue, even if U.S.-Soviet détente did not.[19]

As 1984 started, the Soviet Union sought to punish the Federal Republic for NATO's INF deployments. Militarily, it began implementing its announced countermeasures of placing additional shorter-range Soviet SS-21s, SS-22s, and SS-23s in East Germany and Czechoslovakia. Politically, it revived its 1970s accusation that West Germany was engaged in "revanchism," or threatening to recover former German lands awarded to Poland at the end of World War II. None too subtly, Soviet political cartoons once again depicted West Germans as bloodthirsty SS monsters with fangs.

Yet this time East Berlin conspicuously failed to echo Moscow. Honecker scarcely waited for the ink to dry on the Bundestag's yes to stationing before he dropped his previous dire warnings and instead urged "damage limitation," a "community of responsibility," and perseverance in the efforts of "medium-sized" countries to revive détente despite superpower confrontation.[20]

Most remarkable, Honecker barely veiled his dismay at the prospect of accepting and, unlike the West German recipients of American missiles, paying for the latest round of Soviet missiles in the GDR. Even after the Soviets stalked out of the arms control talks in Geneva, declaring they would not return until the new Western missiles were removed, Honecker puckishly suggested that Moscow would come back anyway, even without the West's paying a price.

By summer 1984 the differences between the Soviet Union and the GDR burst out of the closet. *Pravda* ran an attack on Bonn that was a barely disguised rapping of East German knuckles for consorting with West Germany. The Federal Republic, *Pravda* charged, was trying to undermine the GDR's sovereignty and socialist system. Good East-West German relations, it further cautioned, could not be divorced from bad overall East-West relations.[21]

For the first time the SED party newspaper *Neues Deutschland* retorted with polemics of its own, however veiled. The Hungarians, the Romanians, and even the Bulgarians cheered the East Germans on.

Clearly Honecker felt entitled to his modest self-assertion and his wish to be respected by Moscow as a senior communist leader. He thought East Berlin's zealous past support of Soviet positions now justified a bit more discretionary space for the GDR in local foreign policy, and a probe to see how much scope it might win from the third ailing Soviet leader in as many years. In dealing with West Germany in particular, Honecker also presumed that his own judgment was superior to that of the Russians, and he was certainly tired of being treated in proconsular fashion by the Soviet ambassador.[22]

At this point Honecker backed his conciliatory words to Bonn with an unprecedented gesture, letting 35,000 East Germans move legally to West Germany during 1984. It was the largest exodus since 1961. He further settled quietly—with a purse swelled by DM 90,000 per capita— the cases of East German squatters in West German embassies in Eastern Europe who were desperately trying to emigrate.[23]

With this gift, Honecker proceeded to schedule his long-sought maiden visit to the Federal Republic in September. The Soviets, who were still intent on punishing West Germany, blocked the trip, first by a highly unusual public disapproval of the visit in the Soviet media, then by a blunt "no" to Honecker's face.[24]

The East German leader accepted the prohibition, but his cheekiness toward Moscow, his antinuclear hints, and his relative social liberalization still seemed to win Honecker a modicum of popularity at home. Most of the top GDR-watchers in the Federal Republic thought they discerned, at last, the development of a distinct East German identity.[25]

Pessimists among Bonn's allies sensed the same growth in East German self-confidence and suspected the worst: a disinformation campaign about purported Soviet-East German strains to deceive the West and lower the Federal Republic's guard. Some voiced the old fear of German "self-Finlandization," or undue West German deference to Moscow in order to buy good East-West German relations.

Chapter 4

Nuclear Angst and Reassurance

To understand why the much-feared West German drift to
the East never transpired—and why the West German
reaction to security issues in post-wall 1990 diverged so widely from
American experts' predictions—one needs to reexamine the politics of the
intermediate-range nuclear forces (INF) controversy of the 1980s. So far,
this has not been done; in the radically different world of the 1990s, the
tendency in the United States is to dismiss the whole INF debate as ancient
history, but it is not. Our less hostile decade owes its very existence to the
difficult NATO decision to station missiles in Europe in answer to the
Soviet buildup of SS-20s, argues one of the shrewdest practitioners of
diplomacy over two decades, German Foreign Minister Hans-Dietrich
Genscher.

"I believe it was only this steadfastness of the West that first made
Gorbachev's policy possible and even made Gorbachev himself possible,"
Genscher asserts. "I am of the opinion that if those in the Soviet leadership
who drove the arms buildup had succeeded, and if West Germany had
gone down on its knees, then the Soviet policy of the old [domineering]
kind would have continued even longer. We would not be discussing today
the [cooperative] subjects we are discussing."[1]

In this analysis, INF deployment forced the Soviet leadership to abandon its efforts to dominate Western Europe, then rebounded to end the
Russians' four-decade domination of Eastern Europe. Without the Euromissile goad, Russian mellowing would have taken much longer.

More specifically, various responses to the INF fight—and perhaps
to Reagan's companion star wars program—helped to fuel the various
revolutions of 1989 and to define Germany's role in the post–cold war era.

Besides Mikhail Gorbachev's extraordinary decision to cut the losses of imperial overextension, these responses included Bonn's probing assertion of West German interests (in relation to both Moscow and Washington), and the growth of a dissident East German peace movement that by fall 1989 would spearhead street demonstrations and topple the Berlin Wall. In this context the INF debates, and the German nuclear angst they revealed, triggered the benevolent cataclysm that followed.

This benign reading of the outcome of the intra-alliance spats of the 1980s is far removed from conventional American wisdom. In the United States, both right and left assume that the American-German Euromissile controversy strained the NATO alliance almost to breaking point, and was resolved only by the deus ex machina of the end of cold war.

This interpretation entails, of course, a generally unacknowledged revision of the prevailing wisdom in the immediate aftermath of November 1989. Then the overwhelming consensus of both right and left was that long-term alliances are unnatural, that only a dependent West Germany's perceived need for American security had held NATO together for those improbable four decades, and that as soon as the Soviet threat demonstrably vanished, so would the alliance.

Either way, today's Americans tend to brush off the INF complexities as irrelevant, and to let the German position, which baffled them at the time, fade into oblivion.

An alternative—or perhaps a corollary—framework advanced by the American left puts all the blame for the 1980s quarrels on cold warrior Ronald Reagan. (Thus far the Reagan right would agree, and praise the presidential toughness that ignored the qualms of the timorous liberals and Germans and forced the final downfall of the evil empire.) But the left then goes on to say, that we can now see that the communist world was already being strangled by its own contradictions in the early 1980s, and Reagan's confrontation with Moscow over the INF, if not dangerous, was at least superfluous. In this school of thought the old Euromissile feuds are also irrelevant.

Even the small clan of arms control devotees downplays the eventual INF treaty of 1987, which covered an infinitesimal portion of superpower weapons, as only a rehearsal for the crowning strategic agreements of 1991 and 1992.

The more maverick perspective of this book is that Genscher is right. The short, happy life of the INF was crucial both for East-West and West-West relations, and while the bickering could have spun out of control if mishandled, it was kept within the tolerable realm of alliance management and never did reach the crisis proportions widely attributed to it.

To be sure, there was an insoluble basic conundrum, in the bipolar world, in the whole irrational edifice of a nuclear extended deterrence that could be justified only by virtue of being less worse than any other conceivable system. This condundrum would lose its urgency only when bipolar nuclear confrontation ended. But everyone lived with that contradiction, and there was no innate transatlantic clash of interest over specific nuclear weapons.

Nuclear Angst

The German nuclear anxiety of the 1980s was all too understandable. For the frontline Germans more than for anyone else, deterrence of nuclear and conventional war rested on the double confidence that the United States would actually commit its strategic arsenal to Europe in any showdown, but that it would not use these terrible weapons lightly. In the early 1980s hardware and politics combined to erode both aspects of this confidence. They split West German government officials, who worried about America's commitment, from ordinary citizens, who agonized conversely about excessive American nuclear zeal.

The Federal Republic was, as Chancellor Helmut Schmidt never tired of saying, only the size of Oregon, but packed with a population a quarter that of the United States. Physically, it was utterly vulnerable to Soviet nuclear missiles, should Moscow ever decide to fire them. It had renounced nuclear weapons of its own, and even if it had not, it could never build an adequate counter to a superpower armory. For deterrence of that Soviet nuclear threat it was totally dependent on the credibility of the American nuclear umbrella. Yet in the early 1980s many Germans came to see that umbrella as more threatening than protecting, especially when the presidential holder of the umbrella seemed to them to be irresponsibly hostile to the Soviet Union and cavalier about the prospect of nuclear war in Europe.

On the face of it, the whole concept of extended deterrence—the notion that the United States should risk nuclear suicide to defend Western Europe—was a preposterous foundation for peace. Yet the stubborn fact, Bonn officials were convinced, was that it worked.[2] Throughout the four decades of bipolar nuclear standoff, Western Europe enjoyed its longest peace since at least the Middle Ages.

The logic of bipolar nuclear deterrence was irrational enough even in terms of the superpower stalemate, in which the threat of mutual nuclear suicide at least had the existential credibility of averting subjugation of one's own society. The logic approached absurdity—said Charles de Gaulle in the 1960s and Robert McNamara and Henry Kissinger after they were out of office—when the threat of joint Soviet-American suicide was extended to cover Western Europe. As the rhetorical question had it, would the United States really risk Chicago to save Hamburg?

Before the 1970s—so long as the United States maintained strategic intercontinental nuclear superiority—such extended deterrence was actually credible to most Europeans. The thinking was that if the Soviet Union matched the United States at any stage of nuclear escalation from tactical weapons on up, the United States would always have sufficient superiority at a higher nuclear level to raise the ante still further, to the disadvantage of the Soviet Union, in what was called escalation dominance. No one expected nuclear war, but the risk of unplanned escalation up the nuclear ladder should deter any well-armed aggressor who might be tempted to launch a conventional attack.

There were, of course, West German demurrals in the mid-1960s when the United States changed its planned reaction to any Soviet invasion of Western Europe from virtually assured massive retaliation with nuclear bombs on the Soviet homeland to more tentative flexible response. The latter might be either nuclear or conventional, and its locale might be either the immediate battlefield or territory closer to Moscow. In subsequent war games the Americans naturally preferred to limit the violence, sought to confine the fighting to Europe for as long as possible, and tended to opt for East European targets rather than Soviet nuclear targets that might trigger retaliation on the United States. The Germans naturally preferred to shift the brunt of any war to the superpowers rather than to restrict all the violence to Central Europe. In theory they stressed prompt nuclear escalation on Soviet soil, although in practice they always emphasized war-deterring over war-fighting capabilities of nuclear arms and became nervous whenever the Americans invented scenarios for actually using nuclear weapons.

The Europeans as a whole also resisted the introduction of flexible response for another reason. Since it would allow for an initial period of conventional defense, the implication was that NATO should enlarge its conventional forces to counter the superior Soviet manpower (which exceeded NATO strength by a ratio of about 1.2 to 1 on the central front) and firepower (in ratios ranging up to 2.5 times more Warsaw Treaty Organization tanks). Otherwise, the West feared that the Soviet Union might be tempted to make a quick land grab of, say, Hamburg, then stop its advance and dare NATO to defy Western public opinion by going nuclear to recover the lost territory. Just such a blitzkrieg was the center-piece of Soviet military operational plans.

The Europeans had to accept their nuclear patron's shift to flexible response, but they could and did reject a compensatory conventional buildup of their own. They begrudged the expense, and in any case they mistrusted a purely conventional deterrence. They remembered all too vividly the failure of a conventional balance in 1940, when Hitler exploited the advantages of surprise and concentration of firepower, launched his blitzkrieg offensive against numerically superior French and Belgian forces, and marched to the English Channel within two weeks. They concluded that having Western conventional forces inferior to Warsaw Pact strengths might actually be preferable to parity. A balance might send a false signal to the Russians that NATO was relying on conventional defense and would never go nuclear. It might make a gambler in the Kremlin think that Europe was safe for conventional war.[3]

Under the flexible response that NATO grudgingly accepted in 1967, the alliance's mainstay shifted away from strategic nuclear missiles. Its new mainstay was not conventional arms, however, but tactical (substrategic or battlefield) nuclear weapons, the new fad that the Kennedy administration had brought in. The Russians lagged behind in this category, and the gap ensured that even after the Soviet Union achieved strategic nuclear parity with the United States, as acknowledged in the first Strategic Arms Limitation Treaty (SALT I) of 1972, European confidence in the American nuclear umbrella persisted. It was not just that the Honest Johns and Davy Crocketts that were scattered so liberally throughout the European continent in the 1960s could offset the East's conventional superiority by preventing the massing of tanks to form attack spearheads (and lucrative nuclear targets). The assurance also came from Western nuclear superiority in the European theater, and therefore escalation dominance in the region.

SS-20s Change the Equation

That theater equation was changed by the mobile SS-20 missiles the Russians began deploying in 1977. These were intermediate-range nuclear weapons that could travel 5,000 kilometers from Soviet bases and reach all of Western Europe and North Africa. They had three warheads each and were much more accurate then the old 2,000- to 4,000-kilometer SS-4s and SS-5s the Soviet Union had deployed in the mid-1960s in a kind of obverse extended deterrence, holding Western Europe hostage against any Western attempt to exploit America's strategic superiority. By the early 1980s the SS-20s (and NATO's quiet unilateral withdrawal of 2,400 tactical nuclear warheads) would help reverse NATO's longstanding theater nuclear superiority and establish a Soviet superiority of four to one in INF warheads.

The SS-20s also turned the spotlight on an anomaly in American and alliance nuclear policy that had previously gone largely unremarked. That was the contrast between what was in effect an American no-first-use policy in strategic weapons, but deliberate first-use policy in theater nuclear weapons. In neither case was there a first-strike policy, that is, a threat of an American surprise nuclear attack in an attempt to disable Soviet strategic nuclear arms by a massive blow. But in Europe the United States was ready to escalate first to the nuclear level should a conventional defense crumble.

So long as this stance remained the preserve of specialists—not because it was secret, but because the general public simply ignored such unlikely scenarios—it created no political problem. As the SS-20 focused attention on the theater nuclear balance, though, and as the fear of war rose in the harsh American-Soviet confrontations of the early 1980s, a growing number of West German voters came to view the first-use policy as more menacing than comforting.

But did the shift to Soviet theater nuclear superiority in warhead count actually increase the Soviet threat? No, said the Americans. NATO's several hundred prime targets were already blanketed by other Soviet nuclear weapons. War simulations might now show no Western advantage—and even considerable disadvantage—from nuclear escalation, but America's suicidal threat of extended nuclear deterrence still remained effective. It rested on the 5 percent Soviet uncertainty, as it was often described, that the United States might in fact act irrationally in the heat of crisis.

The West German government disagreed with the United States, not on military, but on political grounds. No one thought the Russians were about to invade Western Europe. Their advance had stabilized by 1948–49 at the eastern border of the Federal Republic. The real problem, however, was potential Soviet coercion of West European governments—and possible American loss of nerve—under the threat of that Soviet superiority in Europe in conventional and now also in tactical nuclear arms. If the SS-20 deployments went unanswered by NATO, Bonn feared, the Kremlin might be encouraged to bully its continental neighbors.

"Of course the Soviets did not intend to attack us with their SS-20 buildup. But they did intend, step by step, to dominate Western Europe and decouple it from the USA," explains Genscher.[4]

Schmidt shared his foreign minister's judgment. Already the Carter administration had signaled diminished resolve, he suspected, in contemplating a shift away from defending West Germany at its eastern border to falling back and trading Germany's minimal space for time. Jimmy Carter was also willing to give away intermediate-range cruise missiles in the ongoing SALT II negotiations, Schmidt feared, without regard for any eventual need for such weapons on the European central front.

Schmidt therefore gave a landmark speech at the International Institute for Strategic Studies in London in 1977, asking for a NATO response to the SS-20. His audience took him to mean an INF counterdeployment, although some years later Schmidt denied that this had been his intent. In the heat of the INF battle, he asserted that he had wanted sea-based rather than land-based missiles to fill the gap, and even suggested that his real aim had been inclusion of the SS-20s in arms control negotiations.[5] After the INF treaty was signed, however, he returned to seeing in the NATO missile deployment a decisive stimulus to Gorbachev's remarkable ending of the cold war.[6]

In the Soviet Union a senescent Leonid Brezhnev was still president as West Germany fought out the issue of INF deployment. A military hypertrophy in foreign policy had Soviet generals intervening with Cuban troops in Africa and lengthening the Warsaw Treaty Organization's already impressive lead in heavy armor in Europe, which between 1965 and 1980 increased from a 2.3 to 1 to a 2.7 to 1 superiority in tanks, from a 1.1 to 1 to a 1.7 to 1 superiority in armored personnel carriers, and from a 1.2 to 1 to a 2.6 to 1 superiority in artillery.[7] Against this backdrop the Iranian seizure of American hostages—and the Soviet invasion of Afghanistan during America's preoccupation with Iran in 1979—only heightened Western concern that the Soviet Union might in some future confrontation try to exert military leverage in Europe.

Under these circumstances NATO decided on a double-track response to the SS-20s in 1979. Beginning in 1983 it would deploy 108 1,800-kilometer-range Pershing II ballistic missiles and 464 slower 2,500-kilometer-range cruise missiles. The numbers would not be enough to match the SS-20s warhead for warhead, but they would be able to target the European part of the Soviet Union, and, in the case of the superaccurate Pershings, to obliterate even hardened command posts short of Moscow with only ten minutes' warning.

Brezhnev was perplexed. In one conversation with Genscher he objected, "I don't understand at all why the Americans are so upset by the SS-20s. They don't hit the U.S. Why are they forcing you to deploy [INF]?"

Genscher replied, "Mr. general secretary, you completely misunderstand the situation. It's not the Americans who are forcing us to deploy, but we who have requested the Americans to deploy, precisely because [the SS-20s] threaten only Western Europe (and that happens to be where I live, I don't live in the USA). You want to decouple [the Americans]. You want to create a zone of differential security. That is not acceptable."[8]

The Arms Control Barometer Falls

In the four years before NATO's Euromissile deployment was to begin, the West offered Moscow arms control negotiations in what it called its second track. If agreement on East-West equality were reached in that time, the INF stationing would be limited, or even canceled. It was a classic case of arming to disarm, and it was widely greeted in the West with the usual cynicism accorded this approach.

As arms control stalled in the early and mid-1980s, the cynicism of the demonstrators in northern Europe only grew. In the twenty years from the late 1960s to the late 1980s nuclear arms control essentially substituted for a superpower political relationship. Little other intercourse developed, even at the height of détente in the 1970s. Arms control became the barometer of Soviet-American relations, which were good in the years of détente after the SALT I signing, but bad as the U.S. Senate declined to ratify the SALT II treaty following the Soviet invasion of Afghanistan. In Germany, the failure of superpower arms control and the antipathy toward arms control by President Reagan during his first six years in office were thus seen as a dangerous worsening of overall East-West relations and of Germany's position in the East-West balance.

In this context, the very characteristics of the INF missiles that West German generals welcomed as coupling the United States and Europe frightened the West German population. Most fundamentally, European officials wanted modern American missiles capable of hitting the Soviet Union to be stationed on the ground in Western Europe to maintain an unequivocal link with extended deterrence. If push came to shove, they did not want Washington to decide suddenly that this was an exclusively European affair and stand back. If American missiles were involved in the hostilities—and if they were based on the ground in Germany and elsewhere in Europe, avoiding involvement would be hard if the conventional front line buckled—then the United States would have no choice but to back its defense of Western Europe with its strategic nuclear arsenal.

In conjunction with the INF stationing, NATO commander General Bernard W. Rogers conducted the alliance's first rational military analysis of what mix of nuclear weapons might actually be needed to maintain robust deterrence in Europe. He and the Europeans were pleased with what they found. It deterred the Russians far more effectively, they thought, to threaten retaliation against Soviet territory with INF (should the Soviet alliance ever attack West Germany conventionally and look like winning) than to threaten only the Soviet Union's optional buffer in Eastern Europe with battlefield nuclear weapons. To the grateful surprise of the West Germans, General Rogers helped write into NATO's revised General Political Guidelines of 1986 the concept of holding Soviet territory at risk early in any escalation, a principle German defense officials had for years tried in vain to get the United States to subscribe to.[9]

Major portions of the West German public, however, did not view NATO's new INF deployments so benignly. For almost a generation indifferent voters had been content to leave arcane defense decisions to the small coterie of experts. In the late 1970s, however, an uproar in Europe over the latest American gizmo of a neutron warhead—popularized as a weapon that could kill people while leaving buildings intact—had resensitized the average person to nuclear issues. In addition, Reagan's pugnacious rhetoric and zest for nuclear war fighting in Europe frightened the inhabitants of Europe, as did Soviet magnification of the American threat.[10]

In this atmosphere many citizens perceived the Pershings not as linking West Germany to American protection, but as chaining it to American bellicosity. They viewed the new Pershings that were going into their backyard less as a defense than as a Western threat to the Soviet Union, and therefore potential targets for the SS-20s. Their instincts were diametrically opposed to the specialists' deterrence theory and the government's perception of a need for land-based systems in the Federal Republic to couple Chicago to Hamburg in the Russians' minds. Their emotions were strong. A war scare engulfed Germany.

The Peace Movement

The antinuclear movement flourished. Entire school classes made excursions to the peace demonstrations. Young Protestants at their biennial summer convocations wore confession of their nuclear angst as the badge of righteousness. Lutheran clergymen sought to atone for the church's political silence in the Nazi era by antinuclear fervor forty years later. Veterans of the 1968 student revolt, now teachers, reporters, and editors, transferred their view of Vietnam-era *Amerika* to the 1980s, especially in Hessian classrooms, television news magazines, and the weeklies *Der Spiegel* and *Stern*. Some 100,000 marched here, another 250,000 there. At the apex of the protest movement, organizers counted a million heads. For a period, Australian consular offices did a brisk business in applications for emigration out of the Northern Hemisphere nuclear danger zone.

As the new antinuclear democratization in security policy swept Protestant northern Europe, opinion polls in the Netherlands revealed that more than half the voters opposed the new deployments. Polls that posed the question in a balanced way never showed the same clear majority in West Germany, but antinuclear feeling certainly ran strong enough to chasten policymakers. Oxford historian Michael Howard met with instant acclaim when he reminded Schmidt's old forum of the International Institute for Strategic Studies of the forgotten truism that military deterrence of the Soviet adversary avails nothing unless Western citizens are reassured at the same time.[11]

Some revival of the general pacifist backlash of the 1950s to the disaster of Hitler was evident in the West German demonstrations. But more specifically, there was a wave of nuclear pacifism as all the inherent contradictions of the balance of terror seemed to bear down on Germany. The peace movement in the Federal Republic, like its American counterpart, asked all the agonizing moral questions about how reliance on the most horrible weapons ever devised could be reconciled with traditional Christian precepts of a just war: that civilians must not be massacred, that war must be the demonstrably lesser evil in comparison with negotiations or any other available alternative, and that the level of violence must be kept to a minimum.

The questions were even more burning in Berlin than in New York. What was still something of an intellectual exercise on the vast American continent became visceral in the shadow of the Berlin Wall. And the German trait of moral absolutism generated more intensity than did Anglo-Saxon pragmatism. The least ambiguous exorcism of Adolf Hitler's abuse of power was to condemn all use of force by the state, and the states the German demonstrators felt themselves most responsible for as citizens were the Federal Republic and the United States.

To the protesters all the anguishing paradoxes of the system of nuclear deterrence seemed wrong and dangerous: that the crucial taboo on nuclear use must be preserved by one's own determination to employ nuclear retaliation for any nuclear strike; that despite the nuclear taboo, deterrence of any kind of war in Europe is enhanced by a willingness to override the taboo and be the first to resort to nuclear weapons; and that while the only sane purpose for nuclear arms must be war deterrence rather than war fighting, weapons must be credible to deter, and to be credible they must have a clear military function.

These concerns were the same in the American nuclear freeze movement's assault on the whole superpower arms race and the European peace movement's assault on new INF deployments and extended deterrence. But the West Germans' alarm was that much more acute when the West's declared policy in Europe was the first use of these ominous weapons.

There was an additional element in the West German peace movement that was missing in the United States: the unfinished revolt against the residues of Prussian deference to authority. West Germany had no heritage of grass-roots activism, no American habit of absorbing new movements into eclectic political coalitions that are only nominally parties. Instead, Germany had the shameful history of failing to resist Hitler, and a tradition of programmatic parties with hierarchies that in practice did not welcome interlopers, however open their rhetoric might be. Until the success of the environmental Green party in the early 1980s, the Greens complained, amateur agitation for causes was viewed as illegitimate by all the existing parties, even the Social Democratic party.

Almost any protest therefore assumed for the demonstrators the sanctity of opposing the establishment, sometimes with little distinction drawn between an authoritarian establishment and that of an elected government. And for the peace demonstrators the United States was an essential part of the establishment to rebel against, both because it was the Goliath in the Vietnam War, and because it was for so long the father figure in West Germany's postwar modernization. The popular left saw only exaggerated anticommunism in American policy, assumed that Washington dictated Bonn's as well as San Salvador's actions, felt the Germans to be helpless victims, and regarded both superpowers with revulsion.

Such equidistance to the United States and the Soviet Union in turn offended Americans, who tended to regard West German protesters, and even officials, as pusillanimous, unwilling to condemn the Soviet invasion of Afghanistan, driven on the one hand by fear of Soviet SS-20s and on the other by the lure of commercial gain to be made from selling industrial goods to the Russians. The mutual stereotypes reinforced each other. U.S.-European relations as a whole went into a tailspin as the United States tried to apply American law to European companies to prevent them from exporting gas pipeline and pumps to the Soviet Union. It took George Shultz, who became Reagan's second secretary of state in 1982, to retract the American claim to extraterritoriality and restore transatlantic civility.

The Soviet Union

For its part the Soviet Union, in its own two-track approach, played the role of the peace-loving moderate in Europe against the fulminations from Washington—but at the same time continued its occupation of Afghanistan and rattled its SS-20s in Europe. It threatened Rome privately for stationing INF, and warned Bonn publicly that an ice age would ensue if it actually carried out INF deployments. The menace was not as bald as Nikita Krushchev's bluster during the Berlin crisis of 1961 about destroying NATO bases in the "orange groves" of Italy and the "olive groves" of Greece, annihilating Britain with only eight bombs, and "placing in question" the "very existence of the population of West Germany."[12] But it was clear intimidation.

It also was bluff. Of course the Russians hoped to benefit from the popular discontent in West Germany. They would have been overjoyed had their appeal to Western publics over the heads of Western governments made the stationing politically impossible. Their tactics owed less to clever exploitation of the open Western system than to sheer paralysis in Moscow, however. The succession of dying leaders before Gorbachev finally took the helm immobilized the policy apparatus and prevented it from taking any initiatives whatever.

As a substitute for policy, propaganda churned on. Fluent German-speaking Russians circulated at the frequent think-tank conferences at the Protestant academies in Tutzing and Loccum and lunched with their favorite journalists in Bonn. Yet when the Federal Republic, the United Kingdom, Italy, and Belgium finally began deploying the INF missiles and the Netherlands also agreed to future stationing, the Soviet Union had no response but to stalk out of the superpower arms control talks. This let West Germany's beleaguered new chancellor, Christian Democrat Helmut Kohl, argue that it was the Russians, not the Americans, who were blocking progress, and helped him win reelection both in 1983, with deployments pending, and in 1987, after the stationing. Kohl's campaign speeches focused on economics rather than security, but the drop in popular interest in missile issues was itself significant.

To be sure, from NATO's viewpoint a political cost was incurred. The West German Social Democrats repudiated Schmidt and his centrist defense policy, helped break up his center-left coalition in 1982, and donned the antinuclear mantle. The new countercultural Green party entered the Bundestag on the strength of its environmental platform rather than its suspicion of NATO, but the Green members of parliament carried with them their dislike of things military, including the alliance. The West German public, while maintaining its steady 80 percent support for NATO, shifted to oppose NATO's nuclear shield by some 80 percent as well, at least in the rather rudimentary opinion polls.[13] Even the conservatives, after hanging tough on the INF deployment but then finding themselves isolated on nuclear issues, declined to explain their convictions about nuclear deterrence to the public.

The United States and Arms Control

Oddly enough, however much West German popular resistance to the missile deployment shaped the U.S. administration's negative image of Bonn, the INF stationing itself was no more than a sideshow to the Reagan team. Ironically, Assistant Secretary of Defense Richard Perle, the man who in his earlier Senate staff job had masterminded nonratification of Carter's SALT II Treaty, was unimpressed even by the Pershing II and its ability to hit hardened targets swiftly in the European part of the Soviet Union. He thought that the 572 Pershing II and cruise missiles—a tiny percentage of American nuclear holdings—would make little difference in either war or deterrence. For him and the Pentagon, the real game lay elsewhere: in restoring a hardline vigilance against the Russians, breaking out of the frustrations of a continental coalition to the freedom of a unilateral maritime strategy, building up the whole U.S. arsenal after America's post-Vietnam military recoil, commissioning a 600-ship navy, and anathematizing the apostasy of arms control.

NATO did need to deploy the INF missiles, the administration thought, because it had announced its intention to do so, and if the Russians succeeded in their efforts to prevent implementation by fanning the antinuclear mood in West European publics, then Moscow would gain an unacceptable veto over future NATO decisions. In this context holding Bonn's feet to the fire was important. But to Perle—and on such issues he spoke for the Pentagon, despite his modest title—the Pershing and cruise missiles were symbol rather than substance. In particular, as the years rolled on, West German willingness to deploy INF became the test of Bonn's fidelity to the West—a symbolism that West German conservatives rather mischievously promoted in Washington during Chancellor Schmidt's tenure in casting doubts on the Social Democrats' loyalty.

For Perle, however, a far more important goal than INF deployment in Europe was breaking Western policymakers' obeisance to arms control. The right rejected the conventional wisdom of the 1970s that a rough Soviet-American parity existed. The Reagan team judged the American arsenal to be inferior to the Soviet one and called for a military buildup that would not only restore parity but also reinstate American military superiority over the Soviet Union, as the Republican platforms of 1980 and 1984 demanded. It contended further that the misplaced enthusiasm for arms control and squeamishness about planning for nuclear war fighting had contributed to American inferiority and inhibitions about redressing the imbalance.

Specifically, the Reagan administration regarded as defeatist the central arms control precept that nuclear war is unwinnable. Defense Secretary Caspar Weinberger argued instead, in his 1982 medium-term defense guidance study, that America could prevail in a protracted nuclear war (despite his apparent belief in American inferiority).

Indeed, all the arms control verities and restraint the United States had so arduously tried to teach the Russians in the 1960s and 1970s now seemed to go by the board. With the accumulated resentments of hardliners who had suffered during the decade-long ascendancy of arms control and antimilitary backlash to the Vietnam War, the Reagan administration attributed nuclear stalemate not to the technological facts of life but to sheer lack of political will. Reagan's aggressive leadership, they were persuaded, would convince voters to restore American invincibility.[14]

The Europeans, especially the Germans, heard the Reagan administration's utterances with some alarm, anticipating a stormy period in Europe as the arms control barometer fell. The administration scorned such timidity—as well as the Europeans' concomitant reservations about American air strikes in the Middle East and American extension to Europe of the East-West confrontation in Afghanistan. Given this loss of nerve, Washington warned, the clever Russians could easily intimidate the Europeans and achieve their goal of driving wedges between the United States and its faint-hearted German ally.

Nonetheless—largely because the move was deemed tactical, without prejudice to the ultimate outcome—the administration did agree to resume formal arms control talks with the Soviet Union. Administration ideologues were unenthusiastic about the prospect. They bowed, however, to the joint lobbying of European governments, Congress, and State Department moderates, who argued that superpower dialogue was a precondition for public toleration of INF deployments in Europe. They agreed to open Euromissile negotiations in 1981, but insured themselves against a final deal, they thought, by coopting the West German peace movement's goal of a zero option of no medium-range missiles for either East or West. They assumed that the Soviet Union would never give up its newest and shiniest SS-20s, already deployed, for a handful of NATO INF missiles that so far existed only on the drawing board. The dramatic Soviet walkout from the INF and the parallel Strategic Arms Reduction Talks seemed to confirm the Reagan administration's judgment.

Nuclear Reassurance

As Kohl played on Soviet truculence to help sell INF deployment in the Federal Republic, however, Moscow realized it had blundered. It agreed to resume superpower arms control negotiations in Geneva on March 12, 1985, two days after General Secretary Konstantin Chernenko's announced death, but, as it turned out, four days after the interim leader's actual death.[15] Mikhail Gorbachev had been in office in the Kremlin all of one day.

The aim of the new talks was agreed to be stability, a word American arms controllers liked and hardliners did not object to, since it was left undefined. It was a goal the Russians had been reluctant to endorse in the past, because it contradicted the Marxist-Leninist dialectic of very unstable thesis yielding to antithesis yielding to new unstable synthesis in a continuing round, until the ultimate triumph of Soviet-style socialism. However, stability now served particular Soviet purposes as well, since it could be cited as an argument against a new American arms race in space.

At issue here was star wars, Reagan's Strategic Defense Initiative (SDI). In March 1983 the president had suddenly announced his quest for that holy grail of defense against nuclear missiles that had eluded all others in the nuclear age. When found, it would make nuclear weapons impotent and obsolete, he declared. It would be exorbitantly expensive, and, some hardliners boasted, it would ruin the Soviet economy if Moscow joined the race.

The SDI changed the course of history, if not quite in the way Reagan intended. It never produced an Astrodome defense against nuclear catastrophe for the American population, nor did it abolish nuclear weapons. It did help concentrate Soviet minds powerfully on arms control, however.

Initially, the SDI distressed West European governments, which deemed the effort to overturn mutual vulnerability unrealistic and dangerously destabilizing in precisely the ways the 1972 Soviet-American antiballistic missile (ABM) treaty had sought to foreclose in banning the testing or deployment in space of missile defense systems. Yet in the end some of these governments at least would value it as a quixotic accelerator of the evolution of Gorbachev's "new thinking," that is, the necessary application of the precepts of interdependence and tolerance to foreign policy.

For the medium-sized nuclear powers of the United Kingdom and France, a major flaw of star wars was that the partial strategic defense it offered could soon be reproduced by the Soviets, who emulated each new American military technology within a few years. While a partial defense would afford no real protection against any all-out superpower attack, it might well afford an effective shield against a medium-sized nuclear force. The British and French arsenals would then be rendered obsolete.

Moreover—and here the West Germans shared the concern—such mutual damage limitation for the superpowers would weaken the link between NATO theater nuclear forces and American strategic nuclear forces, since Europe could not possibly finance the same kind of damage limitation against the shortest-range theater nuclear weapons. This juxtaposition could only enhance the political leverage of Soviet nuclear superiority in the European theater by neutralizing both superpowers' nuclear forces and rendering incredible NATO's fallback to nuclear first use under flexible response. This in turn could make Europe safe for conventional war in a way it had not been for decades.

Both the conservative British and the Socialist French governments, therefore, quickly urged the United States not to violate the ABM treaty's prohibitions on any significant strategic defense. The reaction was more complex in non-nuclear, frontline West Germany. The Federal Republic, contrary to outsiders' foreboding at the time, had felt no compulsion to go nuclear after Britain and France did so in the early post–World War II years. But in return for its voluntary restraint, written into West Germany's accession to the Western European Union in the 1950s and to the Non-Proliferation Treaty in the 1960s, Bonn expected its security to be preserved on a par with that of its nuclear allies. West German spokesmen therefore echoed the British and French warnings, not because they depended on nonexistent British and French extended deterrence, but because they shared the arms controllers' central concern about crisis instability. If a transition to a regime involving some admixture of strategic defense were to occur, there would be a major risk of miscalculation in the uncertainties of getting from here to there, and the place where any miscalculation would backfire would be Germany.

Summitry

As the dynamic Gorbachev settled into the Soviet leadership and nuclear pacifist sentiment continued to be strong among West European voters, various European governments importuned Reagan to reopen the superpower dialogue. Again they found numerous allies in Congress and among moderates in the State Department. By November 1985 the first superpower summit in six years took place in Geneva.

The meeting was an anticlimax. The two sides pledged themselves to seek an interim INF agreement and endorsed the principle of 50 percent reductions in existing strategic offensive arsenals. Given that the number of strategic warheads had more than doubled since SALT I, halving them would still leave more weapons than the ceilings of the 1972 treaty; and in any case, the counting rules the United States proposed reduced the nominal 50 percent cuts to a real 30 percent. For all the meager results, the Europeans were at least reassured to see the Americans and Soviets talking.

The next summit in Iceland a year later did anything but reassure the Europeans. Although the Reykjavik meeting set the pattern for renewed détente, the tentative INF deal reached there upset West German conservatives, and the bilateral lurch for nuclear abolition alarmed almost all the West Europeans.

Concerning INF, the superpowers agreed in Iceland—with no prior American consultation with European allies—to aim for a quick zero option of no Euromissiles whatever in the 1,000- to 5,500-kilometer range.[16] This deal pleased the Americans immensely; the normally taciturn Secretary of State George Shultz called it breathtaking. To reach parity at zero, the Soviets would have to destroy four times as many missiles as NATO. Equally significant, in Iceland the Soviets accepted for the first time on-site inspection of missile destruction and monitoring of missile factories to verify compliance, along with unprecedented full exchange of data before and after reductions. Moreover, the Soviets confirmed their abandonment, before Reykjavik, of a claim to compensation for British and French nuclear missiles.

On issues of regional conflicts and human rights, too, which the United States had insisted on putting on the Reykjavik agenda, there was promise of accommodation. The Soviet Union was gearing itself up to future withdrawal from the Afghan quagmire, and Gorbachev was on the verge of freeing from internal exile the most famous dissident of all, Andrei Sakharov. A resumption of détente, on the West's terms, appeared to be in the making.

In its final hours, however, the meeting plunged from euphoria to gloom, as two bombshells were dropped: Gorbachev returned to the position that everything, including an INF deal, would be linked and would depend on restraining SDI; and both leaders endorsed nuclear abolition, in premeditated fashion on the part of Gorbachev, impulsively on the part of Reagan. Reagan rejected out of hand any limitation on star wars, and with it the INF bargain. To the dismay of his advisers, however, he spontaneously embraced the extermination of all nuclear weapons, and thus the extermination of the West's nuclear equalizer to Soviet conventional superiority in Europe. This non-nuclear utopia was to be achieved within ten years.[17]

The mini-summit broke up in confusion and rancor. In the Western media, commentary typically wrote off any further summit or any arms control agreement under Reagan and anticipated an intensive Soviet propaganda campaign against the American president. Hardliners and moderates alike tended to view Gorbachev as trying to drive wedges between Europe and the United States by holding Europe's desired INF agreement hostage to star wars, and blaming Reagan's rigidity on the SDI for the collapse of all arms control. People of every persuasion asked if the photogenic Ron and Nancy were now being upstaged by the photogenic Mikhail and Raisa in the White House's own game of glitz and spin control.

This conventional wisdom missed the point. However jerky the process, star wars (and the worst accident in history in a nuclear power plant at Chernobyl the previous April) had finally brought home to Gorbachev the dangers of hair-trigger, first-strike capability in any crisis. He had therefore joined the old American quest for stability in the concrete negotiations, if not yet in his non-nuclear rhetoric. To attain this goal, he was offering what in the perspective of Soviet history were huge concessions, and was running high risks that his own hardliners would repudiate him.

The Europeans, shocked by Reagan's yen for nuclear abolition, were grateful, for once, to Reagan's adamant defense of the SDI for blocking a cosmic no-nuke deal that would have deprived Europe of the protection of American ballistic missiles. Both West German Chancellor Helmut Kohl and British Prime Minister Margaret Thatcher swiftly visited Washington to help reestablish arms control orthodoxy. Kohl, uncharacteristically, made one of the strongest public statements of any European leader in support of the traditional understanding of the ABM treaty, and therefore against the SDI, in saying that its interpretation was a question of cooperative solutions by the signatories rather than of unilateral revision.

The episode revived some fears in West Germany about Soviet-American condominium, along with doubts about Washington's long-term commitment to defend Europe. Even those conservatives who had always considered themselves America's closest friends suddenly saw in Ronald Reagan not a fellow crusader against Soviet empire in Europe, but rather a unilateralist who wanted to write off an encumbering Europe to gain a free hand for solo American intervention around the world.

There was one notable exception to the widespread apprehension in Europe: the West German foreign minister. Hans-Dietrich Genscher was struck by Gorbachev's fresh way of dealing with the West unburdened by the old ideological baggage. He determined to say so in a major speech as soon as the general election in the Federal Republic was over.[18]

INF, Short-Range Nuclear Forces, and Conventional Arms Control

After the ambitious Reykjavik deal exploded in the summiteers' faces, both sides returned to focus on the more modest Euromissile treaty. In Washington the INF endgame served everyone's purpose. Moderates in the administration hoped it would grease the way for the much more important strategic treaty, while hardliners, on the contrary, hoped that the complex Euromissile talks would drain the participants' energies away from the Strategic Arms Reduction Talks in the few remaining months before Reagan's term was up.

In Bonn the picture was altogether different. The opposition Social Democrats endorsed the impending INF treaty not because the Soviet Union would destroy so many SS-20 warheads, but because—they claimed—the treaty showed that the Social Democrats had been right in dumping Schmidt and saying the Western INF was unnecessary. The treaty evoked consternation, however, within the center-right government that had heretofore reveled in its closeness to Reagan.

Here at last was the long anticipated wedge driven by the Soviet Union between NATO partners (and between different constituencies in the single country of West Germany). Ironically, the Russians divided Washington and Bonn not, as expected, by offering an INF deal that the Europeans would desire and the Americans would reject in order to defend the SDI, but by offering the inverse, an INF treaty that both hardliners and moderates in the Reagan administration would desire but the West German government would resist.

The specific bone of contention was an issue that no one had dreamed of before Reykjavik, the "short-range" INF, with a reach of between 500 and 1,000 kilometers. Gorbachev offered in April to scrap all Soviet Euromissiles in this category if NATO would scrap its far fewer counterparts. The United States was willing to do so; the Federal Republic was most reluctant.

The dispute arose as the imminent departure of all the "long-range" INF (1,000 to 5,500 kilometers in range) reminded Bonn of all the advantages of such missiles over the shorter-range weapons that, if used, would explode only in Eastern Europe or, even worse, in Germany itself, whether West or East. Much better to have American missiles based in Europe threaten high-value Soviet territory, they thought, risk Soviet retaliation on the American homeland, and thus advertise to the Russians that U.S. power would be fully engaged from the very start of any European skirmish.

The whole issue was brought home vividly to the Germans while the Reykjavik debacle was still reverberating. In early 1987 NATO plunged into Wintex (winter exercise), its routine biennial rehearsal of allied nuclear consultation. For the first time NATO's new nuclear guidelines would apply. For the first time the alliance would actually have missiles with sufficient range to sweep the nuclear battlefield away from Central Europe to Moscow's doorstep. For the first time, in line with the West German advocacy of two decades, the mock escalation intended to "restore deterrence" would fall heavily on Soviet soil. The threat to use the Pershing II would therefore automatically activate America's nuclear umbrella on behalf of West Germany. That is—contrary to the reasoning of the antinuclear demonstrators, who saw the INF as weapons with which the Reagan administration could wage nuclear war in Europe without risking its own territory—the Bonn government saw any German-based American missile striking the Soviet Union as the best guarantee that the United States would not be a sanctuary, and could therefore not stay aloof from any attack on Germany.[19]

The West Germans had no sooner won NATO over to this approach when their victory evaporated. The very NATO weapons that had the speed and ability to penetrate Soviet airspace were being whisked away in arms control. The concept itself was also abruptly jettisoned, according to West German military sources, as Reagan learned of the course of the winter exercise, objected to the risk of superpower nuclear war inherent in swift nuclear escalation onto Soviet soil, and ordered future NATO simulations to concentrate their escalation west of the Soviet border. NATO's

General Political Guidelines may not have been formally changed, but the policy of their nuclear guarantor certainly was.

Moreover, the Pentagon shortly insisted on radically upgrading and expanding a weapon NATO had never before deemed very important, the less than 500-kilometer-range Lance missiles stationed in the Federal Republic. Even worse, the United States viewed Bonn's approval of the Lance replacement—which if it were ever used would make Germany a nuclear wasteland—as the latest litmus of German loyalty to the West.

As the West Germans saw it, then, they were now being stuck permanently with missiles of ranges that could hit little but Germany. This was the very nightmare of singularization, or special threat, that they had consistently sought to avoid. The nuclear risk to the Soviet Union (and therefore to the United States) was being removed by the withering away of INF missiles and Reagan's rejection of NATO's nuclear guidelines, even as the risk to Germany from the shortest-range systems was being frozen in place.

A remarkable wave of self-pity and feeling of abandonment engulfed the West German center-right. Franz Josef Strauss, Bavarian premier and unquestioned leader of the conservative right wing, asserted that the INF treaty "means a decoupling of Americans from Europe." Conservative member of parliament Bernhard Friedmann went so far as to hint that if the United States were not a reliable defender of West German interests, then perhaps Bonn should look elsewhere.

The usually sober *Frankfurter Allgemeine Zeitung* wrote melodramatically about "the surrender of deterrence by nuclear weapons" and charged that the Bonn government was "raped" into acceding to special vulnerability. Even Chancellor Kohl warned the United States, the United Kingdom, and France in veiled language in the Bundestag that "there must be no lesser security [zone for West Germany], either as between the American and European allies or as between the European allies themselves." Various generals added—sotto voce, since the information was classified—that Washington was putting a disproportionate nuclear risk on Bonn in assigning targets under any general nuclear response, or all-out American-Soviet exchange, to weapons based in West Germany.

"The shorter the range, the deader the Germans," chimed in the traditionally pro-American center-right, with a bitterness that was potentially even more corrosive to the long-standing U.S.-German partnership than was popular antinuclear sentiment.

Against this backdrop Foreign Minister Genscher delivered his bombshell speech at the annual gathering of high-powered politicians and business people in Davos, Switzerland. In his most quoted line, he asserted that the West should take Gorbachev "at his word" in his profession of new thinking about mutual interdependence. Alarmed British, French, and

American officials warned each other and the Germans about the dangers of "Genscherism," or softness toward the sly Russians.[20]

In the United States, William Safire was writing column after column on European parochialism, miserliness in defense, and reluctance to help the United States in Central America. And former national security advisers Henry Kissinger and Zbigniew Brzezinski were leading the calls to cut American troops in Europe to force the allies into shouldering their fair share of the common defense and help ease America's huge payments deficits.

In the INF negotiations the Soviet Union dropped linkage with the SDI and gave way on one point after another throughout 1987. By December the treaty was ready for signing as a summit finally took place in Washington. Within three years all the INF missiles and their associated fuel, nozzles, and the like would be "burned, crushed, flattened, or destroyed by explosion." On star wars, Reagan and Gorbachev could do no more than agree to disagree at the summit. The Strategic Arms Reduction Talks were given a new impetus by the INF deal, however.

Unexpectedly, so were conventional arms control negotiations. The Mutual and Balanced Force Reduction talks had dragged on for fourteen interminable years with no results. They were buried without regret as the twenty-three members of NATO and the Warsaw Treaty Organization discussed opening new negotiations on reducing conventional forces in Europe. The Russians and the West Europeans had long been pressing for such talks. The United States, fearing that deep cuts could deprive the West of its ability to maintain frontline troop densities needed to repel a surprise attack, had long been resisting such negotiations. Now, however, the United States acquiesced, and NATO began working out proposed cuts in armor and major heavy weapons down to equality at 5 to 10 percent below existing NATO levels.

By the time the NATO allies and the reluctant French had sorted out their own differences and the Conventional Forces in Europe talks actually got under way in March 1989, they were fast becoming obsolete. In December 1988, for his own economic and political reasons, Gorbachev had announced startling unilateral cuts in Soviet forces in Eastern Europe, removing from East Germany four tank divisions, close to 4,000 tanks, and the only Soviet air assault brigade in the GDR, and from Czechoslovakia and Hungary two further tank divisions. The total Soviet withdrawals of 50,000 troops from the GDR, Czechoslovakia, and Hungary equaled what the West had been asking for in the Mutual and Balanced Force Reduction talks, while the tank cuts were three times what the West had requested.[21]

Thus, as NATO approached its gala fortieth anniversary celebration in May, East-West tensions relaxed somewhat, but West Germany and its

major allies looked to be on a collision course over short-range missiles
and other irritations. Senior American columnists, recalling the Nazis'
murder of the Jews, warned against an unhealthy recrudescence of Germany, and compared sales of chemical weapons materials to Libya by West
German entrepreneurs with Auschwitz. For good measure, they also cautioned against West German economic hegemony in Eastern Europe.

For their part, the British and French press worried that assertive
Germans might again unbalance Europe. West German commentators
retorted that Bonn had kept its head down for forty years after World War
II, and that it was about time for Bonn to assert itself and wrest back some
of its own sovereign rights to cut maneuvers and deafening tree-top flights
in Germany by allied air forces. A few allied voices responded by specu-
lating that if the West Germans did not want to be protected, perhaps the
allied troops should just leave Germany.

The West German left countered by saying that the United States was
an occupier in Germany for its own interests anyway, and was pulling
innocent Germans into its continuing cold war. The American right complained about Germans' Gorbymania, Genscherism, attempted equidistance, and presumption of moral equivalence between Washington and
Moscow. The French fretted about a repeat of Rapallo. The latest West
German right-wing splinter manifestation, the Republicans, came from
nowhere to win enough protest votes in elections in West Berlin and Frankfurt to take away a critical 6 or 7 percent from Kohl's Christian Democrats.
Kohl dropped sharply in opinion polls, and the strongly antinuclear Social
Democrats began tasting victory in the next general election.

It was this atmosphere that George Bush inherited as forty-first president of the United States.

The NATO Summit

The acrimony over nuclear modernization with the Germans, Gorbachev's continued upstaging of the United States in new arms control
proposals, and Bush's own initial poor ratings in opinion polls all led the
new president to announce a vision of the future to rival Gorbachev's. He
chose the venue of the NATO summit in Brussels in May 1989.

Since Moscow, in the increasingly important conventional arms control talks, had already come close to the original Western proposals for
cutting tanks, artillery, and armored troop carriers on the central front,
Bush decided to move swiftly in acceding to the Soviet wish to cut planes,
helicopters, and, specifically, manpower. He offered more generous 10 percent cuts in U.S. air and ground forces in Europe—or approximately the
amount the United States would withdraw anyway if the West's projected

reduction in armor were implemented—if Soviet forces in Eastern Europe would come down to U.S. ceilings in Western Europe. Such a trade-off would remove about ten times as many Soviet as American troops, although the West—and, interestingly, Moscow—never emphasized this.

At the same time, Bush offered public recognition of West Germany's emerging role as the political as well as economic motor of Europe. Immediately after the NATO summit the president visited West Germany (rather than the United Kingdom) and solemnly described his hosts in a speech in Mainz as "partners in leadership." Their common goal, he suggested, was a Europe "whole and free," that is, including Eastern Europe. To Bonn's relief he also quietly dropped U.S. insistence that the Germans deploy a follow-on to the Lance missile.

Associated with the nod to Bonn was the president's clear endorsement of European integration, a cause that past administrations had not always welcomed in practice. Specifically, Bush invited the European Community to lead a new drive to give economic assistance to Poland, Hungary, or any other East European country struggling to move toward political pluralism. Cynics might argue that this hardly proved the political magnanimity of a United States that was in any case deficit-ridden. However, the equanimity with which Bush looked at moves toward European union—and his subsequent opening of diplomatic relations with the European Community—bespoke a new era. The years of fighting Western Europe over economic sanctions on the Soviet Union and Poland were relegated to the past.

Bush now also acknowledged implicitly that Gorbachev was seeking to move even the sluggish Soviet Union in a proto-pluralist direction, and therefore deserved support.

Suddenly the West had a real policy toward Mikhail Gorbachev's Soviet Union. It went to the very heart of the whole East-West confrontation. If Gorbachev were really reforming the second superpower and correcting its military bias, then it might just be possible to build down that densest concentration of weaponry in the world on the East-West fault line.

The new content and tone emanating from the White House were greeted with immense relief in Europe, especially by Kohl. The chancellor and the German center were strengthened against the antinuclear left, and Lance, the erstwhile alliance buster, was relegated to nothing more than a blip on the screen. The nuclear beast was at least provisionally tamed; the West Germans were finally reassured. The public breathed more easily. Applications for emigration to Australia dropped.

Within half a year politics, not arms control, would be the measure of East-West, and therefore of West-West, relations.

Chapter 5

Meanwhile, Europe

I f German unification had burst upon the scene in the years of Eurostagnation in the 1970s or early 1980s, it could have derailed European integration. Certainly the far-right Republicans in West Germany assumed that national and continentwide aims would conflict even in the late 1980s in their subliminal anti-Europe campaign. Once the Berlin Wall did open, the French all but panicked that Bonn would now turn its back on Western Europe for the more romantic lure of a united fatherland and *Mitteleuropa* (Central Europe).

As it turned out, however, the Soviet empire disintegrated and the Germanies unified only after Europe had relaunched itself in a dynamic new drive for a real common market by 1992. In this context, as Kohl kept pledging, the single Germany became not a brake on a single Europe, but the catalyst that accelerated its achievement.

Europe Improvises

In the beginning—after World War II—Europe had idealism and euphoria as well as devastation and rubble. The dream of Europe without barriers, it was hoped, would replace the nationalism that twice within a single generation had plunged the continent into war. Young West Germans, relieved at being able to drop allegiance to a discredited criminal nation, took to the streets to demonstrate fervently for European unity, until the Federal Republic's world soccer championship of 1954 again unleashed a national jubilation that some Germans (and others) found unseemly.

Certainly in the fifteen years of rebuilding the continent, its patron, America, assumed that a united Europe was the wave of the future. The

U.S. Marshall Plan insisted that the European recipients of aid band together in the Organization for European Economic Cooperation (later the expanded Organization for Economic Cooperation and Development) to design a common plan for reconstruction. Thereafter Washington repeatedly prodded Western Europe—Moscow barred East Europeans from accepting American largesse—to establish a formal economic, and even political, union. In the meantime, the United States undertook a temporary defense commitment to Europe by means of NATO.

Under the guidance of visionaries like French Foreign Minister Robert Schuman and banker Jean Monnet, Western Europe took its first steps toward unity by forming the European Coal and Steel Community in 1950 to remove all trade and price barriers in these key commodities among France, West Germany, Italy, and the Benelux countries. Seven years later the "little Europe" of the Six, having failed to persuade others to join them, broadened their cooperation into the European Economic Community (EEC) with the Treaty of Rome. West Germany was glad to begin its political rehabilitation after Hitler by winning acceptance in these groups; France was glad to hobble West German power with pan-European constraints. London, in the throes of decolonization, stood aloof, seeing its future not in heartland Europe, but in the Commonwealth and in its Anglo-Saxon fraternity with the United States.

The security and stability assured by NATO allowed the EEC the luxury of building its own institutions slowly—agonizingly slowly, it sometimes seemed—until social and economic forces might generate new pressures from below for further integration. Despite pan-European exhortations by French, German, and other elites, the EEC soon reached its popular limit. The average person remained suspicious of anything grander than the most rudimentary cooperation. Initially, habits of thought and behavior remained distinctly national.

At the core of the EEC, France made no attempt to hide its motivation, which was driven less by a desire for reconciliation and partnership with its German archfiend than by fear and the aim of keeping Germany divided, with France dominating its Western part. "I love Germany so much, it makes me happy to have two of them," author François Mauriac declared, uttering an aphorism that would be quoted for decades thereafter. Even before the European Coal and Steel Community and NATO were established, France had led four other European countries in forming the alliance of the Western Union (later, the Western European Union, or WEU) aimed at defending its members not only against the Soviet colossus, but also against any return to a German policy of aggression.

For its part, Bonn operated within the EEC, benefited from this larger market, and generally embarked on the course of taming its power by entangling itself more thoroughly in international bodies than any other industrialized nation.[1] It also pursued an economic miracle of its own, however, that soon made even truncated Germany once again the dominant manufacturer and trader in Europe.

As the cold war settled in, the United States made one last attempt to spur its allies into forming a political and security entity, to be called the European Defense Community. The European Defense Community would recruit armed forces from the not yet sovereign Federal Republic to raise the number of Western troops closer to Soviet bloc levels, but would keep the Germans safely in European harness. It would also, the United States hoped, reduce the need for American forces to stay in Europe indefinitely to guard against Soviet intimidation.

The European Defense Community was dashed on French doubts that Paris could control Germany in the proposed arrangement. In 1954 the National Assembly rejected ratification. On the rebound, the Federal Republic joined NATO and the WEU and began rebuilding an army, to the satisfaction of Adenauer, but over the misgivings both of the French and of the German left. In a unique move, the German military (Bundeswehr) was put under direct NATO command. WEU restraints further barred Germany from producing or owning nuclear, chemical, or biological weapons and set limits on Germany's conventional weapons, including the size of its ships.

In 1956 the Americans blocked French and British recapture of the Suez Canal, which Egypt had nationalized. In 1957 the Six finally formed the EEC proper, in part to fill the vacuum left by the failed European Defense Community. In 1958 General Charles de Gaulle returned to power in Paris and began his long campaign to turn German Atlanticists into Gaullists. In 1960 France exploded its first nuclear device, partly thanks to clandestine help from the United States that remained secret for a quarter of a century.[2] In 1961 Khrushchev backed down from his three-year Berlin crisis, and the GDR built the Berlin Wall, cementing the East-West fault line. That same year, partly in response to American prodding, the United Kingdom (along with Denmark, Ireland, and Norway) applied to join the EEC. The postwar European institutions were now essentially in place.

In 1962 the two superpowers stood eyeball to eyeball over Soviet missiles in Cuba. Khrushchev blinked, and de Gaulle concluded that the United States was now superior, and that the hegemonic power to guard against in Europe was no longer the Soviet Union, but America. At the beginning of 1963 de Gaulle dramatically vetoed the entry of the British "Trojan horse" into the EEC, arguing that it would lead to "a gigantic Atlantic community that would be dependent on and be run by the Americans."

A week later de Gaulle signed a Treaty of Cooperation with Adenauer that he hoped would finally shift Germany's orientation away from America to France. The pact brought to a climax a pageantry of reconciliation that included joint worship by the two Catholic leaders at Reims Cathedral and a theatrical visit to the Federal Republic by the French general. On German soil, in German, de Gaulle pronounced his absolution to a bemused German crowd: "You are a great people, yes indeed, a great people!" In his audience the future '68ers, who had just tasted political power by rallying to defend *Der Spiegel* against the government's jailing of the magazine's publisher, did not know whether to laugh or cry.[3]

A Gaullist Germany was not to be, however. The Bundestag, reluctant to swap the known protection of the United States for the uncertain patronage of France, unanimously qualified its ratification of the French-German treaty with a preamble that could not have offended de Gaulle more. Bonn's overarching aim, the preamble stated, was "a close partnership between Europe and the United States of America." The United Kingdom, it added, should be admitted into the EEC.

Within months Adenauer was forced out of office, in part over the *Spiegel* affair, and at the insistence of the Liberals, who were now commencing their long kingmaker role in coalition governments. The next year America's residual hope of a NATO nuclear multilateral force died. Instead, the alliance's Nuclear Planning Group was formed, with Bonn as a permanent member, but without access to nuclear weapons of its own, even in the form of collective ownership. In 1965 the United States intervened in the Vietnam War in a major way, deemphasized Europe, and drew down its NATO forces to meet its new Asian commitments. Conservative Germans worried about America's priorities and judgment, and the student generation worried about America's morality.

In 1966 de Gaulle enshrined in stone the rule that any EEC member could veto any EEC legislation. That same year he withdrew France from NATO's integrated military command. In 1967 NATO's Harmel report expressed the hard-won consensus that the alliance should strive for East-West détente as well as military deterrence. In 1968, in one of numerous stands that foreigners would construe as the first time since 1945 that Bonn was asserting independence from its allies, West Germany resisted pressure to revalue the strong deutsche mark. The Soviet Union invaded Czechoslovakia, and the United States postponed East-West détente.

In 1969 de Gaulle, demoralized by the 1968 student revolt that engulfed Paris as well as Frankfurt, vanished from the political scene. French-American relations improved. The EC, as the consolidated European Community was now called, admitted Britain, Denmark, and Ireland to its ranks.

Despite attempts in the 1970s to expand economic cohesion to political cohesion through formal "European political cooperation" and direct elections to the European Parliament, the EC lapsed into stagnation for more than a decade. Most conspicuously, the West Europeans utterly failed to agree on any common response to the oil shocks. Academic interest shifted away from the sleepy low politics of European institution building to the high politics of nuclear arms control and the Helsinki Final Act of 1975, which set up the floating thirty-five-nation Conference on Security and Cooperation in Europe.

Economic strains developed between the United States and Germany over Richard Nixon's floating of the dollar, Jimmy Carter's desire for a German "locomotive" to growth, and trade imbalances. Among themselves, EC members constantly squabbled about groceries as Europe's agricultural productivity soared, two-thirds of the organization's budget went to subsidize the growing wine lakes and butter mountains, and Europe became America's chief rival in food exports. The bureaucracy in Brussels grew. West Germany and France defended the continent against the gyrations of the floating American dollar by forming a European Monetary System, but Europe split again as the United Kingdom declined to join the scheme.

In other issues the rule of unanimity essentially kept EC political decisions at the lowest common denominator. In many ways the Community became the excuse for inertia. Any government that wanted to resist action in any area could easily plead that it was blocked by obdurate partners in Brussels. The alibi was only reinforced as the EC took in Greece, Spain, and Portugal in the early 1980s to help strengthen these countries' emerging democracies and had to accommodate the weak Mediterranean economies.

Academic studies of EC stagnation flourished. Structuralists sought understanding by analyzing the technocrats and international civil servants, neostructuralists by dissecting interest groups, realists by investigating the lack of political will in low politics, and others by exploring the failure of either diplomacy or the expanding mail, telephone, and personal links to forge a transcendent identity. None of the schools of analysis predicted anything but continued stasis in the EC.[4]

Rejuvenation in the 1980s

The EC owes its unexpected reinvigoration in the 1980s primarily to five men: West German and Italian foreign ministers Hans-Dietrich Genscher and Emilio Colombo, West German Chancellor Helmut Kohl, French President François Mitterrand, and, to a certain extent, U.S. President Ronald Reagan. The Europeans' contribution was to recapture, almost inadvertently, some of the original impetus toward union, while the

Americans helped scare the Europeans into banding together to protect themselves against the vagaries of their giant ally.

To be sure, Chancellor Helmut Schmidt and President Valery Giscard d'Estaing also deserve credit for inching Europe forward with their European Monetary System in the late 1970s, but they viewed this accomplishment more as a technical solution to prevent turbulence in intra-European trade rather than as the harbinger of some grander supranationalism. In any case Schmidt, an admirer of the statecraft of Marcus Aurelius, focused on the concrete and mistrusted grand declarations of intent, so much so that he was scorned as a *Macher* (a cold-blooded "dealer") by left-wing Social Democrats. He certainly continued his predecessors' emphasis on the European economic coordination that had so clearly benefited German manufacturers. He viewed French-German cooperation as the motor of this coordination, and he even seemed to develop a certain affection for the French in his years in office. However, he was not one to establish lofty future goals for a cohesive Europe that was still a figment of the imagination. He viewed the bilateral Franco-German "alliance within the alliance" as a marriage of convenience between Germany, the economic giant and political dwarf, and France, the economic laggard but World War II victor and perceived moral authority in foreign policy.

In this constellation Britain was a conspicuous outsider, as Prime Minister Margaret Thatcher did not favor the concept of a unified Europe. Thus, even when specific British and German interests ran parallel, as they frequently did, Bonn stuck with Paris. If asked why, German policymakers, in a virtual litany, explained that Britain simply was not a player in Europe, and that West Germany therefore had to cling to France.

It was in the midst of this "Eurosclerosis" that Genscher and Colombo suddenly proposed that the EC write a formal European Act. It was 1980, and to all the *Realpolitiker* like Chancellor Schmidt and the other heads of government, the proposal seemed little more than a harmless attempt to divert public attention from the real political issue of stalemate over Thatcher's complaints about British overpayments to the EC. They indulged Genscher, who was by then the senior foreign minister in the Atlantic alliance, but they viewed the initiative less as a vision of the future than as another example of this consummate politician's knack for searching out policy niches to claim as his own against his chancellor's domestic dominance.

Genscher himself describes his motivation as something much deeper. Even at that point of the cold war, he says, he was thinking of creating the preconditions for drawing Eastern Europe into the West European community. As a young man he had been educated in the GDR before moving to the Federal Republic, and in the years since he had maintained his links with his home town of Halle. It was natural for him to conceive of political challenges more broadly. "We were of the opinion that we must go forward with European unification, because we had to create an island of stability in Europe," he says of himself and his Italian colleague. But their goal did not end at the East-West fault line. "This Western Europe must also now be in a position to give an example—not militarily, but politically and economically—in looking east. The attractiveness of the EC is enormous in the East. For me it was simply a necessity to create as much European unity as possible in the West, but to do it also with a view to overcoming the division of Europe."

Whatever his original expectations, Genscher got the backing of a fellow Europeanist once Kohl came to power in 1982. The chancellor likes to point out that he has advocated both German unification and European integration ever since he jumped into politics as a teenager as class and then school spokesman.[5]

By 1983 the member nations issued the "solemn declaration of European union" that Genscher and Colombo had initiated. The declaration's pledge to cooperate in combating terrorism, codifying human rights standards, and setting the eventual goal of a common foreign and security policy hardly warranted all the fanfare, the conventional cynicism ran, but these were unobjectionable targets. All the members signed.

To nuts and bolts politicians what was much more portentous than any proclamation of union was France's concurrent economic convergence toward West Germany. The Socialists, in power in Paris after decades of writing apodictical programs in the wilderness of the opposition, were quickly sobered by the failure of their prescriptions of reflation in the early 1980s. They offered only token resistance to the French conservatives' joining in the Thatcher fad for deregulation during the period of "cohabitation" in the mid-1980s. At long last they were ready to accept the need for German-style monetary discipline.

This convergence also helped prepare the way for the next advance in the EC: the Single European Act of 1985 that laid out the European Commission's goal of fulfilling the Treaty of Rome's original objective of a real common market by 1992. The project met with general, if modest, approval. Germany, the most environmentally conscious because of the Greens' political clout in the Bundestag, was certainly glad to bring pollution under EC purview. The poor southern states appreciated the announced budgetary shift that reduced northern farm subsidies in favor of more regional assistance. Even Thatcher welcomed 1992 as the pragmatic dismantling of annoying, vestigial cross-border restrictions on banking, finance, insurance, and other transactions that British firms excelled at. The simplified market, she thought, would promote British industry but not pose a threat to British sovereignty.

Once the subsequent harmonization of national laws in 280 specifics got under way, however, "1992" took on an unexpected life of its own. Suddenly business people began treating the prospect of a huge market of 320 million customers seriously, adjusted their investment strategies accordingly, and began driving the process in a way that the slow legislatures were not. Suddenly the procedures that member states had agreed on to facilitate decisions—which included permitting the European Parliament to revise draft legislation and allowing weighted majority voting among member governments in areas other than taxes, movement of people, and work conditions—changed the dynamics of the process. Innovations could be voted in by nine to three, or even eleven to one, and the odd man out— usually Britain—would find itself uncomfortably isolated. Peer pressure now served to wear down the resistance of the most stubborn rather than the initiative of the most ambitious. All at once 1992 began to create an impetus for broader economic, and even political, integration.

Most remarkably, various politicians began to discover that the EC might now be good politics as publics and elites reversed their opinions of the 1950s, and popular support for more integration outstripped the intellectuals' boredom with Europe. Opinion polls in every EC country except Britain and Denmark had long since shown 60 to 70 percent approval ratings for European integration. German automobiles had long sported versions of their national identity decal with the "D" for Deutschland fading into an "E" for Europa. Now others also began carrying bumper stickers with the European symbol of a circle of stars on a blue field, and even British and Danish views caught up with the rest of Europe. When the Danish Folketing rejected the Single European Act, the voters overruled their parliament in a dramatic referendum. People did not cease to feel like Italians or Belgians or Dutch, but they did begin to think of themselves generically as Europeans.

Public opinion polls registered the postnationalism that younger Europeans now took for granted. Thanks to the EC they enjoyed unprecedented prosperity. They ate French brie, wore Gucci shoes, and perhaps had a summer house in Malaga. They direct dialed and faxed each other and transmitted electronic data instantly around the continent.[6] They also traveled incessantly. By 1980 cross-frontier arrivals in Europe numbered 160 million, up from 80 million in 1970 and 40 million in 1960, and travelers increasingly saw customs and passport checks as nuisances.

In commerce, manufacturers now regularly assembled components culled from the length and breadth of Western Europe in a way that would have been unthinkable three decades earlier. The national champions of the 1950s became transnational hybrids that by the late 1970s challenged the old American multinationals. Europeanwide retail chains sprang up. The ratio of trade to national income increased, as did the ratio of European to total trade. By the 1980s every EC member except for Britain conducted two-thirds of its trade within what now came to be called the European Economic Space of the EC and the ring of Scandinavian and neutral countries surrounding it in the European Free Trade Association.

The American Goad

Reagan's role in the EC's development began with the transatlantic dispute over European exports to the Soviet Union in the early 1980s. Europe was uneasy about entrusting its security to this film cowboy in any case, and it was certainly leery of the lurches in policy it had encountered under four American presidents in nine years.

The trade impasse arose when the Europeans contracted to sell pipeline and compressors to the Soviet oil and gas industry at a time when the United States was imposing an industrial embargo on the Soviet Union in retaliation for the invasion of Afghanistan and the Soviet-sponsored imposition of martial law in Poland. The Reagan administration, incensed by this lack of solidarity, threatened to shut off American technology from any American affiliate in Europe that failed to adhere to Washington's embargo. In this issue the United States had no European allies. Even Thatcher, close as she was to her fellow ideological conservative in the White House, defended the Europeans' sovereign right to trade as they pleased. The United States, she said in concert with her colleagues, had no right to exercise extraterritoriality on British or French or German soil, and was displaying considerable self-righteousness in insisting that the allies curb their industrial exports to the Soviet Union (a category in which the United States had negligible trade, while the Europeans had substantial trade), while not curtailing agricultural exports, which constituted America's main Soviet sales. Besides, the Germans added, the Federal Republic's maximum 6 percent dependence on Soviet gas would hardly subject Bonn to Soviet coercion.

Reagan backed down after the emollient George Shultz replaced the abrasive Alexander Haig as secretary of state, but Reagan's threat to withhold American technology from Europe coincided with a new consensus that in the ongoing third industrial revolution what drives economic growth is accelerating innovation. Sclerotic Europe, with a slower growth rate than Japan and a much worse record in job creation than the United States, the Europeans feared, would get left far behind if it did not pool its small national technology funds and know-how and stand up to American blackmail. Under French prodding, the Europeans therefore founded the European Strategic Program for Research and Development in Information Technologies and—after Reagan announced his push for a strategic defense initiative—the Eureka program to develop common laser, interceptor, and space technology.

The French-German Connection

At this point, largely because of French alarm about a possible German drift to the East, the special French-German partnership was energized into becoming the motor for Europe that Adenauer and de Gaulle had foreshadowed. Mitterrand, unlike Reagan, decided that the best way to prevent the feared German drift toward Moscow was not to browbeat Bonn, but to embrace it in a grip that would keep it bound to the West.

By a quirk of history, it was the one-time left-wing French Socialists, in power for the first time in decades, who now counseled the traditionally moderate German Social Democrats not to be so gullible in assessing the Soviet Union. In the 1970s the French elite had worried about the Federal Republic's ban on radicals and resurgent German fascism (and had maintained its own infatuation with Marxism well after the decline of communist enthusiasm elsewhere among Western intellectuals). In the 1980s, with growing nuclear pacifism in West Germany raising the specter of removal of France's German glacis, the French elite flipped overnight to worry instead about potential German neutralism.

French anxiety approached hysteria and had a powerful impact on policy. President François Mitterrand traveled to Bonn to address beaming conservatives and sullen Social Democrats in the Bundestag, urging them to deploy those American INF missiles that a still-Gaullist France would certainly never deploy itself. He and Kohl also activated the forgotten pledge of bilateral cooperation on security in the original French-German treaty of 1963.

Kohl welcomed Mitterrand's support for his INF stand. Such European backing, especially from the left, was helpful in diffusing the peace movement's image of a bilateral American-German confrontation over deployment. For tactical reasons Kohl shied away from facing down his domestic opponents, but he fully shared the horror of one British diplomat who exclaimed, "The dreadful feeling that we defend ourselves to please the Americans is appalling!"

Kohl, who resisted having to choose between Paris and Washington fully as much as Adenauer ever had, also welcomed Mitterrand's warming to NATO as part of France's urgent campaign to keep the Federal Republic in the Western camp. Certainly West German generals, and even NATO commanders, expressed satisfaction in this period with their quiet joint contingency planning with the French for any hostilities in Germany (if not yet for critical use of French airfields and logistics during hostilities).

The French may have ostentatiously barred NATO observers from the showpiece French-German maneuvers in the mid-1980s that were the largest since 1945, but in lower-key bilateral exercises they freely received representatives of NATO's Military Committee in the field.[7]

The French military, which did not have the same complexes about defending Gaullism as the political class did, further gratified the West Germans by edging closer and closer in public statements to promising Bonn automatic French engagement in case of any attack on the Federal Republic. That automaticity, while pledged in the WEU treaty, had fallen away with de Gaulle's withdrawal from the NATO military command in 1966, and the West Germans were most eager to get it restored. Kohl and Mitterrand's surprise establishment of a French-German Defense Council in the mid-1980s fit this pattern.

Pragmatically, then, everyone involved saw intensified French-German collaboration as the means for increasing French cooperation with NATO without forcing on Paris the humiliation of repudiating de Gaulle's withdrawal. Everyone also assumed that this French-NATO cooperation made a difference in the one place where it counted, the minds of any Russians who might be contemplating an attack on West Germany.

To be sure, Paris and Bonn remained at cross-purposes concerning the military specifics of their cooperation. While both worried that the Reagan unilateralists were losing interest in Europe and might call the GIs home, Paris wished to hedge against such an eventuality by enhancing Europe's autonomous nuclear power, while Bonn wished to do so by strengthening France's conventional forces. In particular, Bonn wanted from the elusive French a firm advance commitment to help Germany militarily should the Federal Republic ever be attacked. It also wanted France to provide the operational reserves for counterattack that NATO's thin front line desperately needed early on in any war. To that end West Germany urged France in vain to strengthen the French Second Army Corps and First Army in West Germany and replace its antiquated tanks, fighting vehicles, artillery, and logistical support systems.

The conjunction of these two approaches sometimes produced a dialogue of the deaf. Paris, still viewing nuclear weapons as its trump card in the bilateral relationship, probed offering Bonn a German voice—in return for German funding, of course—in disposition of the *force de frappe*. Paris further floated the idea of extending British and French nuclear deterrence to cover West Germany as a kind of added insurance to the American nuclear guarantee.[8] The Federal Republic, however, convinced by now of the political nonutility of apocalyptic nuclear weapons for any purpose beyond crude deterrence, had no intention of paying for France's nuclear badge of honor, and it certainly had no desire to dump the sturdy nuclear guarantee provided by the American superpower for three decades for some nebulous future guarantee by the French regional power.

The one aspect of French nuclear weapons over which Bonn really would have liked to gain influence was the targeting of French substrategic missiles. If possible, Bonn would have liked to dissuade Paris from even thinking of firing its Plutos, which could reach no farther than Frankfurt, or its forthcoming Hades, which would reach East Germany.

The French were not about to circumscribe their options in such a fashion, and West German solicitousness of East Germany—along with the concurrent revival of elite German interest in Central Europe—only added to French suspicions about West German loyalties. In the end, in February 1986 Paris promised the Germans no more than an inconclusive right of consultation before French nuclear use—should time permit.

Nor could Bonn persuade Paris to shift budgetary priorities away from nuclear to conventional arms, or secure that automatic French commitment to spring to West Germany's defense in case of attack. France did inaugurate a lightly armed rapid deployment force for use in Germany as well as in the third world. It also took various symbolic steps: setting up, besides the bilateral security council, a joint French-German brigade and exchanges for training young officers; arranging for regular meetings of the two countries' foreign and defense ministers several times a year; and conducting bilateral military exercises that conspicuously went beyond de Gaulle's old tacit eastern limit for French troops in approaching the Bavarian-Czechoslovak border.

In addition, France spearheaded the lifting of the remaining WEU restrictions on West German conventional armament by 1984. Paris also twice resurrected the languishing WEU in the 1980s as a convenient, standing, non-NATO forum that France belonged to, was strictly European, and comprised only Europeans who, unlike Denmark and Greece, were serious about defense. After the first revival in 1984 Paris once more lost interest in the WEU as its initial alarm about potential German neutralism subsided. The Euromissile arms control negotiations and German reluctance to modernize short-range nuclear weapons, however, along with the superpower summit in Reykjavik in October 1986, rekindled French fears about German reliability, Reagan's age, and Gorbachev's seductive attractiveness.

The French therefore reanimated the WEU yet again in October 1987 and accepted Spain and Portugal as new members, in part to give the Socialists in Madrid a European cachet to help sell their voters on joining NATO. All members signed a platform that traded Bonn's acknowledgment that nuclear and conventional deterrence were both necessary for France's acknowledgment that all member states needed to have their territorial integrity defended. For their part, the British got a recognition of the need for cooperation with NATO inserted into the platform.

After a turbulent decade in which Europe lurched closer together, the increased sense of community was barely visible to the naked eye. It had grown synergistically, however, both in economics and in common security. By the mid-1980s, in the view of the Royal Institute of International Affairs' senior European analyst, William Wallace, the EC was "transformed from an instrument of Franco-German reconciliation into the key power structure in Europe: a structure of collective leadership."[9] By the time the Berlin Wall opened in 1989, the European framework would be ready to receive German unification.

Chapter 6

Meanwhile,
Eastern Europe

Together, the revival of superpower détente and Gorbachev's progressive extension of "new thinking" even to
the Soviet Union's external empire set off momentous changes in Eastern
Europe. Initially, only Poland and Hungary used the new room for maneuver. The recalcitrant East German, Czechoslovak, and Romanian leaderships resisted the changes in every possible way, domestically, bilaterally,
and in the Warsaw Treaty Organization and the Council for Mutual Economic Relations.

Imperceptibly at first, however, then with a rush, the democratization
that Gorbachev was introducing instrumentally from above in the Soviet
Union turned into a push toward real democracy from below throughout
Eastern Europe. In Russia Gorbachev was launching into unknown territory by resuming the direction the nineteenth century Westernizers had
explored before Stalin liquidated the humanist intelligentsia. In East Central Europe ordinary citizens were reclaiming their familiar European
identity after forty years of alien Soviet orientation.[1]

Initially, then, Gorbachev's increasing permissiveness fostered a re-
surgence of the old European (and anti-Russian) identities of the Poles and
Hungarians, and even a yearning for the novel Western political pluralism
that had not been part of either country's heritage. The Czechoslovaks and
East Germans, who did have memories of a nondictatorial past, but were
initially hobbled by hardline political leaderships installed by Brezhnev,
also began stirring in anticipation of a new era. By 1989 the seemingly
immutable division of Europe would end.

69

The Delegitimation of Communist Leadership

The advent of Gorbachev clearly accelerated the transformation of Eastern Europe in the late 1980s. Equally important domestic factors, however, were the growing social pressures and utter disillusionment with communist rule. East Central Europe had been primed for change by functioning civil societies that, by contrast to the Soviet Union, already existed and did not have to be invented.[2] In this external Soviet empire the drive for modernization and liberalization was reinforced by the dominant nationalism, and throughout East Central Europe economic decline fueled popular delegitimation of postwar communist rule. All this created an explosive mixture of despair and hope in the region.

The degree of disillusionment was new. In the years immediately following World War II, even if most of the communist parties had been brought to power by Soviet arms, most of them could nonetheless claim plausible economic, political, or moral justifications for their rule. Soviet hegemony suppressed Hungarian-Romanian and other ethnic border quarrels in the region. Indigenous communists had a clean record—at least after Hitler attacked the Soviet Union in June 1941—of having resisted the Nazi occupiers (or allies in the case of Hungary, Slovakia, and the Balkans). They succeeded interwar regimes that, except in the model Czechoslovak democracy, were corrupt, authoritarian, acquisitive, and anti-Semitic, and they effectively galvanized hatred of the old capitalist regimes.

In addition, the Soviet alliance insured East Europeans against renewed territorial encroachments by the Germans. Warsaw's communists in particular depended on the Soviet guarantee that the new western third of the country awarded to Poland from old German lands (in compensation, of course, for the eastern third of Poland that reverted to Lithuania, Ukraine, and Russia as the Soviets again seized this territory in World War II) would not go back to the despised revanchist Germans.

Moreover, except in Czechoslovakia and Germany—which before World War II had been among the ten most developed countries in the world—all the communist parties in Eastern Europe promised to industrialize agrarian economies that had perennially lagged far behind the West. Like the Soviet party, they also promised to modernize old, stratified societies through a social contract of upward mobility for peasants and workers and a rising standard of living for the poorest, and to do all this without requiring hard work. Many peasants and workers welcomed this new opportunity.

To be sure, the new social contracts involved heavy costs. Poland, whose top officer corps had already been massacred by the Russians in Katyn Forest, suffered a series of communist (and other) assassinations in the early postwar years. Czechoslovakia and Hungary imported lethal Stalinist purges. East Germany, whose communist ranks had already been murderously thinned out during their wartime exile in Moscow, was stripped of virtually everything that could be packed off to the Soviet Union as war reparations. Czechoslovakia ruined its once thriving light industry as well as its democracy. All the East Europeans, with the exception of the pan-Slavic Bulgarians and the maverick Yugoslavs, lost much of their national character as their economies, societies, and politics were pressed into the Stalinist mold.

Under the circumstances, various populations came to feel that their social and national contracts were being violated. In 1948 the guerrilla hero Josip Broz Tito accused Stalin not only of being too lax ideologically, but also of overriding Belgrade's interests, and broke away from the Soviet camp. In 1953, within months of Stalin's death, East German workers rioted when their production norms were increased 10 percent without commensurate compensation, and they were put down by Soviet tanks. In 1956 a new Hungarian government declared the end of the communist monopoly on power and withdrew from the Warsaw Treaty Organization, and was overthrown by Soviet tanks.

By 1968 Czechs and Slovaks thought that times had changed. Because Brezhnev was beginning a rapprochement with the West, he would surely want to maintain his peaceful image by tolerating careful evolution in Prague, they calculated. If only they avoided Hungary's mistakes and preserved communist rule and their country's membership in the Warsaw Treaty Organization, they reasoned, they could reform the system with impunity and create "socialism with a human face." Yet they too were crushed by Soviet and Warsaw Pact armor. If any socialist country deviates from Marxism-Leninism as interpreted by Moscow, Brezhnev said, the Soviet Union has the right to intervene and restore orthodoxy.

The Poles too rebelled periodically against deficient social contracts and Russian domination: in 1956 as Khrushchev de-Stalinized, in 1968 before their own government neutralized dissent by turning to anti-Semitic populism, and in 1980 in the spontaneous formation of the Solidarity free trade union. Solidarity, the quintessential manifestation of a civil society autonomous of political power, was banned under martial law in 1981, but survived, and even flourished, underground throughout the rest of the 1980s.

Significantly, except for simultaneous Hungarian and Polish unrest in 1956, the various East European revolts followed separate timetables. Such disarray helped the Russians divide and rule—until the late 1980s—by not forcing them to deal with more than one crisis at a time in their client states.

Détente Locks in the Division of Europe

After each protest, the combination of internal coercion, the remnants of the social contract, and inertia—the normal sense of most people most of the time that they have more to lose than to gain by turbulence—helped stabilize East Central European governments. Whatever domestic liberalization superpower détente may have encouraged in the 1970s, the overriding message the East Europeans soon heard was that East-West nuclear rapprochement required stability and the sacrifice of the yearnings of unruly grass-roots protesters. Even the Helsinki Final Act of 1975 and the subsequent CSCE process—which set progressive Europeanwide standards of human rights and would be instrumental in legitimizing dissidence, foreign criticism of internal repression, and an increasing distance between Soviet clients and Moscow—seemed at the time to carry this message.

Nor did détente compel industrial reform. The Soviet and East European economies muddled through without liberalization. The Soviet Union was awash in hard currency from high-priced oil exports to the West. As Gorbachev would say later, this windfall disguised the gathering economic crisis and deferred awareness of it. At the same time, Eastern Europe benefited from favorable terms of trade within the bloc, especially in cheap Soviet oil exports to client states. Poland, and even Hungary, despite Budapest's unique early steps in elementary economic reform, simply followed Moscow's lead in attempting to import Western technology as a substitute for rather than stimulus to fundamental economic restructuring. As small countries with no rich base of raw materials for export, they quickly became ensnared in borrowing beyond their means.

When Western markets slumped following the two oil shocks of the 1970s, Poland and Hungary's hopes for a share of these markets—and for ultimate closing of the perennial economic gap between Western and Eastern Europe—also slumped. When Soviet petroleum prices caught up with world prices toward the end of the 1980s, the extravagant use of energy in the Soviet bloc only increased the financial pain. The most successful economy in the bloc seemed to be the very unliberalized East German one; only later did everyone discover how ravaged even this economy was.

The precise mix of pressures was different in the GDR, Poland, Czechoslovakia, and Hungary. So was the perceived relationship between political and economic reform. However, at this point throughout Eastern Europe, except in the GDR, the public saw the communist economic system in all its possible permutations as bankrupt. It had shod, fed, and schooled the peasants, but it was incapable of implementing even the second industrial revolution of distributing telephones, automobiles, and other consumer comforts widely. It was even less capable of effecting the third industrial revolution of computers and information that was transforming the West and, by the 1980s, even the newly industrializing countries in Asia and South America. Yet the bloc economies were proving all too capable of poisoning the air, the water, and the woods; degrading the infrastructure of housing and hospitals; and in Hungary, even shortening life expectancy. Poland and Hungary looked longingly at Finland and Austria, nations that had started at the same economic level as East Central Europe in the 1940s, but had shot far ahead in prosperity through their links to the Western world economy.

At the same time as economic failure seemed inevitable, so did a breakdown of the social contract. Those peasants and workers who had soared in the party had long since completed their replacement of the deposed prewar elites and were now clinging to their own new sinecures, thereby revealing that the communists' upward mobility was only a one-generation affair. Moreover, the privileges of these communist parvenus now looked shabby even to young opportunists contemplating career choices. Increasingly, apparatchiks were not envied, but ridiculed. All the baubles of better food, bigger apartments, and hopelessly old-fashioned cars looked paltry to the increasing number of travelers who visited the West and saw for themselves the consumer cornucopia there. Concurrently, with the police states' mellowing away from brute Stalinist force, private and civil life increasingly recovered the space it had been forced to cede to politics.

With this confluence of economic decline and social reassertion, popular exasperation boiled over. In many cases the intelligentsia came to articulate and magnify the common grievances rather than—as in Russia—to be viewed suspiciously by the proletariat as the privileged class enemy. Throughout the region, except in the GDR, nationalism resurged to galvanize discontent with an intensity that was all the greater for its sublimation during four decades of Soviet uniformity.

In this atmosphere the despair of the early 1980s about ever catching up with the West's well-being and variety, so long as the old communist system remained, fused with new hope that Gorbachev might actually permit the miracle of change.

Gorbachev's New Permissiveness

Initially, Gorbachev seemed to be as intolerant of deviations in the Soviet Union's external empire as his predecessors had been. As he moved toward economic and political reform at home, however, his approach to Eastern Europe softened. He even began displaying what some of his comrades deemed a reckless optimism in signaling to client governments that they were now on their own, just so long as they maintained control. If they got into trouble with their populations, the Soviet Union would not bail them out.

In tentative expression of this new flexibility, Moscow signed the Stockholm Agreement on confidence building and security measures in September 1986. The signatories of this agreement pledged "to refrain from the threat or use of force in their relations with any state, regardless of that state's political, social, economic, or cultural system and irrespective of whether or not they maintain with that state relations of alliance." The pregnant last phrase was not yet a repudiation of the "Brezhnev doctrine," under which the Warsaw Pact had invaded Czechoslovakia.[3] Moscow still applied self-determination in Eastern Europe, not to peoples, but to communist governments, which could be expected to coordinate policy decisions with the Soviet Union.[4]

Under this stimulus from Moscow, the East Europeans' resignation and cynicism abated somewhat. The outbursts of 1956, 1968, and 1980, they thought, might not have been in vain after all: they had kept alive the civil pressure on politics, they had provided martyrs for the next cycle of popular indignation and grudging official liberalization, they had fed the impatience of younger generations who did not share their elders' acquiescence and memory of murderous Stalinist sanctions, and they now suggested an alternative to passivity.

Surprisingly, Hungary was the pioneer. It was the most advanced of any East European nation in economic innovation because it had been testing market elements since the late 1960s. Yet logically, this experimentation should have hindered further liberalization, since by the mid-1980s Hungary's reforms had disrupted the old system and actually lowered the standard of living of a third of the population. Inflation was rising to 16.0 percent, economists identified 40.0 percent of the population as living below the poverty line, and planners projected an unheard-of unemployment rate of 2.5 percent as more market mechanisms were introduced.

Under any normal East European pattern, these circumstances would have invited the hardliners to restore their power by stoking unskilled workers' envy of higher-paid specialists and the intelligentsia; mobilizing the old workers' militias, secret police, and army; and using the security services' direct ties to Moscow. Veteran party leader Janos Kadar's very success in averting independent political engagement over thirty years by gradually increasing the Hungarians' private sphere had, in any case, preempted reform radicalism and might have paved the way for such reversion. Nor did the fragmented Hungarian dissidents, who issued largely from the last remaining community of Jewish intellectuals in Eastern Europe, have any single focus of opposition comparable to Poland's Solidarity or Roman Catholic church.

Yet radicalization came, initially, from within the Hungarian Socialist Workers' (Communist) party itself. Karoly Grosz, a hitherto orthodox party functionary, promoted swifter reform than Kadar's, and by spring 1988 he had successfully maneuvered to replace his boss, in part, by cultivating West German support and loans.

Significantly, Hungarian politicians took the West German linkage of credits to political change not as impermissible interference in their internal affairs, but rather as an aid to their own efforts to modernize. By now the party, or at least its up and coming "Social Democratic" wing, took for granted that political liberalization was an indispensable precondition for economic reform, without which the desperately needed individual initiative and the traditional Hungarian entrepreneurial spirit would never be released.

Subsequently, Hungary abolished official censorship. It allowed— some suggested it instigated—public demonstrations against Romanian repression of the Hungarian minority in Transylvania. All the independent activists, and an ever growing number of communists, dreamed of emulating Finland's neutrality, or even Austria's pro-West neutrality. Nostalgia for the Austrian imperial house of Hapsburg swept the country.

Poland was in some respects more, in some respects less, open than Hungary as Gorbachev settled into office. Back in 1956 it had already reversed collectivization and evicted the Soviet general whom Stalin had installed as Poland's minister of defense. Back in 1980 it had suddenly forged, in the independent Solidarity trade union led by the charismatic Lech Walesa, a unity of workers and intellectuals that the Hungarians could only envy. Thereafter, Poland had a vigorous, completely free (underground) press that ferreted out official misdeeds and by the end of the decade was ready to articulate interests and perhaps even—should politics mature—aggregate them. It had a ready-made alternative to the communist-structured society and state not only in Solidarity, but also in the age-old repository of the Polish nation, the Catholic church. In an extraordinary display of irrational unity, the entire nation had in effect gone on strike against its rulers ever since martial law in 1981.

Virulent anti-Russian sentiments that harked back two centuries neutralized the opposition to liberalization that hardliners might otherwise have hoped to mobilize among unskilled workers intent on preserving the old leveling down. Instead, Poles directed their resentments toward party officials who were living extravagantly beyond the means of the ordinary person, and showed far more interest in wringing an admission out of the Russians that it was actually the Soviet secret police rather than the Germans who had massacred Polish officers in Katyn Forest in 1940.

Meanwhile, the old anti-German inhibitions against any liberalization that might make Poland vulnerable to the West had faded after West Germany acknowledged Poland's postwar border in the early 1970s. Indeed, this assurance was a precondition for Solidarity's willingness to press domestic confrontation as hard as it did.[5] And after martial law was declared and West Germans voluntarily sent millions of food parcels to Poles, anti–German sentiment turned anti-"Prussian" and focused primarily on the despised East Germans.

In the 1980s the special *Zomo* security forces might beat down the workers' protests as Solidarity was banned; they and the secret police might murder Father Jerzy Popieluszko and some sixty other dissidents; but in the end the axiom would hold that the one thing Poles, like others, could not do with bayonets was to sit on them. The economy plummeted. Workers again staged strikes in spring and fall 1988 demanding the relegalization of Solidarity.

The GDR Bucks the Trend

The GDR, Czechoslovakia, Romania, Bulgaria, and, of course, Albania held out against the winds of change. Even the few dissidents in these countries saw Poland and Hungary not as models, but as exceptions, Poland because it was big and feisty, Hungary because it was small and strategically marginal to the Soviet Union and could experiment without endangering others if its experiment failed. Such latitude was not available to other East Europeans, especially the East German state, the outer bulwark of Moscow's western glacis that the Soviets had bought with the blood of 27 million dead.

In Czechoslovakia the old communist reformers, beaten down by the suppression of the Prague Spring in 1968, had in any case been expelled from the party and their previous jobs and were now stoking coal and washing windows. Noncommunist playwright Vaclav Havel, in and out of prison, was honing his thoughts on the social significance of the lonely truth-teller and becoming something of an underground moral authority. Yet with the old communist leadership in full control and backed by Soviet divisions stationed permanently in the country, the compliant good soldier Schweiks were studiously looking the other way.

In the GDR the mix was different, but equally catatonic. Institutionally, the Socialist Unity party (SED), like other communist parties throughout the Soviet bloc, occupied the leading role reserved for it in the country's constitution, and stifled political competition far more successfully than its Polish and Hungarian counterparts. The state, the government, the economy, and social organizations were totally subordinate to the SED, and a ubiquitous secret police network supplemented hierarchical discipline. The formally noncommunist bloc parties obediently deferred to the

SED, as did judges—some more than others—when party officials signaled a preferred outcome in a case. In the entire history of the Volkskammer before November 1989, only once were contrary votes against communist legislation ever recorded, when some Christian Democrats demurred on an abortion law. So far did the party's power extend that well into the 1980s dozens of children of people caught trying to flee the GDR were seized and farmed out for adoption by politically proper couples.

The one major exception to this lockstep was the Protestant church, the combined institution of Lutherans and Calvinists that was organized in a decentralized fashion, with regional bishops and lay synods, or parliaments. The Catholic church was weaker, and far less inclined to campaign for such goals as a right to conscientious objection to military service or exemption from compulsory military drills in schools.

In daily life, of course, many more hiding places from the planned regime were available than organizational schemas show. Honecker was no Ulbricht. He softened the regime a good deal and shrank the politically sensitive sphere in which conformity was enforced. And even if Prussian communism remained much more regimented than sloppy Russian communism in post-Stalinist practice, the old German sense of civil society was increasingly asserting itself. Discipline within the SED itself slackened. In addition, especially after détente relaxed East-West relations and the 1975 Helsinki Conference set an international standard for human rights, Honecker strove for the kind of adherence to the norm, or appearance of it, that would make the GDR accepted in polite company.

The combination of East-West détente and nuclear tension in Europe thus led to a peculiar blend of *Abgrenzung* that was only intensified by the electricity emanating from Gorbachev's Moscow. In many ways East German society was still vastly more open than Russian society, but in other ways it was becoming more tightly sealed.

For a start, East Germans were almost as open to Western influences as were Poles and Hungarians, even if they could not respond as openly. They were visited annually by up to 8 million West Germans—roughly one Westerner per every two Easterners—with whom they had no language barrier. A good 90 percent of them regularly watched news and entertainment on West German television, where they saw everything from the local "Schwarzwald Clinic" soap to "Dallas" to all the 1950s Hollywood time fillers. Although the East Germans were prone to some eccentric interpretations of news events by experiencing them only in the abstract on the flat screen in front of them, they lived vicariously in that abstract world at least as much as in their own reality. Western glitter, however misunderstood, became for many the standard by which they measured their own deprivation. Such broad exposure to the West would have been unthinkable in Russia, even in Gorbachev's Russia.

Freedom of nonpolitical speech was also the rule in the GDR, and in the early Gorbachev years at least, this was still a much broader category in the GDR than in the Soviet Union. Moreover, the sophistication to take advantage of this freedom was fairly uniformly spread. No huge gap in mentality existed between city and countryside as in the Soviet Union, and there was no inert, suspicious peasantry that might be set against urban activists.

By contrast, the range of public political discussion in the media was much more restricted in the GDR than in Moscow, Leningrad, and other major Soviet cities, where intellectuals vigorously exploited Gorbachev's new glasnost, or openness. With splendid bourgeois prissiness, ideologist Kurt Hager dismissed Soviet glasnost in spring 1987 as an inappropriate model for East Germany, asking rhetorically, "Would you feel obliged to install new wallpaper just because your neighbor installed new wall-paper?"[6] The East German media actually began censoring Gorbachev's speeches and coverage of Soviet developments unless Soviet Ambassador Vyacheslav Kochemasov managed to get Honecker's consent to fuller re-portage in specific cases.[7] By 1988 the GDR absurdly banned imports of Soviet wallpaper in the form of the weekly *Ogonyok*, the youth magazine *Sputnik*, three issues of the German-language *New Times*, and various plays and movies. The exercise was futile, as it magnified the very opinions it tried to expurgate by focusing attention on them in West German broad-casts that East Germans listened to all the more avidly. However, the censorship did demonstrate the party's continued control.

The GDR also lagged well behind the Soviet Union, and even Czecho-slovakia, in having no dissidents of the stature of Havel or Andrei Sakharov. There were, of course, individual ringleaders, as the East German security organs identified them. The isolated rings they led, however, were tiny bands of friends whose offense usually consisted of no more than painting slogans about peace, freedom, and justice on old sheets and then trying to join official communist parades. Those outside the inner circle of friends rarely heard about the ringleaders until the latter were expelled to the Federal Republic. And expelled they were, regularly, in a kind of safety valve, to deprive other malcontents of leadership.[8]

The loss of the activists who cared enough about the GDR to strive to improve it was compounded by the parallel "voluntary" emigration of some of the country's most energetic young people. Much like an inden-tured servant gaining passage to colonial America, a young person des-perate to flee could calculate that if he did not get shot while trying to escape, he would only have to serve some four years in jail before being bought free by West Germany. He—few women deliberately chose this route—could then start his life over in a familiar culture and language and easily find a job on the basis of his past education.

Various reasons were well understood for the general political lethargy of the East Germans who remained. Honecker seemed to have succeeded brilliantly in buying off and intimidating the East Germans into resignation, and perhaps even a certain contentment. The GDR's economy still appeared to be the most successful in the Soviet bloc. There was no (known) crisis of enormous foreign debt as in Poland and Hungary, no slipping standard of living as in reforming Hungary, no plummeting standard of living as in rebellious Poland. Bananas and kiwi fruit may have been scarce, but bread and sausage were not.[9] Few East Germans wanted to exchange their relative comfort for the kind of romantic, spartan struggle of the disdained Poles.

Thus, a quarter of a century after the Berlin Wall stabilized the population, routine orderliness even seemed to be spawning a degree of identification with the state. The cautious expansion of travel possibilities was working. Although the number of applicants was snowballing, the vast majority of those allowed out to visit the West returned home afterward. Many ordinary citizens appreciated the GDR's quieter life, they told questioners. Random violence was far less common than in the West, child care was more available. Many found an old-fashioned neighborliness in the GDR that they felt had been lost in the more hectic Federal Republic. Even the general accessibility of West German television acted as an opiate rather than a stimulant to political unrest for East Germans living in their niches.

The grass-roots political void was reinforced in a negative way by the universal assumption that Gorbachev's novel permissiveness toward Hungary and Poland did not extend to the sensitive GDR, Moscow's high-tech supplier, westernmost outpost, and prime trophy of the Great Patriotic War. Besides, as Lenin already knew, Germans do not make revolutions.

To be sure, Honecker did not entrust the control of society to passive habit, but out of deference to the international climate of the 1980s, he reduced his resorts to force and sheathed them in a velvet glove rather than an iron fist. The results were sometimes bizarre. The killing of would-be escapees at the border continued—more than 200 deaths were recorded between 1961 and 1989—but more antiseptic automatic shooting devices replaced human gunners for a time. After loud protests by West Germans, the 60,000 shooting machines were finally dismantled, and the high cement walls separating the two Germanys were prettified. However, construction of a more formidable inner ring of no-man's-land out of sight of Western cameras offset these cosmetic gestures. At their height, the number of landmines in border regions totaled over 700,000.[10]

Even more bizarre was the counterintuitive expansion of the Ministry of State Security in proportion to liberalization. Westerners (and ordinary East Germans) logically expected the role of the secret police to shrink as society became more open. Instead, it grew. The reason was not only that the *Stasi* could exercise subtler controls, less conspicuously in violation of the Helsinki accords. Increasingly, the leadership resorted to this ministry too as an all-purpose troubleshooter to redress the mounting failings of economic and state institutions.[11]

Yet domestic spying remained the *Stasi's* cardinal task. By the 1980s its Central Analysis and Information Group, the real center of state security, according to GDR foreign spymaster Markus Wolf, was keeping dossiers on 6 million out of 16 million East Germans and 2 million out of 60 million West Germans.[12] It ran "a system of total domestic surveillance," he told one interviewer. "Anyone suspected in any way of oppositional activities was spied on," with oppositional activities defined as ranging from trying to emigrate to having church connections to not voting in elections.[13] As the Dresden citizens' committee investigating the *Stasi* "octopus" in early 1990 would sum it up, the guiding assumptions in this operation were: "1. Each individual is a potential security risk. 2. To be certain, one must know everything. 3. Security takes priority over law."[14]

With its comprehensive mission, the *Stasi* cadre ballooned from 13,000 in 1959 to 53,000 in 1973 to 85,000 by 1989. This full-time staff was supplemented by "the main weapon in the battle against the enemy," 109,000 to 200,000 unofficial collaborators, or paid informers with signed contracts. A further 1 million or 2 million informers operated on a freelance basis, without written contracts or code names.[15] The peep and snoop society, as the East Germans sarcastically referred to the *Stasi*, was more than double the size of the dread Gestapo, but policed a population less than a fifth the number of Hitler's Germans.[16]

The *Stasi* placed open and secret agents at all levels of command and in all liaison staffs in the army and border troops; in the ministries, major industrial firms, the SED, bloc parties, universities, schools, churches, theaters, cultural organizations; and, of course, the small peace, environmental, and human rights groups. In these organizations or circles its task was not only intelligence, but often *Zersetzung*, literally decomposition, disintegration, or demoralization of suspect groups or individuals. It clandestinely opened 4 to 5 percent of the 100,000 mail deliveries in the Dresden postal system each day, and a similar percentage elsewhere, above and beyond the special surveillance of foreign correspondence. The *Stasi's* aura of omnipotence and omnipresence worked effectively: East Germans generally assumed that if three or four friends were gathered together in conversation, one of them was probably an informer.

At its most grotesque, from 1967 on, the *Stasi* even maintained a series of internment camps to herd dissidents into on some future day of reckoning, along with lists of up to 200,000 intended victims. Periodically it conducted exercises to prepare for this final defeat of "counterrevolution," and district administrators of the operation continued to meet and plan for it up through early October 1989.[17] Heinz Eggert—Protestant pastor and then, after unification, Saxony's interior minister—discovered just how up-to-date these plans were kept when he found out that one of the detention centers was to have been located 150 yards from his own house. Eggert joked later to a former *Stasi* officer that he could have walked to the camp. The officer replied, "You, Herr Eggert, would not have reached it alive."[18]

In retrospect, Gregor Gysi, the lawyer who by default would assume leadership of the SED redux in December 1989, would analyze the basic flaw of the *Stasi* system this way: "The real lunacy lay in the idea that an extensive security apparatus could guarantee stability, although this is only possible with broad political acceptance."[19]

The Honecker–Gorbachev Relationship

With Honecker stonewalling and Gorbachev improvising in unpredictable new directions, it was not surprising that relations between the two men were strained. Gorbachev, with his frantic changes and heretical concepts of democratization and pluralism, was an offense to all the old dogmatists like Honecker, explains Günter Schabowski, East Berlin party chief and a member of the SED Politburo from 1985 until the Politburo's mass resignation in December 1989.

"Then there was another element," Schabowski points out: the Federal Republic of West Germany, which had become "the most important capitalist partner" of all the communist states. Because of this development, Schabowski notes, "Honecker had a special position in the [Soviet-bloc] hierarchy. By contrast to all the others he was the greatest expert on the Federal Republic." He thought he had a right to decide East German policy toward West Germany himself. He felt cheated by the earlier Soviet ban on his visit to the Federal Republic, and he expected that Gorbachev, this "young guy" who was in any case "already allowing all possible extravagances" ideologically, would finally set things right and let him visit Bonn.

Honecker put the question to Gorbachev when the Soviet leader attended the SED's eleventh party congress in 1986, Schabowski recalls. "It came to this meeting, in which Gorbachev said directly to him: 'Drop this visit. How could I justify it at home?' And Honecker replied to him, 'How could I justify [not going] to our people, who fear the missiles, when I, Honecker, want to put myself forward to some degree as the messenger of peace?' . . . You can imagine when a politician as obstinate as Honecker has such a fight, it remains, so to speak, dominant in the relationship."[20]

Honecker's "tirades" against Gorbachev became a staple of SED Politburo meetings.[21]

His resentment at having to obey his junior was obvious to everyone around Honecker. From what he took to be his own secure base, he reckoned that a leader as alien to the Russian spirit as Gorbachev would prove to be as transitory as Nikita Khrushchev, and that when this upstart was eventually replaced, the orthodox East German leaders would remain.[22] Nevertheless, he still had to wait until fall 1987—after Gorbachev and Reagan were well into their own summit chumminess—before he could bask in his full protocol welcome from the Bonn government.[23]

Popular East German enthusiasm for that much-delayed visit arose primarily from the expectation that once his dream tour had been fulfilled, Honecker would seek to enhance his newly won prestige by voluntarily allowing domestic dialogue in the GDR. He could safely do so, most commentators thought, without putting at risk the quiescence that characterized his country.[24]

Honecker did amnesty 20,000 prisoners in November 1987 and further relaxed the irritating general ban on foreign travel or residence. The 11,500 persons allowed to emigrate to West Germany in 1987 and the 29,000 in 1988 fell short of the 1984 high, but an expanding 1.2 million working-age East Germans in 1987 and 1.5 million in 1988 were permitted to travel in the West.[25] Most of those allowed out for visits returned home afterward. For a period the leadership could hope that such rationed largesse would assuage rather than whet appetites.

By contrast to this improvement, however, dialogue deteriorated between the party and the would-be reformers who emerged from the semi-approved, grass-roots peace movement of the early 1980s. This had always been a wary relationship at best, but a space had opened for activists so long as they stayed inside the walls of the Protestant church and did not try to carry their campaigns for ecological and social change to the streets. The state was, in effect, honoring the sanctuary of the church.

Immediately after Honecker's return from Bonn, even this space shrank. Police raided East Berlin's Zion Church, confiscated environmental pamphlets, and arrested activists.

Then chief ideologist Kurt Hager repudiated a litmus paper written two months earlier by academics working under the SED's Central Committee and the West German Social Democratic party.[26] The paper asserted that capitalism is as capable of peace as socialism; that *Feindbilder* (enemy stereotypes) must be discarded; and that open, mutual criticism between East and West does not constitute interference in internal affairs. When the statement had been published in full in *Neues Deutschland* the previous August, both would-be SED reformers and the handful of dissidents had hoped for a new era. But now even these mild theses proved too radical for Hager and Honecker. The East German academic reformers who had floated them—without any backing from anyone in the Politburo—were rebuffed.[27] The GDR's clock was turned back further.

This stance was reinforced at the beginning of 1988. A handful of dissidents—inluding artist Bärbel Bohley, balladeer Stefan Krawczyk, and future Bundestag deputy Vera Wollenberger—were arrested, charged with treason, and expelled for joining an official parade in honor of communist martyr Rosa Luxemburg while carrying their own placards bearing her provocative words, "Freedom always means freedom for the dissenter." The indifferent masses hardly noticed.

Harsher treatment was also meted out to the churches for the first time since Ulbricht had left the scene. Pressure to persuade Protestant pastors to curtail their social involvement and protection was stepped up. Authorities censored internal church publications, and security officials even harassed churchgoers by checking their identities.

Subsequently, police beat up rock fans who gathered near the Berlin Wall of a summer evening to catch an open air concert blared from the West, and after a lull, border guards resumed shooting people who were trying to flee to the West.[28]

The crackdown made little difference to West German treatment of Honecker. Politicians in the Federal Republic seemed to share Honecker's own view of the permanence of the East German leadership and saw no reason to stir up trouble over a few dissidents. State premiers and parliamentarians from every major party except the Greens crowded each other out in their rush to be photographed with Honecker. Social Democrats called for an end to the archaic conservative notion of German unification, and in 1988 state governments they controlled stopped paying assessed Länder contributions to the Salzgitter registry of East German border shootings. In private contacts, a number of Social Democrats were ingratiating to East German leaders in a way that came back to haunt them after unification opened the GDR's archives.[29] For their part, West German conservatives continued to ransom political prisoners and would-be wall jumpers and brushed aside as unworldly any criticism of the practice as degrading.[30]

As Honecker retrenched, Gorbachev pushed ahead with his new course. In March 1988 the Soviet leader further defied Jacob Burckhardt and Alexis de Tocqueville's maxim that the riskiest period for repressive governments sets in when they begin to reform. On a visit to Yugoslavia he asserted his confidence in the durability of socialism in many countries in promising "respect for different ways to build socialism" and acknowledging, rather heretically in ideological terms, that "no one has a monopoly on the truth."[31]

Then in June 1988, at the nineteenth conference of the Soviet Union's

Communist party, Gorbachev clearly repudiated past Soviet practices in Eastern Europe when he asserted the principle of freedom of choice and condemned "the imposition of a social system, way of life or politics from outside by any means, let alone military." At that point Gorbachev still seemed to expect that the Soviet–East European bond could be maintained on a voluntary basis, and that the East European yearning for change would not outstrip Russian patience.

Obversely, although the Soviet leaders were prodding the reluctant East Germans, Czechoslovaks, and Romanians to get on with reforms— and in the case of the GDR, from early 1989 on would specifically dissociate themselves from the Berlin Wall—they did not force liberalizing conformity on their clients. In his own domain Honecker could continue to stonewall.

By September 1988 this continuing stasis led Genscher to issue a private warning to his Soviet counterpart, Eduard Shevardnadze, as the two met at the fall session of the United Nations. If reforms did not begin soon in the GDR, he cautioned, large demonstrations would break out there in the coming year. They would affect the Soviet Union directly through the soldiers it had stationed there. They would also affect fellow Germans in the West. This time the Federal Republic's reaction would not be the same as in 1953, when with aching hearts neither the West Germans nor the Western allies intervened against the Soviet tanks in East Berlin. Genscher left unstated just how the response might differ.

At the time Shevardnadze was skeptical. In retrospect, he would tell other European foreign ministers that Genscher was the one who first alerted him to the coming storm.[32]

In December 1988, in a UN speech, Gorbachev dramatically fleshed out his declared commitment to freedom of choice. For four decades Moscow had kept half a million troops in East Central Europe. Now, he announced, the Soviet Union would unilaterally withdraw an impressive 6 tank divisions, 5,000 tanks, and 50,000 assault-landing and other specialty troops.[33]

Chapter 7

Annus Mirabilis

In 1989 the pace of change accelerated. Polish and Hungarian reforms reached a critical mass that went beyond simply helping the existing command system to adapt and survive, and compelled instead ever greater liberalization to keep ahead of the new chaos.

Gorbachev, it was said, told the Hungarians early in the year to deal with the West as they saw fit, just so long as they did it circumspectly, without insulting the Russians, and told Jaruzelski to do whatever he needed to do to avert domestic collapse, just so long as he did not endanger Soviet military logistics across Poland to the GDR.[1] In Vienna in January all three governments, along with the other CSCE members, signed the most ambitious international charter of human freedoms ever written.

In the GDR, by contrast, prophylactic arrests continued. On January 15, Rosa Luxemburg and Karl Liebknecht Day, a few hundred Leipzigers staged a silent march, with candles, in support of "democratization of our socialist state." The police detained fifty-three marchers; prosecutors indicted eleven.[2]

In February Hungarian communist Politburo member Imre Pozsgay secured his party's approval of a future multiparty system, and started the party's reassessment of the 1956 revolt as a popular uprising rather than a counterrevolution. Simultaneously in Poland, after trying to eradicate Solidarity for seven years, Jaruzelski abruptly entered into roundtable negotiations with Walesa and his advisers.

By March the Hungarian Socialist Workers' party was developing a new constitution that would not reserve a leading role for the party. Most Hungarians remained dubious. From Budapest one liberal historian, Maria Kovacs, steeling herself against the prospect that she might again be betrayed, wrote to an American friend:

Over the past decade one has developed instincts that would warn against overconfidence in real change. . . . Just think of the mental-psychological journey of any East European from 1980 to 1989. . . . First, in 1980, Poles seemed to do things that surpassed any imagination. We then had to tell ourselves that all we thought about communism (the party will never divide, let alone surrender power) was wrong. Then came the coup [martial law in Poland in 1981]. We had to tell ourselves that we were wrong to think that we had been wrong previously. We concluded that millions of organized people are not enough to bring about change, and that if the party falls apart, there is always an army. The lesson was that there was no way out of a communist dictatorship. Then, only six [or] seven years later, the dictator is offering seats to the defeated opposition while in Hungary, the Politburo goes out of its way to talk (repeat: talk) about sharing power.

As for the public, Kovacs continued:

Of course people hate communism. In principle. Not in practice. They do not like their tyrants, they do not like the police, they do not like the Russians. But they do like the comfort, even if you (or I) have some difficulty visualizing that comfort. Half of the country is old, or aging, at least half of the country does not want to face change. They do not hope for the better economically. Political change intrudes on their life, security, strategies, world-views, compromises, peace of mind. A 50-year-old woman secretary in our department raises her two sons alone, [on] 80 dollars a month. She has no savings, no prospects. But she cannot switch to the private economy. She cannot, and would not, learn anything new. She wants to survive in 'decency,' clean apartment, three meals, one-week vacation. She knows her chances are slim, even if there is no change. If there is change, her chances are minimal, or zero. From her perspective 'change' means she had [put up with] forty years of the regime for nothing. Politics has no meaning for her. Her hatred for party bosses and immediate little tyrants (the little ones are the worst) is meaningless; it does not connect to anything.
      The other half? . . . The generation after me grew up not even knowing what communist orthodoxy and Stalinist dictatorship really looks like. They accommodate to any change, because they have no real experience of the unchangeable. You can push a button, and they become little capitalists, yuppies, neoconservatives, you name it. They become the nouveau riche, with little mustaches and keys attached to fur, always asking for the most expensive import beer in a restaurant, and then leaving half of it, speaking a language that only

remotely resembles the one I learned for Hungarian. But they are clever, and they work, in short, they are the seeds of self-enrichment—marketization—contractualism—autonomous economic power. They are the ones I ought to put my hopes in. I am doing my best to try.

As usual, most East Germans did not even try. On March 15, 850 state security and police officers easily prevented some 300 worshippers at the regular Monday afternoon prayer meetings at the Nikolai Protestant Church in Leipzig from walking en masse to the marketplace. In the lone hint of change, several of the 300, instead of assiduously avoiding provocation, this time shouted "*Stasi* out!" and "*Stasi* pigs!"[3]

By April Pozsgay had persuaded the Hungarian Politburo to relinquish democratic centralism and, in effect, let him organize his own reform faction. Simultaneously, Jaruzelski legalized Solidarity once more and approved immediate semi-free elections in Poland, with the understanding that Solidarity would not seek to take over the government until completely free elections were held four years later. In Tbilisi, Soviet security forces, using sharpened shovels and poison gas, killed several dozen Georgian nationalist demonstrators.

Poland and Hungary Leapfrog Each Other

In May Hungary lived up to its pledges under various CSCE agreements on human rights and began dismantling its iron curtain on the Austrian border, handing out barbed wire souvenirs as proof against relapse. In the same month the Congress of People's Deputies met in Moscow after the first semi-free election in the Soviet Union in seventy years. The slaughter in Tbilisi was a main topic of debate.

On May 7 local elections in the GDR produced an improbable official vote of 98.85 percent for the prescribed candidates. Church observers, who had inexplicably been allowed to monitor polling places, immediately challenged the voting records. For the first time dissidents in different cities coordinated their objections. Some 250 activists filed protests. They were ignored.[4]

In the grand scheme of things, the rigged election was a tiny affront. It rankled, however. More and more East Germans grumbled about *Bevormundung* (guardianship), or being ordered about by the state and party like immature and none too bright kindergartners. More and more East Germans—500 immediately after the elections, 1,250 a month later, perhaps 2,500 by late June—took to joining the weekly prayer meetings for peace that the Nikolai Church had been holding since 1983. Those who were trying to emigrate began chanting, "We want out!" A few voices began calling for honest elections.

On June 4 and in the subsequent run-off election in Poland, Solidarity won all of the 35 percent of seats it was permitted to contest in the Sejm (lower house), and ninety-nine of the one hundred seats in the new Senate. Virtually all the communist candidates were defeated in the initial poll, even when they ran unopposed.[5]

Even as the Poles were rejecting the communists who had led them for four decades, news came in of the massacre in Tienanmen Square of Chinese students who were demonstrating for democracy. The slaughter reinforced the East European reformers in their growing conviction that economic reform without political reform leads to disaster. Increasingly, Poland and Hungary joined forces in defending their still maverick liberalization against their East German, Czechoslovak, and Romanian critics in the various Council for Mutual Economic Assistance and Warsaw Pact meetings.

In June Hungary signed the Convention on Refugees, a move that qualified it for UN aid for the stream of ethnic Hungarians pouring out of Romania, and also turned Hungary into the favored route for thousands of East Germans fleeing to West Germany.

By now it was obvious that even young East German proletarians, children of the system who hardly chafed at the intellectual indignities, felt no loyalty to the GDR. They were unhappy about having to wait twelve or fourteen years to get a Trabant automobile, and they were offended by their imprisonment inside Eastern Europe, with no freedom to travel to the Alps, the Mediterranean, or even next door to West Berlin until they reached retirement age. For many, the escape from boredom and regimentation lay not in reforming the recalcitrant GDR, but in fleeing to the much more relaxed and rich Federal Republic. More and more of the customary vacationers to Hungary took advantage of the blind eye Budapest was now turning to its Austrian border and voted with their feet for new lives in the Federal Republic. This outflow of some of the GDR's most energetic workers began to debilitate the country as much as the outsurge in the weeks before the Berlin Wall was erected in 1961.

In July Gorbachev himself finally repudiated the Brezhnev doctrine, in the reading of East Europeans. At the Council of Europe in Strasbourg he declared that the social and political order of European countries "is entirely a matter for the people themselves and of their choosing." Expanding on his theme of a "common European home," he excluded the "possibility of the use or threat of force, above all military force, by one alliance against another, within alliances, or anywhere else."[6]

In August the Polish government abolished its food subsidies and let the cost of bread triple on the free market. Supplies failed to respond, and lines remained long, however, as production was inelastic. No meat was available in the towns, because the peasants refused to slaughter their animals at a loss. Inflation was by now running at an annual 100 percent and building up toward 300 percent. Per capita income was some 15 percent below that of a decade earlier and falling. Real wages were 20 percent lower than in 1980. Foreign debt had climbed to $39 billion, the highest outside South America, and Warsaw had not made its interest payments for years. Factories had no money to invest in plant or machinery.

After Polish communists reached a stalemate in their attempts to form a cabinet, Walesa mischievously proposed that Solidarity form a government with the two small puppet parties that for forty years had obediently taken their cues from the communists: the United Peasants and the Democratic parties. The noncommunist parties then opened consultations, for all the world as if their numerical majority in the Sejm actually gave them power. To most people's astonishment, the Polish United Workers' (communist) party and the Russians then acceded. On August 19 Tadeusz Mazowiecki—organizer of the Warsaw Club of Catholic Intelligentsia in 1957, thwarted investigator into the killing of strikers by armed forces in 1970, adviser to Walesa since the birth of Solidarity, and "counterrevolutionary" prisoner in 1982—was named Poland's new chairman of the Council of Ministers. He was the first noncommunist to lead an East European government in forty years.

With this the Poles were now violating the sacred Leninist tenet of irreversibility, which held that communists must never surrender power once they attain it. Poland, second in importance only to the GDR in Soviet rankings, historical trigger for two abrupt reversals of czarist liberalization when it rebelled against Russia in the nineteenth century, was showing that now reforms had gone so far as to be irreversible. Instead of the communist nomenklatura's co-opting meatless workers into opposing the sacrifices of reform—the likeliest prospect only weeks before—Solidarity was already co-opting nomenklatura opportunists into becoming entrepreneurs.

So swiftly were things moving that it almost seemed routine a few days later, in the run-up to the twenty-first anniversary of the Warsaw Pact invasion of Czechoslovakia, when the Polish Sejm and the Hungarian communist leadership condemned their countries' participation in the rollback of Prague's timid socialism with a human face in 1968. It almost seemed normal when more than a million Lithuanian, Latvian, and Estonian demonstrators linked hands in a 400-mile human chain to protest the Nazi-Soviet pact of 1939 and demand independence from the Soviet Union; when the Soviets finally admitted the existence of the secret protocol of the 1939 pact that divided Poland and the Baltic states between Germany and the Soviet Union; and when the Sejm unanimously denounced this protocol that had not only dismembered Poland once again, but had opened the way for the deportation of 1.5 million Poles to Siberia.

The Socialist Unity Party Stirs

Against this cacophony, the official silence in East Berlin was deafening. The ongoing exodus threatened to cripple the GDR's industry and did cripple the country's hospitals. For the first time East Germany had a conspicuous and undeniable economic crisis. Yet Honecker continued his denials. A few of the younger Politburo members, men in their fifties and sixties, began to think the unthinkable: their antiquated and rigid leader of almost two decades must be forced to resign before the country was bled of its future.

Within the Politburo, recalls Günter Schabowski, the most analytical of the Politburo members who finally toppled Honecker, there was a period

> of several months in which every individual, without coming to an understanding between us in any exchange, wrestled within himself, some more vigorously, some less so, over this unspeakable and unbearable manifestation of desertion by thousands and thousands of people day after day. There was no need for any special understanding among ourselves. When such a condition develops and its crisis character is communicated so directly to every individual in the leadership, then a situation can arise in which this concern and malaise and also the embarrassment are expressed spontaneously. . . .
>
> We all felt the humiliation, let's say, of our silence in the face of such developments. And this contrasted strongly with our claim that the GDR was at least better than what was running its course in Poland or Hungary or certainly the Soviet Union. That our circumstances weren't so bad. . . .
>
> And this wasn't the first time we had this experience. [The Berlin Wall] was still in everyone's memory. At that time it was relatively easy to ascribe [the exodus of East German workers] not to the essence or weakness of the system, but to the other side [the West], which tried to exploit a certain—let's say—adolescence of the system and in this way seduce people who did not recognize politically why the GDR incorporated the new historical epoch. But [in 1989] this was no longer possible, for several reasons. We had for a long time been seized by an inner insecurity. The system lost its monolithic character . . . after Gorbachev introduced [reforms].
>
> And besides, we now had forty years behind us in which we had expected that as the virtues of the system proved themselves, its re-

jection by the population would diminish. But astonishingly the rejection did not wane, but grew under the influence of the Gorbachev
visions, [which] pinpointed flaws that the people always felt were
failures of the system and wanted to see overcome. And we too, at
least some of us, wanted to overcome them.

All of us suffered under an inferiority complex. . . . It was already, I'd say, a long-term psychological disturbance. . . . Everyone
began doing what he himself thought necessary, after the motto:
whoever can, save himself. . . .

Part of the [GDR] leadership . . . persisted in the view that we
are the best, and the way we're doing things is fine, the only correct
salvation. We must just make sure that if the Soviet Union lets us
drop, the Federal Republic, so to speak, picks us up. Not in the sense
that [anyone] thought of unification. But in the sense that the Federal
Republic would perhaps pay something for, let's say, the good relations
to the other part of Germany which it still wanted, and perhaps over
a longer period we could come to an arrangement with the Federal
Republic. . . .

For some [the growing concern] was connected with pure terror,
with a pure retreat into themselves, for others, naturally, with a tendency to explosion.[7]

The reformers moved too late and did too little to save the communist
system, but once Gorbachev had loosed the forces of change—and withdrawn the support of his bayonets in Eastern Europe—the end to communist rule was preordained. Today Schabowski believes that even if they
had begun to liberalize two or three years earlier, they would only have
hastened the collapse.[8]

Schabowski manifestly did not start out with this view as he concluded in September 1989 that he had to break with the conformity of the
past. He was then sixty years old. His main ally was Honecker's crown
prince, the fifty-two-year-old Egon Krenz. Both were amateurs at this
new game of intrigue. Their habits had been formed in a Politburo of
enforced harmony that as Schabowski describes it was strangely apolitical.

In this world the Tuesday morning sessions of the inner circle of two
dozen were deliberately bland and boring. The absence of controversy was
deemed a virtue, the fruit of good preparation. Typically, the Politburo
would hear droning administrative reports, and in side conversation secret
police chief Erich Mielke would grumble to Schabowski about the poor
job of whitewashing one particular moldy bit of wall outside a downtown
East Berlin bakery that was a fixation of his. Mielke—despite the often
accurate reports about growing malaise compiled by his ubiquitous informers—regarded the country's many other instances of failure to provide

citizens with decent paint, housing, and consumer comforts as purely the fault of incompetent local officials rather than of the system as a whole. Honecker shared this view and saw all dissatisfaction among the people as provoked by nefarious Western forces.

Presumably, various Politburo members besides Krenz and Schabowski also sensed, in some degree, what Schabowski terms this repression of reality. But in Honecker's monolithic, atomized hierarchy no one knew for sure what others might be thinking. "An important tactic Honecker used to assert his power was isolation of individual Politburo members. The worst transgression was faction building. We all subordinated ourselves to this law. We would have more readily been allowed to commit sodomy than to make ourselves guilty of faction building," Schabowski explains. "There was never a group, or even two members, who discussed among themselves matters of principle, or even of an existential nature. No one could be sure whether a revelation of certain complaints or doubts to another Politburo member might not be misdirected [and betrayed]. Honecker in this respect was a great strategist. Even when two or three so much as got along especially well, this was an occasion for suspicion. He then usually played some against others, criticizing some, praising others."[9]

Even socially, Politburo members hardly mixed with one another. In the elite ghetto of Wandlitz each was glad to retreat to his own house and avoid raising any suspicions by being too friendly with the others. Mielke was the only one who would regularly eat breakfast in the common canteen and observe who was doing what each day. Mielke was the person who organized the one de rigeur social event of the year, the annual ball at the Palace Hotel, for which he always hired dowdy (and therefore cheap) Western pop singers, to raise money for his beloved Dynamo football club.[10]

The only colleagues the seventy-seven-year-old Honecker showed any closeness to were Mielke, five years his senior, and the younger but equally rigid Günter Mittag, the sixty-three-year-old economic czar. Mittag, "the Mephisto of the Politburo," Schabowski describes as a man who was "anti-economic to his roots and reduced his policies to a pure command structure."[11]

The Politburo's first tentative nod toward reality came in early September, when Honecker was absent, recuperating from an operation. Krenz too was away on a scheduled vacation that Honecker had insisted he take, despite the mounting crisis. Mittag, on Honecker's instructions, was in the chair. During the session Werner Krolikowski, Central Committee secretary for agriculture, at last admitted that the hemorrhage of East German workers through Hungary was a problem. His proposed solution was to issue an official proclamation on the subject.[12]

Schabowski "spoke up in the discussion and said these three or four points absolutely must be addressed [in any declaration]: . . . the economy, travel, freedom of the media, and meeting the everyday needs of the people. . . . That is how it came about [that we finally began to discuss the crisis in the Politburo], without any prior agreement. It was at this point that [we began to sense] who thought what. That's how late it came. [We didn't yet] draw the conclusions that we finally came to in the fall [to dump Honecker]. But basically this began to formulate itself naturally as Gorbachev began to play an increasing role."[13]

Yes, he felt guilty about this unheard-of deviation from party discipline, Schabowski acknowledged, but the crisis overshadowed his inhibitions. As it turned out, he was backed, cautiously, by the fifty-eight-year-old Siegfried Lorenz, party secretary of Karl Marx Stadt, then by the party secretaries of Halle and Cottbus. Yet no one pushed through to a final resolution, and future debate was postponed until Honecker's return.

While the Politburo fiddled, East Berlin burned. However traumatic the rethinking might have appeared at the top of the hierarchy, the average person saw no movement whatsoever in the political leadership. Many feared that the country would soon be emptied yet again of an entire generation of young people.

The Protestant Church

The Protestant church now began to fill the policy, as well as the moral void, in the forums of the Nikolai Church and a series of synods. Increasingly, the church expanded the sphere of begrudged quasi-public discussion. This devolution was a natural continuation of the kind of social responsibility the Protestant church had embraced after 1945 in both East and West Germany. The failure of the mainstream church to oppose Hitler was seared into the Protestant conscience. Many pastors sought to atone for this lapse by embracing a social mission and establishing, for the first time in Lutheran history, a critical relationship to the state.[14]

Back in the 1950s, the East German church's original stance of sharp confrontation with zealous antireligious communists reflected a close identification with the West German Christian Democratic government rather than a civic opposition to the East German government. As significant numbers of West German pastors began endorsing the Social Democratic message of pacifism, individual conscience, and social compassion in reaction against Chancellor Konrad Adenauer's hierarchical rule and rearmament, however, East German pastors mellowed into an arm's-length modus vivendi with the very different kind of command socialism practiced in the GDR. By the time East Berlin compelled its Protestants to break away from the pan-German church organization in the late 1960s, the Eastern Protestants were ready to characterize themselves as a "church in (though not of) socialism" and to work pragmatically to ameliorate the lives of its adherents.[15]

After the emergence of the grass-roots nuclear pacificist and ecological movements in the early 1980s, many pastors increasingly saw the church's solicitude for the weak and the poor as best manifested not only in the traditional hospitals, old people's homes, and kindergartens, but also in providing a sanctuary for those social activists harassed by the state. The religious flock dwindled from 82 percent of the population in 1950 to 40 percent by 1970, and then dropped further in the 1980s to 23 percent.[16] However, the church's political significance grew for all East Germans as younger clergy in particular—"the church from below"—applied their Christian conscience to the country's glaring social problems and articulated a freer alternative to Socialist Unity party practices. This inclination was magnified as various articulate young men and women who resisted the compulsory conformity of the state chose to study theology as the one field in which they could most freely explore a range of ideas and express their views.

Strains within the church inevitably arose from the old tension between Protestant individualism and conscience on the one hand and the traditional Lutheran "state positivism" and "teaching of the two kingdoms" on the other.[17] Some senior pastors admonished their juniors not to return to confrontation and not to reduce the church's pastoral and spiritual role to a purely secular and social one. Others urged caution as a tactical aid to maximize the church's good offices in intervening on behalf of East Germans caught in the cogs of the SED machine. Only if the church cultivated civil relations with the communists and the *Stasi* could it use these relations to ameliorate the treatment of activists or others who fell afoul of the system.

Still others found such ambiguous relations suspect. In the poisonous police state in which those who wanted to help victims of repression had to deal with the powerbrokers to be effective, the line between illicit and licit collaboration with the *Stasi* was a fine one. Even within a church built on trust between fellow Christians, and indeed between fellow human beings, no one could be confident that others were the persons they seemed to be and were not informers. As Professor Richard Schröder pointed out in retrospect, it was a peculiarity of the closed East German society that one could no longer rely on one's own instinct and direct experience to judge another person's character. Rumors and suspicions about this or that pastor's or church official's cooperation with the secret police abounded.[18]

A less convoluted, but increasingly important, field of tension in the church by early fall 1989 was the growing ill will between those who wanted nothing more than to quit the GDR for good, and those new-left activists who in early September began chanting, "We're staying here," and arguing that everyone had a moral obligation to remain and improve society.[19]

Pastors, some of whom had deliberately moved from West to East Germany at considerable personal sacrifice to tend the needier flocks there, tended to sympathize more with the latter group. They implored their compatriots not to desert the GDR, and they felt some embarrassment as the Monday night meetings in Leipzig became a magnet for frustrated East Germans who simply wanted to escape. Out of Christian duty, however, they offered succor to all, even if their petitioners professed no faith, and even if the church disapproved of the supplicants' positions.

Under these circumstances the church was constantly walking a tightrope. Yet to a remarkable degree it managed to maintain its balance, articulate grievances, prod the state to redress them, and keep alive a niche of integrity, a space for individual conscience, and the parliamentary arts of discussion and compromise. As the church responded to the increasing demands placed on it in fall 1989, it set forth demands more assertively than ever before at the Eisenach synod in mid-September. East Germans should be allowed to travel abroad and to return for visits if they chose to become citizens of the Federal Republic, the synod declared. They should be offered free elections with a choice of candidates and parties, should have the opportunity to read a variety of realistic press reportage, and get adequate health care and a clean environment. The GDR should allow its citizens to demonstrate peacefully without being beaten up by the police, should treat them as adults capable of making their own decisions, and extend to them the protection of the CSCE declaration of human rights that the GDR had signed.

Only tangible evidence of improvements in this direction could persuade East Germans to stay home and contribute to society, the Protestants argued. Only this way could the GDR construct a "socially just and democratic society, peaceable at home and abroad, and compatible with ecology."[20]

At this point others joined in the chorus. For the first time a prominent Roman Catholic churchman, Georg Sterzinsky, the new bishop of Berlin-Brandenburg, also called for far-reaching reforms. Rock musicians derided "the unbearable ignorance of the party and state leadership." The East Berlin chapter of the Writers Union, most renowned for its persecution of writers who did not toe the communist line, now suddenly disparaged "repression of reality." And workers in East Berlin's Bergmann Borsig factory called on the country's trade union chief to end propaganda harangues.

In a stunning turn of events, Bärbel Bohley, back in East Germany after a compulsory term of exile, joined other new-left activists on September 9 to solicit more support for socialist reforms by founding New Forum, the first countrywide dissidents' club.[21] The group applied for official registration as a political organization, but was denied recognition and labeled subversive and antistate. The following Monday, for the first time, the chanters of we're staying here outshouted the we want outs in Leipzig.[22]

Similar proto-parties founded in the next three weeks around core discussion groups from the Protestant chambers—Democracy Now, Democratic Awakening, United Left, and the Social Democratic party— were also banned. All pursued their political discussions regardless.

Meanwhile the massive emigration continued. On September 10 Hungary moved beyond just looking the other way at the Austrian border and explicitly annulled its old pact to bar East Germans from escaping West. Within three weeks 40,000 more young Germans quit the GDR via Hungary (and within a discreet period Budapest received DM 1 billion in credits from Bonn). The hardliners in Prague then rallied to help Honecker by turning back East Germans who tried to cross from Czechoslovakia into Hungary. A few of those thus barred found an unguarded riverbank and swam the Danube. Many more drove to Prague, abandoned their Trabis in the street, entered the elegant, rococo West German embassy, the Lobkovic Palais, and refused to budge until East Berlin gave them permission to go West. This tactic had worked periodically since the mid-1980s. The Bonn government had tried to discourage the practice, but had made a point of not evicting anyone and had always ransomed each successive wave of squatters. In the end East Berlin had always made a deal.

Now the latest desperate leavetakers calculated that Honecker would have to let them go too if he did not want to spoil the GDR's gala fortieth anniversary in October, and figured that after the celebration it would be too late, as all doors would again close.

The official East German news agency ADN angrily blamed the contretemps on a "crusade of imperialism against socialism," and with stunning hypocrisy castigated Hungary's "ice cold trade with GDR citizens" for "pieces of silver." The Czechoslovak press compared the Federal Republic's reprehensible luring of East Germans West with Nazi intrigues. Even *Pravda* railed against the West's "provocation," campaign against the GDR, and "violation of international law."

Despite the heated rhetoric, Honecker quickly gave in. To avoid embarrassing publicity he promised exit visas to the 250 East German squatters in Prague if they returned home first. They did so, and their places were promptly taken by another 400, then 500, then 1,000 imitators. A further 100, then 400, hopefuls similarly occupied the West German embassy in Warsaw and mission in East Berlin.

Again Honecker sent the legendary East Berlin lawyer Wolfgang Vogel to assure the would-be emigrants that if they would just return home quietly, they would be given exit visas in due course. Vogel had a record that should have inspired trust. He had been the broker for Bonn's discreet ransom of 33,755 East German political prisoners between 1963 and 1989 for commodities and payments worth DM 3.5 billion, or approximately $2 billion. He had also been the chief Eastern negotiator for the major East-West spy swaps during the last two decades of the cold war.[23]

By now, however, the time had passed for such a slave trade. There was no margin of trust left. Most of the voluntary refugees refused to leave the Prague chancery, even when the East German government upped the ante and promised that the refugees' relatives could also leave the GDR and their belongings would not be confiscated. Few accepted the deal.

In the war of nerves that now ensued, there were soon more than 5,000 impromptu guests in the Lobkovic Palais, sleeping in shifts, in twos and threes with their children, on the double-decker beds that crowded every nook of the halls and the emergency tents in the back garden. There were few toilets. Cold rains turned the grounds into a sea of mud. Sanitary conditions deteriorated, and fears of an epidemic grew. And still more tried to press into the compound. One West German diplomat who slept in the embassy overnight described his sensation on tossing himself awake in the early morning hours and feeling as if the entire building were heaving with the thousands of Jonahs it had swallowed whole.

On September 21 the Interior Ministry formally ruled New Forum illegal. Already 3,000 people had signed its appeal.

By September 25 the Czechoslovak leadership importuned Honecker to do something about the intolerable situation as ever more East Germans cluttered Prague's narrow cobblestone streets with their abandoned Trabis and clambered over the fence into the teeming Lobkovic garden. If the refugee invasion of Prague were not soon stopped, the leadership warned, the Czechs too might become infected with the virus of discontent. For the first time, that evening the 6,000 to 8,000 people who assembled in and outside the Nikolai Church marched around the inner city ring road.

Honecker stonewalled for a few more days. East German Foreign Minister Oskar Fischer lectured the UN General Assembly that those governments that presume to represent the citizens of other states provoke conflict and endanger peace. Meanwhile in the UN corridors West German Foreign Minister Hans-Dietrich Genscher appealed for help to his Soviet colleague, while U.S. Secretary of State James Baker, at Bonn's request, spoke to the Czechoslovak and Hungarian foreign ministers.[24] As West

German television, day after day, showed East Germans passing children and teddy bears over the back fence of the Lobkovic embassy, then scrambling over it themselves ahead of the Czech police, Honecker finally relented.

On September 30 Genscher, knowing in his heart that he was witnessing the end of the GDR, flew to Prague for a dramatic balcony scene.[25] The cheering broke out before he could even finish announcing that his ecstatic audience would be allowed to emigrate but would first have to board a special train that would travel through the GDR.

Honecker's purpose in setting this prerequisite was to strip the emigres of their identity papers en route, and then claim that they were not fleeing, but that, as a press spokesman phrased it, the GDR was expelling these "irresponsible antisocial traitors and criminals."

The precondition was a mistake. One West German escort, traveling with the emigrants to reassure them that the GDR would not double-cross them, also sensed that East Germany's days were numbered as he witnessed the train's surreal passage through the GDR. Person after person in field and city waved white handkerchiefs at the passing train in spontaneous solidarity. A few inside the train, visibly moved, wondered aloud if they were doing the right thing after all. But in the station where the train halted for the collection of old passports, the passengers displayed their contempt by flinging onto the platform not only their identity cards, but also their worthless GDR bills and coins. Although the station had been sealed off to the public and was swarming with the dreaded *Stasi*, one railroad official on duty removed his cap and one railroad worker his hardhat in deference to the travelers. When they rolled across the border of the Federal Republic several hours later, the new West Germans chanted, "Freedom, freedom." The old West Germans were alternately touched and embarrassed by this display of civic faith in their own less than perfect democracy.

The only discernible response by the East German hierarchy to the growing *cri de coeur* of its people was to condemn those who were fleeing the country as scum and ingrates, aroused by the machinations of Western intelligence agencies, or else drugged and shanghaied against their will. The ominous word "counterrevolution"—a phrase that automatically summoned communists to defend the revolution in violent class warfare— was in the air. The government gave no sign of compromise. On the contrary, its motto seemed to be the prophetic warning by Otto Reinhold, rector of the Central Committee's Academy of Social Sciences and, in effect, the country's ideological pope. Any concession to reform would be dangerous, he counseled, since it would remove East Germany's whole raison d'être as a separate socialist identity and would inevitably lead to the GDR's absorption into the bigger and more dynamic Federal Republic.[26]

In West Germany Chancellor Helmut Kohl and his fellow conservatives agreed with this assessment, but drew the obverse conclusions. Rubbing their eyes in disbelief, they reveled that the reunification they had been preaching ritually for forty years was suddenly really on the agenda.

Chapter 8

The October Revolution: Dresden and Berlin

To the watching world, East Germany, communism, and the cold war all seemed to expire when the Berlin Wall disintegrated into rubble. In reality, they had died more quietly a month before that drama. In Dresden and Leipzig in the first week of October, private moral courage came face-to-face with official demoralization, and won. "It was a revolution," maintains Friedrich Schorlemmer, pastor in Wittenberg, and throughout the 1980s a spokesman for grass-roots peace and civil rights groups in the East German church. "It was astounding that this people suddenly set aside its fear and in masses became self-confident. Also that it became conscious of its power. . . . That was a revolution, a regaining of dignity."[1]

At the time, hardly anyone realized the import of the people's reclamation of dignity. But after October 9 there would be no going back. Nor would there be violence.

As the month began, all eyes were fixed on Saturday, October 7, the forty-year jubilee of the German Democratic Republic. Some 100,000 young East Germans had deserted their country since the summer, and still the aging, ill Honecker insisted on hailing the GDR as the best of all possible worlds. Any internal report that suggested otherwise was quickly suppressed, its author disciplined. Typically, Honecker personally inserted into the key ADN wire service editorial the most vitriolic of the official condemnations of emigrants "who through their conduct trampled on moral values and shut themselves out of our society. One should therefore shed no tears over them."[2]

In Prague the 5,000 or more vacated spots in the West German embassy filled overnight with a new 5,000 or more East Germans demanding escape from the GDR. By now New Forum, in some two weeks of official nonexistence, had 6,000 signed-up members. On October 2 the Leipzig Monday night prayer meeting and demonstration swelled to more than 10,000 people, who again marched along the city's inner ring road. It was the largest number of protesters in one place since 1953, and its character was changing. "We're staying here" was already established as the dominant chant; it was now joined, in this 200th anniversary year of the French Revolution, by "liberty, equality, fraternity." The attendant city police and secret police were augmented by units from the *Kampfgruppe*, the SED's own paramilitary workers' militia, which, people said, had recently been trained in street fighting. There were some clashes and some arrests.[3]

Oblivious, the East German media continued to feature glowing accounts of overfulfilled production plans and awards bestowed on heroic achievers. *Pravda,* despite the Soviet assistance in persuading Honecker to be conciliatory, blamed Bonn for stirring up the refugee crisis, and labeled this an "undisguised attempt to interfere in the internal affairs of the German Democratic Republic."

On October 3 Honecker accommodated his fellow hardliners in Prague and closed the last door, reimposing the requirement of exit visas for travel even to Czechoslovakia, the one foreign country East Germans could still visit spontaneously, without first being vetted by the secret police. In 1989, as back in 1961, the citizens of the German Democratic Republic were again confined to their claustrophobic 200- by 300-mile jail.

Dresden

On October 3 Honecker also announced that the last East German squatters in Prague would be allowed to travel by sealed train through the GDR to the Federal Republic. Two or three thousand other desperate East Germans, fearing that their chance for a new start would end forever with the October 7 deadline on tolerance, crammed into the Dresden station to try to stow away on the passing sealed train. That night the train never came.

By 10:30 P.M. one tired five-year-old pleaded, "Mummy, I want to go home." She might have been speaking for all the children kept up long past their bedtime in this alien, tense atmosphere.

"It's too far away," countered the mother. She might have been speaking for all the anxious parents, who more than anything else wanted to give their offspring the opportunities to study, travel, and play that they had been denied.

"Why do we have to wait here so long?" the girl persisted.

"Because we're going on a trip."

"But where?"

"I'll tell you when you're grown up."

At 11:30 the loudspeaker ordered everyone to leave the station. The crowd whistled derisively and chanted, "We want out." One church worker tried to dissuade a young man from leaving: "You're wasting all this energy on a train platform just to get out. Why not use it in this country instead? Answer me! You can help change things here!" The youth was silent. "Freedom and travel, is that all you want out of life?" the churchman persevered.

"Yes," replied the man.

At half past midnight police and regular army soldiers surrounded the station and set to with their clubs, with a brutality that was new in scale.

The next night 10,000 people—many of them East Germans from other parts of the country who had tried to drive to Prague the previous day but had been stopped at the border—gathered around the station to await the delayed train from Prague. Some threw stones and Molotov cocktails at the police, burned a police car, and vandalized the station. Again, security officials set to with truncheons and made multiple arrests.

In the following days of continuous turbulence the Protestant super-intendent for Dresden, Christof Ziemer, Saxony Bishop Johannes Hempel, and others made strenuous efforts to turn back the spiral of confrontation. Only three days earlier Ziemer had counseled an impatient Dresdener that the protesters should practice nonviolence for four or five months before they would be mature enough to graduate from church naves to city streets. But they no longer had the luxury of rehearsal.

Christians, summoning up the spirit of Gandhi's civil disobedience, the American civil rights campaign, and their own nuclear pacifist move-ments of the early 1980s, began chanting "No violence" and carrying lighted candles as a symbol of peace. The police continued their brutality, but gradually the crowds began to respond to the church's exhortation to voluntary discipline. On October 7 the hordes that had milled about the train station for four nights formed for the first time into a more orderly procession.[4]

Berlin

The four Politburo members who were sufficiently distressed by the course of events to break at last the ironclad ban on faction building were Egon Krenz as leader, Günter Schabowski and Siegfried Lorenz as sup-porters, and, apparently, Erich Mielke.[5] Ironically, Krenz and Schabowski, the key plotters, were the very emissaries Honecker had chosen to send to

Beijing to express East German solidarity with the Chinese leaders after the Tienanmen massacre the previous June. In fact, Krenz was in China at the beginning of October, being strengthened in his resolve not to repeat such violence in the GDR, he later told Schabowski. Lorenz, the party chief of Karl Marx Stadt, and therefore only an occasional visitor to the center of activity in Berlin, allied himself with Krenz early on but did not help shape the palace coup.

General of the Army Mielke, GDR minister for state security, and proud holder of the Soviet orders of Lenin, the October Revolution, and Hero of the Soviet Union, was, along with Günter Mittag, part of Honecker's inner circle. He was an old comrade of Honecker's from the days when communism was illegal in the 1930s. He was the person the East German leader always closeted himself with after Politburo sessions.[6] His worldview had been formed in the days of the Spanish Civil War and had changed little thereafter. So far as is known, his sole criticism of Honecker's policy before the palace coup harked back to 1980, when he and Prime Minister Willi Stoph secretly faulted Honecker for being too soft and unprincipled in courting West German capitalists and neglecting the interests of the Soviet Union.[7]

Of the four, Mielke's role in deposing Honecker is the most shadowy and, as of this writing, can only be inferred. Neither Krenz, Schabowski, nor Mielke himself has ever talked about it, and Schabowski most likely did not even know about it.[8] Honecker takes it as a given, however, that only Mielke and "the Soviet advisers in his ministry" could possibly have overthrown him, Honecker, in a colossal act of betrayal.[9] Colonel General Markus Wolf, the legendary East German spymaster who was one of Mielke's deputies for two decades until Wolf's resignation in 1987, also takes it for granted that Mielke must have been involved, presumably because the octopus (as the *Stasi* was popularly nicknamed) had its tentacles everywhere and could have exposed the plotters at an early stage, or at least greatly complicated execution of their plan, had it chosen to do so. Karl Wilhelm Fricke, the (West) German author most knowledgeable about the *Stasi*, seconds this judgment.[10]

What is known is that by late summer of 1989 Mielke's burning desire, as he lectured his senior officers, was to fight Western "fascistization," to stamp out dissent, and to stop the exodus of the "dirtbags" who were abandoning the GDR under the influence of Western "swine dogs." Yet at the same time he was anxious about the volatile situation and worried that a wrong step could trigger a repetition of the trauma of the East German workers' crushed revolt on June 17, 1953.[11]

The problem for Mielke was that the world he knew was disintegrating before his eyes, as internal *Stasi* reports documented only too vividly. The party could no longer prevent thousands from leaving nor other thousands from agitating for change. Even the *Stasi* no longer inspired deterrent awe: with every passing week more demonstrators simply stopped caring how many informers might be listening as they shouted their blasphemies. And as Gorbachev had made abundantly clear, this time the Soviet army would not rescue the East German or any other East European leader.

Under the circumstances disorientation set in, and *Stasi* morale sank. Many agents were incredulous at their new helplessness. One major, Reinhardt O. Hahn, later told an interviewer, "We had hope up to the last day. [We thought] it must all be a mistake, maybe even a gigantic hoax. Now we watched uncomprehendingly as the so-called 'people' shouted without cease. Sometime, surely, things must return to reason."[12]

As weeks rolled by and things did not return to reason, however, Mielke's dilemma increased. He still had the means to crack down. Besides his thousands of regular agents and the other security forces that reported to him, he had a division-size "watch regiment" armed with far heavier weapons than Western intelligence realized at the time. He had often boasted that, if necessary, this regiment could hold Berlin on its own. Yet if he loosed violence on the increasingly testy crowds, he would indeed risk another June 17. With the Russians staying aloof, the blood would be on his hands, and he could not even be sure of final victory. A show of force was one thing, but if that failed to intimidate protesters as it had for the last thirty-five years, shooting would be quite another thing.[13]

Under the circumstances, did Mielke calculate that it would be better to abandon the obdurate Honecker and gamble on cautious reform under Krenz? From today's meager knowledge one cannot answer this question definitively. Wolfgang Herger, director of the Central Committee security department and a confidant of Krenz, reportedly told *Stasi* officers at the end of October that Krenz would not have deposed Honecker if Mielke had not supported this action.[14] In a gossipy aside, long-time Soviet Ambassador to the GDR Pyotr Abrasimov recalled that Mielke carped about Honecker in Moscow in a way he would never dare do in East Berlin.[15]

Otherwise, the only advance clues that Mielke might condone the overthrow of Honecker—and that Krenz might be banking on such tolerance—are negative. In the first instance, four weeks before the palace coup, Mielke circulated to eleven Politburo members—most unusually, since the *Stasi* were not authorized to meddle in the party apparatus—an analysis by his ministry expressing concern about spreading discontent in the GDR. Honecker, who had not yet resumed work after his operation, was not one of the recipients.[16] Second, in early October Krenz was sufficiently unconcerned about possible discovery by Mielke to slip a strategy paper to Schabowski at a meeting at *Stasi* headquarters that Mielke himself was conducting.[17] The third clue would have to be the striking absence of any thought by Krenz that the plotters' demand for the resignation of the inner circle of Honecker, Mittag, and media czar Joachim Herrmann should logically extend to the powerful Mielke. Certainly when the Politburo showdown came, Mielke was prepared. He immediately backed the ouster of Honecker, berating the party chief and threatening to release compromising information about him if he did not step down.[18]

On the crucial fortieth anniversary weekend, a week before the Politburo finally eased Honecker out, Mielke's holding action on the streets seemed to consist of deploying large numbers of *Stasi*, police, workers' militia, and the army to contain the rot until new SED leadership might restore party control.[19] It was important to Mielke to prevent mob rule, but it was also important to him not to introduce a level of violence that might make the country truly ungovernable.

Demoralized though they were, the East German security organs followed these guidelines. Notably, the *Stasi* never split into factions, with some hardliners acting as a rogue force. No one outside the *Stasi* could be sure of this discipline in advance. The potential for provocation was a constant anxiety throughout October, early November, and even into December. Yet by the time the *Stasi* majors woke up and realized it was not some huge joke after all, they no longer had any organized power to rally. Citizens' committees were occupying their once almighty headquarters in half a dozen cities.

The Plot

The whole *Stasi* aspect is conspicuously missing in the only two published accounts that give any details about the palace coup, Schabowski's *Das Politbüro* and *Der Absturz*. Schabowski focuses instead on his and Krenz's plan, the centerpiece of the exercise. However Mielke arrived at his own conclusions—and whatever his initial doubts about whether Krenz had the necessary backbone to succeed Honecker—it was certainly this plan that Mielke fell in with in the end.

To an outsider, the most striking aspect of the Krenz-Schabowski conspiracy is its gossamer nature as it evolved between late August and mid-October. In its entirety the plot consisted of maneuvering a mild statement through the Politburo that some things in the GDR did need improvement after all, and then using that statement as a lever to win a Politburo vote requesting the resignation of Honecker as someone too old and rigid to effect such improvement. In the minds of the plotters, the aim was not a coup as such, but an acceleration of generational change.[20]

Schabowski saw Krenz as the only possible successor to Honecker if the shift to the next generation were to proceed smoothly. Krenz was sufficiently concerned about the deepening disaster to enact reforms, yet having been groomed by Honecker, he had all the orthodox credentials that would make him acceptable to the old apparatchiks. Schabowski therefore took the opportunity in the few late-September days in which Krenz was in Berlin between his vacation and his trip to Beijing to urge Krenz not to let himself be overshadowed by Günter Mittag. From then on, Schabowski believes, Krenz regarded him as an ally and not just a potential rival.[21] A third possible candidate for the succession identified by Western analysts—if the situation deteriorated badly—was Hans Modrow, the Dresden party chief who had earlier fallen out with Honecker and been exiled to Saxony, where he cut a relatively liberal figure with his modest living and unusual dialogue with intellectuals. Modrow was a very dark horse, however, since he was not even a member of the twenty-six-man Politburo.

The celebrations on October 6 and 7 opened with a torchlight parade of 100,000 that was eerily reminiscent of old Nazi pageants, and was followed by a thunderous military roll-by of tanks and missiles along Karl Marx Boulevard in East Berlin. Gorbachev was present, as protocol required him to bless the pomp personally however much he might dislike his client's mode of governance.

On Saturday the GDR's entire Politburo met with Gorbachev. Characteristically, the Soviet leader, without directly criticizing East German practices, reviewed all the Soviet tribulations and mistakes. "When we fall behind, life punishes us immediately," Gorbachev concluded.[22] His words, despite the subsequent notoriety they acquired as a disavowal of Honecker, were low key. The Soviet leader clearly expected Honecker or some other Politburo member to respond with some self-criticism of his own, but he was far from pushing Honecker off the throne.[23]

Honecker flushed, but made no reciprocal confession about the GDR's failures. Instead, he painted a radiant picture of the country's successes.[24] What he said behind closed doors was a carbon copy of what he was saying to the choreographed crowds at Marx-Engels Square: the GDR was a "humanitarian state entity." Its four decades "were forty years of heroic work, forty years of successful struggle for the rise of our socialist republic, for the well-being of the people."[25] The East German economy was among the top ten in the world.[26] Especially noteworthy was East Germany's triumph in developing a four-megabyte chip (which Honecker's economic managers were already cursing for the millions of marks it diverted from other investment and its instant obsolescence once the West relaxed its electronics embargo on the Soviet Union).

Gorbachev responded to this flight from reality only by exhaling with an audible snort. Everyone rose from the table. Schabowski and Krenz exchanged glances. At the reception that evening, independently of each other, they hinted to Soviet visitors that things would soon change.[27]

Together, the two stepped to a window where they could hear demonstrators across the Spree shouting "Gorby, Gorby," but apparently did not catch the first cries of "We are the people!"

The chants faded, and the pair concluded with relief, Schabowski says, that there had been no special repression that might complicate their plans.

They were wrong. Special repression had indeed taken place. Many of the estimated 5,000 peaceful demonstrators (and not a few bystanders) in East Berlin were severely beaten near the Gethsemane Church, a center of dissident activity, by an estimated 3,000 members of deployed security organs that included not only the usual police and *Stasi* plainclothes officers, but also the *Stasi*'s Feliks Dzierzynski Regiment, antiterror units, and "battalion" of Free German Youth toughs.

Provocateurs (identifiable as they were about to be arrested, when they produced identity cards and were suddenly allowed to pass unhindered through police lines) instigated fights. Many of the demonstrators chanted "No violence," however, and under the inquiry commission's probe, the official reports of fifty-seven injuries to police officers shrank to four, none of which was attributable to the demonstrators, and one of which involved broken hand bones after the police officer in question punched a demonstrator too hard. By contrast, at least fifty-eight protesters suffered serious injuries from kicks, punches, and beatings with sticks. Two pregnant women were hit with clubs and some demonstrators had a particularly powerful tear gas or other substance sprayed in their eyes.

The same pattern was repeated in Leipzig, Dresden, Plauen, Karl Marx Stadt, and other cities. Throughout the country an official 3,500 people, including children, were arrested or detained. Many were not given drink or food or allowed to go to the toilet for hours, were not permitted to sleep, and were forced to stand against garage walls with splayed legs throughout the cold night. In Berlin some three dozen were kept past the twenty-four-hour limit on detention without a charge. The injured, sick, and dizzy were refused medical attention and were threatened with worse treatment (and, implicitly, even death in some cases) if they complained. Mothers were neither released nor allowed to telephone relatives to ensure that their children were being cared for.[28]

When asked later how the massive security operation that Saturday night could have escaped his attention, since he was East Berlin party secretary and also listened to Western news on Deutschlandfunk every day, Schabowski replied that security was in the hands of others, and that even Deutschlandfunk at first reported only that some arrests had taken place. It was thus not until Sunday afternoon that he began to hear about the extent of the crackdown.[29]

For his part, Gorbachev flew out of Berlin before the violence got into full swing. On his way to the airport, Krenz says, casually citing "credible reports," the Soviet leader told his East German hosts, "Act!," an injunction Krenz implies was intended to encourage the conspirators.[30] Schabowski finds this anecdote improbable, because the escorts accompanying Gorbachev to the plane were the hardliners Mittag and Hermann Axen, the last comrades Gorbachev would ever expect to oust Honecker.[31]

On the morning of Sunday, October 8, Krenz used what Schabowski termed a "banal" meeting Mielke had convened at *Stasi* headquarters to slip to Schabowski his five-page draft of a Politburo statement for publication in the party newspaper, *Neues Deutschland*. Its centerpiece was an unprecedented expression of regret over the loss of every East German who had fled to the West. Its intent was to ease the way for Honecker's removal. On this day, for the first time, Krenz and Schabowski discussed how to recruit possible sympathizers on the Politburo. Krenz said that Lorenz was already with them and agreed to sound out Mielke, Stoph, and several others, while Schabowski took on trade union boss Harry Tisch and others.

On the afternoon of October 8 Krenz presented Honecker with his five-page draft, as was customary for any item to be placed on the Politburo agenda. The East German leader took it as a personal affront, but in the end let it be forwarded for discussion in the inner circle the following Tuesday.[32] On Sunday evening security forces in East Berlin again roughed up some of the thousands of demonstrators.

In the intervening thirty-six hours before the next Politburo session, two developments occurred in the provinces that were hardly noticed in East Berlin, but would have a decisive impact on the GDR's future. In Dresden, church intermediaries succeeded in starting a dialogue between an impromptu "Group of Twenty" demonstrators, party secretary Modrow, and city mayor Wolfgang Berghofer on the evening of October 8. In Leipzig no fewer than 70,000 people marched peacefully on the evening of October 9 without being attacked by police or *Stasi*, despite explicit threats beforehand that this Monday night prayer meeting might turn into another Tienanmen.

Dresden, October 8

In Dresden on Sunday the peaceful street protests began at 3 P.M. and were still going on six hours later. By 9 P.M. many demonstrators had already been arrested and taken off to prison. The police surrounded yet another large group of demonstrators on the Prague Street pedestrian zone in the usual prelude to arrest, but three churchmen, including Superintendent Ziemer, finally succeeded in persuading the police to let some protesters talk to the mayor instead.[33] In a breakthrough, the police loosened their human chain, the crowd selected twenty representatives, virtually at random, and the protesters fanned out to four churches to coordinate their approach to the talks.[34] It was the first peaceful end to a demonstration in that city in a tense six days. The country's pioneer roundtable, though it was not yet so christened, began the following day, with pastors helping the inexperienced and often angry new tribunes to translate their apodictical principles of freedom and environmental protection into concrete, pragmatic, negotiable demands.[35]

In hindsight it is tempting to think that various turns of history are inevitable: that in this case the voice of the people had to be heard, and that Modrow was the one preordained to listen. At this point, though, it was not at all clear whether "the people" would in fact align themselves with the activists, or just vanish to West Germany, leaving Honecker with a passive rump population. The demonstrators were increasing in numbers, but they remained a minority, and might still have proved ephemeral.[36] Nor had the pastors succeeded in cooling mob passions during their six days of preaching moderation. If any nervous police officer (or the even less trained paramilitary workers) had resorted to firearms, it might well have sparked a very different conflagration.

Nor had that great white hope Modrow shown himself particularly accommodating in the preceding week. To be sure, by his own account he had begged the central authorities in East Berlin to retract their "crazy decision" to route the Prague train through Dresden, and had "again and again" counseled restraint on those who held power in East Berlin.[37] Yet Dresden's district operational leadership, which was under his chairmanship, condoned the arrest of some 1,300 people and the abuse of many of those detained. The leadership may not have ordered the actions—ascertaining the truth is hard, since the relevant documents were destroyed before citizens' watchdog groups got to them—but it certainly did nothing to stop the show of force in the first six days. Modrow himself, after initially denying that he had ordered the police violence in his city, acknowledged in his 1991 book that in the "complicated situation" of that week he did work jointly with the Berlin ministers to commission security measures in the Dresden train station "to prevent the worst."[38] (This meant, as he defined it, to ensure that trains could go through without endangering people's lives.) Modrow further personally asked Defense Minister Heinz Kessler for some additional security personnel from the army, for the first recorded instance in decades in which the military was employed in constraining civilian demonstrators.[39]

In his personal dealings Modrow was by various accounts a decent man, but a person of limited education and experience. At the end of World War II he was no cynical communist apparatchik who had watched

Stalinist terror stalk the halls of the Lux Hotel, but a scared seventeen-year-old Soviet prisoner of war, a boy from a rural German village who drank in antifascist ideals as his political credo and equated capitalism with Hitler's atrocities.

Especially in the fog of revolution, then, it was hardly predestined that the volatile confrontation would deescalate. Yet in the end Modrow did become the first nationally known politician to sit down and talk civilly with the demonstrators.[40]

Chapter 9

The October Revolution: Leipzig and Berlin

The atmosphere in Leipzig was, if anything, even more explosive. To be sure, the city had had a modest Protestant-communist dialogue for some years, perhaps because of particular personalities, perhaps because Leipzig, site of the world's preeminent East-West trade fair, was more cosmopolitan than the rest of Saxony. The Nikolai Church was such a magnet for dissent, however, that the authorities seemed intent on making an example of the city. The crackdown on October 7 had been as severe in Leipzig as in East Berlin, and over the weekend ugly rumors were circulating in schools, clinics, and public offices—and in various conversations that *Stasi* agents conducted in the region—that Monday, October 9, might produce another Tienanmen.

Leipzig, October 9

East Germany's effusive support for China's successful defeat of counterrevolution the previous June certainly lent some credibility to the rumors. On his visit to China Krenz stressed that both countries "follow the same social goals," and his hosts reciprocated with thanks, "especially for the support and understanding of the comrades in the GDR for China's action in defeating the counterrevolutionary disturbances." Honecker, Mittag, Hermann Axen, Erich Kleiber, and other Politburo members repeatedly echoed these sentiments. On October 9 Honecker was welcoming Chinese Deputy Premier Yao Yilin to East Berlin and agreeing that they could both learn basic lessons from the counterrevolutionary insurrection in Beijing,[1] and State Secretary for Church Affairs Kurt Löffler had just noted pointedly to two Protestant officials at a weekend reception in Berlin that China was far away "only geographically."[2]

Extensive local preparations for a showdown supplemented the ominous general allusions to Tienanmen. Extra blood plasma was distributed to Leipzig hospitals. Regional National People's Army (NVA) units were put on alert, and this information was spread among the demonstrators, who believed this was the first time in a generation that the army was to be used against civilians. One paratroop company of Air Attack Regiment Forty was deployed in the Leipzig area, according to company officers a year later. They also reported that 200 men of Watch Regiment Two, 300 men of Watch Regiment Berlin, and a motorized guard battalion were put on heightened battle alert status in the area; the helicopter squadron in Brandenburg was put on alert level three; 400 border troops and a divers' unit were upgraded to alert; and the military medical academy and clinic in Potsdam were issued additional beds.[3]

A total of twenty-eight companies of mobile police with eighty conscripts each were also deployed in Leipzig, along with the regular police, workers' militia, special units, and the usual *Stasi* contingent.[4] The mobile police had just been purged of about 10 percent of its recruits who were considered too unreliable politically to serve on Monday nights, or who had been observed fraternizing with demonstrators. Political officers had briefed the remainder: "Comrades, from today on it's class war. The situation corresponds to June 17, 1953 [the day of the East Berlin uprising]. Today it will be decided, either them or us. So be class watchful. If sticks aren't good enough, use firearms. [If children are in the crowd, then] too bad for them. We have pistols, and we don't have them for nothing!" On hearing these words, five of the mobile policemen told a New Forum interviewer, many of their colleagues lay on their bunks and cried.[5]

Some workers' militia units had been run through an exercise with district party functionaries in September in which they were told that "day X" would take place on October 7. They were then put on higher alert the morning of October 9, kept incommunicado from their families, and told that special medical centers had been established for their care. Some feared they would die.[6] Other members of the workers' militia in nearby Gera were ordered to clamp snowplow-like equipment onto trucks. (The workers, assuming the contraptions would be used to scoop up demonstrators, refused to obey the command.)[7]

With this massive backing, at least some *Stasi* officers were primed for decisive action against counterrevolution on October 9. One anonymous man identified as a high-ranking ex-officer from the Ministry for State Security who was interviewed on ZDF television on April 11, 1990, and in *Die Welt* in a ten-part series from May 21 to June 13, 1990, for example, gave testimony supporting plans for a bloodbath.[8] In his sensational allegations the officer said that after a planning meeting on October 8—apparently the one at which Krenz gave Schabowski the draft of the *Neues Deutschland* statement—the *Stasi* were told to use all force short of shooting on October 9 in Leipzig. He described the operation as the high point of years of preparations to stamp out dissidence. He attributed to Krenz the order to shatter counterrevolutionary structures in the GDR.

In the end, none of the security forces used firearms, and despite the conspicuous show of force, no specific order to shoot was apparently given during that tense extended weekend.[9] For some months many in the West German media presumed that such an order had been issued, and they spun isolated tidbits of information or misinformation into contradictory speculation about whether local renegades, Krenz, Honecker himself, or the Soviet army might have countermanded the order at the last minute. West German intelligence found no evidence either of such an order or its retraction, however, or any indication that written instructions to shoot might have been deliberately destroyed, as other security documents were in the turbulent final weeks of 1989.[10]

Nonetheless, Mielke's orders of October 5 and 8 certainly implied the authorization of violence, at a level that might escalate to shooting. On October 5 the minister sent a "top urgent" telex to all branch *Stasi* offices saying that protests by those denied exit to Czechoslovakia and other "enemy-negative activities are to be decisively thwarted." On October 8, after the clashes of the night before, his tone was even more urgent, and a message from Honecker to all regional party secretaries backed his commands. All *Stasi* branches were to go on full operational alert, those authorized to carry weapons at all times were to be sure to do so, "all appropriate means" were to be used to deal with protesters, and local commanders were to keep enough reserves on hand to take "offensive measures to thwart and break up conspiratorial assembly."[11] Furthermore, those receiving these orders interpreted them as so imperative that many told their squads to prepare for the class war that would crush the dreaded counterrevolution.[12]

If it was not supported by a specific order to shoot, was the massive threat on October 9 primarily a disinformation campaign to scare away protesters? Or did the astounding number of protesters—seven times the previous Monday's turnout and some twelve times the number of demonstrators in Berlin—persuade Mielke that continued violence, even at the level of beatings and kicking, would now risk another June 17?[13] And if such a decision were made in Berlin, how was it communicated in time to the thousands of local security officers primed to combat counterrevolution? Or did the center simply abdicate at the critical moment and say nothing?

So far, none of these theses can be proved conclusively. At the time, astute West German diplomatic observers viewed the spread of rumors about a Tienanmen primarily as a war of nerves, and in retrospect this hypothesis is plausible.

Nevertheless, however real or artificial the threats were, they generated serious risks. The tense buildup of the previous weekend, combined with the psyching up of security officials before the event, risked a fatal misjudgment by any jittery policeman or even less well trained workers' militiaman in a moment of crisis. Such a volatile situation was also open to provocations by *Stasi* hardliners or to impulsive acts by impassioned demonstrators, especially at the point in each march when the protesters rounded the Dittrich Ring in front of the hated *Stasi* headquarters. Both history and crowd psychology offer far more precedents of such a charged atmosphere exploding into violence rather than calming down to fraternization.

Peter Zimmermann, one of the prime movers to nonviolence on October 9—and a theologian and professor who had cultivated contact with party apparatchiks for some years—finds all but irrelevant the distinction between a formal authorization to shoot and a tense confrontation without clear guidelines constraining the use of weapons. "There did not have to be a specific order to shoot. Psychopolitical preparation to expect the counterrevolution with no explicit ban on the use of weapons leaves the decision to shoot with each individual, according to the motto: what is not forbidden is permitted. I myself observed on October 7 how a mobile policeman, asked when he would take the muzzle off his dog, said, 'When it gets tense.' And we can only be happy that there were apparently policemen in Leipzig who reacted differently from the day before in Dresden and Berlin."[14]

Under the circumstances, it took real civil courage—a quality that has rarely distinguished the Germans—for the 70,000 Leipzigers to gather on October 9 in the country's largest demonstration since 1953 and to press for democracy and the legalization of New Forum. Until then the demonstrators had to a certain extent hedged their bets and not broken with their everyday world. The Monday night assemblies had been a model of German orderliness, starting only at the end of the workday in the Nikolai Church at 5 P.M., beginning to march (as of September 25) at 6 P.M., then breaking up by 7 P.M. in time to go to the theater or feed the children and tuck them in for the night. Protesters had not yet committed themselves to overturning their lives in the service of reform.

October 9, following the violence of October 7 in Leipzig and elsewhere, was different. The 70,000 were frightened, but they marched anyway, with little hope that they would succeed. It was less the heralding of a new era, commented one West German observer, than an act of despair. Yet at the last minute the police held back, there were no *Stasi* provocations, and the event proceeded peacefully. "Wir sind das Volk!" (we are the people) the crowd chanted, uniting that night behind what would become the rallying call of the revolution.

"We Are the People!"

The ambience—and at the climax the dissolving of hostility into precious dialogue—is best conveyed by eyewitnesses interviewed by New Forum members in Leipzig:

> Ewald Diehm: From a friend, a member of the SED, I learned that during a party meeting it was announced that there was a ten-point program of the Central Committee of the SED under which the counterrevolution was to be suppressed on October 9 in Leipzig. . . . I feared the worst. . . . Around 6:00 P.M. I, my wife, and my daughter got into the car and drove to the city center to join the demonstration, whatever might happen. . . . We fell into the procession at Dittrich Ring [where battle-dressed mobile police armed with pistols, machine pistols, and live ammunition were waiting in trucks, with their engines running] with the shout, "Wir sind das Volk." I was impressed by the huge crowd of people. We had tears in our eyes, from joy or from fear? We did not know what would happen to us. We knew only one thing: we did not want to go on living as before, no matter what might happen to us. At Karl Marx Square some *Stasi* members said we might have misjudged the situation in bringing a child along.[15]

> Gudrun Fischer, thirty-two years old, typesetter: We put our daughter—she is six years old—to bed early on October 9. My husband and I had a fight. My husband is very interested in politics, but he kept me more or less separated from political life. But I absolutely had to go to this demonstration with him. Partly out of fear, however funny that sounds. It was crazy, how many police, army, and militia had been deployed since noon. . . . I was indignant, because I had never thought that a workers' and peasants' state would go after workers the way it happened on October 7 and 8. The high alert status of the police made such a strong impact on me that I was afraid, afraid for the future of my child, afraid for my husband. . . . On this day I sought my husband's protection; I held onto his hand. We walked along Quer Street, Gellert Street. There the trucks of the riot police stood. Going by Swan Pond, it was besieged by militia. Up Goethe Street, again riot police, really prepared for battle, with rubber truncheons and these white shields.[16]

Susanne Rummel, thirty-seven years old, housewife: I left the house at 2:30 P.M., conscious that I was becoming a participant in a bloody confrontation. . . . I had to go through an army camp of police and state security. The church was really besieged. . . . It had been full since 1:00 P.M. [I went inside.] From outside, the mighty chorus [of protesters] penetrated through to us: besides whistles and boos and clapping, "Out with the *Stasi!*" "Gorby, Gorby!" and "We're staying here," and the wonderful "Wir sind das Volk!" But loudest the shout, "No violence!" The atmosphere in the church was tense to the bursting point. . . . Then regional Bishop Hempel came—he had already been in the other three churches that also held peace prayers that day— and said he prayed that this night might pass without the worst happening.

None of us wanted to say the word civil war or bloodletting aloud, but it seemed tangibly near to everyone. [Afterward we went outside.] Now the fear in me was so great that I thought I must do something against it. So I went up to the people from the workers' militia that stood at the Opera Park. Other demonstrators did this too. We spoke with them and asked them if we looked like "chaotics" or enemies of the state and if they then would really hit us.[17]

At the time it all seemed a futile gesture. It was transformed into the turning point of the revolution by six Leipzigers who united in a last-minute appeal for calm, however. The six were Kurt Masur, director of the renowned Gewandhaus Orchestra since 1970; Pastor Zimmermann; cabaret performer Bernd-Lutz Lange; and three second-rank party secretaries who had no authorization from above to do what they did and fully expected to be excommunicated from the party for their impudence.

The prime mover, Masur, was not one of those natural politicians— like Solidarity's Lech Walesa in Poland—who occasionally emerge in time of crisis. Instead, he was a Cincinnatus, reluctantly taking an intermission from what he considered the most marvelous profession in the world to perform a civic duty. He brought to politics the same qualities that distinguished his conducting: clarity, proportion, and respect for the individuality of each musical phrase (or each citizen). Ironically, he owed his cherished post in the city of Johann Sebastian Bach to the suppression of the Prague Spring in 1968 and the retirement of his predecessor, who had opposed the Warsaw Pact invasion of Czechoslovakia too openly.

Masur had earlier become involved in grass-roots politics when he had defended buskers who were being harassed by the police. On October 2 he had also bluntly told a West German television interviewer that he was ashamed of the rough handling of demonstrators by security forces, and his orchestra had stood by him in a political meeting the next day.[18] In the wake of the weekend's latest brutality—and the alarming reports that extra hospital beds and blood plasma were being assembled in Leipzig—he now applied all his energies to pleading for utter adherence to nonviolence by both demonstrators and police. Privately, he also contacted high-ranking *Stasi*, NVA, and even Soviet army officers, and was assured that the Soviet army would stay in its barracks.[19] Typically, as soon as the march was over, Masur returned to the Gewandhaus podium to conduct that night's concert.

Pastor Zimmermann had been more deeply involved in politics for several years in his constant wrestling and negotiating with local party officials to protect Christian and other activists, to enlarge the sphere of permitted intellectual and civic enterprise, and to move the GDR toward greater humanity. His partners had been district SED secretaries Roland Wötzel and Jochen Pommert. The latter had resisted East Berlin's increasingly strident branding of Leipzig reformers as counterrevolutionaries, and they readily responded when a third district secretary, Kurt Meyer, asked them to join the plea that was almost as desperate on their part as was the march of "the people."

The three party functionaries were operating in a total vacuum of leadership. That Monday afternoon, their chief, Leipzig party secretary Helmut Hackenburg, telephoned Krenz in Berlin to try to get firm instructions—but Krenz would not commit himself either to a crackdown or to disengagement. Krenz too wanted restraint, he told Schabowski at the time, but he was so preoccupied with his own maneuverings in the solipsistic capital that he did not get around to returning Hackenburg's further urgent call from the provinces until 7:15 P.M., after the terms of contact had long since been fixed.[20] One of the three Leipzig secretaries later wrote: "No one commissioned us [to make the joint appeal], authorized us, or even covered our backsides."[21] Krenz's subsequent attempt to take credit for the peace in Leipzig therefore drew only scorn from the demonstrators, who had taken all the risk themselves. It added to the popular derision of Krenz as a *Wendehals*, the "wryneck" bird that can turn its head 360 degrees, and the instant symbol of opportunistic communists who suddenly proclaimed themselves reformers.

In the absence of any help from Berlin, the six Leipzigers met on their own initiative to draft a joint plea for calm, peaceful dialogue, and a "free exchange of views about the future of socialism in our land." They completed their appeal less than half an hour before the 5:00 P.M. start of prayer meetings and rushed smudged carbon copies through the police cordons to the churches to be read out, while Masur recorded a tape of the statement for the local radio station to broadcast again and again in the next two hours.[22]

After it was all over, the six could hardly believe that their call to discipline had actually worked and, indeed, that spontaneous dialogue had begun that night between demonstrators and security forces. "We are the people" really did ally the population decisively with reforms. The shift in meaning was profound. The people were no longer passive fence sitters, no longer just fugitives from a bankrupt system. Nor were they any longer even just the defiant shouters of "We're staying here," which, as Pastor Zimmermann noted, itself carried an edge of threat.[23]

"We the people," by contrast, constituted an invitation to all the scared mobile police and workers' militiamen to join the protesters as fellow citizens. It embraced the Christian faith that all men are children of the one Father, and therefore brothers and sisters and not enemies. It steered the burgeoning crowds of the next several Mondays past the dangerous face-off at *Stasi* headquarters. Instead of storming the shuttered building, demonstrators obeyed their marshals and contented themselves with the ritual of dripping wax onto the building's windowsills and streetfront and planting their candles there in a mute prayer for light and gentleness.

For twenty-one-year-old theology student Katrin Hattenhauer, the effect of the Monday night prayers was dramatic. Having been jailed on remand five weeks earlier for playing the guitar on the street, she had already become accustomed to prison isolation, and she knew something extraordinary must be happening when, "On October 9 the sound wave of the demonstrators penetrated through to us. There was a real 'prison revolt.' Everybody was tapping on the wall [in the communication alphabet] and jumping around on the beds. And naturally everybody pressed against the wall with their toothbrush cups [to magnify sound] to pick up [information]. People drummed on the walls; people laughed [an act specifically banned under prison regulations]." Four days later Hattenhauer was released, without being charged.[24]

Theo Kühirt, a member of the workers' militia who was on duty the evening of October 9, experienced the epiphany differently: "I must say that at the beginning of the demonstration we were really called names. Expressions came out like 'dirty pigs,' 'communist pigs,' 'betrayers of the workers'. . . . Relaxation of tension began only with the announcement of the appeal by the six personalities. . . . Many honest comrades actually thought this was the mob. Then we saw that they were entirely normal people who were shouting 'Wir sind das Volk!' and we belonged to them too."[25]

Well into the next century historians and psychologists will no doubt still be trying to piece together just why the police and secret police let loose such concerted savagery the previous week, then stood by without intervening on October 9. As of this writing, the best explanation appears to be that local security organs were left without clear guidelines from the demoralized center, then declined to repeat the kind of violence that in crowds of demonstrators swelled by civil courage could easily have led to

a bloodbath.[26] This corresponds with the judgment formed by Kurt Biedenkopf, the one-time West German conservative politician who became
a professor at the university in Leipzig in early 1990, then went on to be
elected premier of Saxony in the first free state election there. His assessment is that the fragile dialogue established in Dresden on October 8 broke
the reflex of official violence and offered an alternative that Masur then put
his full authority behind.[27]

Implicitly, District Secretary Meyer drew the same conclusion when
he returned home exhausted at midnight on October 9, collapsed into a
chair, burst into tears, and confided to his wife, "You know, I have the
feeling that at last I've done something significant that I don't have to be
ashamed of. Whatever happens to me now, let it happen." For two weeks
the SED leadership in Berlin vacillated about disciplining Meyer and his
Leipzig colleagues for insubordination, but in the end did nothing.[28]

With hindsight, many claimed credit for the nonviolence in Leipzig,
including not only Krenz, but also Honecker and some Russians. The new
party secretary's claim was swiftly debunked as people learned that
Krenz's supposed key telephone call to Leipzig came only after the lines
had already been drawn.[29] The rival claim by Honecker that *he* had ordered
Leipzig officials not to use force was also debunked when it was discovered
that his command was issued (at Krenz's prodding, in fact) only on the
Friday after October 9.[30]

Alternative versions assigning the key role to a Soviet military order
to the NVA not to shoot are greeted with more or less skepticism, depending on the hearer. The most prominent proponent of this view was
Willy Brandt.[31] Markus Meckel, the pastor who became the GDR's foreign
minister in April 1990, also believes in retrospect that the Soviets may
have given a specific order not to shoot on October 9. He notes, however,
that he has not really looked into the subject, but bases his view on Brandt's
comments.[32]

Schabowski, by contrast, dismisses the whole idea as a "romantic
legend."[33] Modrow, using almost the same language, similarly discounts
reports of any Soviet military role as a "legend."[34] By implication, so do
East German generals. They would have known of any Soviet orders to
the NVA not to shoot, but have not referred to any such orders. On the
contrary, in their subsequent conversations with West German generals,
they displayed some pride in claiming that they themselves ensured that
there was no army intervention or shooting in the critical October days.[35]
Informed West German sources further say there is no intelligence that
would substantiate rumors of such a Soviet command.

For their part, Soviet political leaders never claimed specific responsibility for the East German restraint, or for the changes in the GDR in
general. The closest they came, in very broad-brush views passed on to

Kohl's foreign policy adviser Horst Teltschik by Central Committee adviser Nikolai Portugalov on November 21, was the signal, as Teltschik phrased it, that "the most recent development in the GDR would have been unthinkable without . . . the Soviet Union."[36] This statement was fully consonant with Gorbachev's laissez-faire policy in all of Eastern Europe, and did not seem to imply any more activist role.

The balance of evidence thus suggests that the 1990 rumors of a Soviet military order not to shoot rested on exaggeration by some Russian intellectuals—and by Germans who could not credit East Germans with making their own decisions or nondecisions—of Gorbachev's undoubted refusal to use Soviet troops to rescue antiquated clients.

Whatever the final assessment, the stunning outcome of October 9 was that the first successful revolution in German history was bloodless.[37]

Berlin, October 9–18

The simplest explanation for the failure by Krenz—the Politburo member in charge of security—to issue any instructions at all before the Leipzig march on October 9 must be his preoccupation with intrigues in Berlin. At noon that Monday Honecker called Krenz in and said he had big things in mind for his protégé in the future. If he persisted in going ahead with the draft Politburo resolution, however, that opportunity would vanish, and Krenz's action would be seen as a serious attempt to split the party. Krenz was still shaken by the conversation when he told Schabowski about it afterward, but he did not pull back.[38]

On October 10 Honecker let Krenz's resolution come before the Politburo as if he himself accepted the idea, but then sidelined it to a committee for revision, naming Krenz and two hardliners to the editing group. Krenz countered by getting Schabowski added to the committee, and the two hardliners, sniffing a change in the wind, did not water down the content significantly.

Honecker thereupon tried another tactic, convening a meeting of regional first secretaries with Central Committee secretaries—including Krenz and Schabowski—for the following day. Honecker opened this meeting with a half-hour lecture charging NATO and other hostile foreign forces with fomenting the GDR's difficulties. This ploy failed too. By now the regional secretaries had experienced clashes in their own cities over the weekend, and they no longer kept silent. Modrow in particular complained about the impossible situation he had been plunged into because of the routing of the Prague train through Dresden. He asked pointedly if the Politburo understood what was happening in the country. Schabowski assured him that the Politburo did not blame everything on NATO, and that it appreciated the Dresdeners' good work. Honecker concluded the session with the old refrain that the GDR must not give counterrevolution a chance.[39]

The following day the Politburo declaration appeared in *Neues Deutschland*, assuring its readers that "socialism needs every individual" and the Politburo was not indifferent to those who had left. However, it still blamed the exodus essentially on the provocation of "imperialist forces," the "hateful campaign" of the West's mass media, and the "illegal intervention" of the Federal Republic of Germany in the GDR's internal affairs.[40] Despite Krenz's nervousness about the daring of the statement, it already lagged far behind "the people" and elicited little but contempt. This was a pattern that would be repeated many times during Krenz's short six weeks as the leader of East Germany.

Simultaneously, the 10,000 people who had by now joined New Forum were inviting their fellow citizens to discuss all problems without taboos, including "justice, democracy, and peace, as well as the protection and preservation of nature."[41]

After the debacle of the anniversary weekend, Krenz and Schabowski decided that things were deteriorating so fast that they could not delay any longer, but would have to depose Honecker at the next Politburo session. Krenz successfully recruited Prime Minister Willi Stoph—the perennial scapegoat for all the residual ills that Honecker did not attribute to NATO but blamed on the GDR's government rather than on the party—to present the resolution demanding Honecker's resignation. Schabowski successfully recruited Harry Tisch, who was to fly to Moscow on October 16 on trade union business, to ask for an urgent meeting with Gorbachev and inform him of the plan. Tisch duly delivered his message. Gorbachev, as anticipated, returned his best wishes for the enterprise's success.

Before this exchange in the Kremlin, one final comedy of errors was still to take place. As a result, Schabowski noted, the Soviet ambassador in Berlin would find out about the GDR's "overdue course correction" before his boss in Moscow. At 9:00 A.M. on October 16 Krenz telephoned Schabowski, and in the cryptic language the conspirators adopted to confuse any eavesdroppers, said that Stoph would play his part only if he could become head of state. Schabowski misunderstood the elliptical message and thought that Stoph was insisting that *Honecker* remain head of state after resigning as party secretary. Appalled, Schabowski rejected the notion out of hand, and decided to solicit the help of Ambassador Vyacheslav Kochemasov, whom he knew would be seeing Stoph that evening, to dissuade Stoph.[42]

The next day, Krenz and Schabowski went into the crucial Politburo meeting counting eleven or twelve people on their side, but still not sure that they could muster a majority of the twenty-six full and candidate members. Yet when Stoph moved to release Honecker from his responsibilities, even Mittag, finger to the wind, turned on his patron. So did Mielke, blaming Honecker for everything that had gone wrong and threatening, if the general secretary did not resign, to release his own secret information, presumably about betrayal of comrades by Honecker in Nazi prisons.[43] In the end, to avoid humiliation and maintain the pretense of leaving voluntarily, Honecker had no choice but to cast his own vote in favor of the unanimous decision to accept his, Mittag's, and Herrmann's resignations.[44] On October 18 the Central Committee held its first spontaneous debate in history, and ratified the Politburo's decision.

A Kremlin or *Stasi* Mastermind?

As of this writing, the available evidence supports the relatively straightforward description of events given here. However, two alternative hypotheses that attribute Honecker's downfall directly either to an interventionist Gorbachev or to the *Stasi*, acting autonomously, should be addressed. These theses have not been argued coherently in print—probably because the evidence for them is so weak—but they crop up again and again as either explicit or implicit assumptions in conversations with specialists as well as laymen, and cannot be ignored.[45] Their persistence is noteworthy; they seem to many who hold them to be a matter of faith more than of analysis. There must have been a pro-Gorbachev faction in East Berlin, runs the typical assertion, the tone of voice suggesting a knowing wink.

The most prominent proponent of this thesis is, of course, Erich Honecker. Even as he enjoyed virtual political asylum in the Soviet Union following German unification, Honecker bitterly accused the Russians of betraying him.[46] His partisan diatribe seems based less on fact, however, than on his sheer disbelief that he could have been outmaneuvered by mere Germans after his eighteen years of blocking formation of factions against himself.

Certainly Gorbachev was responsible for Honecker's fall in the broad sense that once he withheld his active support, Honecker became a target for his adversaries in a way he had not been before. As Genscher carefully phrases it in rejecting theories of more active Soviet string-pulling: "Moscow didn't have to do anything [itself]. You have to recreate the mentality of the GDR leadership of those days: whoever did not follow the line of Moscow was basically, so to say, fair game to shoot down. Over decades people were accustomed to thinking that the Number One, so long as he enjoyed the blessing of Moscow, was untouchable."[47] Once that protection vanished, Honecker was vulnerable to his East German opponents.

Other presumptions of a more active Soviet role rest on the Soviets' habits of forty years and on a few well-known anecdotes. Back in 1971, Brezhnev had clearly compelled Ulbricht's removal. A decade later, in 1980, Werner Krolikowski still went running to Brezhnev when he and other SED Politburo members demurred at Honecker's policies, and Gorbachev issued his famous warning about latecomers in East Berlin a week before the palace coup.[48] Why, then, should the pattern of Soviet ordering about of clients have been different in 1989 than in 1971?

Given this background, the old orthodoxies often drove analysis automatically in 1989, and in the two years following the opening of the Berlin Wall, one additional stimulus inclined Americans at the right end of the political spectrum, in particular, to magnify Soviet intrigues. This was their conviction that Soviet military power was still dangerous, and that a gullible public, which had forgotten this as the cold war ended, must be reminded that Soviet tentacles still extended abroad. The need for such reminders vanished as the Soviet Union disintegrated at the end of 1991, but the tendency to recall the events of 1989 in this light has endured.

Neither logic nor the evidence that is available today, however, justifies the view that the SED Politburo was simply Moscow's marionette. Gorbachev had said repeatedly that he would not intervene directly in Eastern Europe, and he had every reason not to. His absolute priority was his embattled perestroika. He had no intention of endangering domestic reform by getting embroiled in marginal fights abroad that might hand his Soviet hardline critics more ammunition against him. Besides, his persisting faith in dialectics predisposed him to trust "history" to do the job for him in East Berlin. Moreover, logic would suggest that Gorbachev would have acted quite differently had he been the kingmaker. He would have moved earlier to help those mid-level SED officials who after 1985 wanted to introduce perestroika in the GDR, and he surely would have selected as his instrument the mildly liberal Modrow over Honecker's own crown prince, the utterly conventional Krenz.

In testimony by the major players of 1989, Schabowski scoffs at any presumption of more substantial Soviet involvement in the East German leadership shuffles than the minimal contact he has described. He attributes the original palace coup and subsequent developments not to any Soviet machinations, but rather to the juggernaut internal forces loosed by the revolution on the streets.[49] For his part, Modrow states that in 1989 Gorbachev no longer possessed the kind of power to engineer changes in East Berlin that Brezhnev did in 1971, and he notes that East German communists who wanted change regretted the Soviet hands-off attitude.[50]

On the Soviet side, neither Gorbachev, Shevardnadze, nor any other top Soviet official has ever claimed to have manipulated the SED Politburo shifts in autumn 1989.[51] More explicit corroboration of Gorbachev's nonintervention also comes from Ambassador Kochemasov and Aleksandr Tsipko of the Soviet Communist party's Central Committee staff. Throughout the course of 1989 Kochemasov repeatedly told Krenz (as crown prince) that Moscow still thought Honecker could be brought around to accept reforms.[52] Tsipko also told the *Washington Post*'s Don Oberdorfer that the instructions to Kochemasov after the wall fell "were not to interfere, not to exert any pressure, and in fact not to do anything."[53] Pyotr Abrasimov, until 1983 Kochemasov's predecessor as Soviet ambassador (and virtual proconsul) to the GDR under both Ulbricht and Honecker, further told *Izvestia* in an interview in summer 1992 that the GDR's overnight collapse was a great surprise "for Moscow, for our embassy in Berlin, for the FRG [Federal Republic of Germany], for all of the West even."[54]

The few vague exceptions to the general message of noninterference come essentially from Soviet academic advisers in conversation with Western colleagues. Without substantiation, however, such claims look more like self-aggrandizement.

In documentary evidence, in three years nothing has surfaced to indicate direct Soviet steering of Honecker's fall, a telling dearth, since the financial incentives for such sensational revelations would have been the greatest soon after the events.

The other conspiracy-behind-the-conspiracy theory—interpreting the *Stasi* as the main protagonist in Honecker's undoing—takes its most imaginative form in the hands of Henryk M. Broder. This journalist contended in *Die Zeit* in early 1992 that "the revolution in the GDR was the opus magnum of the *Stasi*."[55] His premise was not simply that the *Stasi* had helped unseat Honecker in narrow Politburo jostling. Far more broadly, he claimed that the *Stasi* officers read the plethora of accurate internal spy reports, grasped the miserable situation in the GDR better than anyone else, and orchestrated the demonstrations to force modernization—and ensure that when the crash came, the *Stasi* would still be in control of whatever survived.

Quite a few east Germans, citing the saturation of all the dissident groups by *Stasi* informers—and, with more sophistication, the blackmail possibilities of the *Stasi's* dossiers on functionaries' diversion of public funds to private housebuilding—embrace this explanation of the bewildering events they experienced. If such a master plan had existed, however, the obvious question is why the *Stasi* made such a hash of its scheme. If the ministry itself had engineered the shift to Honecker's crown prince, why did this lead so swiftly to unemployment for the master planners, and why was Mielke himself sacked from the Politburo even before the Berlin Wall fell and then arrested shortly thereafter?

Stefan Wolle, one of the first East German analysts and publishers of the *Stasi* files that unexpectedly entered the public domain in 1990, challenges Broder's theory on documentary as well as on logical grounds. He agrees that the *Stasi* tried to jump onto the bandwagon in fall 1989 and to maneuver its agents into leading positions in the new parties. That tactical reflex revealed no long-term intent, however, he argues; the absence of any records laying out such plans is conclusive, given the *Stasi's* compulsiveness to write everything down.[56] The absurd irony of the whole operation, he concludes, is that the *Stasi* achieved the exact opposite of its intended stifling of any opposition by its ubiquitous infiltration of dissident groups. "It was precisely the Unofficial Collaborators, with their marked sense of duty, who quickly formed the core of the opposition groups through their regular and reliable work in them and through their activities, paradoxically, contributed to their stabilization."[57]

Gerd Knauer, who until January 1990 worked in the *Stasi* press office, comes to the same conclusion after examining a different sort of evidence: the closed mentality of the compartmentalized, elite *Stasi* brotherhood.[58] Opposition to the existing leadership could not have come from the top *Stasi* 1 percent, who were themselves part of that leadership, he contends, nor could it have come from the impotent bottom. If at all, it must have come from the upper-middle layer. Yet this layer did not have access to enough broad information to have formed an overview of the crisis; especially with their religious exclusion of any blasphemous doubts about "socialism," many officers tended to think that problems in their own fiefdoms were simply aberrations that could be corrected with more surveillance. "Not a few [harbored] the illusion that one needed only, bit by bit, to recruit all citizens of the GDR to become Unofficial Collaborators of the MfS [Ministry for State Security], and then socialism would function properly." And those in the *Stasi* who did hope for change through Gorbachev let him become an "alibi for their own waiting things out." For all *Stasi* officers, then, the failure of the top leadership to act in response to the exodus of mid-1989 led above all to demoralization.[59]

Freelance adventures of the sort Broder fancies would also have diverged sharply from the established institutional hierarchy in the GDR. It is true that the Ministry for State Security wielded enormous police and financial powers. It operated in secret, without even minimal feedback from the industrial ministries. It was exempt from ordinary laws in its sweeping "battle against ideological diversion, counterrevolutionary activities, and political underground activity," as the secret guideline 1/79 of December 8, 1979, put it. The minimal 1950 legislation establishing the ministry neither limited, nor even described, its authority. Moreover, *Stasi* dossiers, disregarding an official ban on the practice, extended even to selected SED members.[60]

However, ever since internecine accounts had been settled in the wake of the June 17, 1953, East Berlin uprising, the party's "shield and sword," as the *Stasi* was designated, had been totally subordinate to the SED. It was no independent state within the state on the old German military model. Its unswerving allegiance to the SED did not mean, as Honecker supposed, personal allegiance to its general secretary.[61] However, it did mean that Mielke had no compunction about agreeing with other SED barons on the Politburo when the realization came that the ossified Honecker had to go for the sake of the party.[62]

More convoluted speculation would have the *Stasi* acting not independently, but as a tool of the Soviet Committee for State Security, the KGB. This thesis builds on the known ties between the two secret services, and probably also on the mystique that Markus "Mischa" Wolf enjoyed in the West as the world's wiliest espionage chief until Mielke forced him out of office in a personal feud in 1987.

Stasi loyalty to the KGB "Chekists" in the Moscow center of "world socialism" was, of course, seen as fully compatible with loyalty to the German communists. That double fealty was regarded as the norm for a child of the KGB, especially one in a regime unable to make its own appeal to national feelings for fear of adding to West German attractiveness. KGB instructors, later called advisers, were active in the *Stasi* throughout the 1960s, and the Soviet chief adviser had to approve every *Stasi* decision until at least 1957, four years after Stalin's death.[63] No secret service in Eastern Europe had closer links with Moscow,[64] and none felt more shocked when Gorbachev followed his announced precepts and did not intervene to save the old regime in 1989.[65]

The thesis of KGB manipulation founders, though, on the dilemma of which side KGB chief Vladimir Kryuchkov might reasonably have intervened to support, and through whom. Kryuchkov, who would become one of the hardline coup plotters in Moscow in August 1991, would presumably have favored Honecker over his opponents, and would hardly have stepped in on behalf of the East German coup makers. On the East German side, Colonel General Wolf openly promoted Gorbachev-style reform, but he was an outsider to the GDR leadership and by then even to the state security apparatus. He never mended fences with Mielke, and there is no hint whatsoever that he might have hijacked the *Stasi* apparat from under Mielke's nose.

The best judgment at this point, therefore, remains that the SED Politburo acted on its own on October 17, 1989, within the overall context of Soviet-East German relations, to be sure, but especially within the context of the hemorrhage of the GDR's population to the West.[66] The *Stasi*'s utter loyalty to and dependence on the SED and the KGB left Mielke's formidable state security without any brain to direct it, once the Soviets disengaged and the SED became paralyzed in late summer 1989. Like a headless chicken, the *Stasi* could only run about maniacally, doing automatically what it had always done, but with no clear purpose or strategy.

People Power

The sensational toppling of the undisputed East German leader of eighteen years—coming on top of the rejection of communist tutelage in Poland and Hungary—broke for good the East Germans' four-decade-old habit of fear and resignation in the face of the immutable. On October 23 and 30 the crowd of demonstrators in Leipzig quadrupled again, to some 300,000 increasingly self-confident representatives of the *Volk*.

As one of his first official acts, new General Secretary Krenz met with church leaders on October 19. The same day the party instructed the Interior Ministry urgently to draft a more liberal law on travel abroad. Two days later, in the Dresden Synod, Bishop Hempel challenged the SED's claim to leadership and demanded that the party apologize for the brutality of the security forces and name an independent commission to investigate the beatings. The day after that the SED inaugurated Sunday talks, in which the public could pepper party representatives with questions. Two days later the Volkskammer obediently voted in Krenz as chairman of the State Council, or head of state; however, for only the second time in that parliament's history, opposition votes were recorded.[67]

On October 27 Schabowski held his first semiofficial meeting with New Forum representatives to negotiate the organization's legalization. That same day the State Council announced an amnesty for those who had fled the GDR, and the cabinet announced that as of November 1, East Germans would again be able to travel to Czechoslovakia without passports or visas. Predictably, on November 1, as Krenz paid his inaugural call on the Kremlin as general secretary, the number of East Germans seeking refuge in the West German embassy in Prague again rose. On November 2 Harry Tisch resigned his post as trade union chairman; Honecker's wife, Margot, resigned her post as education minister; and in Dresden legal proceedings were initiated against seventy security officials for brutality against demonstrators a month earlier.

At this point both Krenz and Schabowski clearly were betting that they could ride the tiger. Reformed communist parties were still assumed to offer the most feasible route to liberalization, after all, in all of Eastern Europe except for Poland, and the Solidarity government there was still thought to be something of a freak response to Poland's peculiar conditions. No one expected the Prussian Socialist Unity party—of all parties—to disintegrate.

When the East Berliners decided to show that like their Saxon brothers to the south, they too could defy authority and vent their grievances, the party responded with unprecedented generosity. It not only gave official blessing to the theater workers who applied for a permit to stage a pro-democracy rally at Alexanderplatz on November 4; it also unveiled an action program of major reforms of its own on the eve of the rally. And the two communist politicians who considered themselves the most liberal, Schabowski and Wolf, even invited themselves to speak at the gathering. The measures that Krenz announced with great fanfare included the resignation of five of the oldest Politburo members, an end to compulsory military training in schools, the recognition of conscientious objection to military service, the introduction of a public smog alarm in the most polluted regions, the institution of a constitutional court and of courts for appealing administrative decisions, the reform of education, the tolerance of dissidents, and the communication of full information to "mature citizens" (a phrase acknowledging the dissenters' earlier protests against *Bevormundung* and election fraud).

Even two weeks earlier this package would have been breathtaking. Now it was already too little too late. The 5,000 demonstrators of the anniversary weekend swelled to 500,000—some claimed it was a full million—on that glorious fall Saturday, and these protesters no longer accepted the communist monopoly on power and the right to dole out favors to minions forced to be grateful. What they wanted instead, their hand painted placards proclaimed, was: "Allow New Forum," "Free elections," "Let us fly to Hawaii," "Election falsifiers to court," "*Stasi*, get a real job," "SED into the opposition," "For clean air," "Long live the Prague Spring," "Distrust is the citizen's first duty," "Free surfing in the Baltic," "Asterix to the Politburo," "No protection of the *Wendehals* species," and, from a twelve-year-old, "No school on Saturdays!" Schabowski and Wolf were whistled at and jeered. Incredibly, East German radio and TV carried the entire proceeding live and uncensored. Police and workers' militia sat in their loaded trucks a few discreet blocks away, with instructions to halt any rush toward SED headquarters or the Berlin Wall.[68]

Ironically, although the peaceful pattern established in Leipzig on October 9 and maintained in the intervening weeks meant that the Berliners were hardly risking life and limb in the way the Leipzigers had, Berlin on November 4 was the place where the participants generally began conceiving of their happening as a revolution. Many even nicknamed it the October Revolution, in wry reference to the Russians' 1917 October Revolution, which also took place in November—and which the East Germans viewed far less as a revolution than as a restoration of Ivan the Terrible.[69]

In one sense the Berliners were merely piggybacking onto what the braver Leipzigers and Dresdeners had already accomplished, now that it did not cost anything. The Leipzigers marched because they were scared; the Berliners marched because they were no longer scared. But in another sense the Berliners were advertising to the SED that the whole country was now equally exasperated, that those in the capital could no longer be pacified with their privileged position in the allotment of scarce investment, apartments, and consumer goods. With their November 4 showing, activists began a deliberate campaign to politicize the north too, spraying taunts onto freight cars heading toward Mecklenburg and West Pomerania that were intended to goad readers out of their lethargy.

"The terror regime became an encrusted bureaucracy, with no real terror. Then at some point that had to be the end," explained one West German Social Democrat in retrospect. "People discover that the bureaucracy can be blackmailed [in this case, by squatters in the various West German embassies]. At such a moment the emperor has no clothes. The regime becomes ridiculous," people no longer fear it, and panic sets in among the powerholders.

That point was reached by November 4. Unlike the Leipzigers on October 9, the demonstrators in East Berlin had the heady feeling that "people power" really counted, and that their march would help make history, East German history. Virtually none of the demonstrators interviewed by Western reporters said they wanted unification with the Federal Republic. Yet within five days it would be too late for an independent East German course.

Chapter 10

The Wall Falls

D*ie Wende*—"the turnaround"—was not a very precise concept, but it was instantly understandable in any context. Negatively—unlike the *Wende* of the *Wendehals* bird—it was neither superficial nor easily reversible. Positively, the turnaround covered everything: the giddiness of revolution, the succession in the SED leadership, the ebbing of fear, the disintegration of the Communist party and paralysis of the *Stasi*, the heady possibility of saying honestly what one thought, the political awakening of the passive GDR citizen, and the profound transformation of the collective East German mentality. Above all, *die Wende* meant the paradoxical sense of being master of one's own destiny after sixty years of authoritarian rule, yet simultaneously being caught up in a torrent of events that were rushing forward autonomously, far beyond any actors' ability to control them.

The seal on the *Wende* was the fall of the wall. Before, some lingering doubts had remained. Afterward, a wonderful, scary new world opened up.

The warm-up to the opening of the wall began on November 4, when ADN announced that East Germans who wished to emigrate could do so by driving through the western tip of Czechoslovakia into Bavaria. Within hours bumper-to-bumper Trabis were on the route, despite pastors' impassioned pleas to everyone to stay home and help build the new GDR.

Two days later, the East Berlin leadership proclaimed an extension of travel privileges to the West to thirty days a year for everyone, but made no foreign currency available and still required bureaucratic approval that officials could use to block trips arbitrarily. Throughout the country close to 750,000 demonstrators protested this and other half-measures, and demanded free elections. Blue-collar workers, who were sure that they would never be able to scrape together Western money and resented others' ability to do so, threatened to strike.

On November 7 even the rubber-stamp Volkskammer rejected these travel regulations as too timid. The entire cabinet resigned. And in the most startling act of all, a new parliamentary commission actually began investigating the security organs' behavior on October 7 and 8. The activists, who had already launched their own investigation and lodged charges against any police officer they could identify, strongly suspected a cover-up and diversion from their findings, but in the end cooperated warily with the official commission. Mielke, seeing the writing on the wall, sent out one of his last commands to district *Stasi* directors, ordering them to destroy, in the strictest secrecy, all sensitive documents, especially those dealing with domestic informers.[1]

On November 8 Chancellor Helmut Kohl included eleven surprising sentences in his state of the nation address to the Bundestag at the request of an East German middleman.[2] In this section, Kohl called for East-West German dialogue "with all political forces in the GDR," promised Bonn's "comprehensive help" if the GDR instituted "thoroughgoing reform" (and not just "cosmetic corrections"). "The SED must give up its power monopoly, allow independent parties, and assure binding free elections," the chancellor stipulated. If so, Kohl promised "a fully new dimension of our economic aid."

The same day the entire Politburo resigned, although key party barons, not including Mielke, were immediately reappointed, netting eight holdovers among its thirteen full and candidate members. Hans Modrow was recalled from provincial exile to join the new Politburo and was nominated to be the new prime minister. Krenz promised free, democratic elections and proposed separation of party and state. For his part, Politburo member, Berlin party chief, and new party press spokesman Günter Schabowski told reporters that the Interior Ministry was now willing to register New Forum. Something more dramatic was clearly needed, however, if the new team were to salvage the sinking morale of the party and the state as tens of thousands of refugees continued to desert the GDR.

Krenz and Schabowski now realized that that something had to be a general right to travel abroad. If they could, with a stroke of the pen, legalize the refugees, this might turn the fugitives into simple tourists. Their exodus would no longer mock state authority, stability would be restored, and the communists could place themselves in the vanguard of the ongoing changes. Besides, this channeling of traffic over the East-West German borders would relieve the pressure on Czechoslovak party General Secretary Milos Jakes, who was threatening to close the Czech-GDR border himself if the SED did not stop East Germans from streaming into his country and emboldening Czech dissidents.

Implementation lagged behind intention, however. The Politburo was not used to acting fast, and it was certainly not used to leaping into the unknown. It ruminated, and while it ruminated everyone else demonstrated, including, by now, the disgruntled, noisy communist rank and file.

The Council of Ministers, commissioned by the Politburo, lumbered into the breach and came up with a new travel proposal, which it handed to Krenz on November 9. Krenz, as on October 9, was preoccupied with his own political maneuvering, in this case the day-long Central Committee plenum that was calling a special party conference for mid-December while resisting the grass-roots communist pressure for a full party congress that could replace the Central Committee. As Schabowski recalls, Krenz passed two pages of the draft on to him as he checked with the general secretary before briefing reporters that evening. Without explaining the proposal's status, Krenz commented, "This could be a hit," and Schabowski, who had been absent from the plenum while tending to press duties, assumed that the pages had actually been approved.[3]

The Wall Falls

Not wanting to deflect attention from what he deemed the day's most significant news, the upcoming party conference, Schabowski waited until the last few minutes of his hour-long press conference to drop the real bombshell: "Private trips abroad can be applied for without preconditions. . . . The sections responsible for passport and residence registration in local police offices in the GDR are instructed to issue visas for permanent exit without delay. . . . Permanent exit may be made over all border crossing points from the GDR to the FRG or to Berlin (West)."

Schabowski stumbled as he came to the reference to Berlin, since the city was under four-power, not German, competence, and in that split second he wondered if anyone had remembered to check with the Soviet Union. Then a reporter asked if the new regulations were in effect now, and Schabowski, reading the word "now" on the pages in front of him, answered in the affirmative.[4]

Unaware of the earthquake his words would loose, Schabowski then returned home routinely to Wandlitz. It was not until hours later that he got a telephone call alerting him to the peaceful storming of the wall. He drove back into town, inspected two of the checkpoints, and ascertained that the East Berliners were dutifully displaying their GDR identity cards as they crossed to the West. As he saw this, he "thought the GDR was saved: although citizens can move freely, they aren't sweeping away this border, but respecting it."

He went to sleep content that the masses were acknowledging the authority of state and party. And he persisted in this view the next day, even when he ran into a gloomy "hangover mood" in SED headquarters. "The opening of the wall was the only measure that won for us for a short time the almost unanimous approval of the majority of the population," he argued. "People were happy. The damned restrictions were gone. With that it was possible for us for the first time to get shoulder-to-shoulder with the people and their expectations. . . . We hadn't a clue that the opening of the wall was the beginning of the end of the Republic. On the contrary, we expected a stabilization process."[5]

Struggling to retain the party's control, Krenz swiftly spread the word that the party had actually intended to open the border crossings on November 10, and that Schabowski had inadvertently jumped the gun by his "small mistake" in saying that the new rules were to take effect right away. This version quickly became the standard reading of the event in the West.[6]

Modrow—who had just been named to the Politburo the day before the wall fell and would become prime minister the following week—contests Krenz's account. The opening of the wall could not have been a "prepared and planned decision," he says, since no final decision had been made by those responsible in the government, outgoing Prime Minister Stoph, and the Volkskammer, nor had there been any negotiations with the Federal Republic or West Berlin about legal or financial questions, or any advance notice given to the unsuspecting Soviets.[7] In fact, no draft travel legislation was ready for the Volkskammer until December 1.

The West German government confirms Modrow's observation that no East German official so much as hinted at the fall of the wall before it occurred. Prior talks between Krenz and the designated Chancellery negotiator, Rudolf Seiters, had dealt only with increasing two-way movement through the wall.[8]

Schabowski too seconds Modrow's judgment, saying the only expectation connected with November 10 was that on this day East Germans could begin applying for exit visas at police stations. It is a measure of the fog of revolution that it was only many months later that Schabowski, the main actor in the episode, figured out to his own satisfaction what actually happened that night.[9]

For the ecstatic throngs, of course, it mattered not a whit which particular political interplay produced the open sesame. For everyone who lived through them, those glorious days of the breaching of the wall were intensely personal, and political only in that they ended the communists' claim to proscribe private as well as public life. Yet this experience also constituted a growing-up ceremony, an initiation out of *Bevormundung* into political adulthood. From it the people drew just the opposite lesson from Shabowski's impression that at last the GDR was saved. They concluded instead that people power really can move mountains, and that even the

GDR monolith could not stand against it. After all, the people had gotten rid of Karl Eduard von Schnitzler, the most loathed television performer, for his thirty-year program excoriating the Federal Republic. The people had carried banners in Leipzig demanding "Schnitzler to the Muppet Show," and after 1,518 installments he had indeed finally vanished from the screen a few days before. The people had dumped the unmovable Honecker. They had even pried open the impregnable wall. If the people were united, what concessions could they now not extract from the SED? A daring few even began to dream the preposterous dream of unification with West Germany.

The Drive for Unification

Recoiling before this prospect, Bärbel Bohley—still one of the real heroes of the whole civil rights movement—publicly charged the GDR government with ineptness in opening the borders prematurely on November 9, before the East Germans had completed their own revolution. Her New Forum cofounders phrased the criticism more diplomatically, but shared her basic fear that the masses, if left to their untutored devices, might expunge socialism and become "rent slaves" and the "back courtyard and source of cheap labor" to the West.[10]

New Forum and other new-left spearheads of the East German revolution had not gone as far as their fellow Polish, Hungarian, and by now Czech dissidents in rejecting Soviet-imposed "socialism" altogether. In part out of guilt over Nazi Germany's victimization of Russian and other communists, in part out of revulsion at various bourgeois West German manifestations, they still held to their socialist faith, and their ideals still reflected Russian communist rhetoric more than West European social democratic precepts. They acknowledged that the one-party dictatorships of the SED and the Communist party of the Soviet Union had left their countries in shambles, but they argued that flawed practice did not invalidate worthy goals. Salvation lay in finding a third way, like Dubcek's aborted socialism with a human face from the Prague Spring of 1968, a way that would exhibit more compassion than either heartless capitalism or the heartless SED.

The moment New Forum protested the opening of the Berlin Wall, it relegated itself to the political sidelines. The vast majority of East Germans wanted nothing more to do with anything called socialism. They resented being lectured, in a new intellectual *Bevormundung*, that they were not yet mature enough to travel wherever they pleased. And the unification that New Forum eschewed looked increasingly attractive to them.

Modrow read the mood better. As the first East German official to lay down any markers in relations between the two Germanys, he called for a "contractual community" in his government declaration of November 17. The precise meaning of the phrase was vague, but the prime minister clearly envisioned carrying good East-West German relations beyond Honecker's negative "community of responsibility."[11] One deputy from the National Democrats (a bloc party set up after World War II to attract demobilized German soldiers) immediately trumped him in the subsequent parliamentary debate and floated the idea of a German confederation.

On November 19, in interviews with Soviet and Israeli media, Krenz, Modrow, and Foreign Minister Oskar Fischer all categorically ruled out German unification as an option. Yet by the next day one group of demonstrators in Leipzig did begin demanding precisely that, modulating "Wir sind *das* Volk" to "Wir sind *ein* Volk" (We are one people [or nation]).[12]

This was new. Before the opening of the Berlin Wall, East Germans had not shown any craving for unity. Western interviews with demonstrators and various opinion polls—however shaky the database in a society unused to giving honest answers to strangers—had indicated strong support for preserving the GDR as a separate state. As late as the beginning of December, one survey commissioned by ZDF television and *Der Spiegel* would still find that 71 percent of East Germans thought that the GDR should remain a sovereign state. This poll was skewed, but it did reflect, in this fast-changing environment, an earlier phenomenon.[13] The divergence between grass-roots indifference to unification in early November and enthusiasm for it in late November can probably be attributed not to deception by those polled, but rather to their initial incredulity, after so many decades of East-West German hostility, that unification might be a realistic option.

Typically, one demonstrator in Leipzig at this stage answered with a putdown of the left's assumptions when he was asked if he was not concerned that the GDR might be sold out to the Federal Republic in a merger. The selling out of his country had happened long since, he responded sharply; whatever took place next could only be an improvement.[14]

Moscow already sensed the change. On November 15, less than a week after the opening of the wall, Gorbachev, speaking to a Soviet student audience, referred to possible German reunification in public for the first time. He said this was not a current issue, but he did not exclude it, and he did not repeat his earlier standard postponement of the possibility to a distant century.[15] Then on November 21, to the astonishment of the Kohl government, Nikolai Portugalov, a Central Committee member and adviser on Germany, told Kohl's foreign policy adviser, Horst Teltschik, that even the Soviet leadership was thinking the unthinkable about all possible outcomes, and could conceive of a German confederation in the medium term. On his own authority—not Gorbachev's in these particulars, he specified—he raised issues of unification as well as of a peace treaty formally ending World War II, East German membership in the European Community, and "alliance membership." Teltschik was "electrified."[16]

On November 23 the Christian Democrats-East became the second party in the GDR to call for a confederation that would reflect "the unity of the nation." By now the word "confederation" was on everyone's lips in both East and West Germany, even though no one had any concept of what this might mean in practice. The most common comparison was with the customs union in the mid-nineteenth century between independent German states, but the analogy was never laid out concretely.

At this point Krenz too bowed to the new terminology. On November 24 he repeated to the *Financial Times* that reunification was not an option, but he distinguished this from a more acceptable confederation. He did not exclude, his interviewers wrote in an indirect quote, a "move towards a form of confederation if NATO and the Warsaw Pact were to dissolve in coming years."[17] This timing softened, slightly, the old Soviet call for a joint end to the military blocs, a parallel treatment that NATO always rejected, since the Warsaw Treaty Organization was no real alliance of sovereign nations as was NATO, but simply the formalization of a Soviet hegemony that in the old days would have continued with or without the Warsaw Pact.

Two days later Max Schmidt, the director of the East Berlin Institute for International Politics and Economy and a sometime launcher of SED foreign policy probes, went even further. The two Germanys should work for confederation, he suggested, and aim for treaties to strengthen cooperation that "actually perhaps could have reunification in view."[18]

By now the ground swell was too much for the new left. The same day, East German intellectuals issued a major appeal against selling out to West Germany, and called again for a "socialist alternative to the Federal Republic."[19] The summons fell on deaf ears. The following day, a significant minority of Leipzig demonstrators waved East German flags with the GDR's emblem cut out to leave only the West German tricolor. Growing numbers chanted "We are one people" and, from the forbidden words of the GDR's anthem, "Germany united fatherland."[20]

After the fairy tale opening of the wall, the old innate prudence no longer set narrow bounds on popular aspirations. Unification seemed ever more plausible. Soviet opposition no longer created the taboo it would have even a month earlier. For the Leipzigers who kept seeing their Monday night slogans set the agenda for Krenz's political concessions of the following week, the Soviet Union's—and East Berlin intellectuals'—objections to unification simply became irrelevant.

East Germans, initially defining themselves on the streets by what they were against, now realized that what they were for was what the Federal Republic already exemplified: democracy as well as prosperity. For the first time since 1848, the drives for German unity and individual freedom were not in conflict. Forty years of decaying apartments, bans on holidays in the Alps, constant nagging by the state, and a standard of living only half that of West Germany had totally discredited the illiberal political option. It was not chauvinism that drove the Leipzigers to display pan-German flags. It was the utilitarian reckoning, which swiftly became a consensus, that unification would be the fastest way to acquire the economic and political perquisites that West Germans took for granted.

The new Social Democrats-East did not make the same mistake as New Forum and the intellectuals. As one party organizer observed, voters who turned out for the novel political rallies that now sprang up first asked if German unification would be on the agenda; if not, 70 percent of them left immediately, without even taking off their coats. By the beginning of the new year the Social Democrats-East too would endorse "the unity of the German nation," and compel the reluctant Social Democrats-West to follow.

Kohl's response to the gathering East German sentiment for unification—once the chancellor got his act together—was to seize the initiative and assume the mantle of a twentieth century Bismarck for the election year 1990. Initially he groped for, and failed to find, the right tone to capture the popular imagination, despite the Christian Democrats' litany about unification over the years. The pall of his disastrous drop in the opinion polls the previous summer still hung over him. Three long weeks passed in which Liberal Foreign Minister Hans-Dietrich Genscher and Social Democrat Willy Brandt (despite his ambivalent party) both did much better than Kohl at articulating the growing together of all the Germans.

But then the chancellor made a speech in the Bundestag on November 28 to rally the Germans, yet reassure other Europeans of his continuing commitment to accelerate pan-European integration. In ten points he proposed forming joint East-West German economic, environmental, and other commissions that could lead to "confederal structures"—a vague terminology he used to avoid getting trapped into a permanent confederation of two separate states—and then, in the unspecified future, to "state unity."[21]

As he spoke, Kohl already had East Berlin's quiet consent to form these commissions. Modrow was pleased that Kohl's speech picked up his phrase of "contractual community" and noted that the chancellor expected to reach his ultimate goal of unification only after "a rather long time."[22] Modrow was correct in this assumption. At that point Kohl envisaged union in perhaps five years, a brief time compared with previous expectations, but an eternity compared with the actual rush of history.[23]

To his audience of East German demonstrators the chancellor tried to give the prospect of an orderly progress toward union that could avert any desperate calls for more radical measures and, if possible, stem the exodus of young workers. He did not want the so far heroically disciplined Leipzigers to get carried away by frustration and patriotic fervor, provoke the Soviet Union, and spark a dangerous, unpredictable confrontation, or even just swarm to the Federal Republic in such numbers that the GDR's economy would collapse.[24]

If Kohl's outline satisfied impatient East Germans, it most decidedly did not satisfy other Europeans. The chancellor's speech was widely seen abroad as a deliberate, and possibly reckless, acceleration of events. In Moscow, whatever the evolution in Soviet thinking so far, Shevardnadze warned a visiting Genscher that Germany must not skip stages in building the European house, and that "realities must not be lost from sight." These realities, he specified, included the existence of the two alliances, the inviolability of existing borders, and "the persistence of two German states."[25]

Given twentieth century German history, any goal of German reunification was bound to alarm Germany's neighbors, but Kohl also exacerbated their reaction by failing on November 28 to give his allies the kind of diplomatic briefing that normally precedes major policy statements. After the fact, the chancellor justified the lapse by saying that no one should have been surprised, since he was only replaying conventional wisdom in envisioning modest confederation at that point.

The more pertinent reason for his secretiveness, however, was domestic—and especially coalition—politics. Kohl was determined to seize the high ground, and he did not want any premature leaks to let Brandt or media star Genscher preempt him in leading the march toward the confederation that the main German actors were now converging on.

Kohl's political management was rewarded. The chancellor became the undisputed pilot of German union. Ironically, other Europeans' objections to what they perceived as his headstrong lunge for reunification only helped establish his domestic reputation.

The one crucial exception to official dismay among the allies was in the United States. A week earlier, Bush and Baker had reaffirmed to Genscher in Washington their support for German self-determination and unity. They had agreed with him that unification from below was driving the process, and that it might go much faster than anyone anticipated. Robert Zoellick and Frank Elbe, the two foreign ministers' right-hand men, had also agreed that stability in Europe might be more endangered by going too slowly than by going fast.[26] Now the Bush administration deliberately welcomed acceleration.

The pattern was set for the whirlwind diplomacy of the next eight months. Upheaval of a magnitude normally effected only by war would this time be accomplished without bloodshed. Kohl, minus Bismarck's mystique, would lead the process. The Germans would reclaim their identity. The cold war, with its division of Europe and of Germany, was over. Its "long peace" remained, and would expand to Central Europe, if not to the Balkans.

Chapter 11

Taming the Stasi

Kohl's offer of eventual unification came just in time to provide an alternative to what looked to many, in the first week of December, like approaching chaos in the GDR.

On December 1 the parliamentary committee investigating the abuse of power made its first report to the Volkskammer. Curiously, perhaps because more serious issues were still too sensitive, the committee focused not on the tens of thousands of deaths and unjust imprisonments caused by the regime over the decades, but on its relatively modest corruption.[1] Revelations showed no Ceausescu-type megalomania, but rather such perquisites as villas; payoffs ranging from tens of thousands to hundreds of thousands of marks; cars made available immediately rather than after a dozen-year wait for sons of the mighty; hunting lodges where game was all but led on a leash in front of the elderly rulers' rifles; and access through special stores to video players, fresh fruit, and other goods that any middle-class West German family could buy at will.

Despite the triviality of it all, in a society that had boasted of its egalitarianism, the preaching of water and swigging of wine shocked East Germans who had assumed that Prussian (and even Saxon) communists were immune to the temptations of power. In this light, the discovery of their leaders' petty greed made a mockery of their own sacrifices of forty years.

An even greater shock was administered on Saturday, December 2, as activists and fledgling investigative journalists unearthed a secret cache of weapons at the IMES firm near Rostock on the Baltic Sea. The company had been selling arms clandestinely to the third world, including (as had arms dealers in so many other countries) both sides in the Iran-Iraq war. The arms sales were a going concern, with the next export shipment scheduled two weeks hence. Among other iniquities, IMES had casually stockpiled explosives with few precautions—which especially alarmed local citizens—in an area of low-level military training flights.

Investigations quickly revealed that the firm belonged to a vast, shadowy business empire functioning both inside and outside the GDR under the Coordinating Committee (Ko-Ko) directed by Alexander Schalck-Golodkowski. Schalck was well known as East Germany's chief financial fixer, the genius at accumulating the GDR's desperately needed hard currency. But for Ko-Ko's profits in deutsche marks and dollars, Schalck later testified in the West, the GDR would have suffered as severe a financial disaster as its East European neighbors.[2] Ko-Ko's imaginative methods of acquiring that hard currency included plundering art treasures from East German museums to sell abroad and taking rhinoceros horns from natural history museums to grind up and market in Hong Kong as a potency enhancer.[3]

Schalck was officially a state secretary in the Foreign Trade Ministry and the sophisticate with whom Franz Josef Strauss and other West German politicians cozily arranged West German bank loans and other transactions. Indeed, the very day of the discovery of the IMES weapons, Schalck had been in West Berlin on behalf of the East Berlin government negotiating details of a forthcoming visit by Kohl. His activities took on sinister new overtones, however, when the public learned that he held the secret rank of state security major general.

More aware than anyone else of the GDR's utter bankruptcy and fragility, and fearing that the public, the *Stasi*, or the party leadership would make him the scapegoat for it, Schalck appeared before the Politburo at the end of November to give a report, and burst into tears. "The precipitous change from the self-confident, dispassionate expert to a discouraged man was eerie and terrifying," comments Schabowski. "'Comrades, help me,' he said. 'I can't go on like this any longer. My wife and I are getting death threats. I can't say who is behind them.'" Just before the meeting (Schabowski found out later from the West German press), Schalck had received a phone call telling him to "forget" his link to the *Stasi*. Despite his services, Schalck told the Politburo, he was now being "branded as a criminal in my own land. The prosecutor is after me. Just tell me what I am supposed to do." At that point he felt abandoned by the Politburo and considered suicide, he later told Western interviewers. During Schalck's outburst in this top-level session Schabowski had the premonition, "If things are like that with Schalck, the expert on finding ways out [of difficult situations], then goodnight GDR!"[4]

Despite the evidence of IMES's violation of East German law, the state prosecutor delayed until Sunday in issuing the order to arrest such a prominent personality as Schalck. In those few hours of grace Schalck slipped into West Germany, and popular indignation forced the prosecutor to resign. Schalck spent a brief period in remand in West Berlin, then went free. The Bonn government punctiliously refused to extradite him, arguing that the mood toward old officials in the GDR was so ugly that he could not be sure of a fair trial. To the frustration of the East German activists— who suspected collusion between East and West German powerholders— Schalck quickly gave the West German intelligence agency some 800 transcript pages of information, took up residence in a villa on Bavaria's Tegern Lake near the agency, and accepted the agency's protection. He would not again be pursued by (West) German prosecutors and parliamentarians until 1991, and then the Bonn government would withhold the records of Schalck's debriefing.

As Schalck's flight became known, several thousand communists gathered in front of the Central Committee building in East Berlin once again to demonstrate on behalf of radical renewal of the SED and to demand the Politburo's resignation. The next day the demoralized Politburo indeed gave up all pretense of governing and resigned, along with the entire Central Committee. Just before doing so, the Central Committee plenum expelled Honecker and eleven other top officials from the party. A working group was named to run the SED (contrary to all party statutes), and the party congress was advanced to December 8.

In the first days of December, activists and journalists also discovered that the *Stasi* were systematically destroying their files, tapes, and videos. The burning and shredding of records, combined with Modrow's perpetuation of the state security organ under the new name of the Office for National Security (AfNS)—and with exactly the same leadership, apart from Mielke—roused alarm that the *Stasi* might either maintain their hidden control system even inside the more open society that was now developing, or, failing that, might destroy all evidence of their own past wrongdoing. No one knew as yet about Mielke's order of November 7, or about the supplementary instruction to destroy documents issued on November 27 by Mielke's successor and former deputy, Wolfgang Schwanitz.[5] However, the activists did realize that incriminating evidence was rapidly disappearing. Citizens' committees formed spontaneously and, generally with the cooperation of the regular police, occupied *Stasi* offices in East Berlin, Leipzig, Dresden, Erfurt, Gera, Suhl, and Greifswald on December 4.[6]

One example will illustrate the ad hoc nature of the whole extraordinary exercise. In Greifswald a few New Forum activists issued an appeal late Monday morning for volunteers to form a round-the-clock cordon around the SED and *Stasi* headquarters to block further removal of documentation. They got the agreement of First Deputy Mayor Jonas to this step and to securing evidence for use by a future investigative committee.[7] By 1 P.M. 200 people had gathered to set up a human chain around the building. They were too late to catch one truckload of documents they saw being driven off to regional *Stasi* headquarters in Rostock, but Jonas, four citizens, and the district prosecutor did corner the local *Stasi* chief, who after a short discussion permitted them to secure the remaining material. The group toured the premises together, and the prosecutor sealed seventy locked files or safes. Nine citizens, who changed shifts every hour, then occupied the building's entryway, cellar, and three floors to monitor activities. When those outside saw ashes coming out of the chimney at 2 P.M., the inside monitors rushed to the furnace and retrieved the remains of papers that had not yet completely burned. They also found piles of documents that had been ripped only two or three times and were able to reconstruct them. In all, they recovered, in addition to administrative orders and reports, 22,000 to 24,000 personal dossiers, that is, files on every third or fourth Greifswalder.

In agreement with Jonas—and with the later blessing of the city council—representatives of New Forum, the Social Democrats, Democratic Awakening, Independent Students, and other groups then formed an investigative committee to analyze the *Stasi* and SED files. This procurement of local government sanction was especially noteworthy in that it occurred in the north, in a city in which the old fear of the *Stasi* continued to grip people, where the local Protestant bishop had been sycophantic to Honecker and had tried to smother the church from below, and where a "security partnership" between protesters and police had not existed for weeks after such tolerance had been achieved in the south.[8]

The official Greifswald disposition of the impounded documents excluded them from the later nationwide sealing of *Stasi* files against public, or even official, access until after their evaluation over years by the special *Stasi* commission that parliament would set up. The Greifswald haul, analyzed and reproduced in part in the Greifswald committee's report, thus provided some of the earliest public information about the *Stasi*.[9]

The Greifswald experience exemplified the alchemy at this point as terror turned into anger as well as ridicule. The palpable fear of decades had been consciously defied by a minority of activists on October 7, 8, and 9 (and, with less risk, on November 4), and had then largely vanished for the average person on the street the night of November 9–10. More subtly, by the beginning of December even the subconscious inhibitions and self-censorship were also fading. Not all the risk was gone: the *Stasi* lived on as an autonomous nervous system, and would continue to do so long after the citizens' committees thought they had the octopus under control.[10] However, their lack of direction following the collapse of the SED's leadership meant that their domestic control mechanism lost its cohesion. Within three days of the bold sit-ins in *Stasi* offices, Mielke was put into prison on remand, and a colonel general and a lieutenant general, both former deputies of Mielke, were dismissed from the Office for National Security along with seventeen other high-ranking *Stasi* officers. Lieutenant General Schwanitz, however, stayed on as chief of the organization.

On the same day as the occupation of *Stasi* offices, the Christian Democrats and Liberals both resigned—to be followed by the Democratic Farmers the next day—from the SED-commanded Democratic Bloc of Parties and Mass Organizations. Prime Minister Hans Modrow, Foreign Minister Oskar Fischer, and Egon Krenz (who would still be chief of state and chairman of the National Defense Council for three more days) traveled to Moscow for a Warsaw Pact summit. There Gorbachev, ignoring the lame-duck Krenz, congratulated Modrow in private conversation on the fact that the GDR had now cleared the way for its own perestroika.[11]

Degeneration and Regeneration

Implosion would have been more accurate than perestroika. Modrow, the man so often viewed as the East German Gorbachev, was to preside not over a communist renaissance but over the final demise of Marx in his own fatherland.

The SED, reversing the eighty-year legacy of the split in the Socialist International between revolutionary communists and reforming social democrats, tried to revert from a hierarchical, vanguard dictatorship into a democratic socialist party at its December party congress. Symbolically, it changed its name to Socialist Unity Party–Party of Democratic Socialism (SED-PDS, later just PDS) and selected the personable lawyer Gregor Gysi—the one-time defender of Bärbel Bohley—as its chairman. It further swore to accept whatever minority role voters might accord it in a free election.[12] Whatever it did, however, it only underlined its growing irrelevance to a population freed from the explicit and implicit state violence that had underpinned the SED's privileged position for forty-four years. East Germans hardly credited the overnight conversion to democracy at a party congress at which abstract Stalinism was condemned, but neither Gysi nor anyone else ventured to criticize the party's record of forcing the Social Democrats to merge with the SED in 1946, suppressing the Berlin uprising in 1953, building the Berlin Wall in 1961, or inflicting mass imprisonments and even murder on the population over the years.

Nor did the reform party congress hear any hint that the whole authoritarian SED system, and not just its flawed leaders, might have been responsible for what speakers acknowledged to be the greatest crisis in the history of the GDR. Instead, every communist below the top three or four or five dozen villains (the number grew with the indictments) was treated as an innocent victim rather than an accomplice to the power structure. And despite the legal abandonment of the party's leading role a few days earlier, even Gysi continued to assume that the SED would keep on running things; he made no reference whatever to compromising with other parties or groups.[13]

As the rigid governing structure of four decades evaporated and the state prosecutor filed charges against Honecker, Mielke, Stoph, and three other ex-Politburo members, and as (exaggerated) reports came in of civilian incursions into East German and Soviet army installations, orderly Germans in both East and West feared anarchy and mob justice in the GDR. Modrow said there were up to twenty bomb threats a day.[14] Some worried that if the winter were cold and the distribution system broke down, as seemed to be happening in the Soviet Union, people might even start plundering the shops. Government and church leaders therefore appealed anxiously for peace and calm and nonviolence.

In this tense atmosphere both the SED and the opposition rallied to shore up Modrow and prevent a plunge into dangerous chaos and instability.[15] The new roundtable met under church auspices for the first time on December 7.[16]

This roundtable, described by one of its three Protestant and Catholic moderators as the "school of democracy," had been weeks in the making. The first informal contact group began contemplating possible ways to bring the energies of the new movements to bear on politics as early as the end of October, then increasingly focused its thinking as the ancien regime collapsed in November and early December. The communist leadership at first resisted such dilution of its power, but then came to see in the roundtable an ally that might even help prop up that waning power.

After some procedural wrangling, the roundtable was set up with parity representation between the old forces and the new forces. The former, consisting of the SED and the four old bloc parties of the Christian Democrats, Liberals, Democratic Farmers, and the National Democrats, plus representatives of the trade union, the Association for Mutual Farmers' Assistance, and the small Slavic minority called Sorbs, had fifteen (later nineteen) votes between them. The latter, made up of New Forum, the Social Democrats, Democratic Awakening, Democracy Now, the Green environmentalists, Initiative Peace and Human Rights, the United Left, and, from the second session on, the Independent Women's Association, had fifteen (later nineteen) votes between them. Decisions were by simple majority. The potential deadlock was quickly broken as five of the votes on the old side shook themselves loose from SED suzerainty and supported the new democrats.

Politically, virtually all the new-force delegates, many of them pastors, represented opposition from the left rather than from the right. They deemed a merger with West Germany as an evil. Their aim instead was continuation of a separate GDR that would pioneer that exemplary third way of better socialism, or socialism with a human face. When the trade union delegates, in the first session, threatened a general strike, anarchy, and bloodletting if the question of unification came up, they found considerable sympathy among the new forces in ends, if not in the more extreme means.

With time, the roundtable established rules of debate on the model of the Protestant synods, but initially discussion was chaotic. At the first session, disorderliness was further magnified by anti-*Stasi* demonstrators outside, who some feared might try to force their way into the church building where the roundtable was meeting. Yet for all the tumult, the first session accomplished a great deal: scheduling the first free election on May 6, 1990; laying out principles of equal opportunity in campaign, party, organization, and press regulations; agreeing to draw up a draft of a new constitution; demanding dissolution of the *Stasi* successor organization under civilian control; and, above all, giving citizens a sense that their voice was being heard and that events were not totally out of control.

It was now clear that the SED and bloc parties, and the Volkskammer, lacked any legitimacy whatever. But it was also clear that while the self-selected roundtable and new forces enjoyed the legitimacy of the street, they also lacked real democratic sanction. At the beginning the representatives of the new movements were acutely aware of this deficit and insisted that the roundtable not act as an ersatz legislature, but only as a kind of veto organ against the SED. The first session agreed that the roundtable was to exercise no parliamentary or governmental function, but was to constitute an "element of public oversight" and serve as a kind of advisory council in offering "suggestions to the public for overcoming the crisis." Typically, Wolfgang Ullman of Democracy Now, a theologian and one of the most articulate participants, perceived the role of the roundtable not as a vice-parliament, but as a task force of people with certain middleman skills who might operate as a lobby for the people in relation to the government.

As the old regime continued to disintegrate, however, the roundtable found that it had to take over some parliamentary functions, such as writing the detailed election rules and blocking the perpetuation of the *Stasi*. By the time the roundtable could turn its functions over to the new, freely elected GDR parliament, many in the new forces would be claiming a special moral legitimation as those few who had had the courage to set the revolution in train—and they would be complaining bitterly about the injustice of being shunted aside by the people in the 1990 election.

The *Stasi* Confrontation

The roundtable's first great service was taming the *Stasi*.[17] Originally, Modrow's continuation of the Ministry for State Security with only a cosmetic name change was uncontroversial. Certainly most Volkskammer deputies agreed with the prime minister's explanation that every state has its foreign intelligence and domestic criminal investigation services, and Modrow had presumably stopped the worst abuses when he ordered an end to internal political spying on November 29. However, the series of scandals at the beginning of December alarmed the new forces, and at the December 7 session the roundtable declared the AfNS to be an unacceptable "institutionalized and personal successor institution to the Ministry for State Security." The roundtable demanded dissolution of the AfNS, under civilian oversight, and insisted that the government also inform the public immediately about any other security services and its plans for them. Furthermore, it told the government to ensure that all destruction of documents and tapes end so the *Stasi* could be held accountable for their misdeeds.

On December 8, the day after the first roundtable session, Modrow announced that he was setting up government commissioners in all regions to work closely with local officials and representatives of citizens' committees to consult on all questions concerning the AfNS. On the same day the police put guards into the central *Stasi*/AfNS headquarters in East Berlin to monitor comings and goings.

Ominously, on December 9 some anonymous state security officers in Gera tried to incite other state security officers to armed resistance to democratization. New Forum acquired and made public this call to action addressed to "comrades, battle companions, patriots here and abroad, citizens of the GDR." It invoked "the wisdom of Lenin in questions of power" and asserted that "the armed organs of our common homeland, the GDR," should act "to unmask and paralyze the hate-filled machinations against the organs of state power." The appeal was in accord with Mielke's earlier boast that if the need arose, his single *Stasi* regiment could take control by itself.

Yet the Feliks Dzierzynski Regiment and the close to 1 million men under arms in the country's army, border guards, secret police, regular police, and worker's militia remained paralyzed. That the Gera summons went unanswered was due largely to the roundtable's doggedness in forcing on the secret police the kind of transparency and accountability that the furtive *Stasi* system could not survive.

Modrow did not take the roundtable probes seriously at first and did not want to demean what he still regarded as his rightful authority by subordinating his government to the upstarts. Initially he neither appeared before the roundtable nor sent to it the ministers responsible for security matters. He did not speed up the dismantling of the secret police; he did not disarm the 60,000 who remained in active service; and he continued to pay their old salaries (for a promised three years) to the 25,000 who had already been dismissed, arguing that they should get compensation if they could not find new jobs at their level of qualification.

On December 14 the Council of Ministers suddenly gave in and issued an order to dissolve the new AfNS within six months. No reason was given. On the same day, however, the press office of the Interior Ministry complained that attacks and threats of violence had mounted "to a worrying extent" against former members of the AfNS, SED functionaries, and police officers. That same day, too, Modrow announced his intention of perpetuating the *Stasi* under yet another name change, this time adopting the titles of the West German external intelligence agency (Federal Intelligence Service) and criminal investigation agency (Office for Protection of the Constitution).

On December 17 an oversight committee was formed, composed of representatives of the parties and citizens' movements in the roundtable, prosecutors, and police.

On December 19 there was an interlude as Chancellor Kohl met Prime Minister Modrow in Dresden; granted him additional financial help of DM 3.5 billion; received promises from him about market reforms; and, in front of church ruins left from the allied firebombing of Dresden, addressed enthusiastic demonstrators waving homemade West German and Saxon flags. Before the Dresden trip, Kohl had insisted on not moving toward unity too fast so as not to scare Germany's European allies; he had turned down a proposal by then Interior Minister Wolfgang Schäuble to offer Modrow a currency and economic community at the meeting.[18] In Dresden, Kohl, a press-the-flesh kind of politician, was greatly moved by the Saxons' manifest yearning to join the Federal Republic, but he still sought to dampen the chants for a unified Germany among the demonstrators. In particular, he primed a cantor to stand ready to seize the microphone should the crowd burst spontaneously into "Deutschland, Deutschland über alles." If so, the cantor was instructed to get everyone singing instead Bach's familiar "Nun danket alle Gott." The deflection was unnecessary. At the end of the impromptu rally an effusive East German grandmother darted up to the chancellor, kissed him, weeping, and effectively closed the assembly.[19]

Still in his mode of caution on his return to Bonn, Kohl counseled patience on his television interviewers, saying "We need time."[20] Today, however, he cites the unification zeal of the Dresden crowd as one impetus to his own subsequent acceleration of the rush toward union.[21]

Showdown

By its fourth session on December 27, the roundtable still had not received satisfactory answers about the secret service from the government, despite the announced breakup of the *Stasi*. It therefore registered its protest at this point, asked the government to suspend the formation of a new security agency until after the free election, and requested written answers to its outstanding questions.

Still Modrow balked. The *Stasi* and SED now tried a tack that many feared might succeed in perpetuating the secret police: they cried wolf about rising neo-Nazism in the GDR and said a security service was needed to counter it. Specifically, they responded to anti-Semitic graffiti on the Treptow memorial to fallen Soviet soldiers—who wrote the graffiti was never clarified, and many suspected the *Stasi* themselves—by staging a demonstration against "neofascism and anti-Sovietism" at the monument.[22] At the same time the criminal police briefed the press on growing neofascist activities in the GDR, and the *Junge Welt* newspaper carried an anonymous interview on rising neo-Nazism in the country.

Had such extensive official stonewalling on the *Stasi* not preceded this gambit, it might well have drawn the sympathy of the left opposition groups at the roundtable. The word "neo-Nazi" was a red flag to leftists in both West and East Germany, and after decades of repression of all views other than communist ideology, the existence of rebels who seized the first chance to air neo-Nazi slogans was not surprising. Treptow smelled suspicious, however. The citizens' groups, Social Democrats, and even the former bloc party Christian Democrats boycotted the action. The SED's antifascist campaign of the next two weeks—accompanied by reports of armed *Stasi* and workers' militia units in various localities—only made the roundtable more determined to get rid of the *Stasi* once and for all.

The first of the two final showdowns between Modrow and the roundtable came on January 8, 1990, at the roundtable's sixth session. The prime minister sent only second-level officials to testify, and these men spoke only in evasive generalizations. Peter Koch, the Council of Ministers' civil commissioner for dissolution of the AfNS, and Walter Halbritter, state secretary under the Council of Ministers, told the roundtable flatly that "in the interest of the population" they could not answer the questions put to them. They refused even to say where the state security's central computer records were located.

Outraged, the opposition broke off the roundtable session and issued an ultimatum to the state prosecutor, the interior minister, and Modrow himself to appear before the roundtable within two hours—later extended to one week—to report on internal security.

In the interim, the street demonstrations, which had continued in the large cities, stressed not only unification, but also prevention of any revival of the *Stasi* or perpetuation of SED-PDS rule. Yet on January 11 Modrow still told the Volkskammer of his intention to build a new security service and strongly rejected unification.

Even as parliament met, construction workers mounted a warning strike—this time during the day, not after working hours—to demand faster "democratic renewal" from the SED-PDS, "swift reunification," and "disbanding" of the AfNS. To emphasize their views, they hauled down the flag in front of the Volkskammer and slashed the GDR emblem out of it. The next day East Berlin taxi drivers went on strike, honking their horns for the same goals. The Social Democrats began talking about organizing a general strike. By now even the old bloc parties said they would leave the "coalition" government if the secret police were not totally eliminated.

At this point Modrow retracted his government declaration of the day before, promised to wipe out domestic spying completely, and said he would not establish any new security service before the election.[23] Just to be sure, New Forum called for a demonstration on January 15 in East Berlin against the *Stasi* and *Nasi* (the latter being the protesters' preferred acronym for the AfNS because of its clear allusions to both of the organization's notorious forerunners, the *Stasi* and the Nazis). On that day, even though he had asserted until the last minute that he would not obey the summons, Modrow had a change of heart and put in a surprise appearance before the roundtable. He announced that he had fired Koch, repeated that he would not organize any new security organ before the election, promised to accelerate the dismantling of the AfNS, and even offered to let roundtable delegates participate in civilian oversight of the dissolution.

That afternoon the demonstration proceeded anyway, and this time erupted into what was initially called a storming of the *Stasi*/AfNS headquarters on Normannen Street. Protesters shattered a glass door, charged into the building, and vandalized offices, photogenically tossing papers out of the windows and down the stairwells. As soon as they heard about the riot, both Modrow and roundtable participants issued appeals for calm, then rushed to Normannen Street to calm tempers. Information that became known later—apparently the front door was opened from inside rather than forced open, and a company from the Dzierzynski Regiment, dressed in mufti, led the demonstration and steered it away from the most sensitive offices to an unimportant wing holding exotic *Stasi* groceries— suggested not so much popular passion as *Stasi* red herrings. Whether the intent was to justify a future law and order crackdown or to divert the public from issues of political repression to less damaging ones of privilege was not immediately clear.[24] It was, however, the last such provocation that *Stasi* officers attempted.

The following week Modrow again appeared at the roundtable session and repeated his good will toward it. The roundtable, while appreciating the sentiment, nonetheless passed a stern resolution that declared: "Peace in our land depends at the moment to a decisive degree on the credibility of the government. That applies especially to the measures for dissolution of the state security service." The roundtable "urgently demanded" that the government release officials from previous rules of confidentiality in testifying before the roundtable; make clear the legal consequences of any perjury (a concept that had never before applied either to the Volkskammer or, of course, to the roundtable itself); prosecute those destroying evidence; and make no decisions about dismantling the AfNS without the agreement of the roundtable's newly formed working group on security. Specifically, it again asked for detailed information about the structure and work methods of the former *Stasi* and about current activities of former *Stasi* officers. It further demanded the opening and securing not only of *Stasi* archives, but also those of the SED-PDS and National Defense Council (in its domestic side), and complete lists of all *Stasi* facilities, means of communication, and eavesdropping installations and targets.

It would still take until February 8 for the Council of Ministers to set up a state committee for dissolution of the *Stasi*/AfNS and order the final systematic dismantling of the secret police, and even this order would be implemented sluggishly.[25] However, as the government at last responded to the roundtable's demands—and as the roundtable was then able to progress from groping in the dark to using its incipient knowledge to formulate ever more precise questions—a flood of dramatic information poured forth in subsequent days and months. Its content astounded even those Western experts on the *Stasi* who were paid to worry about worst-case scenarios, and it fueled ever more popular indignation toward the secret police.

Some of the revelations were surprising in degree, including the high figures of 85,000 full-time *Stasi* employees, the thoroughness with which *Stasi* agents had penetrated all social organizations, and the 1 million or even 2 million free-lance informers in a population of 16 million. The division strength of the Dzierzynski Regiment and its armament with heavy weapons was previously unknown, as was the full extent of the sponsoring and training of Arab terrorist groups. The number and seniority of spies in the Federal Republic was also an unpleasant surprise for the West. Those named included the woman who was still preparing the top-level daily evaluations for the Federal Intelligence Service, the head of counterintelligence in the Office for the Protection of the Constitution, the deputy chief of military counterintelligence until 1984, and a senior correspondent for *Der Spiegel*.

Other *Stasi* practices that the West German public had known something about but generally forgotten included the executions of political nonconformists in the 1940s and 1950s, along with mass imprisonments in jail or old Nazi concentration camps; and the forcible separation of children from parents who had tried to flee to the West and their distribution to adoptive parents.[26]

Still other *Stasi* practices that came to light had been unsuspected. The most sensational of these was the harboring, and in some cases training, of at least ten West German fugitives who were on the Federal Republic's most-wanted terrorist list. Others included the clandestine training of West German Communist party cadres in small arms and explosives at a GDR military camp for future sabotage, and the committal of sane dissidents to psychiatric wards on the Soviet pattern.

Rooting out all the petty *Stasi* mafiosi who spun off the state security apparatus, sold themselves state property at cheap rates, and tried to transfer their skills to cutthroat capitalist competition would take a long time after the roundtable revelations. The compulsory resignations of new East German politicians suddenly confronted with their pasts as Unofficial Collaborators of state security would also be a periodic occurrence for years to come. Nevertheless, the fact that *Stasi* officers dispersed into business (and politics) rather than conducting the armed putsch that the Gera secret police so earnestly tried to instigate was a tribute to the roundtable's effectiveness in publicizing and neutralizing the workings of the once all-powerful state security.

Chapter 12

Acceleration

A t this point in January both Modrow and Kohl, in their very different ways and for different reasons, decided to accelerate the process of democratization and unification. Their various allies looked on, transfixed.

The United States, from the beginning, was totally supportive of reunification and played a crucial activist role in achieving it, both in reversing British and French opposition and in persuading the Russians that they could survive German unity with their dignity preserved. Oddly, conventional wisdom in the United States discounts the American activism and presumes that the extraordinary unification of Germany on the West's terms came about almost accidentally. The reasons for this blind spot lie, perhaps, in the Bush adminstration's fixation on the Gulf War as the main show, in the left's reluctance to attribute skills in foreign affairs to Bush, and in the right's reluctance to acknowledge that Bush's "soft" solicitude for the Russians (and trust of the Germans) in this period was the right policy.

Whatever the reasons, the assumption is now firmly embedded in conventional wisdom that the Bush administration did little to manage the end of the cold war and simply benefited from it as the apple fell into its lap. Typically, the lead article in the Fall 1991 issue of *Foreign Policy*, in offering a critique of Bush's foreign policy of inaction and passive watching over the liberation of Eastern Europe during his first year in office, never once mentioned German unification or Washington's part in it.[1] So common was this American evaluation that Dutch-Canadian political scientist Alexander Moens was moved by the end of 1991 to contest explicitly two "popular and persistent misconceptions": that "German unification was a 'runaway train,' beyond the control of even the major players," or that the Bush administration could have, but didn't help "shape events."[2]

The thesis that will be developed in the next four chapters is the standard German government view (but maverick American view) that the Bush administration did in fact act decisively in helping to shape events in Germany, and that the outcome would have been very different were this not the case.

Germany's other main allies, the British and French, were less solicitous of the Germans. Prime Minister Margaret Thatcher and President François Mitterrand were both alarmed at the prospect of unification, but in the face of American-German solidarity, they would decide they had no choice but to accede to this third rise of Germany in a century. For their part, the Soviets resisted the trend, but in the end would be pragmatic and not try to thwart the inevitable.

Bonn, in the eye of the storm, was the first capital to regain its bearings after the fall of the Berlin Wall. The Federal Republic began groping its way toward resolution of the conundrum of forty years: how to let the Germans grow together, as they apparently wished to do, without upsetting the stability of the cold war stalemate that had given Western Europe two generations of peace, whatever the cost in division of the continent. The West, Chancellor Kohl and Foreign Minister Hans-Dietrich Genscher felt, must seize the historic chance for a new beginning arising from the conjunction of Soviet domestic preoccupation, loss of Soviet will to maintain an external empire, the bankruptcy of the communist system throughout Eastern Europe, the determination of people emerging from four decades of repression to salvage their lives quickly, and the dynamics of a newly rejuvenated European Community (EC). "The window of opportunity in which it was possible [to get unification] was very limited," Kohl notes in retrospect.[3] It required a fast tempo.

At this vertiginous speed, however, East and West together had to find a new concept of stability that could no longer mean prolonging the vanished status quo. Instead, a rough balance would have to be maintained for all nations riding the whirlwind of change.

Internationally—especially in view of Germany's dark history and the latter-day economic and political well-being bestowed on the Federal Republic by interdependence with the West—the new dynamic stability required the coming unification to be embedded in continuing European integration, the West German government reasoned. And in any case, only a strong Western Europe could remain a magnet for Eastern Europe and keep up the impetus of democratic change there. In Bonn's view, widening the EC toward the East and deepening the joint operations of its current Western members, far from being contradictory (as the French were arguing), were actually complementary. Kohl, applying this logic, dropped his previous resistance to France's pet European Monetary Union and central European bank, though he did insist on German terms of bank independence and on implementation only after the West German election at the end of 1990.

The Soviet Nyet

As the chants of "We are one people" swelled in Leipzig, so did the misgivings abroad. The Soviets, who stood to lose the most in prestige and were the most alien to the thought processes driving the Germans, were the most negative. (Some West German diplomats, exasperated by the French, and especially the British, hostility to unification, would contest this judgment and call the Russians quite cooperative by contrast.) Gorbachev had grossly underestimated the forces his permissive new thinking would unleash in client countries that already possessed, to a greater or lesser degree, the civil societies and individual initiative that he was trying so desperately to graft onto the Soviet body politic. He still thought in terms of perestroika, not of utter rejection of the communist system, in Central Europe.

An additional block to Gorbachev's comprehension of the dynamism of German events was psychological. After all of Gorbachev's and others' revelations about the nasty Afghan war, the Soviet Union's technological backwardness, Brezhnev's stagnation, the Soviet massacre of captive Polish officers at Katyn, and Stalin's murder of millions, the Soviet Union had only one success it could still claim from seventy miserable years: the incredible heroism with which it had endured and finally repulsed German invasion and occupation in World War II. The role of Moscow's GDR client in symbolizing this triumph was far more important in the missile age than its dubious geopolitical role as a Soviet glacis. All the Eastern superpower's nuclear might could not erase Russian awe of German military technical prowess, and all the Federal Republic's willingness to help develop the Soviet Union economically could not erase the humiliation of watching the GDR slip out of the Soviet orbit not only into neutrality, but as looked increasingly likely in early 1990, into alliance with the Western adversary.

Gorbachev had improved relations with the Federal Republic sufficiently to endorse "the right of peoples to self-determination" on his visit to Bonn in June 1989, and free-wheeling Russian intellectuals had flirted with the idea of German federation or eventual union when talking to Western listeners.[4] But Gorbachev had consistently dismissed the idea that history might change the existence of two Germanys in anything under a century.[5]

It was hardly unexpected, then, when Shevardnadze and some other Soviet commentators briefly resuscitated the old bogeyman of German "revanchism" in fall 1989, and even used the phrase "neo-Nazi" in September in private conversations with the Americans.[6] Or when Soviet Foreign Ministry spokesman Gennady Gerasimov, in the wake of the opening of the Berlin Wall, lauded the GDR as Moscow's important "strategic ally,"[7] and warned after Kohl's November 28 speech that "there is not one country in Europe today which would endorse reunification."[8] Or when Shevardnadze expressed great concern about the "attempt of some circles in the FRG [Federal Republic of Germany] to place the question of the reunification of Germany on the agenda" and cautioned against the danger of destroying postwar "realities" in seeking German self-determination.[9] Or when Shevardnadze and Gorbachev, talking with Genscher in Moscow, rejected Kohl's ten points as a "*diktat*."[10] Or when Gorbachev himself declared that realities must be recognized and that reunification was not a current policy issue.[11]

Within days after Kohl set forth his ten points and the old Socialist Unity party collapsed, the Soviet Union suddenly proposed the first high-level four-power meeting in Berlin in eighteen years. Its manifest intent was to impress on the Germans that the World War II victors still held residual rights and responsibilities for Germany as a whole and for Berlin, and expected to exercise them on the issue of German unification. West German media, with some bitterness, registered the attempt to prolong occupation constraints on German sovereignty forty years after the end of the war.

Through all the Soviet churning, however, West German government analysts kept noting optimistically that while the Russians were ruling out German merger now, they were not ruling it out in the future. The Federal Republic's allies reserved judgment.

The British and French Nyet

British officials were not as blunt as their Soviet counterparts, but their desire to see German unification postponed as long as possible was unmistakable. Prime Minister Margaret Thatcher swiftly consigned German union to the distant future after the turn of the century, when all the neophyte democracies throughout Eastern Europe might have fully demonstrated their capacity to sustain pluralism. For good measure, she also opposed French-German plans to deepen political cooperation within the European Community; seizing the tactical opportunity, she cited the tumult and uncertainty in Germany as a reason for retarding this process.

At the special EC summit in early December 1989, Kohl ran into an "icy climate" on the part of the British, French, and indeed most Europeans. Thatcher, he notes wryly, was at least "more honest" than most in voicing outright her opposition to German unity.[12]

Within a few weeks Thatcher shared her honesty with the public as well. In an interview with the *Wall Street Journal* published on January 26—and with no advance notice to Kohl—she warned that if German unification went too fast, it could have the disastrous effect of toppling Gorbachev. It would in any case disrupt the economic balance within the EC, where Germany already dominated. Kohl and Genscher, she continued, should subordinate their "more narrow nationalist goals" to Europe's long-term needs.[13] West German diplomats fumed that she wanted to preserve the status quo of a divided Germany, and even to revert to a nineteenth century balance-of-power play against Britain's ally of forty years. Kohl was equally furious.[14] The Dutch and Belgians quietly applauded their English spokeswoman.

Until the last minute, Thatcher lobbied for "four plus two" rather than the "two plus four" negotiations that actually evolved to resolve the external aspects of German unity. That is, she wanted a forum in which the Germans would be present not as full participants, but as guests of the four World War II victors.[15] In mid-February she was still stressing the importance of continuing the four-power rights and responsibilities that, she underlined, had preserved West Berlin's freedom for four decades. In the German perception, even after consenting to the two plus four conference, she still did not fully accept for another week and a half that the result would be unification.[16]

After finally bowing to the inevitable, Thatcher still sought to exorcise the German demons somehow. In March 1990 her cabinet office called an urgent secret seminar of academics to tutor it on the German soul. "Angst, aggressiveness, assertiveness" began the arch summary list of Teutonic characteristics that would leak to the press four months later, to the embarrassment of the government and the cost of one cabinet resignation.[17] Symptomatically, Secretary of State for Trade and Industry Nicholas Ridley—taking just the opposite view from those Frenchmen who sought to cage the Germans by means of European integration—would publicly call plans for European monetary union "a German racket designed to take over the whole of Europe." He would compare the surrender of sovereignty it would entail with giving up sovereignty to Adolf Hitler, and chide the French for "behaving like poodles" toward the Germans.[18]

Nonetheless, Britain had other strong foreign policy interests beyond Germany, including the Commonwealth, however tattered, and the old special relationship with the United States that never quite vanished. The latest rise of Germany did not threaten its core identity.

It did threaten French identity. The French had not suffered as many deaths as the Poles or the Russians in World War II, but they still carried the resentments and fears of three German occupations and a century of French-German animosity. The growth to adulthood of a new generation had recently brought the large majority of the French public to regard Germans as normal human beings, and to favor reunification, but historical memory still preserved aversion to Germany among France's powerful political class.[19]

The consternation of the elite bureaucrats was all the greater because the winds of change were sweeping away their Gaullist dreams of French rather than German leadership of Europe. For four decades the division of Europe had been good to France. It had effectively solved the old problem of how to cope with the greater Germany that Napoleon had awakened, a land more populous than France and industrially more dynamic. It had reduced the West Germans to a number about equal to the French, and it had turned the Federal Republic into a buffer for Paris against the newer Russian threat. It had also kept France a great power, in name at least, in its victor's rights in semisovereign Germany and Berlin, and in the prestige the cold war had conferred on the possessors of nuclear weapons. It was perhaps unfortunate in attracting American hegemony in Western Europe as the only possible counterbalance to Soviet hegemony in Eastern Europe, but apart from that—and the awkward fact that France was not among those who carved up Europe at the 1945 Yalta conference—Paris had been quite happy with this provisionally permanent postwar settlement.

The definitive ending of the cold war on November 9 closed this chapter for France. With unification, Germany would gain a fourth in population over its erstwhile peers of France, Great Britain, and Italy. France would never catch up with its next door neighbor economically, as it had still hoped to do in the 1970s. A finally sovereign Bonn would not need to continue its political and moral dependence on Paris for legitimacy in foreign policy—and perhaps not even its dependence on the EC, the French feared. The geopolitical center of the continent would shift eastward with the Poles', Czechoslovaks', and Hungarians' rejoining of Europe and give Germany a further advantage over France. The end of East-West confrontation would, in the phrase of Dominique Moïsi, devalue the French nuclear bomb while revaluing the German mark.[20]

In the early 1980s President François Mitterrand had decided that the most prudent policy toward a troublesome Germany would be to hug the West Germans as close as possible to avert any drift by them to the East. France had, of course, along with all other NATO members, solemnly endorsed German unification yet again as recently as the alliance summit the previous May. And as late as a few days before the Berlin Wall came down, when his rhetoric did not yet cost anything, Mitterrand had declared that he could imagine German unification within ten years if it occurred democratically and peacefully, with due regard for neighbors' interests, with concurrent acceleration of European unity, and in a context of broader adjustment throughout the continent.

Once the specter of unification actually loomed, he behaved more shrewdly than Thatcher. He led the realists—Spain and Italy joined him—in accepting the fact of coming unification, and he avoided counterproductive public opposition to it. His true, negative feelings were never in doubt, though. On November 10 he immediately told reporters that France had nothing to fear from German unification. Thereafter he increasingly stressed the necessary conditions, however, and focused on insisting that deepening the EC must take precedence over widening it, and on warning Bonn against setting up any conflict between German and European union.

Widening the EC to take in the emerging East European democracies, as Bonn increasingly wished to do, would forfeit deepening it politically and condemn the EC to remaining purely economic, he argued. He therefore pushed on an open door in the Federal Republic in nagging Bonn to support a European Monetary Union and a European central bank ("Eurofed"). Bonn's subsequent endorsement of the European Monetary Union and Eurofed at the European Council meeting in Strasbourg in mid-December was widely seen in France as a quid pro quo for France's acquiescence to German merger. For Paris, establishing a European central bank would not be surrendering sovereignty over national currency—in practice France had long since ceded this role to the Bundesbank—but rather regaining some share in the currency and interest rate decisions that governed all of Europe.

Mitterrand's and France's emotional reaction was much sharper than this cerebral policy suggested, of course. The Foreign Ministry in particular—and some of Mitterrand's advisers—clung to the old suspicions of Germany. Within days of Kohl's ten points, Mitterrand, in an ostentatious snub of Bonn, told an American newspaper before telling Kohl that he would visit the GDR on December 20.

This breach of etiquette irritated the West Germans, both because it tended to prop up the discredited Krenz, who was still in office at the time of the announcement, and because it constrained Kohl's own schedule.[21] The chancellor would eventually manage to be the first Western head of government or state to visit new Prime Minister Modrow (after Krenz's fall) only by nipping into the GDR the day before the French president. Mitterrand then compounded the affront by flying to Kiev to see Gorbachev in early December in pointed reversion to that amoral nineteenth century balance-of-power maneuvering against Germany, and by declining Kohl's invitation to join in the ceremony opening Berlin's Brandenburg Gate.[22] Various versions of the Kiev meeting circulated afterward, the juiciest one of which had Gorbachev rebuffing Mitterrand in telling him that the Germans had a right to unification.[23] The French president also took some pleasure in quoting Gorbachev's comment to him in a telephone conversation in late November: "On the day Germany unites, a Soviet marshal will be sitting in my chair."

Moreover, as the Soviet, American, British, and French ambassadors to Germany met in the Allied Control Council building in West Berlin on December 11 in response to the Soviet summons, both France and Britain appeared to welcome the opportunity to hide behind Soviet skirts. Their clear message was that four-power rights would continue and the four should decide Germany's future themselves and then inform the Germans. Furthermore, Mitterrand, in his New Year's address, proposed a vague European confederation that looked as much like a framework to control Germany as a pacifier to Central Europe and a bid to the Soviet Union to join a new grouping that would exclude the United States. [24]

Numerous West Germans read into the French and British reactions economic envy of Germany, along with some nostalgia for the lost glory of empire that lingered on only in those four-power rights (and in permanent Security Council membership). Christian Democratic parliamentary leader Alfred Dregger reminded West Germany's allies of the 1954 deal under which the Federal Republic entered NATO and the NATO allies committed themselves to seek German reunification. The normally thin-skinned Kohl, for his part, said nothing publicly, but waited until such time as more Cartesian analysis might show Mitterrand that his original promotion of a French-German alliance within the alliance was indeed the correct course and that there was no alternative.

For the Germans, the one bright spot in European reactions to the new prospects came from the EC bureaucracy. As soon as the Berlin Wall opened, EC President Jacques Delors lent his support to East German self-determination, and expressed confidence that Bonn's enthusiasm for EC political union would continue unimpaired. By contrast, Vice-President Frans Andriessen worried that the Germans might now forget about advancing "1992" in the West as their orientation shifted eastward, but Delors's optimism was the dominant voice. As early as January 1990 Delors invited the GDR to accede to the EC without the regular entry procedure on the strength of its old, EC-allowed, duty-free link with West Germany. He also seconded Kohl in expecting the German-German and West European integration processes to be mutually reinforcing rather than competitive.

In February 1990 the European Commission set up a working group, which included a delegate from the German-German team negotiating union, to assess the impact on the EC of German economic and monetary union and to help Bonn ease the GDR's entry into the EC and slow emigration from East to West Germany. In March the commission also pressed forward with revised or new proposals on the "1992" targets, on EC economic and monetary union, and on expanded political cooperation.[25]

The American Yes

Among Bonn's allies, adjustment to the turbulent new era was least difficult for Washington. Ahistorical America regarded flux as the norm in any case, and for decades the distant, huge United States had felt much more relaxed about the prospect of German unity than had Britain, France, and Italy. The United States believed in self-determination, it felt no threat from a larger Germany that would still be only the size of Montana, and it stood by NATO's repeated postwar pledges of support for unification should the Germans choose this option.[26] "The Americans were the only ones without complexes" toward Germany, notes Kohl.[27]

By fall 1989 the highly favorable European environment had also reinforced America's democratic instincts. German unification would have looked utterly different had Europe not already agreed on a single market by 1992 and, implicitly, political integration thereafter, and had Gorbachev not already decided to cut radically his half million troops in Eastern Europe. In this context West Germany was fully anchored to the EC and was pulling East Germans along with it rather than itself being lured to the East. The United States had the exhilarating conviction that, as one National Security Council (NSC) staff member put it, the "great game" of ending the cold war had finally arrived, and the West was winning it. Momentum was on the side of Western values. The United States could confidently let the impetus of democracy and free choice carry the day. Besides, the United States recognized very early that the Germans were going to unify in any case, and it could have been folly for Washington to stand in the way, or to let Germany be "singularized" as an earlier Germany was in the punitive Versailles peace settlement.

Given this rare coincidence of principles and obvious tactics, State Department Counselor Robert Zoellick describes the basic decision to work actively for unification as an easy one.

> It was the right thing to do, a slam dunk. A U.S. leadership role would also enable us to better achieve our interests. In some cases it's hard to determine the tactics that will effectively achieve your goals, [but in this situation] deference to democratic choice would unify Germany. And our strong support for that process would make it more likely that the German people would voluntarily stay within Western structures. In this case we would stand firmly for unification

of Germany through democratic means. In the short term, if Germany were treated properly, it would voluntarily stay within the Western structures. Indeed, long-term discrimination or singularization would only plant the seeds of future trouble.[28]

The decision was rendered even easier by the Bush administration's determination on coming into office to start with a tabula rasa, discarding the foreign policy preconceptions of the previous administration, and even of America's professional diplomats, whom it tended to regard as fusty bureaucrats. As early as March 1989 National Security Adviser Brent Scowcroft's aides (especially Robert Blackwill) dueled with outgoing Assistant Secretary of State Rozanne Ridgway over her contention that it would be premature and destabilizing for the United States to return the German question to the international agenda, and formally advised the president to do just that. Secretary of State James Baker, his Counselor Robert Zoellick, and his Director of Policy Planning Dennis Ross, orienting their fresh reassessment of America's long-term alliances with West Germany and Japan to the winding down of the cold war, subsequently reached the same conclusion. The relationship with Bonn had to be put on a new basis, they decided, given the appeal of Gorbachev to the Germans, the reduction in Soviet arms in Europe, and the Germans' new chafing under the constraints on their sovereignty left over from the post–World War II occupation.

The inherited preconceptions the Bush administration threw out included, therefore, the old Reagan and Carter administration angst that Moscow might play a German card in sponsoring unity in return for German neutrality, thus Finlandizing the Federal Republic and driving wedges between it and its NATO allies. Bush exhibited little of the anxiety of his predecessors that the Federal Republic might succumb to peace euphoria and cut defense budgets irresponsibly, and none of Reagan's alarm over West German trade with the Soviet Union and Eastern Europe. Nor did the administration perpetuate the tendency of an older generation of American commentators to hang the sins of Hitler's Germans on their grandchildren's necks, regarding Germans in general as untrustworthy and as genetically liable to produce a Fourth Reich.[29]

In particular, the Bush administration deliberately set aside the Reagan administration's feud with Genscher over Genscherism, or perceived softness toward the Soviet Union, and over Lance missile modernization. Bush hardly proclaimed himself a convert to Genscher's thesis that Gorbachev was serious in wanting better relations with the West and should be taken at his word, but he did move increasingly toward Genscher's view in the course of 1989.[30]

In personal terms, in their sparring over Lance at the NATO summit of May 1989, Baker and Genscher—and their respective right-hand men, Zoellick and Frank Elbe—developed a healthy respect for each other's professionalism and political instincts. Baker, an almost European type of foreign minister in being no specialist on foreign affairs but rather a domestic politician entrusted with the international portfolio, was anyway predisposed to understand Genscher the politician. And he consciously shucked the Reagan administration's habit of ignoring Genscher and dealing almost exclusively with Kohl and his foreign policy adviser, Horst Teltschik.

Political analysis and personal style thus worked together to produce the deliberate, early American support for German unity. Bush specifically backed unification in an interview with the *Washington Times* in April 1989, and again in a press conference in September. Then in October, after Honecker was toppled—but a good two weeks before the wall fell—he discussed developments with Kohl on the telephone and afterward endorsed merger yet again in an interview in the *New York Times.* "I don't share the concern that some European countries have about a reunified Germany because I think Germany's commitment to and recognition of the importance of the [NATO] alliance is unshakable. And I don't see Germany, in order to get reunification, going off onto what some are concerned about, and that is a neutralist path," the president stated.[31]

During this period Washington curbed the enthusiastic predictions of rapid German unification by its ambassador to West Germany, Vernon Walters, not because it had doubts about unification, but because it was not the time tactically for Americans to be seen as stoking the process. National Security Adviser Brent Scowcroft is said not to have seen why the United States should break any lances for German unification, but he did not oppose it vigorously.

A corollary that policymakers introduced by mid-November was that unification must essentially be left to the Germans; there must be no four-power intervention in or Soviet veto on the German process. In this precept the Americans diverged sharply from the French and British, who still wanted to stretch out four-power rights to impress on the Germans their obligations to their European neighbors, including avoidance of precipitous change.

This postulate by no means enjoined passivity on the United States. On the contrary, it required active American engagement in shaping the circumstances of unification to avoid dangerous instability in the transition or in the end result. Risks during the transition were that Soviet hardliners might react violently to the loss of the GDR and might order their still mighty twenty Soviet divisions in East Germany into action,[32] or that the hitherto restrained East Germans might provoke an incident at a Soviet military base that could escalate, or even that discipline might break down among Soviet forces in the GDR. Risks in the end result were that German euphoria about the breakout of peace might prematurely dismantle the NATO alliance that had so successfully deterred war and blackmail, even though the residual threat of a Soviet Union with nuclear weapons—or of Soviet rumps with nuclear weapons, or of blood feuds between hostile East European nationalities—remained.

Certainly the United States was in a strong position to influence the conditions of unification. Its unique superpower relationship with the Soviet Union let it reassure Gorbachev—as Bush immediately did—that Moscow would not be isolated and humiliated in the ensuing readjustment, and that Soviet security interests would not be impaired. Its engagement in Europe implicitly reassured Germany's neighbors that the United States would be on hand as a counterweight to ascendant German power. At the same time, the United States' unqualified support for unification helped assure Bonn of a smooth transition despite other Europeans' misgivings, and let the United States utter some hard truths about the need for NATO's continuance that the British and French, by their resistance to unification, had disqualified themselves from saying.

The State Department, the NSC, and the President

The top levels of the State Department were fairly relaxed about the security outcome and anticipated that, as events progressed, Bonn would in any case see its own interests in the light of the West's axioms. The NSC, by contrast, in parallel with some working-level American diplomats, perceived an urgent need to get Kohl and Genscher to sign on explicitly to the importance of the Western alliance. From their different starting points, however, both institutions combined to insist on the continuance of German membership in NATO as an essential guarantee of security for all of Europe.

The combination of rivalry and cooperation between these two competing offices was characteristic. Their coordination of the politics of German unification would be a major achievement, thanks largely to Secretary of State Baker's closeness to the president, NSC Adviser Brent Scowcroft's willingness to be a good staff officer rather than a star, and the tireless liaison of Robert Blackwill, special assistant to the president and NSC senior director for European and Soviet Affairs. Both institutions would be represented and work together well in the two plus four talks about the international aspects of German unity, once the formal negotiations began. And after German unity was consummated, Zoellick would turn over the complete State Department files to NSC Director of European Security Affairs Philip Zelikow to write the official classified history of the case, without fearing that the State Department's role would be slighted.

So close-knit were the NSC and the State Department that they would on occasion have a better overview of the fluid diplomacy of 1990 than would either of their bickering counterparts in Bonn. There interagency relations were very strained. Such tension was inevitable in a political landscape in which the foreign minister came from the junior coalition partner, one that had been kingmaker for a quarter century, but had to fight for its life in every election to get the 5 percent minimum vote to make it into parliament. The personalities at play also exacerbated the strains. Genscher was senior to his chancellor in office, having conducted foreign affairs in the center-left coalition before his Free Democrats (Liberals) had defected to form the center-right coalition in 1982. One of the shrewdest politicians in the game, he was a consummate artist at staking out nuanced positions that would give his party profile against its larger partner, and at hinting whenever the jostling got especially rough that his party might again switch sides and topple the government. Kohl, whose strength was more iron control of his party than broad policy, left day-to-day diplomacy to his Foreign Ministry, but asserted himself on such issues as the French-German partnership, Europe, and German unification.

In this situation the Foreign Ministry sometimes withheld from the Chancellery information it passed on to the State Department, while the Chancellery sometimes withheld from the Foreign Ministry information it passed on to the White House staff. The two Washington offices, by contrast, consistently profited by pooling their knowledge.

To be sure, there was one major split between the NSC and the State Department, not over German unification as such, but over Soviet policy, and therefore over the pacing and mechanisms of German unity. There was also a considerable divergence in motivation and nuance behind their joint support for unification. At the State Department the political level trusted the West Germans and, in a totally different way, was starting to trust the reforming Russians much more than did the NSC. The NSC fretted a good deal about both.

Baker's growing confidence in Shevardnadze's reliability began with the Soviet foreign minister's visit to the United States in September 1989, shortly before the German issue really exploded. Shevardnadze flew out to Baker's ranch in Wyoming, and in their relaxed exchanges there and en route both men concluded tentatively that they might be able to depend on each other's word.[33]

By contrast, the NSC—whose top Soviet expert, Robert Gates, had come from the Central Intelligence Agency and shared the views of that agency's hardline rather than pragmatic wing in relation to the second superpower—was much more suspicious of Soviet intentions. It still saw in Gorbachev's new thinking a dangerous magnet that might draw Western Europe away from the United States. The NSC worried, therefore, that Baker might be so eager to cultivate a good working relationship with the Soviets that he would make excessive concessions and give Gorbachev a trump hand in the German negotiations. It counseled going slow to avoid making any mistakes.

A third point of view that shaped Western strategy in relation to Moscow was the West German analysis. Bonn, after years of bilateral frostiness, had finally established a certain rapport with Gorbachev during Kohl's visit to the Soviet Union in October 1988, and especially during Gorbachev's return visit to the Federal Republic in summer 1989. By 1990 both the Foreign Ministry and the Chancellery discerned in Gorbachev's stated goal of a common European house a real yearning to be part of Western Europe, and not just a trick to push the United States off the continent. As one aspect of opening up to Western pluralism, they were persuaded, the Soviet leader was ready to cut his losses and let the East Europeans, even the East Germans, go their way. However, he needed time and the forthcoming party congress to overcome conservative opposition to this unorthodox course, the Germans thought.

Despite their varied assumptions, the German and the top-level State Department prescriptions for dealing with Moscow over the next six months would dovetail nicely.

Between the NSC and the State Department, there was a further divergence in instincts about the Federal Republic. In Washington Zoellick had the reputation of being an ultrapragmatist, a kind of lawyerly engineer, and he certainly had no special background in German affairs. Yet there was something more to his approach to the unification issue than sheer cold analysis, he conceded in retrospect. He was a fifth-generation German Midwesterner. As a child he had heard German spoken by both sets of grandparents, and he brought an innate cultural trust to bear that was quite different from the negative burden of proof put on the Germans by the Reagan administration (and the French) to demonstrate constantly that they were not going to sell out the West to the Russians (or, alternatively, turn neo-Nazi). The Germans found in Zoellick a sympathetic ear.

The NSC was by no means Reaganite, but, in common with a number of professional Foreign Service officers, it worried that politics might turn volatile in the Federal Republic. In particular, it feared that an already weakened Kohl might be defeated in the 1990 election by a quasi-nationalist Social Democratic campaign calling for national sovereignty to be asserted against American military rights in Germany, and that Genscher might be so convinced of Soviet benevolence that he would let NATO wither away prematurely and induce a dangerous security vacuum.[34]

There was, finally, a philosophical or temperamental difference between Zoellick, the State Department's key player on the German issue, and the NSC. The NSC had a more dramatic view of the importance of concrete, specific policy targets, and of success or failure in achieving them. Zoellick tended to see history as a stream that flows on without being shifted decisively by critical highpoints.

Far from crippling policy decisions, these discrepancies initially served to unite the NSC and the State Department tactically. Despite its wariness of Soviet propaganda, the NSC tended to believe that the time was generally propitious for negotiations, since Gorbachev was weak and adrift politically, and therefore susceptible to pressure by a United States that knew what it wanted. The NSC also welcomed the potential of the unification issue to bolster Kohl against the Social Democrats' subliminal charge that he was simply America's poodle, and to plant the United States clearly on the side of virtue in the eyes of the German public. Moreover, their very depth of concern about the Germans prompted the NSC staff to make special efforts to prevent leaks about their misgivings; otherwise, they feared, the French and British alarm might only be reinforced and poison the whole alliance at this delicate moment.

The result was a united American front as Bush went into his get-acquainted summit with Gorbachev in Malta on December 2 and 3. Gates was muzzled and made no more public speeches stressing continuing Soviet dangers. Bush left the Soviet president in no doubt about his interest in German unification, but he assured a Gorbachev who was not yet sure where the American president stood that he too (and not just Baker) desired a positive, comprehensive superpower relationship, and that he wanted to avoid isolation of the Soviet Union as the Germans unified.

At the summit Gorbachev still maintained publicly that it was "the bidding of history" that "there are two German states in Europe today."[35] Privately, however, he confirmed the Soviet desire for a continued American presence in Europe that he had already implied in his speech in Strasbourg the previous July, and he persuaded the NSC that on the German issue he would be pragmatic and flexible.[36]

In later conversations Gorbachev would frequently refer to the importance of the Malta meeting in clarifying American policy and laying the groundwork for a cooperative approach to German unity. Among themselves, American officials would refer to this meeting as the beginning of the conditioning of the Soviet Union to accept unification.

In a brief stopover scheduled hastily after the opening of the Berlin Wall, Bush flew from Malta to NATO headquarters in Brussels and set forth a four-point framework for unification. His intent was not only to promote merger (his first point), but also to soothe the anxieties about it among Germany's allies (by calling for gradualism, his third point), and at the same time to make clear to the Germans what external conditions were essential to prevent instability (a continued NATO alliance, with German membership, and the commitment not to change existing borders by force, his second and fourth points).[37] Everyone understood the last guideline to rule out any German reclamation of western Poland. The allies, including the West Germans, immediately endorsed these principles and incorporated them into their next European Council summit of EC heads of government on December 8.

In Brussels Bush conspicuously held a private dinner with Kohl, assured him of U.S. backing, and agreed to confine the imminent four-power meeting in Berlin to Reagan's Berlin initiative of two years earlier that proposed that Berlin become a major world air hub and be otherwise rejuvenated. A week later, in the Soviet-summoned session of the Allied Control Council in Berlin, the United States took pains to specify that the four ambassadors to Germany had no negotiating authority and would do no more than listen to Soviet views and talk about Reagan's initiative. In this way the United States was signaling that the four victors of World War II would not dictate terms of settlement to the Germans.

Influential portions of the West German media, however, read the session as an attempt at just such a *diktat*, willed not only by the Soviet Union, but also by the United States. The tabloid *Bild Zeitung* ran a bitter banner headline, "Now We Know Who Our Friends Are," and lumped Bush, Thatcher, Mitterrand, and the Italians together as treating Germany like a banana republic.[38] The erudite *Die Zeit* compared hypocritical Western support for German unity with Christians' desire to go to heaven, "but not too soon."[39] Editor Rudolf Augstein of *Der Spiegel* blamed contemporary German division—as he had for forty years—on superpower complicity at the Potsdam Conference in 1945 and later.[40] The weekly *Stern* complained: "The more Germans in both states strive for new unity . . . the more unambiguously the erstwhile victors lay stones in the way— above all Soviets and Americans. In unison they swear by 'stability.' "[41] For *Stern*, stability still meant the status quo, and the United States was still trying to perpetuate American hegemony by stuffing NATO membership down German throats.

The Bonn government considered the meeting a public relations disaster, shared some of the resentment at having Germany's fate decided in council in the absence of Germans, and determined from then on to insist on full German self-determination in securing union. U.S. policymakers decided on the rebound that some mechanism other than four-power councils would have to be found, and redoubled their efforts to avoid being painted as the hindrance to unification in their nuclear, NATO, or troop stationing policies. That possibility was "our nightmare," one American official recalled later.

On the following day, December 12, Baker placed NATO in a larger context in a speech in West Berlin and called for creation of a new European architecture involving not only NATO, but also the EC and the Conference on Security and Cooperation in Europe (CSCE). He further described Bush's four points as presupposing stability, German consultation with allies and neighbors, respect for Soviet security needs, and—yet again—continued membership of any united Germany in NATO. The Bonn Foreign Ministry interpreted his speech as signaling a major American shift away from suspicion of the CSCE to openness toward an expanded role for it.[42]

More unexpectedly, in a last-minute decision acceding to the advice of the U.S. ambassador to the GDR—and overriding the U.S. ambassador to the Federal Republic—Baker paid the first, and certainly last, visit by a senior American official to the German Democratic Republic. As always, he refused to acknowledge East Germany's incorporation of the eastern half of the nominally four-power city of Berlin, and instead met Prime Minister Modrow—and, separately, Protestant Consistorial President Manfred Stolpe—in the suburb of Potsdam. The visit was a judgment call, intended to help boost Modrow's authority enough to avert the anarchy that so many Germans feared, but not so much as to prolong senescent communist rule. As the American secretary of state, Baker was conscious that he represented freedom to the ordinary East German as well as prestige to Modrow. His intent was, without being provocative, to encourage the prime minister to continue on the road toward elections and self-determination and to convey Washington's understanding that this road would lead to unification.

Some of the small community of American specialists on Germany—who were conspicuously shut out from Baker's inner policy circle—suspected that the secretary of state also wanted to beat Kohl in talking to the new East German leader. The Chancellery and Foreign Ministry, which were consulted in advance, perceived no such slight in the contact, however.[43]

On December 19 Kohl made his first visit to Modrow in Dresden and got the kind of popular crowd reception he could only dream of in West Germany. On December 22, in pouring rain, Kohl and Modrow opened the Brandenburg Gate as the latest Berlin crossing point for the public. As the chancellor walked from the Reichstag in the British sector to the history-fraught monument, the British commandant intercepted and greeted him, and the British military band broke into a lusty rendition of "The British Grenadier." "I'm not sure this was such a friendly gesture," commented a senior West German diplomat.

By Christmas Eve all East German political prisoners were released.

The New Sobriety

In the new year sobriety set in in both East and West Germany. The dismantling of the old structures in the GDR continued: on January 1 the army's Main Political Administration ceased its functions, on January 2 the ADN news agency carried the announcement that the elite Wandlitz ghetto would be turned into a "rehabilitation sanatorium," and the leadership began to admit that the GDR generated some of the worst industrial pollution in the world. However, now that union seemed more and more likely, people began to worry about all the conditions: the looming unemployment in East Germany's uncompetitive industries, the buying out and export by speculators of subsidized goods from the GDR, the potential reclaiming of houses and lands by West Germans who had been dispossessed of their holdings forty years earlier, and the eventual worth of ostmark savings in "real money."

The cordiality between Kohl and Modrow also suffered strains.[44] The Bonn government—which was ready to pay whatever it took to bring about an economic miracle in the GDR, but believed that private investment had to provide the bulk of the money—had been pleased with Modrow's promises in December about moving toward a market economy. In particular, Kohl welcomed Modrow's intention, as he understood it, to allow majority foreign shares in small and medium-sized joint ventures. However, he felt duped when Modrow's subsequent government declaration on January 11 did no such thing, and even sounded, as one West German official put it, as if Honecker could have written it.[45] Bonn, already giving the GDR millions of deutsche marks for environmental and telecommunications projects, became chary of pouring grants down a black hole, and as more data became available, both Western analysts and ordinary East Germans began realizing how much blacker the hole was than anyone had imagined. Most notably, many firms simply could not pay their debts.[46] Bonn's mistrust of East Berlin was also fed by Modrow's attempt to perpetuate the *Stasi*.

As a last straw, the East German prime minister now confided to Kohl that when he gave orders, nothing happened. The bureaucracies simply ignored them, and were in any case vanishing. The paralysis of local government was becoming serious as more and more community apparatchiks resigned or were jailed, and as those who remained at their posts proved incapable of making decisions in the absence of the old centralized command.[47] East Berlin could not even manage its own garbage collection and asked the West Berlin senate to take on the task. Dresden, on the upper reaches of the Elbe River, was grateful for the enlightened self-interest of its partner city at the mouth of the Elbe, Hamburg, in getting Dresden's sanitation in order after two years in which its raw sewage poured into the river untreated. Similarly, Leipzig looked to Hanover, Schwerin to Schleswig-Holstein, Thuringia to Hessen, and Saxony to Baden-Württemberg for money and know-how, as a kind of grass-roots knitting together proceeded without waiting for any formal arrangements at the top.

The economic and administrative news was bad enough. The human news was even worse. In a transparent signal that the average person had no confidence whatever in Modrow's half-hearted measures, emigration to the West now doubled. Some 344,000 East Germans had moved west in 1989; an untenable average 2,000 a day continued the trek in January.[48] The only way to persuade the remaining GDR citizens to stay home was to give them some hope of orderly progress toward unification.

Now the worry was not disorder, but sheer disintegration. At this point the Bonn Chancellery telescoped its previous expectation that unification would take some five years to a one- or two-year process. The immediate priority was still prodding for free elections in the GDR as soon as possible to get a government that could act and work with the Federal Republic to stabilize the East German economy and stanch the population drain. The expectation now, however, was that a freely elected government would want swift unification.[49]

For its part, the Modrow team resented Bonn's financial miserliness and presumption to speak for East as well as West Germans. Increasingly, Modrow—and the roundtable—interpreted Bonn's stance as intervention and bribery of East German voters with promises of money only if they supported the conservatives in the impending election.

Yet even Modrow saw that drastic measures were needed to stop the rot. On January 28 the roundtable decided to shorten the period of limbo by advancing the free elections to March 18 and to form in the interim a "government of national responsibility" that both new and old forces would join.[50] The next day Modrow told the roundtable that the crisis was deepening, that the economic situation was becoming ever more threatening, and that the state's authority was ebbing away.

On the following day Modrow flew to Moscow, and the Soviet Union and the GDR accepted the inevitable. Just before receiving Modrow in the Kremlin, Gorbachev declared to journalists that "no one ever cast doubt in principle on the unification of the Germans."[51] Two days later Modrow presented his own plan for "reconstitution of the unity of Germany," but set German neutrality as a precondition.[52] The West rejected this proviso, Moscow was deafeningly silent on it, and the East German prime minister promptly downgraded his prerequisite to nothing more than a basis for negotiations.[53]

Exhilarated, but worried that social stagnation could be far more destabilizing than a political dash forward, Bonn now accelerated the pace of developments with a dramatic offer. Picking up the couplet of Leipzig demonstrators, Kohl declared at the beginning of February, "If the DM [deutsche mark] doesn't come to Leipzig, then the Leipzigers will come to the DM." He was now ready to make the proposal for an East-West German currency and economic union that Interior Minister Schäuble had first floated in mid-December. Overriding the vociferous objections of the Bundesbank, on February 7 Kohl proffered the GDR the mighty deutsche mark even before political union.[54] He also began talking about joint elections as early as 1991.

To the many German and European challengers who criticized him for rushing things indecently, Kohl kept citing the folk adage: "We must get the hay into the barn before the storm." On occasion he also quoted Napoleon: "S'engager, puis voir."[55]

Chapter 13

Two Plus Four Equals One Germany

After the fact, Bush administration officials circulating in the innumerable seminars on the subject would explain their success in the German-American steering of unification in 1990 with the deprecatory quote from Yogi Berra, "We didn't make the wrong mistakes." This observation contained a good deal of wisdom, and a tribute to a policy that in the midst of tumult always stayed two jumps ahead of Gorbachev and of those Germans who wanted a united Germany to distance itself from the Western alliance.

The American decision in mid-January to let unification rip ahead as fast as possible—despite British and French foot-dragging, and despite Baker's own precept of gradualism propounded in Berlin a month earlier—was one of the West's preemptive leaps. The Genscher plan and "two plus four" were others.

The Genscher Plan

At this hinge of history any vigorous Soviet bid to veto NATO membership for a united Germany might well have succeeded. Most opinion polls were inconclusive in that they did not measure one value against another; both NATO and unification enjoyed consistently high approval ratings in West Germany.[1] There was a widespread assumption that the Soviet threat had evaporated, however, and that NATO had fulfilled its work and would not be needed in the future. Conventional wisdom equated fewer weapons with more peace, and many voters (ranging from

40 to 50 percent to 80 to 90 percent depending on the phraseology in the questionnaires) were distressed by NATO's reliance on nuclear deterrence.

Moreover, German self-pity—this time over the real lack of support for German unification from France and Britain and a perception by the elite of a lack of support from the United States—had not yet dissolved into the energies devoted to the myriad practical tasks of union. This environment too could have strengthened West Germany's urge to part with allies if unity were really at stake.

Certainly in East Germany street interviews suggested that public opinion almost universally rejected NATO membership.[2] Foreign policy, so long as there was no risk of war, was no urgent concern of citizens preoccupied with reorienting their own daily habits of forty years. It was taken for granted, though, that the two Germanys would end membership in their respective military blocs as soon as they merged.

Thus, assessing the mood in early February, analysts from across the political spectrum in West Germany believed that if a collision between NATO and German unity arose, NATO would lose. Here the Social Democratic party (SPD) was not the only question mark. Among West German conservatives there were vestiges of old Gaullist longings (associated in the 1960s with Bavarian potentate and nuclear enthusiast Franz Josef Strauss). Some Western diplomats and the National Security Council (NSC) feared that even Kohl, whose instinct for the political jugular was his most highly developed faculty, might sacrifice NATO if anti-NATO sentiment developed in the Federal Republic or if Gorbachev told Bonn that his domestic survival depended on keeping a united Germany out of NATO. They noted, among other clues, that in his ten-point speech on November 28 the chancellor did not refer to the Western alliance except to thank it for its commitment to unification. Chancellery sources dismissed such speculation as misplaced. From the beginning, they said, Kohl was determined not to accept unification without firm Western ties. However naive its hope might have seemed to others, the government was operating with a "metaphysical optimism," as one official put it, "that we could convince the Soviet Union of its interest in NATO membership" for Germany.

As it turned out, latent Gaullism on the right never found a spokesman. Misgivings about NATO on the left did, in the persons of Egon Bahr on the SPD's left and even Karsten Voigt, an SPD Bundestag member who for years had been active in NATO parliamentarians' assemblies. Moscow would never tolerate the GDR's slippage into NATO membership, they contended. Gorbachev was already making so many concessions to the West that hardline domestic opponents were attacking him for losing Eastern Europe. If the GDR added insult to injury by not even turning neutral, but actually joining the adversary alliance, that could be the end of Gorbachev and of détente in Europe. It was much too dangerous a gamble.[3]

The corollaries were implicit: if a united Germany could not be a member of NATO, that meant that West Germany would quit the Western alliance, and if the Federal Republic withdrew from NATO, Congress would surely pull back U.S. forces deployed in the Federal Republic and elsewhere on the continent. That hundreds of thousands of GIs remained in Europe forty-five years after the end of World War II was in any case a wonder. It would not have taken much to trigger their return home.

Yet a continued U.S. presence in Europe was essential, allied strategists agreed. Only the American superpower could provide insurance against the Soviet nuclear missiles still targeted on Europe, and only the United States could also carry out the last of NATO's missions as described by the alliance's first secretary general, Lord Ismay: keeping "the Russians out, the Americans in, and the Germans down."

By 1990 the issue was no longer keeping the democratically reformed Germans down as in the 1940s. But there was a more subtle need—which the West Germans themselves accepted—for the American counterweight to growing German might to assure the anxious French, Italians, and Dutch that the Germans would not overwhelm them. And for a West Germany whose legitimacy in foreign policy was still overshadowed by the memory of Hitler, there was a more subtle need for a partner whom Bonn could work with in launching its own initiatives.

For a quarter of a century France had performed this function in Europe in a symbiosis in which the Germans provided economic clout and the French provided licitness. With this new ascent of Germany in 1990, however, France became too small and parochial to be Bonn's main partner in dealing with extra-European affairs. Only the United States had the size and the range of global contacts with the Soviet Union, for example, and the will, to be able to affect Soviet conduct on German unification.

Against this backdrop Genscher rushed—the day after public Soviet acceptance of unification—to avert a contest in the minds of German voters between unification and continued German membership in NATO. Even after German merger, he proposed, NATO should forswear military extension onto the territory of the then GDR in peacetime. During a transition period of several years the Federal Republic should also refrain from moving its forces assigned to NATO, as the bulk of them were, to that area. Further, the Soviet Union—which was already having difficulty absorbing Soviet soldiers returning from Hungary and Czechoslovakia and was housing tens of thousands of them in tent cities—should be able to keep troops in the GDR for another three or four years before removing them all.[4]

The last point was as much arrogation as promise. Even half a year earlier, no Western leader would have presumed to "offer" Moscow the opportunity to keep in East Germany for a few more years the forces it had stationed there for decades.

Two Plus Four

Genscher immediately flew to Washington to present his new plan in person, and on that visit "two plus four" was born. On February 1, in a brainstorming session, Zoellick, Ross, and Elbe wrestled out what kind of international framework might accommodate the domestic German union that was now racing ahead.[5]

With those twenty top-category Soviet divisions in the GDR, with nuclear weapons always hovering in the background, and with the peace of agreed stalemate of the past twenty years now turned unpredictable, this need was no mere procedural detail. In a negotiation in which every country involved except the United States had an emotional stake in the outcome, a good bit of the all-important quotient of final satisfaction or resentment would depend on getting the terms of participation right. In the Soviet Union Gorbachev might have just consented personally to German merger—and might be painfully aware that another Soviet resort to force in Eastern Europe would destroy perestroika—but his political longevity was always in doubt. Although he had performed his breathtaking high-wire act for five long years on the premise that there was no alternative leader and no alternative domestic policy to grudging compromise between radical reformers and reactionaries, his base for consensus was getting narrower and narrower. The loss of the GDR might render it razor thin.

Certainly Russia had a long history of violent conservative reversal whenever reform and Westernization went too far and a popular yearning for "order" set in. And psychologically, however irrational any neo-Brezhnevite turn might seem to Westerners, the sober reckoning of potential gain and risk is most prone to emotional distortion when an autocrat is losing (rather than gaining) power, and sees only a desperate now-or-never choice before all power vanishes. Indeed, the first concrete warning of such a backlash, in domestic criticism of Gorbachev for letting the GDR get out of control, was already looming at an enlarged plenum of the Soviet Central Committee on February 5. The hardline discontent that would culminate in the attempted coup of mid-1991 was already mounting.

In the longer run too there was a danger of humiliating the Soviet Union now in the way Germany was humiliated after World War I, and thus inviting some future Soviet Hitler to avenge the shame. Both Bonn and the political level at the State Department therefore consciously sought to avoid creating a Soviet pariah that might one day seek violent revision of the post–cold war order.[6]

The NSC saw things somewhat differently. It agreed, as Bush would stress, that the United States should not gloat over Soviet misfortunes, but since events were nudging Gorbachev aside anyway, the NSC opposed prolonging Soviet superpower pretensions by showing Moscow any deference in the unification process.

One further hazard, as some British, French, and American officials worried, was that Gorbachev might now achieve through weakness what he had failed to achieve through strength: German neutralization through a conclusion by euphoric German voters and politicians that all threat had now vanished. The Soviet leader had yet to define the terms of unification he would accept, and he certainly had not modified Shevardnadze's assertion of the previous November that with no Warsaw Treaty Organization, NATO would not be needed. Modrow had further specified neutrality for a unified Germany, and the NATO alliance looked outmoded or untenable even to many in the United States. Moreover, at this point the Bonn government itself had not made a clear public commitment to continued full NATO membership.

The challenge, then, was to design a mechanism that might reconcile the internal and external aspects of unification, persuade the Soviets to withdraw their divisions from the GDR and give up their residual four-power rights in Germany, and still avoid all the pitfalls.[7]

The Soviet Union certainly had its own ideas about how to proceed. Since mid-November it had been pressing hard for four-power management of the German transition. Washington thought it had fobbed Moscow off with the December 11 ambassadors' meeting, but on January 1, and again on January 10, Shevardnadze wrote to Baker proposing another four-power session at the ambassadorial level or higher.

In response, the United States, backed by Britain, rejected any meeting of the four above deputy ambassador level and insisted that the Germans be present at any discussion of Germany's future. For reasons of both justice and politics the United States wanted to.end the period of the Federal Republic's incomplete sovereignty—a relic of World War II and Bonn's postwar need for foreign security guarantees—and give the Germans a full voice at whatever international table might be set up.[8] Such a maturation was overdue, and would be healthy in turning debate about Bonn's security policy from a foreign (and latently anti-American) issue into a domestic one. The Federal Republic too thought the time had come for full sovereignty, as Genscher made clear at the end of January.

A four-power instrument excluding the Germans was therefore out of the question. So was a decision by the two Germanys alone that would not settle the leftover four-power rights. NATO was equally inadequate. The

Western alliance would include West Germans, but it would exclude the Soviet Union, thus ignoring the Soviet army in the short run and isolating Moscow in the long run. Nor was the thirty-five-nation Conference on Security and Cooperation in Europe (CSCE) the proper venue. That body reached agreement by consensus, and no one wanted to give Liechtenstein and the Vatican gratuitous vetoes over German unity. Nor would a final, unwieldy peace conference of the three dozen World War II belligerents (including such unlikely participants as Uruguay) be appropriate. Bonn absolutely ruled out a formal peace conference in any case; it refused to be put in the dock four decades later as the successor to the German Reich and to be dunned by all and sundry for more reparations than it had already disbursed voluntarily. Washington backed Bonn in this determination, and worried lest Moscow suddenly call for a peace conference as a propaganda circus.

In mulling over the dilemma, Dennis Ross's State Department policy planning staff had written a paper floating the notion of a "two plus four" conference attended by the two Germanys as full participants, and the four World War II victors in Germany: the Soviet Union, the United States, Britain, and France. Such a grouping would be small and flexible and would fold into the process the still "balky" British and French, as well as the Soviets.[9] If set up carefully—with the United States insisting from the start that the end result must be a totally sovereign unified Germany—it would give the Germans a full voice in their own destiny. On February 1 Zoellick and Ross raised the idea with Elbe. Elbe, who thought they were proposing a generic council of the six without pinning down the level of German participation, sounded out Genscher on the ride into town from Dulles Airport on February 2. Genscher approved, so long as the configuration was clearly two plus four, with equal rank for the Germans, and not some four plus two relegation of the Germans to a second-class side table as at the last peace conference in Geneva in 1959.[10]

Within a week of Baker and Genscher's agreement on two plus four, Baker flew to Moscow, stopping off at Shannon Airport on the way to discuss the latest initiatives with French Foreign Minister Roland Dumas. On February 8 and 9, he basically sold Gorbachev on two plus four as a process that would keep the Soviets engaged in Europe rather than letting them get pushed out by the tumultuous events. It was a gamble. "What one didn't know, the big wild card, was what the Soviets would do," Zoellick noted in retrospect. The administration nonetheless brought "maybe a belief in rationalism" to its approach to superpower relations from its experience in developing mutual trust with Shevardnadze. "We saw with Shevardnadze, if we could explain what we called 'points of mutual advantage,' and we had momentum going for us, we [could advance]."[11]

At this point Baker made a rare slip in a late night press briefing in Moscow in which he spoke—contrary to firm American policy by then—of possible German "association" with NATO as an alternative to full membership. To correct the gaffe, the State Department briefer stressed to American reporters traveling with Baker at the next stop, Sofia, "It's membership, membership, membership!" Back in Washington the NSC staff made personal calls to embassies in Washington to read off Baker's later (correct) references in the same press conference to full German membership in NATO. And in one of the several saving instances in which the Russians trailed American reflexes by a critical month, Gorbachev failed to exploit Baker's error and press immediately for some associated status for Germany in NATO.[12]

Hot on Baker's heels were Kohl and Genscher, who flew to Moscow to see Gorbachev on February 10. Bush sent Kohl a letter on February 9 intended to reaffirm Washington's total support for unification and to stiffen Kohl's resolve not to yield on the issue of the Western alliance even if Gorbachev should stage a major crisis over the issue. In the letter Bush described specifically the firm measures the United States would take to block any attempt to use Soviet rights and responsibilities in Germany to slow down realization of German national aspirations. In addition, he set forth American views on what the West needed on NATO. The overall message, one American official suggested, was persuading Kohl "to keep his sights high and to keep him from a determinist view of history." In subsequent conversations with the Americans Kohl would refer to Bush's letter several times as a landmark.[13] The same day Baker, after his own talks in Moscow, sent Kohl another letter debriefing him on the Soviet-American conversations, discussing tactics, and explaining why two plus four was a good idea and would not slow down unification.

The joint Soviet-German declaration in Moscow said both sides agreed "that the Germans themselves must resolve the question of the unity of the German nation and themselves decide in what kind of state system, in what time frame, at what speed and under what conditions they wish to bring about this unity." The chancellor, having gone to Moscow with the multiple Russian warnings about German unification still ringing in his ears, was ecstatic about the results of the trip. His foreign minister, having partially discounted these warnings already as aimed more at Kohl and the Christian Democratic Union than the Germans in general, was less surprised by the Soviet openness, but by the same token was less impressed by this specific leap of progress. On the flight home Kohl popped open the champagne bottles, a gesture Genscher thought overdrawn. Shortly thereafter Teltschik, to the scorn of the Foreign Ministry, declared that the key to German unity now lay in Bonn. Genscher, bouncing from the tarmac to a television talk show, began steering public discussion away from NATO toward economics, stressing that Bonn would fulfill all the commercial contracts the GDR had had with the Soviet Union.[14]

Even at this late date, the NSC and the European Bureau in the State Department, largely unbeknownst to each other, both resisted the two plus four concept. They feared that Kohl might interpret it as a shift in U.S. policy toward unacceptable four-power intervention, that it would unnecessarily restore lost influence to the Soviet Union, and that it would enable the Soviets to slow down the course of unification sufficiently to preserve old Soviet levers in the new Germany. In particular, they worried that Moscow, while posing as the champion of unification, might be able to impose unacceptable conditions that would cast the United States as the barrier to union, perhaps demanding a nuclear-free Central Europe or a presence by Soviet forces in Germany so long as American forces remained there.

This rift between the NSC and the State Department's European Bureau on the one hand, and the State Department's political level on the other, would be the most serious interagency clash over Germany in the administration. The NSC opposed two plus four vehemently, but lost out to the Bush-Baker connection as Baker got Bush's oral approval of the concept at the last moment in an Ottawa-Washington telephone call.[15] Long afterward, one NSC member—who noted that with hindsight two plus four did seem to be the obvious solution—expressed heartfelt relief that the depth of the differences within the administration never leaked to the press at the time.

After the whirlwind diplomacy in Washington and Moscow, the various foreign ministers now set out for an "open skies" conference of NATO and Warsaw Pact states in Ottawa. The formal business of the conference was another stage in the conventional arms reductions talks, this time centered on confidence building through surveillance overflights over the adversary's territory, and on a new American initiative to cut superpower troops in Europe even more.

The latter was important to the West as a way to transform the old concept of East-West parity to a new principle of inequality between the sturdy NATO and the rapidly disintegrating Warsaw Treaty Organization. During the previous forty years, when the West's persistent aim in Europe had been to reduce Soviet superiority in heavy ground weapons, the goal of equivalence had provided a useful public shorthand in arms control. However, now that Gorbachev had agreed to parity (even if he had not yet signed on the dotted line in Vienna)—and now that the East Germans, Hungarians, Czechoslovaks, and Poles were further reducing the Warsaw Pact's strength by deserting it—the West wanted to signal that its voluntary political alliance should not be equated with the compulsory Soviet military alliance. NATO would not vanish just because the Warsaw Treaty Organization was disappearing, and the West intended to preserve a qualitative, and not just a quantitative, balance between the Soviets who would be withdrawing their troops only 600 kilometers across relatively easy land lines of transport, and the Americans who would be withdrawing their troops 3,000 miles across the sea. Washington therefore proposed—and Moscow accepted surprisingly quickly—lower ceilings for the number of superpower soldiers in Europe that would keep 195,000 American and 195,000 Soviet troops on the central front, but would allow the United States to keep an additional 30,000 troops elsewhere in Europe.

This achievement was upstaged, however, by the full international acceptance of German unification at Ottawa on February 13. The Germans themselves would determine the "internal aspects" of unification without outside interference. A peripatetic two plus four conference would be set up to regulate, in legally binding terms, the "external aspects" of German unification and the security of neighboring states. There would be no formal peace treaty ending World War II, but all the leftover four-power rights and responsibilities in Germany would cease. The West further specified that Germany should have full sovereignty at the moment of unification: there would be no special status for Germany and no limitation on its choice of alliance membership. Furthermore, by the date of unification Soviet forces should be committed to a withdrawal from Germany by a stated deadline.

To make sure that the Soviets would not use the two plus four talks to obstruct or delay sovereign German unity, Washington also insisted to Moscow that while the two plus four delegates could discuss anything, they could negotiate only how to end the four powers' residual rights in reaching this goal. On all other matters the forum could act only as a clearinghouse in parceling out issues to various other bodies for resolution. Two plus four would present its final results to the CSCE for that institution's endorsement, but neither the CSCE nor any other council would have the power to alter the terms of German unity.

Suddenly it dawned on the public that German unification was going to come very fast indeed. The smaller European nations felt steamrollered, especially when Genscher snapped at the offended Italian Foreign Minister Gianni de Michelis at Ottawa, "You're not in the game."

The NSC, after sounding out Kohl's reaction, now realized that two plus four was a fait accompli and turned its energies to delaying the first foreign ministers' gathering until after the March 18 East German election, to pinning down precisely what two plus four could and could not do, and to eliciting from Kohl the firm commitment on terms of NATO membership it felt had previously been lacking. On the last point the NSC's concern was heightened by a domestic squabble in the Federal Republic about the military regime that would prevail on the territory of the former GDR once unification took place.

Bonn Politics

The Bundeswehr, looking at the specific regime the Genscher plan would establish in eastern Germany, was appalled. The suggested constraints, it seemed, could prohibit the defense of what would soon be a part of the Federal Republic. Senior levels of the West German armed forces, feeling that the West German foreign minister had outmaneuvered them too many times in the past, now prodded Defense Minister Gerhard Stoltenberg to challenge Genscher, establish the principle that there be no zones of "unequal security" in Germany, and stake out a claim to east German access for regular Bundeswehr officers and men.

Genscher sharply rebuffed Stoltenberg. Kohl, objecting to a major row in his cabinet so close to the GDR election, instructed his head of Chancellery to settle the quarrel. In consequence, Stoltenberg was muzzled. The odd joint declaration of the two ministers on February 19 carried explicit self-renunciation even further than previous vague formulations in stating: "The sentence that no units and institutions of the Western alliance will be moved to the present-day territory of the GDR refers to the NATO *and non-NATO* assigned forces of the Bundeswehr."[16]

In retrospect, after Stoltenberg's vision of a Bundeswehr command operating in the ex-GDR became the uncontroversial military regime in the united country, Foreign Ministry officials would explain Genscher's initial rough rebuke of Stoltenberg as no opposition in substance, but rather a silencing of unhelpful public discussion at a delicate period. The top reaches of the State Department were inclined to appreciate this sensitivity to helping Gorbachev save face.

The NSC was more suspicious, both of Genscher's public remarks and the German foreign minister's stress in private talks with American emissaries on what the Soviets would never accept. It did not yet know its own mind, but it knew it did not like what it heard from Genscher. It therefore sought to shift the focus from prejudging what the Soviet reformers could bear to ensuring that the NATO security guarantee would cover the former GDR, whatever the eventual military regime there. It also made sure that the name for this concept was neither Genscher's original formulation nor Teltschik's subsequent reference to the GDR in one briefing as a future "demilitarized" area, but rather NATO Secretary-General Manfred Wörner's vaguer anticipation of a "special military status" in the former GDR. After some ambiguity about future east German conditions on Baker's part in early February, the NSC pinned down Wörner's coinage as the standard in Bush's letter to Kohl of February 9.

This package quickly became NATO's official position, regardless of the Genscher-Stoltenberg statement of February 19. It extended NATO protection to the former GDR upon unification, yet still offered unilateral restraint. This could, the West hoped, let Gorbachev argue to his domestic critics that NATO was not taking advantage of the Soviet loss of empire.

It also gave centrists in the West German Social Democratic party a graceful way out of the left-wing position that a united Germany could not belong to NATO. Party Chairman Hans-Jochen Vogel quickly stated that neither neutrality and a German *Sonderweg* nor "extension of NATO at the expense of the Warsaw Pact" was the proper course. Instead, Germany must be embedded in a pan-European peace order that would take the place of the opposing alliances.[17] Even the countercultural daily *Tageszeitung*, while hardly becoming a fan of NATO, noted the alliance's benign constraints on Germany.[18]

The potential collision between NATO and German unity was thus deflected to a very different collision, should any develop, between full or limited German sovereignty. It was no longer a case of the United States insisting on German membership in NATO as a precondition for unification. It was, instead, the United States insisting that Germany have full sovereignty, including, as the CSCE treaty specified, the right to choose its alliances. In this context Washington would not be blamed for blocking German unity, but Moscow would be if it refused to let the Germans choose membership in NATO.

There remained then only the need, the NSC thought—the political level at the State Department was much more relaxed about the issue—to elicit from Kohl an explicit declaration of Germany's desire to stay fully active in NATO to ward off any dilution of German military participation in the alliance in the course of negotiations with the Soviet Union. The next opportunity for such a statement was Kohl's visit to Camp David for shirtsleeve diplomacy on February 24 and 25. The means was a joint press declaration that the NSC prepared for Bush to read in the name of both leaders. The gist was that a united Germany would remain a full member of NATO, continue to assign German forces to the alliance's integrated military command, and continue to host "substantial U.S. nuclear and conventional forces." Kohl concurred, and the NSC gave the declaration wide publicity.[19]

Timing

With the two plus four mechanism and Western policy guidelines now in place, a tactical issue of timing remained to be resolved. Some working-level American, British, and French diplomats, and some of the smaller European countries as well, felt they were being bulldozed by the Germans' speed. Policymakers in Washington did not share these misgivings. The NSC, in common with Kohl's Chancellery, wanted to go as fast as possible on internal unification to create an irreversible fait accompli for Germany's neighbors, including the Soviet Union. The State Department's European Bureau was inclined to defer to Bonn on pacing in any case. The political level at the State Department also favored letting the Germans proceed as swiftly as they wanted, but thought that getting the two plus four process going was essential to include the Soviets before they were completely shut out by the rush of events.

Among American and German players, the NSC was the party that wanted to go most slowly on opening two plus four. Its object was to delay these external negotiations relative to rapid domestic unification so as not to give Moscow a lever for slowing down that unification.

In these various calculations Western policymakers believed that in the short term time worked for them, but in the undefined medium term might work against them. In the short run, as the momentum of free elections propelled the Germans toward union, Moscow would realistically have to adjust, they thought. They dismissed cynical American media commentary that assumed that Moscow could just keep its army in Germany until it got its preferred terms. They believed that troop defections, demoralization, and possibly even dangerous clashes between these forces and the East German population would create their own pressures for Soviet retreat. Yet they thought there was only a limited window of opportunity to secure Soviet consent to unthinkable German unification before Soviet hardliners yanked Gorbachev back, either with or without his acquiescence. The trick would be to let unification proceed fast enough for the impetus to persuade Gorbachev to cut his losses by voluntarily consenting to the process, and thus remaining a player, but not so fast as to trigger the explosion by reactionary forces in Moscow that Genscher feared. In this balancing act the very speed of developments helped both the West and Gorbachev, who were much faster on their feet than the rigid Soviet conservatives.

Deciphering Soviet Policy

In dealing with the Soviet Union at this point, the approaches of the American and West German bureaucracies thus differed, but again served to reinforce rather than militate against each other. In Bonn both the Chancellery and the Foreign Ministry stressed the importance of offering carrots to Gorbachev and Shevardnadze to sell unification to Soviet hardliners. The incentives would eventually include billions of deutsche marks and technical and organizational assistance. But they started with the more intangible mutual trust that Kohl and Genscher both felt they had established with the Soviet leaders. Gorbáchev and Shevardnadze were treated with scrupulous dignity as members of the "common European house" and not as aliens.

As Genscher summarizes it, "Basically, my strategy was to say to the Russians that for them a united Germany in NATO would be better than the German division that always stood between us. I always said to Shevardnadze, the relations you could have with a united Germany will be more important for you than the sum of your relations with the GDR and us." He kept pointing out further that "German unification is no isolated process, but will change the situation in Europe more rapidly and fundamentally than the division of Germany did. . . . We could create a new relationship between the alliances."

The American approach to the Soviet Union was more skeptical, but in practice complementary. The Americans were certainly making every effort to hear from Gorbachev and Shevardnadze what sort of rhetorical changes they needed to make to "de-demonize" NATO in Soviet eyes. They, along with the Germans, were very happy to have NATO "extend the hand of friendship" to the Soviets and state explicitly that the latter were not viewed as enemies. They were glad to have invited Shevardnadze, the first Soviet foreign minister to be so honored, to address the NATO Council in Brussels on the surprisingly early date of December 19, 1989.

Much more than the Germans, however, the Americans continued to view the process of rapprochement with their old superpower rival as conditioning, or educating, Gorbachev and Shevardnadze as well as other Soviets, and not just as easing the two leaders' selling of NATO to their hardline colleagues. The Americans judged Gorbachev's top priority to be perestroika, and saw the Soviet leader's acceptance of a cooperative relationship with the West as a necessary and welcome tool to that end, but not yet a cornerstone of Soviet policy in its own right. American tactics therefore entailed, far more than did German tactics, persuading the Russians that successive faits accomplis were being created on the ground in Germany, and that the Soviet Union should accept these voluntarily if it did not wish to shut itself out as a player. In less polite phraseology, Washington relied on Gorbachev's sense of reality to convince the Soviet leader at each point that his less worse step would be to bow to the inexorable.

From their somewhat different premises, then, Washington and Bonn coordinated their policies toward the Soviet Union in exemplary fashion. "Gorbachev cared about only two countries, Germany and America," notes Genscher. So long as their policies fit together seamlessly—as they did in

1989–90—the Germans were covered. "If America had so much as hesitated [on backing Germany], we could have stood on our heads" and not gotten anywhere, he adds.[20]

An anomalous several months would follow, in which Soviet spokesmen would consistently reject German membership in NATO and float various half-hearted alternatives. Yet they did not object vigorously to NATO membership in the early stage, when such objections would have had the strongest impact on West German voters. And time and again various Soviet officials and others indicated privately to Western visitors that Moscow actually would prefer not to leave an enlarged Germany as a loose cannon, but would like to see it balanced in some way by the continued presence of American troops in Europe.[21] Gorbachev would not be able to voice such a preference out loud, the moderate Soviets surmised, until after the battle for authority was fought out at the forthcoming party congress in July.

During this period the West found it hard to decipher which was the real Soviet policy. This was an old conundrum, of course. Ever since Moscow had decided that the oil crises of the 1970s were not the death throes of capitalism and that a minimum of cooperation between the two systems was necessary for economic well-being as well as for nuclear survival, contradictory motives had been at work in Soviet policy toward Germany and Western Europe.

Defense, intimidation, security overinsurance, and feelings of superiority and inferiority all fed into declaratory policies that might develop in any of several directions. So did justifying Soviet hegemony in Eastern Europe; maximizing Soviet influence in Western Europe; gaining a Leninist breathing space now the better to combat capitalism later; holding Western Europe hostage against U.S. strategic missiles; exorcising the trauma of World War II occupation; keeping the Americans in Europe to restrain the Germans; deciphering the sometimes enigmatic American superpower; persuading Europe to persuade America of particular policies, tapping Western technological wizardry; and simply muddling through the multiple Soviet domestic crises.

By 1990, puzzling out Soviet policy was made even more difficult for the West by the lag of official statements behind the logic of Gorbachev's "new thinking" and by the new cacophony of voices under Gorbachev's glasnost. It was hard for Western military analysts to believe that the Soviet superpower, with its strategic nuclear arsenal and the largest army in Europe, really feared an utterly tame Bundeswehr that was under firm civilian control. If it did, however, and especially if it wanted to avoid any urge by Germans to acquire their own nuclear weapons, then it would have been much smarter for Moscow to bind Germany to NATO rather than detach it. This certainly was the explicit preference of the Poles,

Hungarians, and Czechoslovaks, expressed both unilaterally and in an unprecedentedly captious Warsaw Pact foreign ministers meeting in mid-March.

In this context the vehement public Soviet opposition to German membership in NATO that eventually emerged seemed inexplicably counterproductive. It could only increase the stakes in terms of Soviet prestige and make it even harder for Gorbachev to reverse course eventually without losing face. Yet Gorbachev's and Shevardnadze's negative pronouncements and backtracking continued.

Thus, even though Gorbachev had accepted in 1989 the guideline of bringing Soviet and Warsaw Pact heavy ground weapons down to NATO levels, in 1990 he balked at completing the Vienna negotiations to confirm this. Though Shevardnadze had agreed early on in contacts with the United States and West Germany that a formal peace treaty ending World War II was unnecessary, he resumed talking about just such a treaty at the first two plus four ministerial meeting in May. Although the Soviet foreign minister had paid an unprecedented, friendly visit to NATO headquarters one day, he sought a loosening of Germany from it the next in requesting German membership in both military alliances, or perhaps political but not military membership in NATO on the French pattern, or perhaps Soviet membership in NATO.[22]

The Soviet Union further slowed down its unilaterally planned troop withdrawals from the GDR in 1990, and spokesmen vacillated between attributing the deceleration to technical problems or to bargaining pressure on the West. Moscow proposed, variously, having an international referendum on German unification, neutralizing and demilitarizing a united Germany, having the CSCE take a leisurely decision on German unity in a year's time, arranging for oversight by the Soviet Union (and other World War II victors) even over domestic aspects of German union, leaving external security arrangements ambiguous even after the two Germanys merged, abolishing nuclear weapons in Europe, reducing nuclear weapons in Europe to a minimum, retaining a Guantanamo-type enclave of residual Soviet forces in eastern Germany, pulling out all American troops from Western Europe as all Soviet troops left Eastern Europe, and continuing to station Soviet and American troops on German soil.

All the Soviet suggestions seemed almost random, however: they never added up to any coherent alternative to the Western proposal. Nor did Gorbachev take advantage of the obvious opportunities to reinforce Modrow's insistence on neutrality or to go over the head of the Bonn government to court the West German Social Democrats as the Soviet Union had done in the early 1980s. Whether out of preoccupation with Kremlin infighting, the floundering Soviet economy, and Lithuania's gathering independence movement, or from a hunch that German anchoring in NATO would actually best serve Soviet interests, Gorbachev initially let the issue ride. The most precise expression of the core Soviet concern was Gorbachev's assertion in late February that while the two Germanys had a right to unity, Moscow too had an inalienable right to ensure that reunification did not lead to "moral, political, or economic damage" for the Soviet Union.[23]

Interpreting the Soviet response was made even harder by the pluralism of unofficial Western conversations with Russians. Vyacheslav Dashichev of Moscow's Institute of the Economies of the World Socialist System—the man who had correctly prophesied the end of the Brezhnev doctrine—told the newspaper *Die Welt* in March that the NATO issue was not a major problem.[24] Yet his voice was only one among dozens of contrary hardline comments, and the latter issued from the more authoritative Soviet specialists on Germany, including current and former ambassadors to Bonn and the senior Foreign Ministry official on German policy.[25]

NATO: If It Ain't Broke . . .

As they sifted the evidence, numerous senior Western analysts became convinced that the Kremlin would not yield on NATO membership, and they began advocating either alternatives or inaction. The father of containment, George Kennan, one of the first to react to the opening of the Berlin Wall, urged the United States to proceed with the utmost caution and postpone all decisions for several years.[26] Former National Security adviser and current Georgetown University professor Zbigniew Brzezinski envisaged an even longer period of perhaps twenty years in which NATO and Warsaw Pact forces would stay on in their respective Germanys.[27] Historian John Lewis Gaddis argued that the best solution would be double German membership in both NATO and the Warsaw Treaty Organization.[28]

Stanley Hoffmann, chairman of Harvard's Center for European Studies, foresaw the end both of an American-dominated NATO and of German acceptance of American occupation of Germany. He advocated emasculating NATO to its 1949 origins, before an integrated military command was set up. In his scenario the United States would maintain the American nuclear guarantee and a conventional presence in Europe, but the superpowers' main institutional link to Europe would be a strengthened CSCE that would also keep both great powers at arm's length. A new Western European defense organization would asume primary responsibility for Western European security, and the British and French would supplement American deterrence by extending their own nuclear umbrella over Germany.[29]

Hoffmann's Harvard colleague, Samuel Huntington, proposed that Germany belong to NATO but be largely disarmed.[30] University of Chicago strategist John Mearsheimer, worried that the stable bipolar world was now going to revert to an unstable scramble for balance-of-power advantage, went so far as to advise Germany to acquire its own nuclear weapons.[31] Columbia University political scientist Jack Snyder, concurring in the widespread view that NATO was bound to vanish as the Soviet threat and Warsaw Treaty Organization vanished, proposed primary supervision of German confederation by the European Community, warned against any union of the two German armies, and sought the perpetuation of two German states with guarantees of their sovereignty by the superpowers.[32] Various others, presuming that the Germans would ask American forces to leave once the country was unified—but also presuming that stability required the continued presence of U.S. forces in Europe—contended that France would have to give up its quarter-century distance from the NATO military command and invite American divisions to France.[33]

European recommendations were equally diverse, ranging from Otto von Habsburg's proposal for a full European federation, to German Social Democratic plans to substitute a CSCE system of collective security for NATO's collective defense, to Mitterrand's ambivalent wish to ensure the continued presence of American troops in Europe while reducing America's (and Germany's) political influence through his pet East-West European confederation with Gaullist overtones.[34]

In the end Bush rejected all radical innovation in NATO on the basis of the old American adage, "If it ain't broke, don't fix it." He raised smirks for stating that now that the Soviet Union was not the threat it used to be, NATO's main enemy was instability. But this longest lasting alliance in history did give the United States a familiar channel for insuring Western Europe against any Soviet return to military intimidation, acquisition of nuclear weapons by militant Soviet minorities, ethnic shoot-ups between East Europeans no longer restrained by the pax sovictica, or even an overbearing Germany. Moreover, NATO existed and had become a habit in American foreign policy. It did not have to be invented, and American public support for it did not have to be created from scratch. U.S. troops would clearly be reduced in Europe under the new conditions, but voters' willingness to pay for the ones that remained would not have to be generated anew.

Throughout this period Bonn too opted to interpret each new Soviet rejection of German membership in NATO primarily as rhetoric for domestic Soviet consumption, and to stick to the Genscher plan without budging. In countering the Soviet abhorrence of German membership in his own multiple meetings with Shevardnadze, Genscher also played to some extent on Soviet anxiety about that potential loose cannon. His "strongest argument was always . . . we must not do anything provisionally. . . . There must be no questions left open for a united Germany."[35] After each meeting with his Soviet counterpart, Genscher accentuated the positive to reporters and observed that the Russians had not yet said their last word.

The Conference on Security and Cooperation in Europe

To help encourage that desired last word, both Americans and West Germans sought to maximize the area of East-West cooperation. One obvious arena for this was an enhanced CSCE. Beginning in February, Genscher energetically lobbied the United States to offer the Soviets a kind of pan-European security council that would guarantee them a voice in European affairs even after their troops left Eastern Europe.

Baker was skeptical. The CSCE had been a political football in the United States ever since its initial Helsinki conference got caught up in the ideological battles that eventually brought Ronald Reagan to the White House. The American right considered the Helsinki Final Act of 1975 a sellout that legitimized Soviet-imposed postwar borders in Europe.

Yet in the intervening years, the minimal statement on human rights inserted into the Helsinki agreement at the insistence of the West Europeans had stimulated astonishing ferment inside the closed East European regimes. A series of ad hoc review conferences had kept the spotlight on repression of dissidents, and governments that finally acknowledged the legitimacy of foreign states' interest in their human rights performance had kept releasing political prisoners in order to avoid international criticism. This, in turn, emboldened more citizens to discover and speak their minds.

The fateful Hungarian decisions to dismantle the barbed wire on the Austrian border in May and not to force East German emigrants to return to the GDR in August 1989 could both be traced in part to the moral suasion of the CSCE. More broadly, Western assurances at Helsinki that the East-West borders were inviolable (though not unchangeable if peaceful means were used) had allowed Solidarity to spring up and demand domestic change in Poland without fearing exploitation of any resulting Polish crisis by German "revanchists." Helsinki—and the rise of the unorthodox Mikhail Gorbachev to lead the Soviet Union—paved the way for the peaceful revolution of 1989 throughout Eastern Europe.

In retrospect, the Americans acknowledged the CSCE's political virtues. In the realm of security, however, they certainly did not want utopian ideas about vague collective security among erstwhile adversaries to replace NATO's proven commitment to collective defense among democratic friends. Initially, also, they were wary lest Genscher try to substitute the CSCE for NATO, or let Soviet troops stay on in the GDR without any departure deadline in an effort to help Gorbachev. Such an ambiguous arrangement, Washington thought, could threaten stability by generating pressures—from German citizens wishing to be rid of the Soviet forces—to get rid of Western allied troops as well as a price for hastening Soviet withdrawal.

The United States therefore rejected any grandiose ideas of a European security council with real powers. Once the Americans were persuaded that Genscher intended the CSCE to supplement rather than supplant NATO, however, and that Bonn would eventually pin down Moscow on the removal of Soviet divisions from the GDR, they saw no harm in elevating the CSCE modestly. They agreed to the CSCE summit at the end of 1990 that Moscow had proposed—if the Vienna agreement on conventional arms control were already signed and ready to be endorsed by the summit. They reckoned that giving the floating CSCE conferences some regularity—and even permanence in the form of a small secretariat—would not challenge the rationale of NATO. If this then helped Gorbachev sell Soviet retreat from East Germany and Eastern Europe in the Kremlin, so much the better.

Still, no Westerner knew where the Soviets might, in the American phrase, draw the line in the sand. Some said at the preservation of the Warsaw Treaty Organization. Some said at the line of demarcation between the Soviets' external empire in Central Europe and internal empire in the Baltics. No one knew for sure. In the end even the most optimistic Westerners would be surprised that the Soviets did not drive a much tougher bargain.

Chapter 14

Meanwhile, Domestic Politics

On February 13 and 14, with the sensational news about two plus four still reverberating, Prime Minister Hans Modrow and representatives of the roundtable made their first and last official visit to Bonn. To Kohl, Modrow was already nothing more than a footnote in history. He was dragging his feet on liberalizing the economy; he was manipulating the election laws, Kohl thought, in trying to shut West German politicians out of the campaign; he had done his best to perpetuate the *Stasi*; and, as he now told the chancellor, he no longer got any response from the bureaucracy when he issued orders. Collapse threatened, and Modrow could not avert it. Kohl received his counterpart brusquely, and did not bestow on the GDR the gift of DM 15 billion ($9 billion) that both Modrow and the roundtable suggested would be useful.

As a result, during their exchange in Bonn, the two sides did little more than set up a joint commission to plan details of financial, economic, and social union. Back home, the disappointed roundtable resumed drafting a new East German constitution that would not only enshrine democracy's traditional negative freedoms from coercion, but would also perpetuate all the positive socialist rights to work and housing that liberal constitutions eschew as unenforceable. Meanwhile Kohl got on with coordinating joint tactics on the external aspects of unification with Bush. Inevitably, the external aspect most in the public eye was Poland.

The Polish Complaint

The one great postwar reconciliation still pending in 1990 was that between Poland and Germany. Israel and West Germany had long since

192

developed their special relationship.[1] France and West Germany had long since concluded their alliance within the alliance, even if Mitterrand was currently possessed of the seven-year itch. Even the Soviet Union and the Federal Republic had worked out a modus vivendi, and by the late 1980s Bonn was in many ways Moscow's most understanding partner in the West.

Only Poland, the country that had suffered the highest percentage of casualties at the hands of the Nazis, remained unreconciled with West Germany. Relations were correct, but far from cordial. The reason was the legally unsettled Polish–East German border, left over from the Yalta and Potsdam conferences' awarding of the eastern third of prewar Poland to the Soviet Union, with compensating German lands attached to Poland in the west.[2]

In reality, the Polish boundary had been a nonissue in the Federal Republic for a long time. Despite occasional fiery rhetoric from the older generation, the once powerful West German associations of the 12 million postwar expellees from the eastern territories had by the 1980s been tamed into folklore and nostalgia clubs. The Federal Republic's overwhelmingly middle-class voters had no interest whatever in recovering poor, polluted Silesian provinces. Bonn had pledged not to change the boundary by force, both in its treaty of 1970 normalizing relations with Poland and, more generally, in the 1975 Conference on Security and Cooperation in Europe agreement.

The Federal Republic had always maintained, however, that final legal recognition of the Oder-Neisse border would have to await a government that could speak for a united Germany. The West German conservatives, in particular, had stressed this position after they came to power in 1982, and some of the Bavarians in the Christian Democratic Union's (CDU) sister party of the Christian Social Union were even insisting that the 1937 German boundaries—with Silesia, Pomerania, and the Sudetenland as part of Germany—were the proper legal ones.

Kohl himself, while certainly not endorsing the claims of the handful of extremists, had always avoided confrontation with them. He had never joined Foreign Minister Genscher and one bold Christian Democratic member of parliament in wanting to give Poland firm political, if not legal, guarantees on the permanence of the border.[3] He had also displayed insensitivity in fall 1989 on his goodwill visit to Poland in scheduling a meeting with ethnic Germans at the site of German-Polish boundary skirmishes in the 1920s.

Even after the opening of the Berlin Wall, Kohl did not change his public stance. He did not address the boundary issue in his ten points of November 28. He went slightly further than ever before in mid-January, telling an audience at the French Institute for International Relations in

Paris that Bonn supported "secure borders" for Poland. With an eye to the far right Republicans' 5 percent threshold, however, he still did not specify that those secure borders must run along the existing Oder-Neisse line.[4] Instead, he left it to his entourage to say privately that even the expellee organizations would soon have to admit that forfeiting claims on Polish lands was the necessary small price to pay for the incredible unification of the German heartland. The realization would just need a certain time (as well as Republican losses in regional elections) to sink in, his advisers noted.

The new noncommunist prime minister in Poland, Tadeusz Mazowiecki, was eager to turn his country away from Moscow toward the West, and knew that Bonn was the key to this shift. He was by nature pragmatic and was initially disinclined to prod Kohl into what the chancellor considered politically risky statements. As one of his first acts in office, Mazowiecki even joined other Polish and German Roman Catholics in a placatory gesture in September 1989, signing an unprecedented expression of sympathy for the suffering of German expellees in the mid-1940s.

The sudden prospect of German unification and the bolt-out-of-the-blue two plus four announcement in February, however, strained Mazowiecki's patience. He now campaigned to get a Polish seat at the negotiating table, a full peace treaty with the Federal Republic, and an unambiguous boundary settlement before unification day. As media alarm about a new Yalta mushroomed in Poland, he no longer accepted Kohl's distinction between legality and politics on the frontier issue. By February 21, in the run-up to Kohl's visit to Washington, he went so far as to tell reporters that Soviet troops should stay on in Poland as a guarantee against "the German problem."[5] Even West German officials favorably disposed to Poland were irritated.

For his part, Bush believed Kohl's private assurances that Bonn had no intention of revising the border, whatever the sensitivities about a public commitment to the Oder-Neisse line, and the American president told Warsaw so bluntly. As a favor to the Poles (in Chicago as well as in Krakow), he was willing to address the issue in public, but he was not willing to pillory the Germans over it. Nor was he willing to back the Poles' insistence that the boundary be nailed down legally before German unification. This restraint was appreciated by the Germans, criticized by numerous American commentators, and identified later by various American officials as one of the correctly judged nuances in U.S. support for German unification.[6]

The whole feud burst upon the American scene on February 25, in the joint Kohl-Bush press conference at which the National Security Council (NSC) was engineering Kohl's declaration of support for membership of a united Germany in NATO. The joint statement proceeded as planned, and then reporters bombarded Kohl with questions about his position on the Polish border. "No one has any intention of linking the question of national unity to the change of existing borders," he asserted, but he would not make an unambiguous pledge not to do so. Instead, he reiterated that only a freely elected parliament representing the whole of Germany would be the "legally competent sovereign" able to declare the permanence of the boundary. Bush intervened to state American recognition of the existing Polish border, but declared that he saw no difference between Washington and Bonn.[7] The American media focused on the dramatic Polish border issue almost to the exclusion of the NSC's carefully crafted declaration on NATO.

Back home, Kohl did accede to another Bundestag declaration that Germans had no claims on Polish territory, and committed his government to joint Bundestag and Volkskammer political declarations about the inviolability of the Polish boundary after the GDR elections.[8] However, he then offset this concession by linking it to a renunciation of German war reparations for Poles and to a treaty guaranteeing the rights of the German ethnic minority in Poland. In fact, the West Germans had given generous sums (some called it ransom) to buy the emigration of 200,000 ethnic Germans from Poland to the Federal Republic in the 1970s, but Bonn had never been willing to pay token compensation to Poles whom the Nazis had impressed into forced labor. To Poles the raising of the issues of money and the German minority sounded like cheap haggling, and even awakened memories of Hitler's championing of German minorities in the 1930s.

Something of an international firestorm broke over the question. Few went as far as Lech Walesa in implicitly envisioning a nuclear strike by neighbors on the Germans should the Germans again destabilize Europe.[9] But those who suspected the worst of the Germans saw their fears confirmed and vented all their anxieties in almost cathartic fashion. West German diplomats asked under their breath—the old Foreign Ministry-Chancellery frictions were again apparent—whether the Germans had gotten so close to their goal of unity only to have Kohl rekindle all the old mistrust of Germans throwing their weight around.

In the end, the tempest served some useful functions. It did win for the Poles a seat at the two plus four table for any discussion of their western border (if not, as they had hoped, for discussion of Germany's military status or for any formal peace treaty). It put outside pressure on Kohl that he could use to help persuade his right wing to give up idle Silesian dreams for real Brandenburg and Saxon unity. It sparked public discussion about what needed to be changed in the West German constitution to forswear irredentist claims in the future. It chastened the West Germans into somewhat more subdued conduct in diplomacy. It induced the Bonn government to be more meticulous in soliciting European tolerance for each new step toward unity rather than confronting Germany's neighbors with a fait accompli each time. It convinced Kohl that however unfair he might think it for foreigners to hold the Federal Republic to more exacting standards than other governments forty-five years after a war and holocaust that were not the doing of today's Germans, this judgment was a fact of diplomacy; to indulge in self-pity over it would only aggravate resentments. Eventually, the tempest even elicited identical statements from both German parliaments renouncing claims on Polish territory in pledges that awaited only the final seal by the future united German government.

The Polish diversion may also have marked, finally, the return to normality for the Germans after World War II. It did not and could not remove the special demand for contrition by the Germans for the sins of their grandfathers, nor the special responsibilities (as distinct from guilt) that German statesmen see history placing on them for decades to come. Yet when it was all over, with the Oder-Neisse line guaranteed after all, with the united Germans still in NATO and still leading the drive for postnational European integration, a new era began. Germany was no longer a political dwarf.

The Polish affair also gave the French—or could have given them—a means to reposition themselves as Germany's friends after their sulk of previous months. Mitterrand, however, instead of assuming the role of quiet counselor to Kohl on behalf of the Poles, played the issue to the grandstand against the Germans. He had no more intention than did Thatcher and Gorbachev of sharing the prestige of full two plus four seats with lesser nations, but on March 9 he ostentatiously met with Mazowiecki, Polish Foreign Minister Krzysztof Skubiszewski, and even the communist president of Poland, Wojciech Jaruzelski. He told reporters that the Bundestag declaration of the day before—which had again failed to name the Oder-Neisse as the border—was insufficient. He called for international regulation of the Polish boundary before unification, talked of a four-power role in guaranteeing the boundary, and promoted the equivalent of the peace treaty that was anathema to Bonn.[10] Then just before the East German election (which everyone still expected to favor the Social Democrats), Mitterrand received in Paris Kohl's likely next Social Democratic challenger, Saarland Premier Oskar Lafontaine. Various commentators speculated about a new Paris-Warsaw axis.

Like Mitterrand—but even more insultingly, since her remarks came a week after the GDR election—Margaret Thatcher also used the Polish issue to rap German knuckles. In an interview with *Der Spiegel* on March 26, she cast doubt on Kohl's willingness to recognize the border, offered a British guarantee for it, and declared German signing of a boundary treaty with Poland to be a necessary precondition for German unity.[11]

The Election Upset

Such external issues hardly impinged on the campaign for the March 18 election in the GDR. The feud about Poland's western boundary did not bother the East Germans, who tended to be more anti-Polish in personal contacts than the West Germans but certainly had no designs on the opposite banks of the Oder and Neisse rivers. Nor did the whirlwind of two plus four diplomacy find much resonance among voters already focused on pocketbook issues. Similarly, Kohl's curt treatment of Modrow and rejection of the GDR's request for DM 15 billion seemed to agitate West German media rather more than East German citizens.

What did count in the election was unification, yet what this would mean in party terms was far from clear. All the opinion polls indicated a victory for the new and untainted Social Democrats, and much of the media commentary pointed out that such an outcome would be a natural resumption of the region's prewar, pre-Nazi tradition.[12] The communists' formidable wealth and organization could not be written off, however, and the imminence of the election hardly gave the fledgling parties time to recruit staffs, let alone sort out policy prescriptions.

Even master politician Kohl was at first uncertain how to proceed. He paid no more attention than any other Western politician to Modrow's and the roundtable's ban on West German interference in the East German campaign and party funding, but he hesitated before deciding precisely how to engage in GDR politics. He did not want to tarnish his West German Christian Democratic Union by identifying it with the East German CDU bloc party (which in early 1990 was pulling only 7 percent in rudimentary opinion polls), nor was he sure where Lothar de Maizière stood after the new CDU-East chairman had joined and stayed in Modrow's government and told television interviewers (in mid-November) about his enthusiasm for socialism in the GDR. Certainly the CDU-East wanted to proceed with unification much more slowly than the CDU-West. By the opening of the GDR's election campaign, the Western Christian Democrats solidly backed immediate East German accession to the Federal Republic under article 23 of West Germany's Basic Law (constitution). The Eastern Christian Democrats were still contemplating using article 146, as the Social Democrats were advocating. The latter route assumed a tabula rasa: the new constitution for Germany as a whole would be written from scratch by the joining parties.

Kohl solved his dilemma by knocking East German heads together in early February and forcing a coalition, Alliance for Germany, between the CDU-East and two small new parties, the Democratic Awakening and the German Social Union, a conservative party to the right of the CDU in the mold of the Bavarian Christian Social Union. The Alliance thus allowed the conservatives to benefit from the inherited organization of the CDU-East, while still denying that the Alliance had any past as a satellite of the Socialist Unity party. A week before the election the Eastern Christian Democrats finally accepted the route of article 23.[13] Just days before the election Kohl's forcing of a conservative coalition almost backfired, when it was revealed that the chairman of Democratic Awakening had been a high-ranking informer for the secret police.

However murky the Eastern parties, the campaign clarified the choice in the election. The conservatives favored fast, uncomplicated unification, with the extensive West German social net, but without all the GDR's nurseries, uneconomically low rents, and guaranteed jobs for all who conformed to the system.[14] They ruled out, as they kept reminding voters allergic to the term, any kind of socialism, and they lost no opportunity to hang on the neck of the SPD-West the albatross of the party's earlier eagerness for dialogue with the old SED. They also had the advantage of controlling Bonn's purse strings and of personifying the respected authority of the Federal Republic in Chancellor Helmut Kohl.

The SPD-West faced an obverse dilemma to Kohl's in deciding whether or not to support the total unknowns who had founded its namesake party the previous fall. It quickly concluded that it had no choice but to do so, and Brandt even preceded Kohl in campaigning in a major way in the East. On the controversy over article 23 versus article 146, the West German Social Democrats generally favored article 146, arguing for a slow process that would preserve the GDR's identity, allow fundamental rethinking, and perhaps reopen all the old political issues of expanding the Federal Republic's social guarantees constitutionally. The left-wing leader of the SPD-East, Ibrahim Böhme, agreed, and although his coworkers were split on the issue, East German voters saw the choice as black and white. The Social Democrats only reinforced this image by targeting the conservatives rather than the hated communists as their primary opponents, and by the constant disparagement of unification by West German chancellor candidate-apparent Lafontaine.

As it turned out, the takeover by West German parties of the GDR campaign seemed to attract rather than repel the voters. They knew the Western politicians from television better than they knew their own, formerly reclusive, politicians, and they certainly trusted the West Germans more. In this sense Kohl's and Brandt's appearances in Erfurt and Rostock served to reassure the East German public that Christian Democratic Chairman Lothar de Maizière and Social Democratic Chairman Ibrahim Böhme were not pawns of the communists. Random interviews suggested that voters complained about interference by West German politicians (if at all) only in the case of parties they opposed, but found it natural that

Bonn politicians from whatever party they supported should help their colleagues in the East.

Once the parties made their basic decisions, the campaign ran largely as might have been expected. With the fear of a communist restoration almost gone—it would take the palpable sensation of the free election itself to vanquish fully the angst of decades—everyday worries dominated. Saying that there was a sobering of euphoria would be inaccurate, since—apart from the very personal emotion of November 9 and a curmudgeonly grumbling about the lack of support for unification from allies—there had been no national euphoria to begin with. What did reign, though, was a sober, utilitarian yearning to hitch onto the Western prosperity and freedom to travel. East Germans fretted that they might get left behind in the unfamiliar Western free-for-all, but they calculated that the one thing worse than being exploited by West Germany would be not being exploited by West Germany. They therefore opted for what the orthodox left derided as "deutsche mark nationalism," but the revisionist left welcomed as a gain in common sense and a vast improvement over the old chauvinism.[15]

The communists, in their new incarnation as the Party of Democratic Socialism, resigned themselves to a future minority position even before Modrow was voted out. They adopted the stance of a populist opposition ready to lead strikes and highlight all the social and economic inequities of whatever transition the new government might attempt. In the Volkskammer they used the last days of their majority to pass a series of dubious laws—such as letting the old communist bureaucrats review their employment dossiers to destroy incriminating material, and writing trick clauses into legislation to channel profits from foreign industries secretly owned by the party into party and not state coffers—that further revised the once favorable Western view of Modrow. "A wonderful party!" mused SPD parliamentary leader Richard Schröder later about the communists, as more and more such sleights of hand came to light. "Idealists at the top and all 'slit-ears' [con men] down below!"[16]

On March 18, in defiance of the forecasts, the East Germans echoed Konrad Adenauer's old campaign slogan of "no [more] experiments." They voted against raw, reformed, or any other kind of socialist experiment, and for the known economic and political success of the Federal Republic. The impressive 93 percent who cast their ballots gave a landslide 48 percent plurality to the conservatives, 5 percent to the Liberals (who, as in West Germany, immediately joined the conservative coalition), and only 22 percent to the Social Democrats. The revamped communists of the Party of Democratic Socialism got 16 percent. The new-left Alliance 90 and Greens/Independent Women, who prided themselves on having started the East German revolution, got 5 percent between them.

The voters thus signaled their wish to unify Germany as fast as possible. Yet they also put a check on both East and West Germany's ruling conservatives in the form of a strong Social Democratic minority that the conservatives would need to engage before they could attain the two-thirds majority required to amend the GDR's constitution. It was a textbook democratic finish.[17]

A bitterly disillusioned Bärbel Bohley saw the conservative triumph as the end of the GDR's infant democracy, "with the voter behaving like a sheep again, yet fondly imagining he is taking part in his first free elections."[18] East Berlin communist reformers, still regarding political harmony as the desired norm and mistrusting a naked clash of interests as dirty, also echoed, unconsciously, Bertolt Brecht's sardonic comment after the 1953 uprising that the government needed to elect a new people.

Yet for the majority the process was profoundly moving. One woman said she felt almost giddy as she voted. A companion said he felt awe at doing something that really mattered as he declared his political faith in democracy with his ballot. An octogenarian had a sense of seeing the world put right as she voted again in a free election for the first time since 1933. A nineteen-year-old political neophyte approved the clarity of the outcome.[19]

Moreover, after forty years and the loss from the GDR of three and a half million people, a fifth of the population, the ultimate vote of confidence was registered by foot. Emigration from the GDR after March 18 dropped to a third of its preelection rate. Apparently most East Germans still saw a chance of establishing their identity, as fully franchised citizens of a united Germany.

De Maizière, the most stunned of anyone by his election as prime minister, fit the axiom that East German conservatives were more left, Social Democrats more right, than their West German counterparts. He turned out to be a typical violist, amateur musicians noted, just irascible enough to stand up to the Christian Democratic paymasters in Bonn when he felt East German interests required it, but in the end helpless to resist Bonn's sheer power. One of his main Social Democratic partners, Richard Schröder, fit the axiom as well. Together, right and left in East Berlin formulated common positions on the approaching currency union, harmonization legislation—and even "provisional" NATO membership, if NATO changed—with a minimum of crises.

In its first sitting, the Volkskammer asked Israel for forgiveness for the Nazi holocaust against the Jews and for the "hypocrisy and hostility" of earlier GDR governments on the subject. In his first government statement, de Maizière approved full economic and social union with the Federal Republic by summer.

Within days after the election, Böhme, like Democratic Awakening Chairman Wolfgang Schnur just before the election, had to bow out of politics as his long career as a *Stasi* informer was revealed. The more pragmatic remainder of the SPD-East voted to form a grand coalition with the conservatives to build a two-thirds majority, amend the GDR's constitution, and prepare for unity. East-West German negotiations were quickly concluded and July set as the date for economic and social union; new negotiations began on the final treaty of full political union.[20]

As the new dispensation settled in, there was no night of the long knives against the former rulers. There were, however, continuing revelations about the cruelties of the old regime and its Soviet patron. Only after the election did people who had been confined to psychiatric wards by the *Stasi* have the courage to recount their histories. Only after the election did mothers whose children had been seized from them and put up for adoption fourteen years earlier—after the mothers had tried to "flee from the republic"—dare to tell their stories. Only after the election was it revealed that the uranium mining operations of the Soviet-German Wismut Joint Stock Company in Saxony had killed thousands of locals and produced radioactive toxic waste that would persist for 1,600 years. Only afterward did accounts come out of staged accidents to kill off East German sports stars who defected to the West, of forced sterilization and lobotomies of mental patients, of rushed delivery of terminally ill patients to East Berlin's *Stasi*-connected Charité Hospital so their organs might be used posthumously. Only afterward did those who had witnessed mass burials by the Soviet occupiers in the late 1940s dare speak out about them. Graves at Bautzen, Fünfeichen, and other stations of the German gulag were dug up. Bones were unearthed, not only of old Nazis, but also of "class enemies" from the "bourgeois elite," an estimated 50,000 in all, who had been killed or succumbed to famine and disease as prisoners' rations were deliberately reduced to below subsistence level in internment camps.[21]

The Left's Complaint

One of the unsung accomplishments of the East German revolution—which gradually became apparent after the election—was the tentative rapprochement between right and left it offered Germany, through the agonizing crisis on the left. Reconciliation had begun with the common joy of November 9. The revolution was greeted instantly as the answer not only to the division of 1945, but also to the aborted revolution of 1848, to Europe's long "civil" war that had started in 1914, and to the Germans' failure to resist Hitler during the twelve years of the Third Reich. It was further seen as the answer to the bad conscience of the West Germans, who had never seized democracy for themselves, but had been handed it as a gift by their Western conquerors and occupiers.

Now the peaceful revolution in the GDR showed that Germans too could, in the cause of democracy and freedom, shed their excessive deference to authority, and could demythologize and nullify their own authoritarianism without waiting for others to do it for them. It also reassured a rather self-doubting West Germany that its own values were worthy of admiration and emulation. And it gave any restless souls who might be yearning for a metaphysical identity plenty to keep them busy in the enormous task of rebuilding the East German economy and polity.

Approaching German unity strengthened the West German center by assuring Kohl's reelection and steady German adherence to the Western alliance. The chancellor shot up in opinion polls as the incumbent (and beneficiary of a booming economy) when the miracle occurred, and as the keeper of the grail of unification over the years.

In electoral terms, imminent German union also bound the swing-vote Liberals to Kohl's center-right coalition and neutralized the far right, which could have played a spoiler role had it passed the 5 percent hurdle of votes needed to enter the Bundestag. Liberal allegiance was not a real question, of course. The voters' preference for stability and the backbiting within the Free Democratic party that accompanies each defection of the Liberals from the conservatives to the Social Democrats and back has established a decade as the rule-of-thumb length for Liberal alliance with right or left. A switch back to the Social Democrats was therefore unlikely to be posed until 1992, midway between elections, ten years after the Free Democrats had last jumped from left to right. In this context the prospect of unity only reinforced the trend by giving the Free Democrats the added incentive of wanting to stay in the government and share in the glory of managing unification.

The threat to Kohl of the far-right Republicans looked more serious before November 9. They were no Aryan supremacists, no nationalists in the old sense of seeking German dominance over neighbors. Indeed, their dislike of ethnic Germans from Kazakhstan, and even East German immigrants, was as strong as their dislike of Turks and Yugoslavs. In domestic politics they resented equally the competition of all guest workers for jobs and housing within West Germany. In foreign policy their bland slogan of putting Germany before Europe veiled chauvinist resistance to European integration.

Given the rise and precipitous fall of the far-right National Democratic party twenty years earlier, mainstream politicians were confident that the Republicans too would eventually fade away. They worried, however, about how long the decline might take. They feared that the Republicans might well peak during the December 1990 elections, enter parliament, and deprive Kohl of a working majority.

As it turned out, Kohl's rush toward unification in 1990 (and, he seemed to think, his verbal ambiguity over the Polish border) totally preempted the Republicans' subliminal nationalist appeal. In retrospect, it became clear that the Republicans had peaked in the first half of 1989 in the West Berlin and European Parliament elections, then dwindled even in local votes to 3.4 percent in the Saarland in January 1990 and less than 2.0 percent in North Rhine–Westphalia and Lower Saxony in May 1990.

Beyond sheer electoral mathematics, approaching German unification also began to bridge the whole right-left schism that had bedeviled West German politics to a greater or lesser extent ever since Adenauer had forced his countrymen to choose the sure defense of the Western alliance over the chimera of Soviet-sponsored neutral reunification.[22] The first West German chancellor's thesis that only an unambiguous Western identity could eventually secure German unity had been mocked by left nationalists over the years as a Rhinelander's anti-German casuistry that had forfeited unification. Social Democrats under Kurt Schumacher had deliberately seized on this issue to establish the patriotic credentials of their party, which had previously taken a drubbing for its international priorities. In the early 1950s, in the name of reunification, the SPD had bitterly fought West German rearmament and membership in NATO. Thereafter, there had always been a certain tension for the Social Democrats—sometimes tacit, sometimes explicit—between their security and German policies.

To be sure, the SPD had made its peace with a West German army and Western alliance in the landmark Bad Godesberg program of 1959 rejecting dogmatic Marxism. In the 1970s, it was conservatives much more than Social Democrats who had polarized politics by branding Social Democratic Chancellor Willy Brandt's conciliatory *Ostpolitik* as a betrayal, until the conservatives regained the Chancellery in the 1980s and themselves adopted Brandt's policy of "small steps" in dealing directly with Honecker.

Nevertheless, the ideological nostalgia and bitterness of the West German left remained. The left admired what it saw as the old-fashioned, unspoiled idyll of East German villages; thought the division of Germany was fitting moral punishment for the Holocaust; maintained a utopian view of the GDR's possibilities; and hoped, in common with prominent East Berlin intellectuals, for that compassionate third way. In moments of stress, the SPD longed to get back to its original pacifist ideals, even if this reversion risked shaking the domestic consensus on security and loosening Bonn's ties to the West.

In this vein, during the feud over deploying new American nuclear missiles in Germany in the early 1980s, the SPD's left wing and the Greens deplored the American nuclear presence in the Federal Republic as a victimization of Germans that was little better morally than Soviet hegemony in Eastern Europe. The party opened a dialogue with the SED as if the latter held no repressive monopoly on government but were a fellow party in a pluralist system, and signed joint appeals with the SED for various nuclear- and chemical-weapons-free zones that ran counter to Western alliance policy. Some revived the old charge that Adenauer's alliance with the West had sacrificed German unity, while neutrality might have won it from Stalin. Some even came close to considering peace and continued alliance with the West as incompatible. With political attitudes among twenty- to forty-year-olds shaped during the wave of revulsion at U.S. intervention in Vietnam, this new left frequently made blanket condemnations of the United States—in mirror image of the Reagan administration's condemnation of it—that carried overtones of German hubris in the early twentieth century about the spiritual superiority of German culture over Western civilization.[23]

Among prominent politicians this inclination was most marked in Oskar Lafontaine, the SPD leader in the Saarland, who in the early 1980s was being groomed to become the party's candidate for chancellor in 1990. At that time, while other SPD spokesmen were qualifying their opposition to NATO's new nuclear missiles by pledging continued support for the NATO alliance, Lafontaine was vigorously advocating West German withdrawal from the NATO military command on the French model. He dropped his bid for West German aloofness from NATO only after Kohl was reelected in 1983, Reagan and Gorbachev subsequently moved toward agreement to scrap all the superpowers' intermediate-range missiles, and nuclear weapons ceased to be an acute issue in the Federal Republic.

In early fall 1989, in the opening skirmishing for the 1990 election, the SPD again began gearing up for what could have turned into a major quasi-nationalist campaign, running against limitations on German sovereignty imposed by the British, French, and, especially, American allies in low-level training flights and against the extensive damage to property during maneuvers. With the Soviet threat gone, they argued, it was demeaning for the West to continue these impositions on the Federal Republic.

Paradoxically, the left nationalist corollary in the German question turned out to be increasing SPD insistence that Bonn recognize the permanent division of Germany into two states. Egon Bahr, the architect of *Ostpolitik* under Willy Brandt, articulated the view that German unity could be achieved ultimately only by accepting the reality of two equally sovereign states for the foreseeable future, and by persuading the Soviet Union, through sweeteners if necessary, to let each of the two go its own way. In this view, the key to German unification lay in Moscow, and Moscow had to be assuaged.

Though the Greens and one portion of the Social Democratic left criticized the SPD for ignoring the suppressed human rights of East German dissidents, the more numerous antinationalists among the left Social Democrats found Bahr's position compatible with their own. For their part, centrist SPD leaders did not contest such an abstract policy, as everyone still deemed it, of such low salience. Upgrading East-West German representation to formal ambassadorial level and canceling the Federal Republic's offer of instant West German citizenship to any East German asking for it became SPD policy almost by default.

With November 9, however, the left's world was shattered. Adenauer's original hypothesis was vindicated. The now risible SPD dialogue with an SED that East Germans themselves rejected gave Kohl a handy stick with which to beat his rivals. And once censorship was lifted and the East Germans began voicing their pent-up grievances, it became clear that in the supposed idyll of the GDR a fifth of the apartments were certified uninhabitable; a fifth of its water was certified undrinkable; sulphur dioxide air pollution was quintuple West German levels; official blackmail, instead of prosecution, of criminals was routine; East Berlin's Schönefeld Airport was a center for drug running; the GDR harbored West German terrorist fugitivies; and the country's main nuclear reactor near Greifswald had an alarming history of hushed-up accidents, one of which had come within a hair of meltdown.[24]

Both main planks of the West German left—that is, West German sovereignty in military affairs and full recognition of the GDR—were thus rendered obsolete by the gathering German unification. The first was eclipsed in the minds of voters by the much more gripping issue of union, and was then preempted by American insistence—to the Soviet Union, as well as to Britain and France—that the unified German state indeed gain complete sovereignty. And the bankruptcy of the SED regime left nothing to recognize and made the West German left's romantic vision look naive.

Under the circumstances, a fierce row erupted on the left over fundamental orientation and operational policy. West Berlin novelist Peter Schneider, writing in the Berlin countercultural daily *Tageszeitung*,[25] and (more sensationally) Brandt's wife, Brigitte Seebacher-Brandt, writing in the conservative *Frankfurter Allgemeine Zeitung*,[26] began the debate only days after the Berlin Wall fell.

Schneider, a Maoist back in the halcyon days of 1968, faulted his fellow leftists for having cast a blind eye to the inhumanity of the old East German regime. Seebacher-Brandt contended that while the left might remain ideologically pure in opposing German unity, it could do so only at the cost of again being repudiated by public opinion. Novelist Günter Grass, rebutting Seebacher-Brandt and other left revisionists, argued, on moral grounds, that Hitler had forfeited any German right to patriotism.

Yet philosopher Peter Sloterdijk asked, with some surprise, "When were the Germans less ugly than today?" Writer Hans Magnus Enzensberger challenged the left's (and his own previous) contempt for quotidian bourgeois concerns and contrasted the "hysteria" of elite left intellectuals after the Berlin Wall fell to the "dimension of insight and common sense" displayed by middle-class East Germans "in an extremely tense and potentially dangerous situation."[27]

No policy consensus emerged from the left polemics in time to help the SPD in the elections, and the party conducted both its East German and its pan-German campaigns in a kind of schizophrenia. On the one hand, Willy Brandt embraced German unity as a natural development. He became an elder statesman, and even developed a certain personal closeness to Chancellor Kohl.[28] On the other hand, Oskar Lafontaine, though a favorite political "grandson" of Brandt, continued to resist unification. He appealed to discontent among West German taxpayers about having to bankroll East German immigrants immediately and a rise in the GDR's standard of living later. Still other Social Democrats, fearing that their party would repeat history and again alienate voters by an antinational stance, proposed even faster confederation than Kohl was advocating.

The SPD's manifest difficulty in coming to grips with the German question and its implications was only part of a broader crisis that beset the intellectual left with the fall of the wall.[29] That crisis was the more acute since the intellectual mainstream in the Federal Republic had flowed to the left ever since the Nazis had discredited the right, and so—unlike in Czechoslovakia, Poland, and Hungary—had the mainstream in the GDR. West German literati were by no means all disciples of the new left gurus Herbert Marcuse, Theodor Adorno, and Max Horkheimer. Nor had they ever embraced the communist faith in the way French literati did (or experienced the obverse loss of faith and revulsion toward communist dogma as the French did under the impact of Solzhenitsyn in the 1970s). Nevertheless, the views of the antiestablishment 1968 generation—replete with disillusionment with the United States and guilt about unearned German prosperity and insufficient purgation—dominated within the articulating class. A sometimes healthy, sometimes unhealthy, skepticism about the practice of democracy in West Germany prevailed, and there were even echoes of the Weimar intellectuals' disastrous contempt for politics.

The impact of this left orthodoxy was greater than any comparable intellectual fashion in the United States because of the greater deference to intellectuals in Germany, the greater homogeneity of the shapers of public discourse—in a continuum encompassing the writers of belles lettres and many of the more popular political commentators—and the German proclivity to certainty and abstraction. Well into 1990, the romanticizing of the GDR's potential (and then lost potential) that Peter Schneider and others decried continued to complement West German intellectuals' mistrust of the Federal Republic's democracy. Moreover, anticommunism was a sin that few intellectuals wanted to be accused of.

Bitterly protesting the moral and political risks of such cerebration, one elderly Polish Jew who had lost most of his family to the Nazis complained pointedly, "When a forest burns, German intellectuals spend all their time discussing the deeper meaning of fire instead of helping to put the damned thing out."[30]

Unification broke this orthodoxy of the left. The shift was first evident in the pages of Die Zeit and Der Spiegel. As more and more revelations of the GDR's chamber of horrors came to light, Die Zeit's editors explicitly retracted their earlier rosy depictions of the GDR as a society that, unlike the commercialized West, still had time for humanity. Die Zeit's literary critic, Ulrich Greiner, also devalued East German novelist Christa Wolf's work, saying it had received inflated praise because Western critics had wanted to support East German writers in their delicate situation and had therefore treated them with kid gloves.[31]

Der Spiegel, in which irony is all and sacred cows are identifiable by their conspicuous exemption from irony, made no such confessions of past errors, but changed its views nonetheless. Editor Rudolf Augstein, who had happily satirized everything but Gorbachev and the peace movement in the 1980s, not only failed to satirize the notion of German unity after November 9, but even made impassioned appeals for it. In addition, the magazine increasingly opened its pages to left revisionists like Hans Magnus Enzensberger, Patrick Süskind, and Martin Walser, who now came to see West German democracy less as an imperfect system whose failures demanded constant ridicule, and more as an imperfect but honorable process whose failures deserved correction. Süskind, in a rueful flash, even saw the dethroning of the old left's certainties as a mid-life crisis of the '68ers.[32]

Every other serious German publication also joined the political and intellectual polemics that broke out as the collapse of the Soviet empire, the end of the cold war, and German unification invalidated the old mental constructs. The feuds pitted right against left, left against left, structuralism against postmodernism, ideology against esthetics, East German writers who stayed in the GDR against East German writers who emigrated, eighteen-year-olds (and thirty-year-olds) against fifty-year-olds.

In this debate Richard Schröder, who turned out to be as much essayist as pastor, philosopher, and parliamentarian, was among the most eloquent in arguing against nostalgia for an imagined GDR that had never existed. If family life was warmer in the East, that was simply because it had to be the refuge against an inhumane system, he contended. A much more telling difference between the two Germanys was that in the West one could basically judge another's character from personal experience, while in the old GDR one never knew whether one's closest friend was a secret *Stasi* informer. It was unworthy for privileged postmaterialists, he continued, to demean East Germans as deutsche mark nationalists who voted for bananas when they should have stayed pure and poor. The human longing for a more comfortable and varied life was legitimate, he maintained, and it might behoove leftists who championed the common man in the abstract to show a bit more affection when they met him in the flesh.[33]

By spring 1990, the various quarrels coalesced around the reevaluation of Christa Wolf, and especially her latest work, *Was bleibt*.[34] This was a bittersweet elegy for a vanishing GDR, cast as a characteristically subjective exploration of her experience in being tailed by the *Stasi* ten years earlier. She had written the essay at the time, then put the manuscript away and revised unidentified parts of it just before its 1990 publication. The experience of being shadowed had been an exception to her generally elite status as an intellectual and party member, and was certainly mild by comparison with the constant harassment of less favored writers or their expulsion from the country. Her own answer to the question of "what remains"—her ambiguous title that could also mean "something remains"—was "mourning, remorse, shame."[35]

Critics asked why Wolf had waited to publish this book until it no longer required courage to do so, what parts of it she had rewritten, and why she had not spoken up in defense of other persecuted writers over the decades. Defenders saw in such criticism a "witchhunt" (Günter Grass), "Stalinism of the West" (East German playwright Heiner Müller), "terror" of the West German media (East German writer Stephan Hermlin), and "postmodern McCarthyism" (the presidium of the West German PEN Club). Wolf herself saw a "monsterization" of the GDR. Everyone accused everyone else of hypocrisy.

Frank Schirrmacher, the young literary critic of the *Frankfurter Allgemeine Zeitung*, expressed some understanding for the way literature had come to be a surrogate for politics in the oppressive GDR. Nonetheless, he excoriated the post–World War II substitution of ideology for esthetics as the test of art in both Germanys.[36] Widening his fire to include other East German literati, he also opposed the "evil rationality of a Heiner Müller" who could write in December 1989, "Without the GDR as a grass-roots democratic alternative to the FRG [Federal Republic of Germany] democracy upheld by the Deutsche Bank, Europe will become a subsidiary of the USA." Schirrmacher commented, "Naturally, none of them defends the totalitarian brutality of the abdicated regime. But they all but avoid speaking about that at all. They talk [instead] about the stupidity of the abdicated [old] guard and clearly about the evil of the Western system."

Widening his fire still further, Schirrmacher called for an end to literature's fixation on German guilt and championed neo-postmodernism over old left conservatism.[37] For the West German '68ers, this was perhaps the unkindest cut of all: to be cast into the role of the mid-life establishmentarians the young were rebelling against. Süskind's diagnosis of a "mid-life crisis" hit the target.

Both the political and the literary left would carry the scars of this "paradigm change," as some of them termed it, into the united Germany.

Chapter 15

Denouement

G erman unification would not be a barrier to, but a "catalyst" for European integration, Kohl had promised in late
1989. In January, February, and March 1990 his optimism looked hollow.
From April on, it began to look prophetic as France and even Britain
sought refuge from the unsettling new realities in a larger European framework.[1]

Until a few weeks after the East German election and a few weeks
before the first two plus four foreign ministers' conference, both London
and Paris resisted bestowing unconditional sovereignty on a unified Germany. Beginning in early 1990, relations between Mitterrand and Kohl
even cooled so much that they dropped the extra tête-à-têtes they had held
regularly in 1989 to ensure that they met at least once a month. Then after
the East German elections the French began negotiating with the provisional government in East Berlin as if it had long-term authority, and they
would continue to do so through early June.

In mid-April President Bush used bilateral summits with both allies
to lobby for full German sovereignty, and both then accepted the inevitable.
British diplomats, freed to exercise their full skills in two plus four by
Thatcher (whatever her own lingering reservations), thereupon made their
peace with the new situation and became active negotiators. They had in
any case feared economic rather than political gigantism in a unified Germany, and now they quickly concluded (mistakenly) that diffuse economic
power did not confer focused political power, especially when the Federal
Republic would have so many problems in reconstructing the ruined GDR
that Britain would have five years or more to build its trade defenses.

With this shift, the various London bureaucracies again became players in the game of reshaping Europe. Close on the heels of the Foreign
Office, the British army, nimbly averting obsolescence in a world without
the Soviet threat, began working out a new NATO concept of a rapid

reaction corps that would give Her Majesty's forces the most prominent role.[2] Within half a year Britain would accede to the European Monetary System that it had scorned for a decade; a month after that, a Tory revolt would give the United Kingdom a new prime minister who was far readier to join Europe.

French recovery from the German shock took longer. The French had a gut feeling that, in the aphorism coined by philosopher Bernard-Henri Lévy, "Germany doubled equals France halved." Despite all the efforts over a quarter of a century to build a self-sustaining bilateral cooperation, this zero-sum reflex prevailed in the French business and political elite, and would disorient even Mitterrand, not for months, but for years. After energetically promoting European Community (EC) economic union in fall 1989 and then floating the notion of a pan-European confederation at the beginning of 1990—when German unification still looked far enough off to allow years of preparation—Mitterrand turned indecisive on both ideas as German merger accelerated.

His hesitancy was understandable: whatever his joy that the revolutionary ideas of 1789 were triumphing again in the world, French room for maneuver was shrinking. All options looked unpalatable. The French heard Kohl say yes to the European Monetary Union and a European central bank, but worried that Finance Ministry and Bundesbank grumbles showed that Bonn did not really mean it. Yet they also heard Genscher's enthusiasm for the idea and worried that the Germans really did mean it. Either way, whatever constraints an integrating EC imposed on Germany, it would also impose on France; whatever freedom of action it allowed Paris, it would also allow a much more powerful Bonn. The French feared German might unrestrained by the EC, but they also feared German might magnified by the EC.

Similarly, the French feared an American withdrawal from the continent that could leave them alone with the Germans, but they also feared a tactical German-American alliance against the French. They were uncomfortable in harness with an expanding Germany—but they mistrusted their alternative of greater nuclear cooperation with a United Kingdom that was too close to the United States. They flirted with a return to an unalloyed balance of power, yet they feared that such a free-for-all could push the Germans into the Russians' arms, or else make the Germans feel so insecure that they would want nuclear weapons of their own. Finally, the French feared German economic and financial monopoly in Eastern Europe, but they disliked the obvious remedy of inviting East European members to join the EC, since this would require open markets and agricultural competition for French farmers.

France's initial hopes of binding Germany to a deepened EC thus came to be besieged by doubts about whether this framework would actually suffice to curb German dynamism. Under the strain, the Gaullist consensus that had held diverse French groups together for so long began to fracture, without regard for party lines. Economists came close to sharing Thatcher's aversion to a European central bank and preference for an *Europe des patries* (a Europe of [strong individual] fatherlands), and from spring 1990 on persuaded Mitterrand to show much greater reserve toward the EC. And "post-Gaullist Gaullists" revived French suspicion of an uncontrolled Brussels—whatever Jacques Delors might say—and especially of qualified majority voting that removed France's veto.[3] They also argued that the more France became entangled in the conundrum of Western European defense, the more France's military autonomy and the purity of its nuclear doctrine would be endangered. One wing of Mitterrand's own Socialist party, under Defense Minister Jean-Pierre Chevènement, shared this view.

The French dilemma about how to redefine French foreign policy now that Germany's useful semisovereign status was drawing to a close was all the harder for Mitterrand to solve because it was accompanied by a profound domestic malaise. In the 1980s he had presided over the modernization that de Gaulle had postulated as the precondition for French greatness, in part by scrapping old socialist dogma. He had, in effect, turned his Socialist party into a Social Democratic party, and he had skillfully emasculated the rival Communist party. However, other wrenching domestic changes were still essential, and after a decade in office Mitterrand was running out of the political energy to produce them. A more flexible decentralization needed to replace the rigid traditional centralism, the whole educational system needed to be revamped to make France competitive in a nonprotectionist Europe, and French farmers had to be faced down and their subsidies cut if money were to be available for more pressing EC tasks. This further modernization seemed out of reach.

The seriousness of the French dilemma finally sank in as the East German election returns became known on March 18. Mitterrand himself now saw his reception of loser Oskar Lafontaine in the Elysée Palace on March 16 and the concurrent French fanning of Polish fears about the Oder-Neisse border as tactical errors. The president hastened to restore cordiality with Kohl and launched a joint initiative with him in April to introduce European political union simultaneously with completion of the single market in 1992. And—after a blunt bilateral summit in Florida, in which Bush's entourage told Mitterrand's entourage that American troops would not stay in Europe as mercenaries if the EC shut the United States out of political decisions—the French president muted his opposition to strengthening NATO's, and thereby America's, political role in Europe.

Just as in the old days, a joint French-German initiative sufficed to energize the EC. At their Dublin summit at the end of April 1990 the twelve together warmly welcomed the coming German unification and its "positive and fruitful contribution" to economic growth and European security, and they set the goal of greater democratic legitimacy and a common foreign and security policy for the EC. German unification was indeed acting as the catalyst for European integration.

Two Plus Four Catches Up

From May on, unification proceeded along the track laid down in the frenetic opening months of 1990. Bonn focused on the terms of domestic union, while Washington and Bonn together worked on the kinds of changes in NATO that might help Gorbachev avert a revolt in the Soviet Communist party.

The latter required no less strenuous efforts than the former. To be sure, NATO's transformation was not as radical as the GDR's disappearance from the face of the earth within less than a year. However, any alliance of sixteen very different nations that has gathered inertia over decades puts up even more resistance to a sharp alteration of course than does a homogeneous single country. The speed with which NATO adjusted was phenomenal.

The think tank that was set up within the U.S. government to co-ordinate all the necessary nuclear, conventional, and rhetorical shifts in NATO—it was the one interagency committee the small inner circle let get anywhere near German and NATO policy in this period—was the European Strategy Steering Group. Robert Gates was chairman, Robert Blackwill the chief bureaucratic tactician, and Philip Zelikow the executive secretary. State Department and Defense Department members of the group were hand-picked for their openness to American-style new thinking: from the State Department, Under Secretary of State for Security Assistance, Science, and Technology Reginald Bartholomew and Assistant Secretary of State for European and Canadian Affairs Raymond Seitz joined Zoellick and Ross. The steering group itself managed to stay out of the public eye as it gave the coup de grâce to Lance modernization and planned radical cuts in conventional forces.

The first public launch of the new concepts came with an address by Bush in Oklahoma on May 4. He was calling for a NATO strategy review, he said, to look at the political role for the alliance in the 1990s, the nature of its conventional and nuclear forces, and the future of the Conference on Security and Cooperation in Europe (CSCE).

The following day, the first two plus four conference of foreign ministers assembled in Bonn. Shevardnadze floated the idea of leaving the external aspects in limbo for an unspecified time after Germany's domestic union. He further declared that if the GDR quickly acceded to NATO, the two plus four conference should reconvene within twenty-four hours, and threatened that if it did not, the Soviet Union would act "on its own responsibility." Initially, the French and British were favorably disposed to such continuing oversight by the four powers, and Genscher was ready to accept Shevardnadze's decoupling of the internal and external aspects of unification. Kohl immediately conferred with Bush and Mitterand by telephone, however, and the West united to reject lingering two plus four authority, and to insist that the internal and external aspects of unification be dealt with "in parallel." In rebuffing Genscher, Kohl argued that splitting the two facets would simply invite Soviet meddling in German affairs for an indefinite period.[4]

All participants invited the Polish foreign minister to join the two plus four session in Paris in July that would discuss the German-Polish boundary. During one day the six foreign ministers crisply finished their work, parceled out various tasks to the CSCE and other bodies, and, in accord with the Western strategy of subordinating two plus four to German self-determination, set a leisurely pace for subsequent monthly one-day ministerial sessions.

Out of the two plus four limelight, Richard von Weizsäcker finished the first visit ever made to Poland by a West German president on May 5. It was not a success. Even von Weizsäcker's honed conciliatory skills were inadequate to win him anything other than a cool reception in the absence of a full German border guarantee.

A week later Horst Teltschik suddenly flew to Moscow in the company of two executives from the Deutsche and Dresdner Banks to discuss additional credits for the Soviet Union on top of the DM 6 billion in outstanding credits. The Soviet side was more forthcoming with economic data than it had been previously. Gorbachev was also forthcoming politically in describing frankly the resistance he was encountering to his German policy. Gorbachev further said he wanted to conclude a treaty with Bonn to serve as a pillar of the European house. Politically he would not be able to meet with Kohl to discuss this, however, until after the party congress in July.[5]

On May 15 the West German coalition broached substitution of an all-German election for the West German election scheduled for the end of 1990. Three days after that, the two Germanys signed their treaty on currency union on the basis of a social market economy. The GDR guaranteed private ownership of property, free prices, and dismantling of state monopolies. Again Kohl overruled the Bundesbank and granted such generous exchange values for East German marks that they would balloon wage costs, hasten the bankruptcy of the large majority of East German firms, and magnify East German unemployment—but would at least provide sufficiently high social welfare payments to keep all 16.5 million East Germans from migrating to Stuttgart the day after currency union.

On May 23, Genscher offered an overjoyed Shevardnadze credit of DM 5 billion ($3 billion), with the understanding that it would be part of the final package of German unity.

Summit Diplomacy

At the end of May Gorbachev flew to Washington for the next superpower summit. The Strategic Arms Reduction Talks treaty was not yet ready for signing, and had in any case lost its central role in East-West relations with the end of political confrontation. The main topic was therefore Germany, and also NATO. The United States, on the basis of its own and the West Germans' understanding of Soviet needs from discussions with Shevardnadze and others, bundled its various "points of mutual advantage" into nine listed items: the United States agreed to further negotiations on both conventional and short-range nuclear weapons; Germany would repeat its renunciation of nuclear, biological, and chemical weapons, accept the presence of Soviet troops in the former GDR during a transition period, state that a united Germany would comprise only the current West and East Germany and Berlin, and help the Soviet Union economically; NATO would conduct a strategic review to adapt to the new situation and would not put its troops into the former GDR during the transition period; and the CSCE process would be strengthened.[6]

For its part, Bush told Gorbachev, the West would expect four-power rights to end on the day of German unification, with no discriminatory limitations on German sovereignty. No one in the West wanted to shut the Soviet Union out of the community of European nations, but Moscow might isolate itself if it took negative positions on Germany that ran counter to the wishes of most West and East European governments. If that happened, Moscow would have lost an opportunity to build constructive relations with Germany and the other European democracies.

Inevitably, the hardest pill for Gorbachev to swallow was German membership in NATO. Bush again assured Gorbachev that a German anchoring to the integrated military command of the Western alliance would contribute greatly to European stability and security. At the end of the summit the American president could say that the two leaders agreed that alliance membership was a decision for the Germans to make themselves, in accord with the CSCE agreement of 1975. Privately, the National Security Council thought that with this statement the Americans had achieved a major breakthrough.[7] The State Department was more skeptical, seeing Soviet acquiescence as an encouraging sign, but less than a real decision on NATO membership. Elsewhere, Gorbachev still spoke publicly of some kind of double German membership in both NATO and the Warsaw Pact.

In June the pace quickened. On the first of the month the West German Bundeswehr and the East German National People's Army (NVA) agreed to establish official contacts between senior officers and units. West German Defense Minister Gerhard Stoltenberg specified that the unified Germany would have only one army, and that senior East German officers— who had been trained in the Soviet Union and practiced obedience to their Soviet masters second only to the *Stasi's* devotion to the KGB—need not apply. For their part, West German generals made plans to turn the NVA into a local territorial army and worried not at all that what had so recently been the best East European military machine in the Warsaw Treaty Organization might turn against NATO. Their main concern instead was to preserve the practice of conscription in the former GDR so that no zone might develop that could draw Germans out of the habit of the draft.[8]

In an ironic twist, the loudest protests at NVA cuts came from pastor and former peace activist Rainer Eppelmann, now the East German minister for disarmament and defense, who saw his new duty as preserving the jobs of all the disproportionately high number of generals and admirals under his wing. Professional West German soldiers, offended by Eppelmann's implicit assumption that all military hierarchies are interchangeable, no matter what system they serve—and concerned lest Stoltenberg offer to take on junior NVA officers as a friendly gesture—let it be known that they would refuse to serve under undemocratic NVA officers.

On June 5, the National Security Council's earlier sense of a breakthrough was reinforced. At a CSCE conference in Copenhagen, Shevardnadze assured Baker of Soviet acceptance of German membership in NATO, pending the working out of conditions such as the future size of the German army. Only the timing remained uncertain. Baker immediately notified Genscher, and Genscher hinted on German radio the next day that solutions looked to be within reach.[9]

By now de Maizière and his government finally came to understand that their writ would not last two or three years, as they had anticipated, but only, as it would turn out, 176 days.[10]

On June 7 members of the Warsaw Treaty Organization met in Moscow, vowed to change their alliance into a "treaty of sovereign states with equal rights, resting on democratic principles," and stated that German unification must "take place in the context of a pan-European process" and "preserve the legitimate security interests of Germany's neighbors."[11] The same day NATO foreign ministers came together for the first time since the East German revolution in cold, rainy Scotland. Baker spoke of the importance of not excluding the Soviet Union from the West's deliberations in the future and anticipated that the "overlapping institutions" of NATO, the EC, the CSCE, and others would operate henceforth in the area of security. On the second day of the gathering the foreign ministers jointly "reach[ed] out the hand of friendship and cooperation to the Soviet Union and all other European lands."[12]

On June 8 Kohl flew to Washington to be debriefed by Bush on the Soviet-American summit and to discuss changes in NATO and future German troop ceilings. On June 11 Genscher flew to Brest for his penultimate meeting with Shevardnadze in the year's series of intensive bilateral discussions. At the Soviet foreign minister's request, the two met at the grave of Shevardnadze's brother, a casualty of the German-Soviet bloodletting of the Great Patriotic War. Genscher's entourage understood the gesture as a signal to domestic Soviet opponents that Shevardnadze too had suffered a painful personal loss at the hands of the Germans and that he was impressing on the Germans their burden from the past.

The following day, the United States, Britain, and France agreed to give West Berliners a direct vote in the forthcoming West German (or possibly all-German) election. On the same day Gorbachev again proposed—and Kohl rejected—temporary associated double membership for Germany in both NATO and the Warsaw Treaty Organization.

On June 15 the two Germanys agreed that property nationalized after 1949, when the GDR government took over from the Soviet occupation administration, would be returned to its original owners. The land reform of the early postwar years would be preserved, however, and arrangements would be made to avoid hardship for East German families currently living in buildings that would be repossessed.

On June 18 Genscher and Shevardnadze held what would be their last bilateral consultation before unification, this time with the symbolism not of war, but of peace. At the Rathaus in Münster, where the Treaty of Westphalia had ended the Thirty Years War in the seventeenth century, Shevardnadze's aide, Sergei Tarasenko, handed over a "nonpaper" that expanded on the Brest talks (and on a June 13 Soviet message to Baker) and foreshadowed the final deal. United Germany could stay in the NATO alliance; NATO structures could not extend to the former GDR so long as Soviet troops remained there, but that territory would nonetheless fall under the guarantee of the Western alliance; and Western troops could stay on in Berlin until Soviet troops vacated eastern Germany in 1994. At Genscher's insistence, the Soviet side acknowledged the Federal Republic's right to station Bundeswehr units in eastern Germany before final Soviet withdrawal, but German territorial forces in the east would come under NATO command only when the last Soviet soldier had left.[13]

Further elements of the Soviet package were that the two military blocs sign a treaty regulating their relations, a ceiling be set on German armed forces, membership in one alliance not preclude membership in the rival alliance, both sides renounce first use of nuclear weapons, remaining nuclear weapons under the 500-kilometer range be removed, and Western troops in Germany be cut as Soviet troops there were cut. Shevardnadze described his proposals not as demands, however, but as a basis for negotiation.[14]

Genscher came away from Münster strengthened in his conviction that while from the beginning the natural Soviet preference had been to have all Germans in the Warsaw Pact, Moscow's more realistic second choice was to have the Germans tied down in NATO. The Soviets were finally accepting NATO membership for the united Germany, he thought, but they could not say so publicly until after the party congress.[15]

The Chancellery and the top levels of the State Department remained more skeptical. They appreciated the Soviet flexibility, but still did not discern in it the breakthrough they had hoped for. They did not sense full Soviet commitment to Tarasenko and Shevardnadze's probes, nor did they like the continuing overall Soviet framework of a relationship between the two military blocs. Especially at this late date they refused to equate NATO with the crumbling Warsaw Pact.

For his part, Valentin Falin, chief of the Soviet Central Committee's International Department, was still insisting on neutrality for unified Germany.[16] At the same time the democratic GDR's new Foreign Minister Markus Meckel, in line with his own nuclear pacifist principles, was still insisting on denuclearization of Germany and withdrawal of Western troops from Berlin.

On June 21 both German parliaments passed identical resolutions confirming the Polish border on the Oder-Neisse line.[17] The next day, two plus four convened its second session in East Berlin, listened as the military bands saluted the dismantling of Checkpoint Charlie, agreed to conclude its work by the fall, and heard Shevardnadze's surprise proposal that Western troops quit West Berlin within six months, while Soviet troops stay on in the GDR (and American troops in the Federal Republic) for five more years.[18] The West raised its collective eyebrows at this retreat from the Soviet foreign minister's message in Copenhagen and Münster, and Shevardnadze backed down. In private he explained to Baker that the Politburo had forced him to make the proposal. He then looked favorably— surprisingly so, the Americans thought—on some U.S. ideas on the CSCE that Baker ran past him. The signals were so mixed at this point that no one had any sense of how long it might take to close the final deal.[19]

On June 26, the two German parliamentary presidents paid a symbolic joint visit to Israel—where they were hardly noticed—to assure Jews that they need not fear the new united Germany. The same day *Pravda* published a remarkable manifesto by Shevardnadze that constituted the first public defense of his German policy against, as the foreign minister portrayed them, McCarthy-like zealots who would have avoided losing Eastern Europe by sending in the Soviet army. In the *Pravda* interview, Shevardnadze sought to put German membership in NATO into a more positive perspective after all the years of propaganda about German revanchism. "Here we need to clarify a few things," he said. "First, the FRG [Federal Republic of Germany] has long been a member of NATO. This means it can only be a question of increasing NATO's potential by the addition of the GDR when and if the latter becomes part of Germany. . . . We are by no means indifferent to Germany's future military-political status. But this question will probably be viewed differently depending on the changes which take place in Europe." These changes he presaged as including a less belligerent NATO, institutionalization of the CSCE, and "substantial reduction in troops and armaments in Europe—including the reduction of the German military arsenal—to the level of defense sufficiency."[20] Ten months later Shevardnadze would be even more explicit in his depiction of the hardliners, revealing that some military hotheads had indeed wanted to go into the GDR and restore order with tanks, just as in the good old days.[21]

On June 27, Bonn formally guaranteed a $3 billion, twelve-year commercial credit to the beleaguered Soviet Union.

Regardless of the still murky international status of the future united nation, the two Germanys pressed ahead with their own domestic merger; and history, as the instant cliché had it, went into fast forward. In an organizational tour de force, the two began their currency and social union, without a hitch, on July 1. East Germans picked up their deutsche marks at an average 1:8 exchange rate of East for West marks in private bank accounts, 1:1 for wages and pensions, and 2:1 for business debt.[22] The GDR's four-month-old Treuhandanstalt agency for managing the economic transition was turned into the biggest public holding corporation in the world, with the commission to privatize the GDR's state firms. West German goods flooded East German shops; price gouging appeared. East-West German border checks were dropped, while East German–Polish border checks were stiffened. Overnight the lines of do-it-yourself Polish capitalists buying groceries for resale from cut-rate supermarkets in West Berlin vanished.

With currency union, Soviet troops in the GDR also began getting paid in deutsche marks, which gave them the highest real wages they had ever earned, under Bonn's assumption of the GDR's financial obligations. In the broadest of hints, the Federal Republic also offered to pay for building barracks in the Soviet Union so that the Soviet army could be repatriated soon.

On July 2, the GDR coalition assented to all-German elections in December. On July 3, West Germany reduced military service from fifteen to twelve months.

The same day, pastor-turned-foreign-minister Meckel proposed to the UN Conference on Disarmament placing a ceiling of 300,000 on the combined German armed forces; removing all nuclear, chemical, and biological weapons from German soil; and allowing Soviet forces to stay on in the GDR for five more years. The surprised Americans—who had expected the East Germans to react like the Czechoslovaks and Hungarians in wanting to get rid of Soviet troops as fast as possible—began thinking of the GDR's foreign minister as "more Soviet than the Soviets," Meckel noted wryly in retrospect. He explained his actions as respecting Soviet security needs, and even a year later he seemed not to have grasped just how much Washington and Bonn were doing precisely that themselves, and how much more important this was to Shevardnadze and Gorbachev than the notions of lame-duck East Germans.[23] The West Germans were less surprised by Meckel's policies, but more surprised by his appointment of relatives to ministry posts, and by his insistence on sending a new ambassador to the United States even though the GDR was, by now, on the verge of vanishing.

On July 5 and 6, the NATO summit Gorbachev had been waiting for took place in London. Proclaiming that the Soviets were no longer adversaries, the Western alliance reextended the hand of friendship; invited the Soviet leader to address the NATO Council; said its own task would henceforth be as much political as military; pulled back from its previous tenet of forward defense; announced that it would remove all its nuclear artillery from Europe; and, the most important point, relegated nuclear missiles and bombs to "weapons of last resort."

The French, offended by the downgrading of the nuclear deterrent and American-British-German railroading through of NATO's new agenda, did not realize until much later that the changes had been made at the Soviets' behest to give Gorbachev and Shevardnadze the minimum they needed to neutralize domestic hardliners. Paris signaled its own pique by announcing at the same time as the NATO summit—to the Germans' consternation—that it would pull all of its close to 50,000 troops out of Germany by 1994, would not join any multilateral forces, and would not allow multilateral forces to be stationed in France. Mitterrand did not bother to inform the much heralded French-German Defense Council about this decision in advance.

The peripatetic summit moved next to Houston, where six of the NATO leaders joined the Japanese prime minister for the annual economic wrestling match of the Group of Seven. Despite Kohl's lobbying, the

Group of Seven did not commit itself to any massive aid program for the faltering Soviet economy.

Simultaneously in Strasbourg, the European Parliament made a course correction. As late as May it had still been chiding the European Council composed of the heads of government for accepting Bonn's contention that the GDR's entry into the EC required no revision of existing EC treaties. Now, although it continued to hedge its approval of unification with warnings about necessary preconditions, it passed a resolution anticipating a positive political and economic impulse from unification for the EC's own monetary union and internal market. For its part, Bonn sought to ease fears about an overbearing Germany by letting its partners know it would not seek greater weight within the European Commission, and by pledging to the Mediterranean states that EC aid to the GDR would not come at the expense of existing regional assistance payments.

The Miracle of Moscow

From his ramparts at the all-important Twenty-Eighth Party Congress Gorbachev responded instantly to the signal from London. The ink was hardly dry on the new NATO identity before his staff was on the telephone inviting the alliance's Secretary-General Manfred Wörner to Moscow for a media blitz of explanation of how friendly NATO had become. Wörner arrived in Moscow as the party congress ended on July 13, and was able to pass on a full account of his royal treatment to Kohl and Genscher, who followed him to the busy Soviet capital on July 14. Gorbachev, after a bruising battle, had defeated the hardline Egor Ligachev at the congress.[24] With his new lease on office, he was now ready to deal.

Gorbachev and Kohl opened their talks on July 15 by affirming their shared responsibility as members of a generation too young to have fought in World War II but old enough to remember its horrors. Gorbachev then spoke of the importance of ending the division between Russians and Germans: a task as important as normalizing Soviet-American relations, he added.

Kohl offered the Soviets a comprehensive nonaggression treaty, pledging on a bilateral basis the same cooperation the NATO summit had just proposed, as soon as outstanding issues were resolved. He then described the economic tailspin in the GDR, said that pan-German elections were needed by the end of the year to stabilize things there, and noted that three questions had to be settled to finish the two plus four and CSCE business. These were the drawdown of Soviet troops in the GDR, German membership in NATO, and the future ceiling on German troops. The time for decision was now, Gorbachev responded.

Further discussion of principles followed. Kohl stressed that the United States must not feel shut out by good Soviet-German relations, and Gorbachev again welcomed NATO's declaration that it did not view the Soviet Union as an enemy. The Soviet leader passed a paper to Kohl entitled "Reflections on the Content of a Treaty of Partnership and Cooperation between the USSR and Germany." Then Gorbachev launched into his précis of the two plus four outcome they were working toward: United Germany would consist only of the Federal Republic, the GDR, and Berlin; Germany would continue to abstain from nuclear, biological, and chemical weapons; NATO military structures would not be extended to GDR territory; transitional arrangements would be agreed on for the remaining period before Soviet forces left eastern Germany; and the old four-power rights would end.

The chancellor asked if Gorbachev agreed that united Germany would regain full sovereignty. "Of course," replied Gorbachev. NATO must not extend its authority to GDR territory so long as Soviet troops remained there, he repeated; there must be transitional arrangements. But—he said this "very calmly and seriously," Teltschik recorded—Germany could remain a member of NATO.

Kohl's face betrayed no emotion at this "surprising statement," noted Teltschik, or at Gorbachev's "second surprise": that the Soviets were ready to terminate four-power responsibilities immediately on signing the two plus four agreement. Given a separate agreement on the terms of Soviet troop presence in Germany during the next three to four years, no interim prolongation of four-power rights was necessary.

To ensure against any misunderstanding, Kohl summed up what he had just heard the Soviet leader say. Gorbachev confirmed the summary and restated each point clearly. "The breakthrough is here! What a sensation! We hadn't expected such a clear promise from Gorbachev," exulted Teltschik in his diary. "I'm witness to a historical moment!" He entitled this entry "The Miracle of Moscow."

After a forty-minute lunch and a thirty-minute press conference, the two delegations flew off to Stavropol, then on to Gorbachev's home ground of Zheleznovodsk. There, the next day, the Soviet host formally accepted "full and unrestricted sovereignty" for a united Germany, as he told a press conference, including the right to decide "freely and by itself if and in which alliance it desires membership." The 360,000 Soviet troops, he stipulated, would leave the GDR by 1994.[25]

In return, Kohl promised, Br'er Rabbit-like, a ceiling of 370,000 for the joint German army; a number above what the Bonn government had feared it might have to drop to anyway for domestic reasons. From Moscow's point of view the figure represented almost a halving of the nominal 670,000 West and East German armed forces. From Bonn's point of view the number sufficed to underwrite stability in the new era, and it was a significant improvement over the 250,000 the Soviets had first demanded or the 300,000 floated by Meckel, or even the 350,000 that Shevardnadze and Genscher had already agreed on.[26] The Germans also extended their 1950s pledge not to manufacture or possess nuclear, biological, or chemical weapons. In economic assistance, Bonn promised, in addition to the DM 5 billion in credits pledged earlier, DM 1.25 billion for the costs of stationing Soviet troops in Germany in 1990, and DM 220 million in subsidies for food deliveries to the Soviet Union.

In the Soviet–West German deal, the Genscher plan, as modified in Defense Minister Stoltenberg's direction, was to prevail during the remaining stay of Soviet armed forces in Germany.[27] No NATO structures or troops would enter the territory of the former GDR, but the American, British, and French brigades would remain in West Berlin, and West German officers would assume command of East German troops.[28] Once Soviet forces left eastern Germany, German forces under the NATO integrated command—but no nuclear weapons—could move onto the territory. And American forces could and should stay on in Germany, Kohl and Genscher noted.[29]

On July 17, almost as an afterthought, the two plus four foreign ministers held their penultimate session in Paris, with the Poles in attendance. All agreed that the future German borders would be drawn around the two existing Germanys and Berlin. Germany and Poland would sign a treaty guaranteeing the Oder-Neisse line. The West German Federation of Expellees called the deal a "total surrender of German areas and rights" in Poland and booed Kohl when he addressed the association.[30]

American journalists, inferring that Bonn and Moscow had worked everything out together without Washington—some even began murmuring "Stavrapallo" in a pejorative elision of Stavropol and Rapallo—peppered the secretary of state's entourage with questions about slipping American leadership. Official assertions that the whole process of unification had been very much a joint American-German effort were met with incredulity.

All that remained was mopping up. On August 1 the two German governments agreed on the rules for their first all-German election, which would take place in four months. In August the United States announced that it would cut its armed forces by 442,000 during the next five years. Stoltenberg announced that the new German armed forces would draw 320,000 troops from the Bundeswehr and 50,000 from the old NVA. On August 31 Bonn and East Berlin concluded their unification treaty and specified that articles 23 and 146 be struck from the new constitution.

In early September, at a meeting in Berlin, the two plus four working-level delegates warded off a last-minute Soviet attempt to outlaw all conventional and "dual-capable" nuclear weapons on German territory, and even secured Soviet consent that the two plus four settlement not be construed as impairing German obligations to NATO. This concession was unexpected, an "enormous loophole," commented an American diplomat, interpreting it as even allowing NATO maneuvers on former GDR soil, should a crisis demand them and the German government approve.

The British held out as long as possible for a more explicit right of maneuver and looked askance at the precedent of a non-nuclear zone in the former GDR, while the French regarded with misgiving the Soviet-German negotiations about friendship and troop withdrawal treaties. The Americans, by contrast, were so elated yet again that they did not even bother to get debriefed about the bilateral Soviet-German talks by the top West German diplomat at the Berlin meeting.[31]

On September 12 the foreign ministers sealed the final two plus four agreement in Moscow.[32] The new Germany acknowledged the irrevocable nature of its new borders, declared any offensive war unconstitutional, once more forswore acquisition of nuclear, biological, or chemical weapons, and noted its voluntary commitment under the Treaty on Conventional Armed Forces in Europe to a ceiling of 370,000 armed forces. The four powers terminated their "rights and responsibilities for Berlin and for Germany as a whole."[33] On September 24 East German forces formally withdrew from the Warsaw Treaty Organization. On October 3 the two Germanys merged.[34]

The German-Soviet treaties on good neighborliness and economic cooperation followed on the anniversary of November 9. On November 14 the German-Polish border treaty was signed. On November 19, in Paris, participants signed the Treaty on Conventional Armed Forces in Europe that, in effect, was the peace treaty for both the cold war and World War II.[35] The CSCE summit duly blessed this treaty and all the other transactions and declared its faith in the future with the Paris Charter for a new Europe.[36] On December 2 Germans East and West rewarded the center-right coalition in Bonn with a resounding reelection victory. In mid-December the intergovernmental conferences on EC economic, monetary, and political union began their consultations. In spring 1991, before the putsch, the Supreme Soviet finally ratified the Soviet-German treaties.

No blood was shed. The only iron involved was in those superb machine tools that helped make Germany the largest exporter in the world. It was the most peaceful change of this magnitude in European history.

Chapter 16

Hangover

A las, the Germans did not live happily ever after. Their joy of November 9, 1989, faded. They forgot they could be as spontaneous as Latins. They lost sight of how much of a miracle unification was. The "Wessis" (west Germans) begrudged transfering $100 billion a year to the "Ossis" (east Germans). The Ossis resented their 40 percent real unemployment, the meagerness of productive investment in eastern Germany, and the lemons of second-hand cars they sometimes got stuck with. Many blamed their failure to attain Western living standards fast on the new heartlessness of capitalism rather than on forty years of communist heartlessness.

The German, European, and world economy went into recession, and the combination of Bonn's fiscal gas pedal and the Bundesbank's monetary brakes exported the costs of unification to other Europeans in the form of slowed growth and capital drain. The Danes, the French, and even the Germans got the jitters about the ambitious Maastricht treaty vision of European monetary and political union before the end of the century. Even the old exchange rate mechanism exploded in everyone's face as speculative pressure forced the British pound and Italian lira out of the currency grid. Recriminations followed. Observers asked if this presaged a new Eurosclerosis.

German voters, west and east, became disillusioned with the centrist political parties. Their flirtation with the far right threatened to top the crucial 5 percent of votes at the federal level for the first time since 1945. Kohl's bluff accentuation of the positive—a style that had worked well to inspire eastern confidence during the uncertainties of transition—seemed less suited to rallying citizens to sacrifice for rebuilding. Teenagers at the low end of the social scale, especially in the east, assaulted third world nationals seeking asylum night after night, and while some Germans rallied to protect their foreign guests, other citizens cheered on the skinheads—and initially the police seemed unable to stop the arson and brutality. The grim total for 1992 was seventeen deaths and 2,300 recorded right-wing attacks on foreigners.

The combination of untamed violence and economic stagnation created a discontent that went well beyond the usual German propensity to use pessimism as a tool to identify and solve social problems. Many called this discontent malaise; a few called it crisis; some even called it a moral crisis.

Governance

Administratively, unification went smoothly enough. Previously nonexistent state and local governments were set up in the east and neophyte officials elected to run them. West German politicians flooded in to help fill the many gaps, some out of dedication, some out of flight from deadends at home. Western federal and state ministries and courts loaned thousands of bureaucrats and judges to the east for two years. Training programs for east German diplomats, managers, bankers, bookkeepers, teachers, librarians, local administrators, and a host of other professionals abounded.

Deeds records were reestablished in the east. The Bundestag made a gesture of compensation for wasted lives by paying DM 550 per month of imprisonment to every east German who had been a political prisoner. Symbolically, it also stopped paying compensation to the earlier have-nots, the (West) Germans who had been driven out of Poland, Czechoslovakia, and the Soviet Union in the early post–World War II years. The Central Office for Political Education fanned out to the new states and trained government clerks and petitioners in the exotic art of treating each other politely. The complex West German legal system went into effect instantly—West German unity negotiator Wolfgang Schäuble would consider this one of the mistakes of the union treaty—and drowned the east Germans in regulations.[1] The one saving grace was the east Germans' slowness in becoming as litigious as the west Germans.

A few Baden-Württemberg educators introduced in Saxony the kinds of school reforms they could not possibly have got accepted in the old, more rigid Länder. East German parliamentarians learned on the job, though with few exceptions did not learn fast enough to make much of an impact in the established western parties. Local east German police were modernized slowly from a political control force to a riot and drug control force.

And the National People's Army was integrated into the Bundeswehr in a short nine months. This feat could not solve the Bundeswehr's own problems of identity in a new world in which its mission was not self-evident, but it did illustrate the workmanlike competence the Germans brought to their multiple transformations. The task entailed everything from securing unsuspected depots of arms and ammunition to encouraging East German officers and men to speak up; from stopping Soviet-style hazing of young recruits to advising struggling mayors on prices and environmental cleanup.[2]

Purges of ideologues, *Stasi* collaborators, and sheer incompetents from the heavily featherbedded universities and other positions of public trust took place in the five new eastern states, sometimes with good, sometimes with bad, results. A few of the old icons came out looking much shabbier than their previous reputations. Mischa Wolf, who had in any case never enjoyed the same mystique in the East as in the West, now lost his chic in the West too. Prisoner exchange middleman Wolfgang Vogel looked less like the Catholic altruist of his self-image and more like an ordinary *Stasi* informer who just had classier information than most, and therefore earned more for it, through his lawyers' fees (and, some charged, extortion). Sascha Anderson, the guru of the East Berlin Prenzlauerberg counterculture, turned out to have been a *Stasi* agent provocateur for years—and after a brief furor went back to his old post as partner in the Galrev publishing house. Manfred Stolpe, the popular Social Democratic premier of Brandenburg, came under fire for his contacts with the *Stasi* during three decades as the Protestant church's top lay official.

Mastering the Past

More than any other, the Stolpe case exemplified the most vexing issue the Germans had to face: *Vergangenheitsbewältigung* (mastering the past). This dilemma about how to punish or integrate those who had collaborated with a repugnant regime—and how to sort out the ambiguities and draw the line between agent and victim—was hardly new. Two generations earlier, in the wreckage of 1945, the Germans had faced the same challenge. The GDR had swept the question under the rug by claiming that only the Federal Republic had any Nazi leftovers. The West Germans had indeed, apart from convicting 6,500 people for Nazi crimes, consciously integrated many old Nazi sympathizers.[3] They had also, however, publicly agonized about the ethics, or violation thereof, involved. By 1990 no one argued that the tens of thousands of East German murders and political imprisonments had made the regime as vile as Hitler's, but some of the moral issues involved in dealing with the aftermath were the same.

In a way, the easiest level was the legal one. The courts could never settle the fundamental issues of culpability for the Berlin Wall and *Bevormundung* (guardianship) and ruined lives, of course; but rule of law required some accounting by GDR officials for their violation of elementary human rights. After a fumbling start—former Politburo member Harry Tisch was convicted on a petty charge of diverting modest amounts of public monies for private construction—prosecutors decided to concentrate on manslaughter and to work their way up the chain of command. Several young former border guards were convicted on the grounds that their specific shots had killed specific would-be escapees, and were given sentences that usually corresponded to the time they had already spent in prison awaiting trial. To avoid ex post facto charges on the pattern of the Nuremberg trials, indictments generally cited violation of the GDR laws that existed at the time of the killing rather than universal humanitarian guidelines that had never been codified in specific East German legislation. This concept was stretched, however, to include the GDR's international commitments to human rights under UN and Conference on Security and Cooperation in Europe (CSCE) agreements and also the legal notion of disproportion in the lethal shooting of persons whose only offense was the attempt to flee the GDR.[4]

Subsequent indictments of the top leaders focused primarily on their roles in issuing orders to shoot. Honecker's trial was delayed by the Soviets' smuggling the former GDR leader out of supposedly sovereign united Germany; it had to wait for decisions in Moscow and Santiago to expel Honecker from the Chilean Embassy in Russia and extradite him in summer 1992. It ended in farce when Honecker was suddenly released by one Berlin court on grounds of illness and was flown to Chile, only to be ordered back, in vain, by another Berlin court, whose medical advisers gave a different diagnosis. The trial of *Stasi* chief Erich Mielke also had elements of farce as the overburdened prosecution won time to prepare its real case by keeping Mielke in prison on an irrelevant charge of murdering a policeman in the early 1930s.

Convoluted as the legal reckoning was, it was, by comparison, easy. The much more difficult part of coming to terms with the past was untangling the everyday compromises that so many had to make in a secret police system, and evaluating whether on balance these compromises served more to abet or to subvert repression. In private lives, the consequences were for individuals to draw. In judging a candidate for public or semi-public office, broader conclusions were necessary to determine eligibility or exclusion.

The united Germany approached this aspect of sorting out the past in several different ways. It eventually set up a parliamentary commission of inquiry to explore broad issues of responsibility for what went wrong in the GDR. It also launched routine investigations into the records of officeholders suspected of being *Stasi* informants. As a consequence, resignations from east German state governments and legislatures were a staple of the first years after unification.

By far the most coherent national debate about how to deal with the past, however, quickly centered on what to do with the 125-mile long shelves of *Stasi* records. This unique cache of a police state's documents owed its existence to the speed of events, which left the *Stasi* no time to destroy or alter its files systematically, and to the surprise occupation of various headquarters of the Ministry for State Security by vigilantes that first week in December.[5] Under Modrow, and even under de Maizière— *Stasi* generals Heinz Engelhardt and Edgar Braun and 337 other *Stasi* officers would serve until summer 1990 as "advisers" in de Maizière's committee to dissolve the secret police—*Stasi* officers did remove the lists of agents and some of the most sensitive personal files.[6] In addition, many white-collar *Stasi* agents obtained access to their own employment records to sanitize them before unification. Yet the practical effect of the moles was limited; a very thin Foreign Ministry dossier for an East German diplomat, say, was a dead giveaway, and the Germanic pedantry with which the *Stasi* wrote everything down meant that a secret agent's activity could most often be traced eventually in secondary or tertiary files.

In the fierce public debate at the end of 1991, the most controversial issue concerned access to personal dossiers. West German politicians, media, and intellectuals in the center and left tended to advocate a course of forget and forgive in avoiding inquisitions and revenge by locking up the files and not letting them poison personal and political relationships. Centrists based their reasoning largely on the need for social healing of the wounds of division and injustice. Some leftists contended further that if West Germany had once failed to root out ex-Nazis on the right, it would be hypocritical if Germany now rooted out ex-communists and informers on the left.

The old east German dissidents and ordinary citizens, however— joining together, for once, in an urge to expose the arbitrary forces that had victimized them—insisted on their right to truth, with full access for each person to his or her own dossier. They found an unexpected champion in Wolf Biermann, who used his reception of a literary award to issue a blast at "asshole Sascha," Sascha Anderson.[7] In the fierce ensuing polemics with his erstwhile allies on the intellectual left, "Grand Inquisitor" Biermann (as Günter Grass and various east German writers began calling him) helped turn the tepid Bundestag debate around. By the beginning of 1992, individual *Stasi* files (with other names blacked out, but usually identifiable) were open for victims to read. Within a few months 1.4 million applicants were standing in line for the privilege.

The principle, as explained by Joachim Gauck, the former dissident Rostock pastor who was given the commission to administer the *Stasi* files, was self-determination.[8] If victims, on finding out who their past tormentors were, wanted to sue them in court, or punch them on the nose, or offer private forgiveness, that was up to each individual to decide. The state was not going to institute a new *Bevormundung* by deciding how to handle each case, or by concluding in advance that citizens were not mature enough to bear the pain they would subject themselves to in learning who had informed on them.[9]

In the early period of this experiment there was one suicide of a politician from the Party of Democratic Socialism (PDS) that opponents of the new openness laid at the door of the ongoing "witchhunt." There was one celebrated divorce, after Vera Wollenberger made the searing discovery that her own husband Knud (alias Donald) had for years informed the *Stasi* exhaustively on her dissident and intimate activities. There were bizarre episodes in which ex-*Stasi* officers became public judges on television of whether various accused persons had or had not been secret police informers.

Then there was the Stolpe case. Stolpe—who had been considered a likely future president of the Federal Republic before his secret police dealings became an issue—was one of the two eastern state premiers born in the east. He had negotiated all the Protestant church's arrangements with the regime since the early 1960s. He had also been one of the trusted channels for West-East German government contacts. The complicity or innocence of his admitted connections with the *Stasi*—Stolpe launched the entire controversy by volunteering that he had talked regularly with the *Stasi* over a quarter of a century as part of his job for the church—became the object of intense scrutiny.[10] Stolpe maintained that his equivocal relationship was necessary if he was to expand the church's room for maneuver and accomplish any good for Christians and others sheltering within the church. He further said that if he was carried in *Stasi* books as the informer "secretary," it was without his knowledge. His critics, including many of the church's grass-roots activist pastors, argued that he had made unnecessary concessions, curbed their activities, and helped stabilize an odious system. His defenders, like Richard Schröder, cited the old adage that you cannot rescue a man from a swamp without getting your own vest dirty. The church as a whole emerged with its 1980s moral authority badly tarnished.[11]

Economics

Economically, the outlook for a united Germany was good for the long term, and remains so. Germany has the third largest economy in the world and was (before unification) second only to Japan as a creditor nation; its currency was second only to the U.S. dollar in its use by others as a reserve. It is the undisputed leader of a European economic area that produces a third of global goods and services. It has just consolidated its scattered stock exchanges to make Frankfurt a strong financial center for commercial dealings as well as the home of the Bundesbank. It has already shut down the worst industrial pollutants from GDR days. Vigorous small and medium-sized enterprises are already emerging in the east. By fall 1992—whatever its controversies—the Treuhandanstalt had privatized 9,000 out of 12,000 state-owned enterprises, and was considered enough of a success to have imitators in Central Europe and the Baltics. Wealthy west Germany has the means, and the constitutional requirement, to bring east Germany up to its level.

For its part, eastern Germany has the crucial skilled manpower for modern industry. Like West Germany after the bombing of World War II, it also has the perverse advantage that the bulk of its plant is so antiquated that it must be razed and replaced. As a consequence, by the turn of the century parts of east Germany should emerge with the most modern telecommunications and lean-production factories in Europe.

That is the long term, however. Human beings live in the short term. After the first burst of consumer spending as easterners received real West German marks for their GDR play money, it became obvious that many years would pass before the eastern standard of living could approach western levels. It also became obvious to western taxpayers that they would be subsidizing the east during those years. These discoveries led to mutual recriminations.[12]

Naturally there was some exaggeration in the exposure of this antipathy. New Wessi publishers of Ossi tabloids thought it attracted readers to trumpet the "annexation" of the east by westerners with a "conquistador mentality." Yet the stereotypes contained enough truth to make them hurt. Various easterners bought far more insurance policies from slick Western sales agents than they needed. Many easterners who had toiled and stood in lines for decades to get their homes cozy now found former western owners ogling their property. Eastern mom-and-pop stores were undersold by western chains.

Financial hardship was also a fact of life. The east's low rents quadrupled in two years. Many aged forty-five and above lost their positions and had to resign themselves to living on welfare for their remaining years.

Women, who had held jobs in ratios close to 90 percent in the productive age span, had to adjust to West German rates of half that level. Men who had cheered on the west German labor unions' fight to raise eastern wages to a par with western wages by 1994 gradually realized that with eastern productivity only a third that of western Germany, all the union generosity was doing was scaring away western investors from the east and preserving old jobs in the west for those who were already union members. The goal that everyone was aiming for, self-sustaining growth in the east, kept receding like the horizon.

Kohl at first thought, and preached, that the new demand in the east and overall German economic growth would cover the added costs of unification. Western taxes would not need to be raised. Nor would things get worse for anyone in the east. Just as in the West German postwar economic miracle, so now, consumer drives would help expand production. "The first thing that happens is the [eastern] family gets a car," explains Kohl in one of his favorite homilies. "That's the husband's. Then his wife says, 'You got your car; now what about a new kitchen for me?' And then she says, 'And by the way, we never had a honeymoon. Let's take the grandchildren and go on a honeymoon.' "[13]

As it turned out, the new kitchens and the late honeymoons were not enough to smooth the short-run transition. The important Soviet and East European market collapsed as unification came into effect; the West German insistence on favoring property restitution over indemnification in the unification treaty raised enormous barriers to clear titles and to investment; and the 1:1 conversion from ostmarks to deutsche marks for wage payments, given low eastern productivity, meant that far more firms would go belly-up faster than would have been the case with a more realistic exchange rate. In addition, unified Germany had to pay for the GDR's neglect of its seed capital over ten years and for the prodigious pollution in the east. The net result was a halving of the GDR's industrial production within eight months of the opening of the Berlin Wall—a drop it took the United States three and a half years to accomplish in the Great Depression—and a drop to a plateau of one-third of previous production throughout 1991 and 1992, a feat never achieved in the American depression.

Given the pressures, this collapse was less surprising than the fact that real east German consumption in this period actually rose 9.7 percent for all households, not counting those who moved or commuted to the west. Given generous social welfare payments, an estimated 60 percent of all private households experienced an increase in real income, even as unemployment soared. Sales of video recorders, computers, and freezers boomed.[14] The Kohl government expected an upturn by 1992 that would get eastern Germany out of its trough.[15]

The upturn did not materialize. As of this writing, the government was still waiting for it and still groping for an efficient program to finance reconstruction in the east. Its massive transfers of $100 billion a year—plus perhaps $80 billion a year in private investment—will continue for the rest of the century, but will still not meet requirements there. Its deficits will soar by 1995 as the Treuhandanstalt and other shadow budgets come into the direct federal budget. In the meantime, Germany's public debts and the Bundesbank's compensatory high interest rates are soaking up capital from other Europeans, slowing growth all around, and wreaking havoc with the European Monetary System.

"Anyone Who Doesn't Believe in Miracles . . ."

In Europe as a whole, German unification first propelled the European Community (EC) to set the ambitious Maastricht treaty target of economic, social, and (at Kohl's insistence) political union by the end of the twentieth century—then jeopardized the enterprise through the economic drag of German unity costs.

At the historic European Council summit in Maastricht at the end of 1991, Kohl argued that a common European currency and reserve system could function without fatal strains only if political unity were sufficient to ensure as well a common budget, finance, trade, and social policy. He argued further that other Europeans should build automaticity into European union in order to bind Germans to it irrevocably, allowing no future option that might tempt a new generation in a more powerful Germany to end the frustrations of multination compromises with a go-it-alone policy. The Maastricht course seemed certain enough for the European Free Trade Association (EFTA) states to sign a subsequent treaty on a European economic area assuring the free flow of people, goods, capital, and services in a market of 380 million and for EFTA members Sweden, Austria, and Finland to apply for full membership in the EC. The resulting economic area will account for 43 percent of world trade.

Yet with that Maastricht projection a year after German union, it turned out that the European political elites had once again overshot their publics. Both publics and markets recoiled, with a bare majority against the Maastricht treaty in a Danish referendum and a bare majority for it in a French referendum, and with the weak British pound and Italian lira blasted out of the European currency grid by fall 1992. Even the Germans erupted into worry, as Kohl had anticipated, about sacrificing their "lovely deutsche mark" for "esperanto money."[16] Publications as diverse as Bild, the *Frankfurter Allgemeine Zeitung*, and *Der Spiegel* rallied to defend the Germans' totem of stability and rectitude.

Kohl was not unduly worried about Germans' concerns. He could get ratification of the Maastricht treaty and the two-thirds majority to pass the necessary constitutional amendments easily enough. Whatever the editorialists and consumers might say, all the main parties agreed on the direction of European political union. And, despite the grumbling, most people generally continued to favor economic union. In the worst case, the chancellor could, like the regal Adenauer in introducing the army, ignore popular discontent, refuse to hold a risky referendum, and figure that the voters would be grateful later. In the best case, once a real public debate about the Maastricht treaty finally took place, the Kohl team thought, sheer logic should convince citizens that every mark they spent on the EC and every power they surrendered to a European central bank would only increase their own prosperity.

Kohl could not depend on rallying wary populations abroad in a similar fashion, however. The Italians gave cause for apprehension as they had been model European citizens for many years before the lira was yanked out of the European Monetary System. Now the resulting recriminations threatened to exacerbate domestic north-south tensions in Italy and fan separatism in the richer north. The far more reluctant Europeans in Britain also caused concern, as the humiliation of the pound's exit from the exchange rate mechanism boded ill for any future knitting of the British back into the common undertaking. A bout of German-bashing recurred, with English ire directed especially at the Bundesbank for keeping its paralyzingly high interest rates and for forcing recession on the rest of Europe. Thatcher's old suspicion of the German economic powerhouse also stoked the ill will. How could the Germans be trusted to be good Europeans in a union tomorrow, the British asked, if they were willing today to pursue blinkered national economic interests even to the point of shattering the old European Monetary System? Phrased another way, how could the ambitious currency union work if even the far more modest European Monetary System could not hold together? Unflattering beer hall cartoons of Germans again appeared on editorial pages in London.

As they heard the new grass-roots murmurs, the European elites realized they had neglected the voters for far too long. They therefore began courting their constituents assiduously. The European Commission uncharacteristically started soliciting others' opinions before submitting legislation to the European Parliament. Kohl and Jacques Delors gave speeches vowing to preserve national identity, increase transparency and accountability, and avoid rigid regulation of everything from unpasteurized Camembert cheese to transport of corpses. Devolution or subsidiarity in the English words, federalism and regionalism in the German vocabu-

lary—in plain language, doing everything at the lowest possible level—
would be built back into the Maastricht treaty's design, they promised.
So would some form of democratic accountability, not only against the
Brussels "Eurocrats" whom the public so mistrusted, but also against
heads of individual governments and national ministries who liked the
closed-door deals they could cut in the secretive European Council. National legislatures would be granted more oversight over the process.

Apart from the public relations blitz, Kohl and Mitterrand moved to
salvage what they could from the Maastricht treaty institutionally. Institutions cannot create reality, the pair recognized, but if they bear an or-
ganic relation to the communities they issue from, they can help shape
them. A full retreat from the Maastricht treaty would risk retrogression;
implementation of what was possible could move the Europeans forward
again. This instinct corresponded with the opinion polls, which showed
that Europeans were suspicious of the specifics of the Maastricht treaty,
but still strongly in favor of more integration.[17]

Kohl and Mitterrand therefore refused to reopen the intricate compromises of the original treaty for renegotiation. Instead, they threatened
implicitly, if others would not stick to the goals, to go to the oft-discussed
two-speed Europe. France, Germany, and the Benelux countries—possibly
with the addition of Sweden, Austria, and Finland—could form the monetary core. Other states could join as they followed France in converging
toward Germany's strict anti-inflation criteria, that is, the criteria that had
prevailed before Bonn resorted to Reaganomics to pay for unification.
Unprecedented, successful coordination between the Bundesbank and the
Bank of France in protecting the franc against speculation after the pound
and lira dropped from the grid lent credibility to the threat.

Mitterrand had no alternative. For him the real issue was just the
reverse of that posed by the British. If the Bundesbank was almighty today
as a national bank, then the only way to regain any French share whatever
in that omnipotence and in France's own economic fate would be to form
a European central bank in which Paris would at least have some voice.
Far from surrendering France's by now nonexistent financial sovereignty,
this would restore a modicum of that sovereignty.

Within weeks of its angry flirtation with a return to splendid isolation,
London rediscovered the same verities as Paris. Britain would have to deal
with German economic power in some form, and its own weaker economy
would be most vulnerable if there were no institutional checks on the
German government and the Bundesbank. Even a two-speed Europe
would leave Germany more dominant than would full union of the twelve,
since there would be fewer allies to restrain Germany, and, again, no voice
for Britain. Besides, everyone knew that ecological and economic problems—and speculative capital flows of the sort that knocked out the

pound—could no longer be solved at the level of the puny nation-state. They require continentwide cooperation.

For Kohl, the modifications to the Maastricht treaty following the French referendum were not without pain. He certainly agreed that the EC's "democratic deficit," or lack of accountability to voters, should be addressed. Indeed, he had vainly argued this need all along, even if he had sought an answer more in strengthening the European Parliament than in observing subsidiarity or in increasing national legislatures' oversight. What was far more distressing for him, however, was the new uncertainty about pinning the next generation of Germans to Europe, and the new uncertainty about political union. Widening to take in the former EFTA countries as members would now clearly preempt deepening of political institutions. In particular, a common European foreign policy or army would again be relegated to twenty-first-century dreams, since Kohl could not now exact strict adherence to joint EC foreign policy as the price of admission for EFTA neutrals.

In the end, the Maastricht treaty lost its aura. The day had not yet arrived for a new Holy Roman universalism to supplant the nation-state. As always, however, Europe would advance not by blueprint, but by trial and error: two brave steps forward, one messy step back. There would be less integration than the negotiators had hoped for and more of the residual nation-state, but there would still be vastly more integration by the end of the century than anyone would have dreamed possible in 1945, or even in 1989.

On January 1, 1993, the EC's long-planned single market came into effect, with a few ragged edges. The Americans again looked at the disarray and concluded that a United States of Europe could never come to pass; a millennium of history militated against it. Germany and France again looked at the disarray and decided there was no alternative but to consolidate what had already been gained and press ahead. And statesmen again quoted the first president of the Common Market Commission, Walter Hallstein, who said of his job, "Anyone who doesn't believe in miracles isn't a realist."

Security and Foreign Policy

As Germany unified, its overall external environment improved vastly. In stimulating European integration, unification revived a dynamic the continent had lost a century earlier to the United States, and then to the Soviet Union. It clearly defined the reentry of Eastern Europe to Europe proper, as well as the eventual terms of entry to Europe for Ukrainians, Russians, and other outsiders.

It even, as it turned out, provided something of a model for the Muscovite resistance to the hardline Soviet putsch in August 1991. The Leipzig demonstrators had shown that when the small minority of those with civil courage reaches a certain mass—and intersects with demoralization in the power hierarchy—change is possible. This electrifying revelation, after seventy years of resignation before the claims of gun barrels and historical inevitability, immediately transformed the Bulgarians, Czechs, Romanians, and, with a lag, enough Russians to make a difference. The few tens of thousands who manned the fragile barricades outside Boris Yeltsin's White House in Moscow that August were comically weak by any conventional evaluation. Yet those few privileged city dwellers—who were a far more isolated minority in their society than were the Leipzig marchers in theirs—had witnessed the impossible collapse of power in the GDR and elsewhere in Eastern Europe. Fed by this experience of a miracle, they achieved their own defiance of all the odds of Russian history.

Their victory accelerated the final collapse of the Russian empire and of the Soviet Union itself six months later. This implosion of an empire without any outside pressures of war or catastrophe was historically unique, and it meant that united Germany did not have to inherit the bitter hatreds usually associated with such a breakup. Geopolitically, Ukraine's independence for the first time in 300 years also gave Western Europe a buffer against any renewed Russian imperial pretensions.

In superpower relations, German unification and the end of the cold war further transformed arms control, to the immense benefit of the Germans. From the late 1960s until 1989, strategic arms control was the fulcrum of East-West relations and a surrogate for virtually nonexistent political relations. The fall of the Berlin Wall effected, or at least completed, the restoration of politics to superpower stage center in a way that both Carter and Reagan had tried, but failed, to do earlier. Arms control of all sorts was thus freed to reflect the improved politics. The nightmare of nuclear holocaust vanished, as the United States and the Soviet Union finally signed a Strategic Arms Reduction Treaty in 1991, then within months signed a second understanding that will, if implemented, eliminate land-based multiple-warhead strategic missiles and bring the superpowers' total strategic warheads from 12,000 and 11,000, respectively, down to 3,000 to 3,500 each by the early twenty-first century. Of equal importance to Bonn, both powers also began to remove and destroy their tactical nuclear weapons. The Germans were relieved to see NATO's Lances disappear from Bavaria and to see all East European targets vanish from NATO lists, and were reassured rather than troubled by the remaining 700 American nuclear bombs in Europe. The Germans were even happier to see the more laxly guarded Soviet equivalents disappear from nearby areas of potential ethnic conflict. By mid-1992 all Soviet tactical nuclear warheads were withdrawn from eastern Germany, Eastern Europe, and all Soviet successor states except Russia.

During the Soviet breakup, the United States quickly took steps to avert proliferation, getting fourteen of the fifteen Soviet republics with nuclear weapons to surrender these 27,000 weapons to the more disciplined single successor state of Russia, or, in the case of strategic missiles remaining in Ukraine, Kazakhstan, and Byelarus, to promise to do so in the near future. Together, the United States and Germany also launched a companion initiative to offer jobs to the thousands of unemployed Soviet nuclear scientists to forestall their dispersal to would-be proliferators in the third world.[18]

Even more unexpectedly, after twenty-four years of desultory negotiation, an international treaty was signed banning production, use, stockpiling, and export of chemical weapons. In addition, the old Warsaw Pact and the NATO states finally agreed on the national distribution of their huge conventional cuts and began melting down 33,000 tanks, artillery, and other heavy weapons into scrap metal.[19] At the same time, the other signatories of the Treaty on Conventional Armed Forces in Europe agreed to individual troop ceilings in a pact that no longer left Germany as the only nation so restrained. Soviet forces continued to leave eastern Germany on schedule for meeting the 1994 target of total withdrawal.[20]

This still left old Soviet biological weapons out of international control. President Boris Yeltsin admitted in 1992 that a Soviet program had existed even after signature of an international treaty outlawing these weapons two decades earlier, and he contracted out destruction of Russian stockpiles to the United States. Yet he seemed unable to rein in a rogue Russian military that wanted to preserve the option of biological warheads on delivery missiles.

Nonetheless, after decades as the most immediate potential target of Soviet nuclear and conventional weapons, Germany hardly worried about marginal biological missiles. For Bonn the most important—and still unbelievable—change was the disappearance of those tens of thousands of tanks and artillery pieces in Eastern Europe and the withdrawal of the twenty Soviet divisions in eastern Germany. Any Russian attack was now preposterous, and even if the preposterous happened, advance mobilization would necessarily provide a warning time for any attack of a year instead of the previous few days. To be sure, ethnic battles were erupting throughout the old Soviet empire, but none—not even the carnage in Yugoslavia—carried the risk of a Europe-wide conflagration that might engulf Germany.

For the first time in history, Bundeswehr Inspector-General Klaus Naumann took to saying, Germany had only friends and allies as neighbors, or would as soon as the Russian withdrawal from eastern Germany was completed. For a country with the longest borders in Europe, one whose insecure position in the middle had led to countless wars, this was an inconceivable blessing.[21]

Two major exceptions marred this more peaceful landscape after German unification. The first was in the Persian Gulf, the second in Yugoslavia. In the end, both wars worked to erode the popular hope of the 1980s that if Germany and the West eschewed evil military force, a more peaceful world might result. Both helped shift the German public away from its longing for an ideal international role for Germany like that of a Switzerland writ large, holding itself aloof from the world's, and perhaps even Europe's, troubles.

The earliest test not only of post-wall superpower relations, but also of the new West-West relations in NATO, came with Iraq's lightning conquest of Kuwait in August 1990. Gorbachev had just agreed to the terms of German unity. Actual merger was two months hence. Not surprisingly, Bonn's main focus was not on the Arabian deserts.

The first consequence in Europe of Saddam Hussein's vivid reminder of post–cold war threats was to arrest what some feared could have become a race among NATO members to renationalize their security decisions and disarm unilaterally and precipitously. The second consequence, within Germany—though it was hardly noted abroad—was to split the pacifist-inclined left.

Iraq was an "out-of-area" case with a difference. It contained none of the unilateralism and few of the ambiguities of Reagan's controversial bombing of Libya that had so roiled U.S.-European relations in the mid-1980s. Bush carefully put together a broad coalition against Iraq before moving; the European allies willingly joined in an embargo and, in concert with Australia, in a naval blockade through NATO, the Western European Union (WEU), and EC channels.

For its part the Federal Republic, the old critic of Carter's and Reagan's economic sanctions and unilateral military operations, this time did not censure American and British challenges to vessels suspected of breaking the embargo on Iraq. On the contrary, it sent minesweepers and supply ships of its own to the Mediterranean to free other vessels for the allied expeditionary force in the gulf, contributed an initial $2 billion to the American operation and to those cooperating nations hardest hit by the embargo, facilitated the use of bases in Germany for ferrying troops and matériel to the Middle East, and loaned some unique tanks for detecting chemical weapons to the United States for use in Saudi Arabia. It further—in lieu of direct German troop participation, which everyone agreed was excluded under the long-standing interpretation of the Federal Republic's constitution—donated several more billion dollars to Desert Storm, for a total $6 billion payment to the United States alone. Bonn's own timid military actions, which earlier would have fueled editorial polemics about their constitutionality, roused so little controversy in the preoccupation with German unity that they were all but wiped off the front pages by the concurrent squabble over the date for all-German elections.

To be sure, Bonn did not contribute as much politically to the common cause as the United States would have wanted. What most irritated Washington was the ten-day public silence by the Bonn government in the face of protesters' and media condemnation of the U.S.-led bombing of Iraq that began in January 1991. West German television coverage focused on the two or three American army deserters in Germany and the noble Germans who were hiding them. German peace demonstrators reassembled to the chants of "No blood for oil!" Various Americans retorted by contrasting the American sacrifice of blood to the German sacrifice of a few billion marks, and again singled out German "Auschwitz in the sand" sales of chemical weapons components to Iraq. (America's own contribution to Iraqi armament was not yet known at this time.) A significant number of German air force officers assigned to accompany eighteen Luftwaffe Alpha jets redeployed to NATO-allied Turkey pleaded selective conscientious objection, on the grounds that Turkey had not been attacked, and NATO might be acting provocatively in sending warplanes there.

In the face of all this, the government offered no public defense of the United States or the gulf campaign for those ten long days. Alarmed out-of-office Atlanticists in Germany leapt into the breach to shift the public debate with a major advertising campaign in favor of the allied expedition. Numerous pundits on both sides of the Atlantic concluded that a renationalization of German defense was already under way, and that the American relationship with a Britain willing to participate in military police actions might after all be more special than the American-German economic links.

Yet those initial appearances deceived. The Bonn government, very quietly indeed, provided critical ammunition supplies and massive logistical help to the coalition war effort from the German staging area on the basis of existing NATO plans and practices; the gulf operation would have been inconceivable without this assistance.[22] At the other end of the spectrum the silent German majority (75 percent according to the polls), ignoring the opinion leaders, actually approved of the American coalition's actions in the gulf from the start.

Most important, given the special claim on the German conscience of potential Jewish victims, Iraq's Scud attacks on Israel set off a wave of German revulsion against Saddam Hussein. Memories of the Holocaust suggested that in an imperfect world there might be another moral imperative to overrule the moral imperative of never going to war. Intramural polemics broke out on the left that were even fiercer than the arguments over unification. The peace movement itself split as some charter members accused others of being anti-Semitic and knee-jerk anti-American.[23]

Within six months of the Gulf War, the attempted Soviet coup further contorted the old orthodoxies in Germany by showing how fragile new thinking might be in a land that had once casually exported 1.5 million Poles to Siberia overnight. Afterward, no less a witness than East German novelist Stefan Heym, who had deplored West Germany's swallowing up of East Germany in 1990 (and before that had helped spread the charge that American researchers were deliberately introducing the AIDS virus abroad), confessed that Kohl had "acted correctly and decisively" in seizing the chance to achieve swift union.[24]

The mounting slaughter in Croatia and then Bosnia as the ethnic wars there broke out and ground on unopposed made Germans question even more sharply the virtue of nonintervention. Rudolf Augstein counseled early on in *Der Spiegel*, "There is no doubt but that the great republic Germany must now take more worldwide political responsibility than before."[25] Yet all outside nations shrank from sending their sons to die for Sarajevo, and all the efforts of EC and UN diplomats to broker a ceasefire failed. Night after night Germans watched on television as undefended civilians were murdered, maimed, and driven from their homes.

In this new context the Germans opened a serious debate among themselves by the fall of 1992 about the morality of and responsibility for the use of force. The government sent 140 Bundeswehr medical volunteers to join UN peacekeeping forces in Cambodia and—over the constitutional appeal of the Social Democratic party (SPD)—dispatched a destroyer and three spotter aircraft to join allied patrols monitoring the UN embargo of Serbia in the Adriatic.[26] A consensus began to build that—however honorable the Germans' post-Hitler recoil from the use of force during the previous four decades—the time had come to reconsider the ethical trade-offs. The major parties agreed that the constitution should be reinterpreted, or even rewritten, to allow Bundeswehr units to participate in UN- or CSCE-ordained humanitarian and peacekeeping operations outside the NATO alliance area. The conservatives sought to expand this to potential use of force in peacemaking operations. In the meantime, the slimmed-down Bundeswehr was restructured to form several rapid-reaction battalions capable of undertaking whatever missions might eventually be agreed on: 25 percent of the new army, 20 percent of the air force, and 40 percent of the navy were dedicated as crisis reaction forces to be compatible with NATO planning.

The debate on circumstances under which the Germans might use force clarified that the terms of reference had totally changed. In the end the disappearance of the Soviet threat did not have the impact that the allies had initially feared of persuading the Germans that no army was necessary in the peaceful new world. Instead, the Russians' own vigorous repudiation of the old Soviet foreign policy and Moscow's support for the Iraq operation and various Western peacekeeping initiatives pulled the teeth of the left's former objections to Western power politics.

Thus domestic argument no longer focused on whether a semi-sovereign Federal Republic was or should be acting as the surrogate for superpower rivalries. It centered instead on whether the fully sovereign Germany, the undisputed leader of an integrating Europe, should or could be isolated from its neighbors and choose a new *Sonderweg* of abdication. Significantly, the left's old bogeyman of national interests now became— especially as applied to the agony of the former Yugoslavia—not a temptation for imperial meddling abroad, but rather a sober restraint on any urge to indiscriminate intervention on moral grounds. The whole debate shifted from moral to political categories.

In this framework, the necessary adjustments by NATO and by allied forces still stationed in Germany took place smoothly. Negotiators for a new supplement to the Status of Forces Agreement between the United States and sovereign Germany discreetly kept the talks out of the public eye until after the American presidential election, then turned out to have settled on arrangements that would drastically cut those exercises that irritated the Germans but still keep the United States engaged. American forces in Europe dropped from 300,000 toward some 70,000: a number that seemed large enough to demonstrate commitment but small enough not to attract congressional budget sharks or local German demonstrators. The Germans welcomed the withdrawals of GIs from cities, where their presence was most intrusive. They regretted withdrawals from towns in poorer regions like the Eifel.

For its part NATO drew the consequences of its announced changes and its swiftly cut national budgets, restructured to far leaner forces centered around the multinational, British-led rapid-reaction corps. The Germans won the real NATO military command under the American supreme allied commander, Europe, in the post of chief of staff. The East Europeans quickly became NATO's greatest fans, petitioned for membership, and pulled the alliance away from its premonitions of an early death. The organization's rejuvenation was, in fact, most evident in the invention of NATO's associated North Atlantic Cooperative Council, a hastily created halfway house to draw East European and Soviet successor states into dialogue.

Simultaneously, Kohl and Mitterand sprang a new French-German corps on their surprised defense and foreign ministers—and the Bundeswehr quickly practiced damage control to exact a government pledge that no German troops assigned to NATO would be taken away from the alliance to form the corps. With this, Kohl finally won Mitterrand's retraction of the decision to pull all French forces out of Germany. The French and Americans squabbled over the corps and over concomitant French efforts to reduce American political influence in Europe while still retaining American troops there. This time, however, in marked contrast to the 1980s, the Americans consciously shifted to the reality that the Europeans were the *demandeur* for the American presence; the moment the Europeans did not want them, they warned, they would leave. The French, Germans, and British subsequently conducted a long tug of war about whether the still-phantom WEU forces would constitute NATO's European pillar or the EC's defense component. The outcome would be a rhetorical draw that left the practical sorting out to the future. But even Britain would come to see the WEU as an insurance policy against any American pullout from Europe.[27]

What everyone did agree on fairly soon was that the much vaunted security architecture of the future would be jerry-built, with overlap among NATO, the WEU, the CSCE, and the UN. The CSCE set up a small permanent secretariat and was immediately swamped both by the Yugoslav civil wars and by the bloody breakup of the pax sovietica. NATO offered its services to the CSCE or the UN on a selective basis. The WEU secretariat, over French protests, moved to Brussels, where it would be closer both to the EC and to NATO, and planned for its first maneuvers (in consultation with NATO) in 1993. It was left open whether these would be only staff exercises, or whether the WEU would borrow troops from the French-German corps or NATO under WEU Secretary-General Willem van Eekelen's pet "double-hatting" scheme.

The East-West Gap

Is consensus to be found in a Germany turned upside down? The answer is yes, despite—or perhaps because of—the current malaise. Sufficient alarm has now been raised to jar leaders out of old habits and sterile confrontations. And Germany remains a stable, conservative country, even in adjusting to tectonic changes.

In terms of the most conspicuous division, that between east and west, various participants in the transformation hold that the present gulf is bridgeable. The west Germans are grumbling, but they are paying the $100 billion a year to the east (an equivalent, German officials note, of America's spending $200 billion on the savings and loan cleanup and more each year in real terms than the entire three-year Marshall Plan). They will accept further the necessary cuts in their own second vacations, health benefits, and industrial subsidies. That is, the politics of economics will become fair belt-tightening rather than, as for most of an idyllic quarter of a century, fair distribution of each incremental surplus.

On the eastern side, of course, the required adjustment to the west's whole system is more monumental, and therefore harder. The PDS and some of the old GDR intellectuals, expecting the east-west gap to persist, have formed a lobby and potential new party to press eastern complaints. Yet few observers expect the easterners' sense of being second-class citizens to remain so pronounced as to perpetuate an aggrieved separate eastern identity and return the PDS to the Bundestag in the 1994 general election.

To be sure, Genscher predicts, judging from his native Halle, the growing together will take a "very long time," since the different experiences of forty years cannot simply be swept away. He could conceive of an end to the worst alienation, however—if things begin looking up in the next two or three years—by the end of the century.[28]

Similarly, Wolfgang Schäuble, now leader of the Christian Democratic Union Bundestag caucus, believes that the east-west gap is largely a function of the still staggering economy in the east. Once the economy picks up, he surmises, the psychology too should greatly improve.[29]

If these instincts are correct, and if eastern Germany begins to lift out of its economic trough in 1993–94 as widely expected, the worst of the eastern bitterness could begin to ease fairly soon. Already, in a phenomenon that is common throughout Central Europe, the perception of individuals' own private well-being is much more positive than the perception of general economic trends.[30] Experience of modest but steady improvement could build on this base fairly rapidly to sustain a new optimism.

In such a context, especially after the disappointments of the first two years, the easterners might also scale down their expectations to more realistic levels. Kurt Biedenkopf, the western premier of Saxony whom the Saxons accept as one of their own, keeps urging his constituents to strive for something more attractive than becoming carbon copies of Wessis, and he keeps reminding them that in decades past, when high-tech Baden-Württemberg was still a cow pasture, Saxony was Germany's industrial heartland. Local patriotism is certainly one natural option, given German history, and could help considerably in building self-confidence.

Monika Maron, one of the remarkably few novelists who has dared wrestle with issues of identity in the GDR in retrospect, also prods her former compatriots to snap out of self-pity, lethargy, and a new, self-induced *Bevormundung* of blaming all their new troubles on the west. She has not yet stirred much of a response—at one talk she gave in the east she was reduced to arguing the rebuttal of her accusation herself—but as assurance grows in the east, so should her audience.[31]

The Left-Right Gap

The further consensus required in Germany—one that is far less publicized than east-west alienation—is that between right and left. Here considerable agreement has already emerged since unification. After fierce argument, politicians finally settled on apportionment of costs for reconstruction in eastern Germany between the federal and Länder governments. Funding of homes for the elderly was settled on after a twenty-year standoff, and soaring overall health payments were trimmed. The parties tackled the first major—and long overdue—reform in the university system since the number of students going to university doubled in the 1970s and 1980s. They approved a major twenty-year transportation program to expand the rail network (in preference to roads and polluting automobiles) and to connect it with their European neighbors' rail systems. Management and labor, after a melodramatic clash, have gone back to Germany's exemplary social harmony. Laws against exporting missile and chemical weapons components were finally tightened, as was their enforcement. The Bonn government, after two decades of resisting compulsory adherence to full International Atomic Energy Agency safeguards by all importers of nuclear-related materials, suddenly campaigned for this cause until all major suppliers accepted it in 1992.

The Maastricht treaty was ratified in parliament, and the two-thirds majority needed to implement relevant constitutional changes will be forthcoming. In the process the Länder will have carved out their new restraints on federal authority to cede powers to Brussels. The Bundestag will further amend the constitution to authorize the use of Bundeswehr units outside the NATO area for peacekeeping, and probably even peacemaking, operations.

The naturalization law was liberalized to enable Turks (and others) who have lived in Germany the requisite number of years to become citizens more easily. A more restrictive law on asylum was finally passed that will at least bring German practice more in line with other European practice. This and further changes in citizenship law will end Germany's old anomalies of shutting out immigration while granting a universal right to asylum in the abstract, simultaneously refusing most applicants, yet granting them generous social welfare and rarely expelling them. A further combination of education, police training, and—now that the mobs come from the right rather than the left—tightening of the very liberal 1970s laws governing demonstrations will enable the Germans finally to turn back the skinhead violence against Gypsies and Africans and Turks.

Moreover, the main parties will continue to wrestle out each year the terms for financing construction in the east. Popular unhappiness with the failure to do so earlier is now sufficiently strong that no party dares seek "profile"—making a name for itself by aggressively opposing the adversary party's views without compromise—at the cost of a real solution.

The left's post-unity crisis continues, and in most elements of the new consensus, it will be the left that will yield. Local SPD politicians who want to win elections have importuned Social Democratic leader Rudolf Scharping to revise the platforms party intellectuals have written during the past decade, and he is organizing the retreat on asylum, peacekeeping forces, and other issues. The SPD is not about to reinstate Helmut Schmidt to a position of honor, but it is returning to his centrism.

In the left's most sensitive issue, German participation in UN peace forces, it turns out that the Iraqi threat to Israel and the grisly slaughter in Yugoslavia greatly weakened the left's conviction that German moral abstention from military force would avert rather than perpetuate horrors. Green executive committee member Helmut Lippelt, after inspecting firsthand the "archaic violence" in the former Yugoslavia, explicitly announced the Greens' abandonment of pacifism.[32] The logical consequence of this shift, and of the left's parallel mistrust of Germans abandoned to their own devices, is the left's acceptance—now operationally as well as philosophically—that Germany must indeed be part of the West.

As the single Europe came into effect on January 1, 1993, then, the SPD's reconciliation with unification and the party's renewed preference for the power of office over ideological purity would be compared with Herbert Wehner's landmark steering of the party away from rote Marxism in 1959–60.

Outside politics, the parallel pragmatization of the literary left is so far advanced that some commentators have already announced its demise. Ulrich Greiner, writing an "obituary for the left," declares flatly, "The left doesn't exist any more," and welcomes the new chance to think individually, without the old pressures for intellectual conformity. As one example, he recalls the problems Otto Schily had as a Green parliamentarian in 1985, when he advocated accepting a state monopoly on force as against the left's claim to a higher morality above the law for violent demonstrators. Now, Greiner notes, the left is readier to endorse this orthodox view.[33]

The Voter-Establishment Gap

After east-west and left-right consensus, the final reconciliation outstanding is that between the political elites and the voters. Here the outcome will not be known until the 1994 general election, but certain warning signals and reassurances are already evident. The most obvious warning signals include the widely noted discontent with the existing parties; the appeal of the far-right Republicans, running up to 8 percent or more approval ratings in some localities; and the sanction in early and mid-1992 by thousands of onlookers of skinhead violence against foreigners.

Growing boredom with the centrist parties and their blurred consensus-oriented messages actually predates unification, but it has been exacerbated by the strains of union. Back in 1980 the three main parties together—the Christian Democratic Union/Christian Social Union, the SPD, and the Free Democratic party—took 98 percent of the vote, and 60 percent of their electorate were loyal stalwarts, with only 24 percent floating. By 1990 the three took only 88 percent of the vote, and only 44 percent of their electorate were consistent adherents, with 41 percent floating. Even worse, participation in elections went down during the same decade from 89 percent to 78 percent, contentment with democracy went down from 90 percent to 79 percent, and the number of those doubting the truthfulness of political leaders jumped from 33 percent in 1977 to 40 percent in April 1992. Conversely, those saying they had confidence in the parties dropped from 35 percent in 1984 to 24 percent in 1991, and those expressing confidence in government and parliament dropped from 70 percent in 1980 to 42 percent in 1991.[34]

These might be levels that American parties could only envy, but they represent a serious erosion for the Germans. They also summon the ghosts of the Weimar Republic, with its citizens' disastrous antipathy toward politics. The parties' most celebrated critic, President Richard von Weizsäcker, took up the popular complaint when he reproached the parties for being "power crazy," and asked if they might not be undermining constitutional democracy by their secretive decisions in smoke-filled rooms away from the glare of parliament.[35]

Some of this disenchantment is even reflected within the ruling Christian Democratic Union itself. The trophy of unification no longer earns much credit from voters, and Kohl has now passed the magic ten-year mark at which—to judge from Margaret Thatcher—leaders seem to exhaust their energies. There is probably more muttering in the ranks than at any previous time since the conservatives came to power, and business people make little secret of the growing estrangement between them and the chancellor. Yet his control of the party remains so absolute that Kohl still occupies the throne.

Does this mean that Germany's famous corporate decisionmaking, with change effected in small, frequent, consensual steps, is breaking down in face of the whirlwind of change in the past three years? Are Germans yearning to be done with endless ambiguities and desiring the hard-edge policies of the Republicans? Pending the answer at the polls in 1994, the best guess would be no, precisely because the politicians do seem, at last, to be forging the consensus to act and to show voters that they are solving problems. Economic upturn in the east should favor the centrist parties by election day, and voters who register their protest in favor of the Republicans in local elections will typically return to the mainstream parties in the federal election. The Republicans are as unlikely as the Party of Democratic Socialism to get over the 5 percent hurdle to enter the new Bundestag.

Return to Consensus?

In the past, the Federal Republic's sturdy and resilient democracy has proved itself capable of creating consensus. At this stage, after the cataclysm of three post-wall years, its talent for consensus building has not yet functioned to restore equilibrium and the predictability that is so dear to German hearts. The gravest sign of failure is habituation to violence against foreigners, the disabled, and other weak members of society.

Shock at this failure is now palpable. Already it has summoned spontaneous candlelight demonstrations of solidarity with foreigners by hundreds of thousands of Germans in Berlin, Munich, and elsewhere. Is the shock sufficient to rally a sober new consensus between east and west, right and left, parties and public, and Germans and the many others who put their hope in the Germans?

Despite the burdens, the answer is probably yes. The country's stewards are determined that Germany no longer be "the delayed nation," the rejector of the Enlightenment, the political dwarf, or the purveyor of archaic hate. They long to atone for Hitler and to muster that responsible leadership for Germany, for the EC, and for Central Europe that only the Germans can provide. They now have their chance.

Chapter 17

Agenda for America

F ew generations are vouchsafed the chance to reshape the world. Today they have that opportunity as the old Russian empire continues to disintegrate, German power rises for the third time in a century, and Europe begins a troubled new renaissance.

The United States is not the same colossus now as it was forty years ago. Yet it still holds a unique position as the sole remaining superpower and the necessary balancer of both East-West and West-West relations. Much will depend on its wisdom and skill in managing the present transformation.

The last time a world was shattered, it was indeed America's upstart diplomats who put it together again almost single-handedly, in what awe-struck Secretary of State Dean Acheson called "the creation." Despite abundant evidence to the contrary, they started from the novel premise that peace was not an aberration, but the norm (at least in Europe). They turned their backs on the isolationism of the 1930s and on the sage eighteenth century but dangerous twentieth century advice to avoid entangling alliances. They stationed hundreds of thousands of GIs permanently in Europe and committed the new continent to the NATO alliance to contain the Soviet Union—and deter war altogether, so the United States need not intervene a third time in medias res to rescue the old continent from its civil wars.

Moreover, after World War II the Americans redressed the punitive Treaty of Versailles that had so quickly after World War I led to a new bloodletting. Remarkably, they decided that the way to increase their own well-being was not to hoard jealously their half of world production, but to share it out in order to generate more wealth for all. In enlightened self-interest, they devoted an unheard of 3 percent of their gross national product and 10 percent of their federal budget to Marshall Plan aid to rebuild Europe into a formidable economic rival. To that weary, cynical Europe they imparted optimism and energy as well as money. They also insisted that the Marshall Plan largesse be administered not unilaterally, but multilaterally by all its recipients—including the erstwhile German enemy—in cooperation with each other. This requirement, along with the vision of the Robert Schumans and Jean Monnets, forged the European Community (EC).

The Marshall Plan, along with the Bretton Woods creation of new international financial and trade institutions that could withstand the fatal pressures for protectionism, succeeded beyond anyone's wildest imagining. Despite some false starts, democracy and prosperity became synonymous in the minds of West European voters and shut out the extremes of both right and left. The whole structure proved sturdy and flexible enough not only to incorporate the emerging Japan into the free trade club, but also to incorporate Spain and Portugal (and an errant Greece) into the Western European democratic commonwealth as they emerged from right-wing dictatorships.

At the same time the perverse blessing of nuclear terror outlawed war on that foreign parcel of earth most dear to both superpowers. Western Europe enjoyed its longest peace since the Middle Ages, despite the convulsions of decolonization, and despite the tense cold war confrontations.

By contrast, Eastern Europe, dominated by the Soviet army, paid the price for this precious stability. Eastern Europe was the cruel exception to the continent's long peace. In a nuclear era, prevention of East-West war and miscalculation was all important; after some initial probes the West would no more interfere militarily in the ceded Soviet sphere of control east of the Elbe than the Soviet Union would interfere in the West.

Yet in the end Gorbachev the Intrepid came to power and introduced perestroika. He and his advisers became convinced that guns and remote Afghan passes were less useful than butter and joint ventures, and that old-guard ideologists and rotten Eastern European economies were more a burden than an asset. Increasingly, the East Europeans tested their expanding room for maneuver, until 1989 became the year of democratic (or para-democratic) revolution throughout the region.

For all the brutality in Yugoslavia, the danger now does not compare with the late 1940s, when a savage and possibly mad czar in Moscow, a man who had murdered 20 million of his own subjects, seized a new empire of 100 million East Europeans and acquired the atom bomb. But the Soviet successor states could still degenerate into chaos. The United States might still abdicate from Europe. The EC, in the public rebellion against the Maastricht treaty, might fall into paralysis just at the time it needs to go forward to integrate the new Germany and the new East Central European democracies.

Positively, there is now a historic opportunity to spread the West's cooperative international community eastward—and negatively, there is a risk that failure to do so might import instability into Germany, especially in refugee flows that could warp domestic politics. The United States and Germany are key to the endeavor to knit East Central Europe into Europe proper, the United States because it is the only superpower left, Germany because it is still the European dynamo and the example the East Europeans, the Balts, and the Russians look to as a model for their own modernization. However much they must now focus on domestic reconstruction, the United States and Germany are the only two countries in the transatlantic community that understand that the continent cannot accept perpetual division into haves and have-nots without paying a terrible price. American policy toward Germany is therefore of far more than bilateral interest.

Heritage of Trust

At this stage American security policy toward Germany (and Europe, since the two are no longer divisible) must begin with acknowledging the extraordinary accomplishment in Germany in 1989–90 and building on this foundation. The famous new world order may be a chimera in the third world after a gulf war that was far less of a defining event than German unification, but it is already reality in a Europe that is to some degree postnational, ready to explore new patterns of security, and expanding its system eastward from the sheer attractiveness of its example.

In this new context the job of Washington's leadership—and for all the dated talk of a declining United States, the American chief executive remains what *La Repubblica* calls a "kind of president of the world"—is both harder and easier than during the cold war.

It is harder because the single Soviet adversary has vanished against whom all other rights, wrongs, and policies might be measured, and because Washington will now have to share leadership with, and sometimes defer to, the dynamic new Europe much more than in the past.

It is easier because the acute danger is gone. The nuclear sword of Damocles has lifted; the penalties for mistakes are not so catastrophic, and defense no longer makes such distorting demands on domestic budgets and tolerance. Leadership is also easier because the end of the Russian empire has bridged Germany's old left-right gap over sovereignty and subservience to the United States; has restored the Germans' identity; and has made obsolete such transatlantic squabbles as those over first nuclear use, short-range nuclear weapons, Soviet superiority in heavy conventional weapons, NATO burden sharing, credits to the Soviet Union, and even, to a degree, "out-of-area" interventions. Moreover, it has diffused such arguments as do arise, rendering them discrete and subject to individual compromise rather than cumulative and mutually aggravating.

Already Washington has begun to adapt to the new European order, but it needs to adjust still more. In theory, it correctly sees enlightened self-interest in perpetuating that Euro-Atlantic community of the past half century that began as an ad hoc defensive contract, but ended—in trilateral community with the Pacific Rim—as an unimaginable magnifier of the commonweal. In practice, however, the United States keeps being tempted to break out of that international commonwealth in answer to the calls of protectionism, unilateralism, or preservation of the dominance it enjoyed in relation to the old Europe of separate nation-states.

These temptations are probably weaker than the fundamental American instincts, both popular and official, that favor continuation of a co-operative relationship with Europe (and even Japan).[1] Yet to withstand repeated temptations, this pro-European inclination needs to be anchored in conscious, articulated policy. The United States needs to acknowledge that the progressive integration of a democratic Europe in fulfillment of America's 1940s vision is entirely healthy and positive for the United States, and to build from there eastward. This means, most fundamentally, keeping the United States engaged in Europe. It also means supporting the widening and deepening of the EC into political and eventual defense union if the EC so chooses, rather than exploiting Anglo-Dutch Franco-German feuds for short-term American advantage.

Such a policy requires working out consultation channels between NATO, the EC, and the Western European Union that could permit the formation of a European army and its use in Europe, as the need arises, with the discreet backing of American intelligence and airlift. It entails giving the Conference on Security and Cooperation in Europe (CSCE) some teeth in crisis prevention. It also entails specific Euro-American backing for the efforts of the East Central European and Baltic states to build stable economic and political systems, and specific American backing for the efforts of these countries to join the EC.

This would be a more subtle kind of leadership than the United States exercised in galvanizing its allies to withstand Soviet pressures during forty years of cold war. It would respond to the desire of Germans to maintain the ultimate American security reinsurance, the desire of non-Germans to have an American balance to Germany, the desire of the small European states to have an American balance to the large European powers, and now the desire of East Central Europeans to have American patronage as a buffer against both the Russians and the Germans.

This more modest role for the United States would be a sign of maturity rather than of decline. It would voluntarily shift some of the burden of leadership, both in funding and in initiatives, to the Europeans in general, and the wealthy Germans in particular. It would acknowledge that in the Euro-Atlantic community that already exists policy debates have gone beyond traditional clashes of monolithic national interest to become, in effect, exercises in domestic coalition building between ever-shifting constituencies that now span the Atlantic. It would maintain a U.S. voice in regulating the world economic environment that is now so important for the quality of life, but it should permit a welcome redirection of American resources and primary attention away from foreign policy back toward this country's own pressing problems of education, the economy, violence, and homelessness.

Partners in Leadership

In Europe the Federal Republic is leading the march to the next century, not only because it is the biggest and richest land on the continent, but also because it made the original leap to conceive of a European identity four decades ago. The Germans had to surrender their sovereignty and tribal patriotism in 1945. Their social glue has long since passed beyond heroic nineteenth century (and Nazi) chauvinism to the more humdrum but safer cohesion of consumer satiety and constitutional legitimacy. Today's policymakers in Bonn and Berlin were inoculated against national hubris in their formative years, when they discovered that their parents had tolerated Hitler's murder of Jews and Gypsies in the name of Germany. The much more nationalistic French and English, having been spared such shame, still face the painful loss of narrow patriotism as the European Community assumes more authority.

Moreover, the Germans, with considerable powers already distributed to jealous Länder in a way that was not artificially imposed on them by the victors of World War II but was an outgrowth of centuries of splintered principalities, will adapt nicely to the new regional dynamics as politics devolves downward as well as upward in the new Europe.[2] Neither Paris nor London has yet reconciled itself to such decentralization. Economically, politically, and intellectually, Germany is a country whose time has come in a continent whose time has come again.

In this context it makes sense for the United States to continue to give the priority to its bilateral relationship with Germany that Bush had in mind when he anointed them as "partners in leadership" in spring 1989. Events in the train of unification are creating their own enormous pressures on Bonn and Berlin to exert leadership in Europe in any case. And while conventional American wisdom at unification presumed that the newly sovereign Germany must necessarily flex this new leadership in renationalization of defense—and in rebellion against its irritating European partners and its erstwhile U.S. patron—a strong case can now be made for a contrary thesis of intensified cooperation.

Thus the older Germans who currently hold senior positions feel an urgent need to knit their country into an interwoven Europe before ceding their posts to a generation they fear might be less inhibited by German history, and therefore less European. And many Germans who in the past enjoyed the invisible American security, but felt morally superior because they did not have to dirty their own hands with fighting—just as Americans scorned the British defense of the high seas they passively enjoyed in the nineteenth century—may well gain more appreciation for the United States as they themselves inherit part of the old American security function.[3] Conversely, many Americans who previously deemed Germans cowardly may, in the post–cold war era, gain an appreciation of the German art of reaching cooperative, ambiguous solutions.

Put a different way, Germany may turn out to be postnational, not only in Europe, but also in the Euro-Atlantic community. And in today's more relaxed world, the United States may see differences with Germany and with Europe less as zero-sum clashes of interest (the view that prevailed in the Reagan administration) than as joint searches for the maximum common good (the view that prevailed under Bush). To be sure, many differences between the United States and the Federal Republic will continue, but with a bit of circumspection, policy wrestling matches between Washington and Bonn could turn out to be no different in kind from, say, the rivalry between the U.S. Army and U.S. Air Force or the German Foreign Ministry and the Chancellery.

Europe's Security Architecture

War has now become as obsolete in once war-prone Europe—at least heartland Europe—as slavery or the divine right of kings. The slaughter of two world wars and the horror of potential nuclear holocaust have assured this transformation. The new security task will be to stanch those wars at the periphery—in the anachronistic Balkans and perhaps in the remnants of the Russian empire—and then to spread the voluntary, democratic Western European peace eastward and southward.[4] With no Eurasian adversary superpower requiring the counterweight of the American superpower in Europe, this new security task belongs primarily to the Europeans, and is so understood by them for the first time since 1945.

The tranquility of Europe is also important to the United States, however. The reasons that compelled Washington to intervene, late, in World Wars I and II are all the more compelling in today's world of much greater economic, financial, and informational interdependence. In addition, today's ultimate threat of nuclear annihilation, however successful we have been at neutralizing it thus far, surely counsels preventive engagement to help maintain a benign political system in Europe, rather than another belated intervention after events have spun out of control. America still has an important role to play in the 1990s in reinsuring Europe against remote nuclear risks and providing the kind of outside political balance that Europeans have come to rely on.[5]

The U.S. function at this point is less existential than auxiliary, in assuring a smooth transition to a stable Europe in the new environment. However, as the Soviet empire disintegrates, potentially giving rise to the kind of turbulence that the breakup of the Austro-Hungarian, Ottoman, British, and French empires did, American commitment in this time of transition is still crucial for well-being on both sides of the Atlantic.

The precise architecture of Europe's post-wall system is hard to discern, not only because it has not yet emerged, but also because the multiplicity of overlapping institutions blurs the lines of responsibility. The simplicity of bipolar confrontation—NATO and the EC on our side, the Warsaw Treaty Organization and the Council for Mutual Economic Assistance on theirs—is yielding to a much more nebulous arrangement. Following dissolution of both communist organizations and of the Soviet Union itself in 1991, the EC and NATO continue to be the dominant institutions in terms of security, with the EC assuming ever greater responsibility in an era in which security is increasingly nonmilitary. The Western European Union, the Council of Europe, the CSCE, the North Atlantic Cooperation Council, the World Bank, the International Monetary Fund, the European Bank for Reconstruction and Development, the Group of Seven industrialized democracies, the United Nations, the Organization for Economic Cooperation and Development, the European Court of Human Rights, the Court of First Instance of the European Communities, the European Energy Charter, regional groupings, individual national governments, European and especially German business people, and other actors will also participate in stabilizing the new Europe in ways that will shift with changing circumstances.

The European Community

Even before it enters the confederal European Union targeted for the end of the century, the European Community will be the central organization that all others will increasingly orient themselves to, not only in economics but also in security. The United States should not be deceived by the agonizing birth pangs of political and monetary union—or Europe's inability to halt the bloodshed in Yugoslavia, or the Germans' preoccupation with jacking up their new eastern regions—into thinking that the EC will lapse back into its slumber of the 1970s and early 1980s. All German policymakers and all major German parties now agree that Germany's future can be secured only within a uniting Europe, and they will continue to press for this. All non-Germans agree that German energies can be safely channeled only within the larger framework of the EC. All West Europeans further agree that they can meet environmental and drug-running challenges and migration pressures from the east and south only as a unit.

Thus, following German unification, the EC is condemned to succeed. Its deepening must slow, following public resistance to some aspects of the Maastricht treaty, but its widening to take in new European Free Trade Association and then East Central European members will proceed. In doubling its constituent countries by the early twenty-first century, the EC will set the economic and political norms that applicants must meet in order to join the club. This means not only harmonizing business, trade, and tax laws (the East Central Europeans are already adopting most EC economic legislation), but also observing human rights; protecting minorities; safeguarding free elections; and, of course, renouncing any change of borders by force.

The EC possesses strong incentives and disincentives to encourage such civilized behavior in the neighborhood. Much as West Europeans insisted that Spain and Portugal meet democratic criteria before being admitted to the Council of Europe and the EC in the 1970s, so they will now insist that the East Central Europeans play by the rules. The sanction of withholding EC membership from recidivists should go far toward discouraging, say, reversion to the kind of praetorian rule that prevailed in Eastern Europe in the 1920s and 1930s. The EC will take the lead not only in organizing Western financial aid to the East to undergird democratization—and in opening its markets, perforce, to Eastern exports in place of opening its borders to millions of poor immigrants—but also in educating the new democrats in the difficult arts of pluralism.

The United States can watch these developments with equanimity. Fortunately, it does not have to deal with the difficult problems of redressing the "democratic deficit" of the unifying Europeans, of balancing rival Sicilian and Galician claims to economic stimulation, and of forcing farmers into a real market economy while still preserving village virtues. And it should not worry about EC trespasses on NATO turf.

Indeed, a more cohesive, more powerful, democratic Europe that can take over some of the U.S. security burden on the continent is all to America's advantage, whatever the short-term frustrations for Washington in facing a more or less single ally that is suddenly bigger and richer than the United States. The United States should therefore support the European evolution and increase its direct dealings with the EC in proportion as political unity progresses.

Unitary diplomacy with the EC will, of course, never fully supplant bilateral diplomacy with individual European countries, any more than bilateral diplomacy displaces direct contacts, say, between the U.S. Department of Commerce and economics ministries in European nations. Bilateral contacts will continue, not least with Germany, the benevolent bully of European integration in much the same way that the United States for decades was the benevolent bully of NATO. The United States should no longer insist that European national governments negotiate everything bilaterally and severally with Washington, however, and no longer protest that any coordination of a single European policy before U.S.-European talks would constitute ganging up on the United States.

Such a divide-and-weaken approach maximized immediate American influence in the atomized Europe of the 1970s and 1980s, and one could argue that this hectoring style was often needed to force urgent decisions through sixteen sluggish sovereign parliaments in the clear and present danger of East-West confrontation. In the past the German government, for one, often tacitly preferred this approach, since it allowed Washington to ram decisions through NATO that Bonn actually wanted but could not itself deliver politically. As the NATO maxim had it, the Europeans loved to be led by the United States—just so long as it was in the direction the Europeans wanted to go.

Whatever functions this unequal relationship served in the past, however, preserving it artificially now would be counterproductive. In the 1990s it will be much more useful to have what the United States has always said it wanted: an equal defense pillar in Europe for the transatlantic bridge, and a corresponding shared leadership.[6]

Despite their closeness, the United States and the EC will, of course, have trade disputes that cut across their common security interests. Because of space constraints, this book deals only with security in its classic definition and omits economic, environmental, and social issues, important though these are. In very broad economic terms, however, both the United States and Germany should avoid the trap that many fear in the post-wall era: removal of the former outside restraints on West-West economic squabbles through disappearance of the overarching Soviet threat.

Especially as the fledgling American export lobby grows stronger, the temptation to indulge in all-out chicken or oilseed wars can presumably be avoided by national import restrictions and by continuing the General Agreement on Tariff and Trade negotiations, and the United States no longer worries as it did initially that "1992" could create a fortress Europe. The beggar-thy-neighbor reflex will be much harder to resist after the turn of the century, however, when either the Ecu of a real European Monetary Union or the deutsche mark supplants the dollar as the world's main reserve currency, and the United States can no longer "tax" European and Japanese holders of its debt by inflating the dollar.

Certainly both sides of the Atlantic are aware of the dangers. It should not be beyond the wit of the Americans and Germans in particular, with their stakes of direct investment alone in each other's economies in the tens of billions of dollars, to stop playing chicken short of a collision. There is a problem of world trade issues' being crowded off the German agenda because of Bonn's absorption with eastern reconstruction. But Germany, which exports a third of its national product, and the United States, which exports a tenth of its larger national product for a volume close to Germany's, should be natural allies in wanting as open a world trading system as possible. The American suggestion of a U.S.-EC treaty aiming for a common free trade area should be pursued.

NATO

Before November 9, 1989, the consensus seemed to be that NATO was suffering from congenital, and perhaps terminal, crisis; that American and German interests were bound to clash as postwar Germany and its successor generation came of age; that only Moscow could offer reunification to the Germans, for a price; that (in the right's formulation) Gorbachev was playing the peace and disarmament theme so cleverly that Western publics, swept up in "Gorbymania," "Genscherism," and the fading Soviet threat, would outrace themselves to disarm and leave Moscow to dominate Europe; that (in the left's formulation) the United States could no longer impose bipolar confrontation on Europe; that the Americans would or should tire of paying for European defense and American hegemony and go home; and that the Europeans would or should respond by accommodating themselves to the Soviet Union. Implicit in much of this analysis was fear that the weaknesses of open Western societies would prove vulnerable to the strengths of the Soviet command society.[7]

After November 9, the consensual worry still maintained a kind of half-life among analysts inclined to snatch defeat from the jaws of victory. Even if NATO survived, they thought, a newly sovereign Germany no longer dependent on American security would deem NATO a shackle that was only keeping the Germans down. Surely the united Germans would, in another widely used image, "hollow out" their commitment to the alliance and expel Western allied troops from their territory.[8] Or Germany might revert to aggressive behavior and become, in columnist Conor Cruise O'Brien's term, the "Fourth Reich."[9] Or—under the prevalent international relations theory that national function follows international form—once the opposite pole of the bipolar world vanished, the nations clustered around the American pole would inevitably fall into anarchy, "renationalization" of their defense policies, and amoral shifting alliances of the nineteenth century variety. Under unstable multipolarity, even Western Europe might succumb once more to war as long-suppressed ethnic conflicts exploded in the east and spread west.[10] After all, alliances are unnatural, the reasoning went, and endure only so long as a mortal threat exists. Even today, some serious commentators still think NATO is in deep crisis.[11]

In part, the abrupt ending of German and European division in 1990 has transformed those earlier premises. In part, it has exposed them as false, or at least incomplete, from the beginning. With some surprise, the allied governing elites are discovering that the reports of NATO's demise were greatly exaggerated. The raw need for ready military forces able to repel any standing-start surprise attack—NATO's nightmare for so long—has vanished, but there is an allied consensus that a reinsurance mission remains. And NATO, as the only institution politically able to keep the Americans fully engaged in Europe, is too useful to too many nations to be given up lightly.[12]

Certainly German habituation to the stability provided by NATO's collective defense—and obviation of the need for German nuclear weapons or a large German army—disposes Bonn to perpetuate NATO so long as there is any risk of unpredictable events in the neighborhood.[13] Every Bonn government has explicitly acknowledged this advantage, and Yugoslavia's atavistic tribal wars and the messy breakup of the Soviet Union have now spread recognition of this advantage more broadly among the general public. Moreover, Bush's unstinting support for unification in 1989–90 showed the benefits of maintaining an alliance with a large, distant friend who is not as encumbered by European history as are Germany's near neighbors. The French-German relationship will always have to be the core of the European Community, but the Germans will also need, for a long time to come, a less parochial counterweight to Paris and London.

To be sure, the current West German enthusiasm for NATO could be abnormally colored at this point by gratitude for America's stalwart support for unification against the French and British (and Soviets). But there will probably continue to be numerous issues in which German stakes will coincide more closely with American than with French or British interests, and Germany will value its augmented influence in European councils arising from its American connection in NATO.

Moreover, the horrors of Bosnia show the prudence of retaining for now the option of NATO's military prowess and practiced political crisis management. The Atlantic alliance is still the sole international organization with an integrated military command adaptable to a variety of situations. It is an existing institution that can perpetuate the American habit of political engagement in Europe—with reduced numbers of GIs—without requiring the generation of impossible new popular American support for this involvement. It is a forum the Europeans trust and understand how to use. The Germans and the British realize that perpetuating NATO is the only way to persuade the Americans to stay on in Germany. And after almost three years of balking, the French are finally resigning themselves to the fact that the Americans will not remain in Germany as mercenaries, and that NATO and a continued American political voice in Europe are the price Paris must pay to prolong an American military contribution to European stability.

Thus, in the 1990s, the United States should continue to treat NATO as the primary forum for discussing security issues among the industrialized democracies. The benefit is great, and with the disappearance of the Soviet threat, the costs and risks of maintaining the Atlantic alliance are much smaller and more bearable than they used to be. They will not siphon unacceptable resources away from America's own domestic overhaul. In today's interdependent world, in a nuclear era in which the United States cannot afford to intervene a third time if European wars break out, NATO's ounce of prevention is still worth a pound of cure. Within NATO the United States should also seek to broaden the alliance's reach by proposing that Japan be invited to establish a permanent liaison office in Brussels. It should further promote various other innovations, ranging from adoption of German as one of the official NATO languages to possible nomination of a European as NATO's supreme allied commander.

One old NATO issue—out-of-area intervention—should be mentioned here just because it is no longer the bone of contention it used to be. U.S. and German policies are converging in this respect. In Washington a domestically focused Clinton administration with slashed military budgets and a reduced army is, in any case, much less inclined to resort to controversial, unilateral intervention, while in Bonn the Germans now accept, in principle, the need for occasional interventions abroad in a way they did not earlier. Should a NATO consensus develop that military action was needed in the Middle East, the Germans would certainly provide once more all the logistical staging support necessary for U.S. and allied operations. There would be no repetition of the 1970s fights over confining American forces and equipment in Germany to a restrictive internal NATO role.[14] Moreover, in a sea change for Germany, the Kohl government has already made its own Bundeswehr volunteers available for modest UN operations in Somalia and NATO air surveillance of Yugoslavia.

One new out-of-area issue in which American, German—and EC, Russian, and Chinese—cooperation is urgently needed is in establishing global rules and a monitoring system to prevent the proliferation of missile, as well as nuclear and chemical weapons, technology.[15] There is a related need for German-American leadership to curb third world sales of conventional weapons and to provide the few million dollars of aid to improve the safety of Chernobyl-type nuclear power plants in the former Soviet bloc. Germany is not one of the big five exporters of conventional weapons (the United States, the Soviet successor states, France, Britain, and China) that provide more than 90 percent of all arms transfers. Its general export experience, its familiarity with would-be markets for old East German weapons, and, despite exceptions, its widely observed ban on German weapons exports to areas of tension make it a natural partner in the endeavor to curb conventional arms exports, however. It prodded the big powers to set up the new U.N. registry of arms transfers, and it should be consulted in preparations for the newly instituted meetings of the big five arms exporters.[16]

The CSCE and East Central Europe

Initially, as bipolarity ended in 1989–90, many analysts thought that the NATO system (if it survived) would apply to the Oder-Neisse line, while the CSCE would apply east of the line to the Urals. The NATO universe, with its practice of allied consultation and cooperation, whatever the intramural fights along the way, would constitute a family of shared values and democratic rules for working out compromises. A mutual commitment to active collective defense of the territory of all members against any outside aggression would be maintained. The CSCE universe, bringing together much more disparate nations in a pact of survival at least and mutual benefit at most, would be a much looser regime of collective security in which any sanctions against aggression or intimidation would have to be agreed on ad hoc, and in virtual unanimity.[17]

Within two years this geographical line of demarcation shifted eastward to the Bug River, in part because speedy Soviet dissolution removed the need for kid-glove treatment of the former superpower's former European empire, in part because the East Central Europeans themselves refused to be shunted off to the second-class security of the CSCE. Instead, the East Europeans strove for an ever closer link to the more muscular security of NATO.

NATO declined to grant membership to East European countries and deemed any extended guarantees still premature, especially before the August 1991 coup attempt in the Kremlin. By early summer 1991, however, as the Warsaw Pact formally disbanded and as East Europeans killed off Mitterrand's notion of a European confederation without the United

States, NATO put a tentative arm around the East Central Europeans.[18] In April U.S. Defense Under Secretary Paul Wolfowitz noted in a speech that "European security is indivisible. The United States is committed to supporting the process of democracy, as well as the independence and sovereignty of the Central East European states." In June the NATO summit in Copenhagen issued a promise that "coercion or intimidation" in Eastern Europe would be treated by alliance members as a matter of "direct and material concern."

Most authoritatively, in July Secretary of State James Baker testified before the Senate Foreign Relations Committee that the Conventional Forces in Europe (CFE) Treaty—which, he pointed out, the NATO states had signed—could be viewed as a legal guarantee of the territorial inviolability of East Central Europe, since it "provides that no state party to CFE may station forces on the territory of another without the express consent of that state."[19]

By now, with Poland, Hungary, and the Czech and Slovak republics associated with the EC and the North Atlantic Cooperative Council and already standing in line for EC membership, the CSCE is less needed in East Central Europe. There the EC's far more stringent democratic and free market norms than those of the consensus-bound CSCE are the engine for the spread of the Western system.

Nor did the CSCE process evolve into an effective instrument of peacekeeping in the Yugoslav civil war. That test came too early, of course; the CSCE was empowered to set up a tiny secretariat and Conflict Prevention Center in the summer of 1991 only days before fighting broke out in the Balkans. It was hardly surprising that it was not the CSCE, but the European Community and the United Nations that took on the main responsibility of trying to separate the Serbs and Croats—and failed, given the unwillingness of outsiders to provide military sanctions.

The CSCE remains valuable, however, in enshrining the pledges of all signatories of the Helsinki Final Act not to change international borders by force. Its guidelines of behavior worked out in the 1980s still set the important minimum standard in the Balkans and in the Soviet successor states in respect for human rights, safeguarding of democratic freedoms, rule of law, and protection of minorities. Even with a veto for everyone (or, as now adumbrated, unanimity by all except the country that sanctions might be applied to), the four-dozen-member CSCE will be the chief forum for monitoring and promoting adherence to these guidelines. The genius of the CSCE was and is its successful combination of consciousness raising and more or less voluntary authorization of international prying into domestic treatment of member states' citizens. The United States and Germany together should help strengthen this consensual intrusion into traditionally sovereign matters as the Conflict Prevention Center is activated, not as an exclusive CSCE function, but as one possible resort for aggrieved minorities or individuals lacking domestic redress. In addition, the CSCE's new Center for Democracy, in conjunction with the Council of Europe, is already helping to train lawyers and build legal systems for the new democracies.

In military affairs the CSCE further deserves American support as the most likely sponsor in this volatile period of confidence building and arms control verification measures. NATO should, as needed, lend military forces for such tasks.

Such functions will not impinge on NATO—as the United States feared might happen in 1990—but could usefully supplement it and the EC. After Washington safely navigated the CSCE Charter of Paris in 1990 and agreed to regular political consultations among members—without having German unification slowed or NATO undermined—the United States mellowed toward the institution. It should mellow still more, and, together with Germany, actively use the CSCE process to help the Soviet successor states and the Balkans, in particular, move in the direction of pluralism and civilian control of the military.

Finally, whatever the particular institution or combination of institutions used, something must be done to stop the bloodletting in Yugoslavia and to discourage other territorial grabs of the kind Serbia has now effected in Croatia and Bosnia and Croatia has in Bosnia. Neither the EC nor the United States has performed creditably in this crisis. Primary policing must be the Europeans' task, but the United States can hardly claim credible involvement in Europe if it continues to abdicate in Yugoslavia. At a minimum, the United States too should contribute soldiers to the UN ground forces there and pay up its old Reagan-era UN assessments to help finance current operations.

Conclusions

Managing Soviet collapse, German ascent, and East Central European transition will not be easy. Preserving the congruence among democracy, prosperity, and peace will not be easy, especially in the midst of swiftly rising expectations, world recession, and pent-up nationalist animosities in the Balkans and the former Soviet Union. Yet the means of maintaining essential European security to give positive evolution the best chance— much as the improvised transatlantic security guarantee of the 1940s gave West Europeans the space to construct their economic and political miracles—is at hand.

This new European order still has two powers, but no longer two poles. It no longer has, as in the nineteenth and early twentieth centuries,

two revisionist states, Germany and Russia, that alternately clash or col-
lude, disrupting the concert of Europe either way. Nor does it have to
contend with the mutually repelling poles of the Soviet and American
superpowers. Indeed, the organizing principle of the new ad hoc system is
precisely the Western precept of renouncing force or intimidation in intercourse among democracies; and however alien this may be to the hierarchical experience east of the Czech republic, it is a precept that the Soviet
successor states increasingly understand as the price of joining the West.

In this developing system of the 1990s the two powers on the continent
are the United States and German-driven Europe. They are linked in a
four-decade-old Euro-Atlantic enterprise that the participants are discovering, to their surprise, is a real community and not just a frontier alliance
against the wolves.

The partnership of Americans and Germans that is at the heart of this
community is healthy. The two know they need each other. They have
come through a common baptism of fire since the fall of the Berlin Wall,
and they are both committed to cooperation in minimizing the risks of a
newly unpredictable Europe. In the 1990s, the two will be more equal
than ever before, not only because Germany magnified by Europe is as
big and powerful as the United States, but also because the two foreign
policy mentalities are now converging to some extent. The United States,
while not abdicating from Europe, will be more inward-looking in the
post–cold war decade and less inclined to armed intervention abroad. Germany, though preoccupied with the difficult modernization of its eastern
provinces, faces such turmoil at its doorstep that it is being forced to turn
activist in broader European affairs. It fully intends to share in exercising
leadership in the EC, the Euro-Atlantic community, the Group of Seven,
and in the UN Security Council whenever this is restructured.

In the new Europe, a policy of concentric circles makes the most sense.
A process of democratization is desirable and is now possible in East
Central Europe and, with the help of the Scandinavians, in the Baltic
states. It is hardly viable as yet east of there. Virtue therefore begins with
a pragmatic focus on developing East Central Europe economically and
politically, and letting the energies set free there spill over as Russian black
marketeers and Ukrainian workers flock to the glittering streets of Warsaw
and Tallinn. Economically, it will be important to provide enough development to sustain democratization and ensure that democracy does not
become equated with hardship and chaos.

That means, for Germany, helping the east Germans get onto their
feet first. Next it means, for both Germany and the United States, helping
Poland, Hungary, the Czech and Slovak republics, and Slovenia, then the
Baltic states—and only after that the Soviet and Balkan successor states,
as they develop the discipline to divert foreign aid from mafia pockets into

institution building. Western business people with capital to invest will incline naturally to such priorities, and Western governments will also be forced to do so because of competing demands and their own shortage of capital.

In this endeavor Germany will clearly be the leader, both financially and intellectually. Bonn is already contributing more than half of all international aid to the former Soviet Union and Eastern Europe.[20] The economic development of Saxony is designed to stimulate next-door Silesia and Bohemia in a regional cooperation that deliberately reverses the Aryan contempt for Slavs of half a century ago. German investment and trade in East Central Europe and hiring of cross-border Polish and Czech labor far exceeds the economic involvement of any other country.

In addition, German jurists are already helping Hungary adopt the entire German legal system and offering similar advice to any other interested country. The German Social Democratic, Christian Democratic, and Liberal think tanks of the Friedrich-Ebert, Konrad-Adenauer, and Friedrich-Naumann foundations are sharing the techniques of political and social organization in East Central Europe as they did fifteen years ago in Spain and Portugal. The more liberal German Catholic church has had some impact on the more medieval Polish Catholic hierarchy, and the German Protestants on the Latvian and Estonian Protestants. There are scores of bilateral student and teacher exchanges; training programs for business managers and local administrators; workshops for parliamentarians, legislative staff, and librarians; joint history- and textbook-writing projects; and city partnerships. Grass-roots Polish-German and Czech-German environmental, friendship, and other societies are mushrooming. Riga is awash in German delegations. The Goethe Institute outposts are facilitating the flow by spreading knowledge of the German language, politics, culture, and counterculture.

There is no cause for alarm here, as the French in particular have expressed it, about German cultivation of a special sphere of influence in the region. On the contrary, the United States should welcome the burst of German activity and try to match it with exuberant grass-roots exchanges of its own. The Polish, Lithuanian, and Ukrainian emigré communities in the United States are a great resource and should be encouraged to take their capital, ideas, and can-do spirit to their parent countries, in full cooperation with the Germans.

In terms of economic assistance, the United States should, but probably will not, do more for East Central Europe as the region where aid could spark waiting private initiative and show the fastest returns. This would be much cheaper and more efficient than the military expenditures of the past forty years that maintained a different kind of stability in the region. Washington, mindful of its deficits, has made clear that it will not initiate any new Marshall Plan, however, and realistically, assistance will remain minimal.

While such parsimony may be regrettable, it should not cause serious quarrels with Bonn or with the EC. Germany, the EC's paymaster, is itself stretched in transferring some $100 billion annually to eastern Germany and more than $46 billion over several years to the Soviet Union, for a budget deficit temporarily higher even than Washington's as a percentage of national income. There is potential for irritation here, especially if the United States keeps displaying great generosity in offering to defer repayment of Soviet hard currency loans drawn largely on German banks and governmental guarantees. Yet such spats hardly threaten a transatlantic divorce as some thought the earlier feuds about NATO burden sharing did.

Whatever Western assistance in funds and organizing techniques can be mustered will be needed to avoid the many hazards in the East. The populations there, unlike their Western cousins, are not yet postnational; enforced socialist internationalism simply suppressed ethnic loyalties without mellowing them. In the 1980s these reemerged as benign forces for self-determination and the breakup of the Russian empire, and also as malevolent xenophobia. In the 1990s they could either help democratization by providing cohesion during painful transitions, or they could harm it by lending appeal to the kind of chauvinist strongmen who ruled in East Central Europe in the mid-1930s. Today one can hope that the greater homogeneity of national populations and lower numbers of disaffected national minorities, after the slaughter and forced migrations of World War II, will supply less tinder for radicalism. However, mutual hostilities offer easy scapegoats for economic hardship and uncertainty, and demagogues will undoubtedly arise. In this context the EC's sanction of withholding membership from warring or repressive applicants could be an effective deterrent.

Farther east, of course, the Western governments must provide immediate humanitarian aid—food, medicine, and housing construction—to help soften hardship. Economic assistance in the Balkans and the Soviet successor states will be limited, however, and should therefore focus on specific projects—stabilizing currencies, reconstituting the Russian oil and gas industry, storing and transporting the fifth of the Russian-Ukrainian grain harvest that rots in the fields, and the like—and should involve hands-on project implementation by Western specialists in cooperation with local counterparts. Besides providing veteran experts, the United States and Germany might well sponsor joint peace corps programs and youth exchanges, on the pattern of the successful postwar French-German exchanges, to help lay the foundations for future openness to such development.

This concentric approach may sound—to change the image—like a brutal triage. In face of the enormous need, however, and the rare opportunity in the current flux to help mold new institutions, the West should put its limited resources where they will do the most good. Releasing the energies of East Central Europeans to approximate Western standards of living, freedom, and pursuit of happiness—after their centuries of lagging behind—would give the greatest possible hope to all, including the Soviet heirs.

The east Germans will pioneer the uncharted transformation of a command economy into a pluralist, market society and will provide East Central Europe with examples of successes to emulate and failures to avoid. East Central Europe will do the same for Byelorussia, Ukraine, and Russia. These Soviet successor nations have a very different heritage from their western neighbors: Orthodox, Tatar, anti-Enlightenment, communal serf, Stalinist-totalitarian. They are apt to choose as their savior from the current breakdown not liberal democracy, but authoritarian order. Yet if the transformation works, more or less, in East Central Europe and the Baltic states, the next generation of westernizing Russians, Ukrainians, and Byelorussians may also find a synthesis that can blend their temperament and habits with the individualist, competitive system that is the better modernizer, and they can perhaps be easier to live with in the interim.

In more traditional security terms, the same geographic priorities should prevail. Already the post–cold war vacuum in East Central Europe is being filled by a flow of Western institutions east. For the 1990s, the appropriate ways for the West to enfold the East Central European and Baltic states (and probably Slovenia in the next few years) are to expand on their EC association and participation in the North Atlantic Cooperation Council. The North Atlantic Cooperation Council has a major flaw, however. Because of the unexpected disintegration of the Soviet Union imediately after its founding and the rush of Soviet successor states to join it, the North Atlantic Cooperation Council has conferred no special status on the East Central European states. An interim step before full accession to the EC at the turn of the century—a step that the United States should encourage—would be some kind of associate membership in the Western European Union for Poland, Hungary, and the Czech republic (and Slovakia if it qualifies).

In the rest of the 1990s American and German instincts are unlikely to diverge sharply in dealing with security risks in the outer circle of European states. Neither will want to get engaged in these regions militarily, short of some acute nuclear threat. Both will abhor any military involvement in the Armenian-Azeri or other ethnic feuding. Both will keep intervention essentially at the rhetorical political level that the new states increasingly permit under CSCE monitoring of human rights, and that they accept as the cost of acquiring Western investment and assistance. Any more strenuous intervention—to try to prevent the persecution of minorities from escalating into pogroms or civil war, perhaps—would be economic. In such cases Germany, as the main donor and the Western country closest to the unrest geographically, would also be the main disciplinarian, acting through the EC. Only in an extremity that directly threatened to spill over into Central or Western Europe would or should Western European Union units be deployed—in cooperation with the CSCE—as peacekeepers or peacemakers.

The American-German Bargain

Overnight Germany has become united and fully sovereign, a political as well as an economic giant. Despite its renunciation of nuclear weapons, despite its military ceiling of 370,000 personnel, it is now a major provider and no longer a consumer of security. But by its own choice, Germany exercises its newfound power not as a solo actor, but as the mover of Europe, magnified by the European Community, but also constrained by it.

Nor does the new Germany feel the need to prove its sovereignty, as so many feared, against its American mentor. In this special relationship too it is constrained by the American connection, but also amplified by it, and it is mature enough to recognize this state of affairs. Whatever their parochial relics, the partners in leadership of the United States and Germany-in-Europe consciously share a basic faith in the open exchange of goods, services, and ideas. They will and should work together to promote such an international system. Their feuds of the 1970s and 1980s were episodic rather than structural, discrete rather than cumulative. What endures from their interaction over four decades is common benefit from inspired policy choices made together at critical moments.

Rewriting the American-German and Euro-Atlantic security bargain in the post-wall era, then, should be the easiest part of Europe's task in the 1990s. We have the habit of cooperation; we are enriched by it; and the United States will profit in this decade from having an equal ally, finally, in the new Europe.

We have amply demonstrated that mature democracies do not go to war with one another. We have demonstrated that they can band together in stable alliances for self-defense and that they are not more vulnerable—but much more resilient—than command systems. America, having stood by its German ally in Stalin's Berlin blockade, Khrushchev's Berlin crisis, and Brezhnev's heaping up of conventional superiority, should now see the job through in Yeltsin's coming time of troubles. As we once stabilized the Federal Republic, allowing the Germans to rebuild their economy and construct the first robust democracy in their history, so we should now help the Germans stabilize East Central Europe, the Baltic states, and Slovenia to lay the foundation for greater well-being and self-determination there. A much smaller American effort than was required in the 1940s would now secure the final return on that first self-enlightened choice. And if, in the process, the individualist Americans learn reciprocally some of the German and West European skills in designing a compassionate social net for the underclass, so much the better.

Surely the time has now come to drop the old arguments about pulling back from a Europe that is our own flesh and blood. We, like the Germans, are already postnational. In this interdependent world of potential nuclear annihilation, global warming, and instant communication, our policy differences with German and other European allies can no longer be understood as old-fashioned clashes of national interests. They have become instead virtually domestic debates. The Euro-Atlantic community is already reality.

It awaits only a second creation worthy of the first.

Bibliographical Essay

It is the instinct of journalists to trust interviews, so long as these interviews can be triangulated. The cold document often misses the crucial compromises or interpretations or expectations that went into the text. By contrast, cross-checking of West German, American, and British strategists, say, or of a Lothar de Maizière, a Richard Schröder, and a newly talkative Günter Schabowski, when they still feel the pulse of their actions, can disclose the living, breathing process of policy improvisation (and, in this case, collapse of a state).

Interviews

This book, then, is based primarily on interviews I conducted in Bonn, Washington, Berlin, and other European capitals as a reporter living in Germany since 1977. Persons I interviewed between fall 1989 and 1992 include the following.

West German diplomats, officials, and others

Chancellor Helmut Kohl (March 25, 1992); Willy Brandt, former chancellor (January 18, 1991); Hans-Dietrich Genscher, former foreign minister (August 28, 1992); Wolfgang Schäuble, interior minister in fall 1989, chief negotiator for the treaty of union in 1990, currently Bundestag CDU leader (September 23, 1992); Andreas Meyer-Landrut, chief of the president's office (November 29, 1989; January 15 and May 22, 1990; January 14, 1991; January 15, 1992); Horst Teltschik, foreign policy adviser to Chancellor Helmut Kohl until January 1991 (August 11 and November 16, 1989; January 26 and June 28, 1990, Bonn; January 17, 1991, Gütersloh; September 9, 1991, telephone); Peter Hartmann, foreign policy adviser to Kohl from January 1991 (February 25, 1992); Uwe Kästner, chief of West-East Relations in the chancellor's office (May 15, 1990); Claus J. Duisberg, member of the chancellor's team that negotiated German unity (November 14 and December 6, 1989; May 11, 1990); Michael Mertes, head of section, Policy Unit, Chancellery (October 24, 1991; January 14, April 23, and June 16, 1992); Martin Hanz, counselor, Chancellery (October 24, 1991); Dieter Kastrup, Foreign Ministry political director (January 10, 1990); Klaus J. Citron, Foreign Ministry head of policy planning until fall of 1990 (November 29, 1989; June 1, 1990); Konrad Seitz, Foreign Ministry head of policy planning from fall of 1990 (December 19, 1990); Frank Elbe, head of private office of Foreign Minister Hans-Dietrich Genscher, then head of policy planning in the Foreign Ministry (January 10, 1991; March 24, April 24, and September 29, 1992); Dietrich von Kyaw, Foreign Ministry deputy director-general for economic and European Community affairs (August 15 and November 9, 1989; January 19 and May 22, 1990; January 4, 1991; February 16, 1992); Wolfgang Ischinger, Foreign Ministry legislative liaison (November 21, 1989; January 18 and May 3, 1990); Hans-Otto Bräutigam, ambassador to the United Nations until fall of 1990, then minister of justice in Brandenburg (July 29, October 6, and December 8, 1989, New York; September 6 and December 5, 1991, Potsdam); Hans-Friedrich von Ploetz, ambassador to NATO (December 5, 1989, Brussels); Ernst-Jörg von Studnitz, deputy head of the mission in East Berlin until summer of 1990 (November 13 and December 20, 1989; March 14, March 19, and June 25, 1990; January 7, 1991; January 17, 1992, East Berlin and Bonn); Hans Georg Wieck, president of the Federal Intelligence Service until fall of 1990 (December 4, 1989; January 24, February 9, March 29, and May 15, 1990); Konrad Porzner, president of the Federal Intelligence Service from fall of 1990 (January 8, 1991); Klaus Kinkel, state secretary in the Justice Ministry until January 1991, then justice minister (November 28, 1989; March 12, 1990); Gerrit Stein, assistant to Kinkel (March 12, 1990); Major General Klaus Naumann, then deputy chief of staff, Politico-Military Affairs and Operations, Armed Forces Staff (December 27, 1990); General Franz-Joseph Schulze (retired) (February 6, May 9, and June 26, 1990; July 16, 1991; January 27 and April 29, 1992); Colonel Horst Siedschlag, branch chief, military strategy, Armed Forces Staff (May 28, 1990); Hans Heinrich Weise of the planning staff (February 15 and May 21, 1990; January 15 and February 24, 1991; February 28, 1992); and other officers and civilians at the Defense Ministry; Major General Hubert Marquitan, deputy corps and territorial commander, East (September 4, 1991, Potsdam); Burkhard Dobiey, minister director (November 9 and November 24, 1989; January 10, February 21, and May 11, 1990; January 7, 1991); Manfred Ackermann, chief of the Cultural Section (November 15, 1989; May 10, 1990); Marlies Jansen, section chief, and others at the Intra-German Ministry (May 9, 1990); Birgit Breuel, president of Treuhand-Anstalt (group interview, April 8, 1992, Berlin); Heinrich Vogel, director, Federal Institute for East and International Studies (May 23, 1990); Volker Rühe, Christian Democratic Union general secretary (March 5, 1992); Professor Karl-Heinz Hornhues, Bundestag member and CDU parliamentary foreign policy spokesman (January 16, 1991); Eberhard Kuhrt, chief of German, foreign, and security policy under the CDU general secretary (May 16, 1990); Wolfgang Thierse, SPD deputy chairman, (group interview, June 3, 1992); Karsten Voigt, member of the Bundestag and SPD parliamentary foreign policy spokesman (May 17, 1990); Jens Fischer, adviser to former Chancellor Helmut Schmidt (December 1, 1989; May 10, May 31, and December 28, 1990; January 4, 1991; January 16, April 25, and June 11, 1992); Uwe Stehr, chief of disarmament and arms control section of the staff of the SPD's parliamentary faction (November 8, 1989; May 11, 1990); Karl Wilhelm Fricke, chief of the East-West Section at Deutschlandfunk (July 12, 1990, Cologne; June 11, 1990, and July 18, 1991, telephone); Professor Eberhard Schulz of the Deutsche Gesellschaft für Auswärtige Politik (November 8, 1989); Peter Bender, author (June 4, 1990, telephone); Hermann Rudolph, commentator, *Süddeutsche Zeitung* (February 2, 1990, Munich); Professor Arnulf Baring of the Free University, West Berlin (June 4, 1990, telephone; December 21, 1990, Berlin); Kurt H. Biedenkopf, minister-president of Saxony (group interview, September 6, 1991, Dresden; individual interview, April 6, 1992, Bonn); Berndt Seite, minister-president of Mecklenburg–West Pomerania, (group interview, June 6, 1992); Peter Radunski, Berlin representative in Bonn (March 6, 1992); and ministers, legislators, and other officials in Saxony, Berlin, Brandenburg, Mecklenburg-West Pomerania.

East Germans

Pastor Bernd Albani of the Gethsemane Church, East Berlin (November 3 and November 13, 1989, East Berlin); demonstrators and attendants at political rallies in East Berlin, Leipzig, and Dresden; Günter Schabowski, member of the Politburo of the Socialist Unity [communist] party (SED) until December 1989 (December 29, 1990, and February 14, 1992, Berlin); Wolfgang Vogel, lawyer, confidant of Erich Honecker, negotiator of major East-West spy swaps and ransom of East German political prisoners (March 20 and June 5, 1990, East Berlin); Rolf Reissig, rector of the Academy of Social Sciences under the SED Central Committee (March 16, 1990, East Berlin; telephone, August 27, 1992); Gregor Gysi, chairman, and other members of the Party of Democratic Socialists (former Socialist Unity party) (March 17, 1990, East Berlin); Professor Heinz Kosin, Institut für Internationale Politik und Wirtschaft der DDR (December 21, 1989; March 6, 1990, East Berlin); Karl-Heinz Arnold, private secretary to Prime Minister Hans Modrow, November 1989–March 1990 (June 7, 1990, East Berlin); Foreign Ministry press spokesman Denis Ruh (June 6, 1990, East Berlin); Lothar de Maizière, prime minister, April–December 1990 (January 18, 1991, Bonn); Richard Schröder, parliamentary leader (June 6, 1990, East Berlin), Stefan Finger, member of the executive board, and other members of the Social Democratic party (March 16, 1990, East Berlin); Markus Meckel, foreign minister, April–August 1990 (group interview, September 2, 1991, Bonn); Vera Wollenberger, dissident and then Bundestag member (June 2, 1992, Bonn); Erich Iltgen, president of the Saxon Landtag (September 6, 1991, Dresden); Deputy Mayor Reinhard Keller, Dresden (September 6, 1991); Thomas Meyer, physicist, member of New Forum, leader of the investigating committee's section on Greifswald University, and, after the 1990 free city elections, president of the City Council (July 24, 1991, Greifswald); members of the Christian Democratic Union and National Democratic Party of Germany; and journalists.

American diplomats, officials and ex-officials

Vernon Walters, ambassador to the Federal Republic (January 8, 1990, Bonn); Richard Barkley, ambassador to the GDR (December 20, 1989, and June 4, 1990, East Berlin); Robert Kimmitt, ambassador to the Federal Republic (March 6, 1992); J. D. Bindenagel, minister to the GDR (December 20, 1989, and June 4, 1990,

East Berlin; telephone, Washington, July 29, 1992); John Kornblum, minister of mission to NATO (December 5, 1989, January 11, February 13, April 10, May 4, June 20 and July 2, 1990; June 3, 1991, Brussels and telephone); Robert Zoellick, counselor, State Department (May 13 and June 26, 1991, Washington; and October 10, 1991 and July 31, 1992, by telephone); Reginald Bartholomew, undersecretary of state (December 11, 1989, Washington); Robert Hutchings (March 28, 1990; June 23, 1992, Washington), Philip Zelikow (December 8, 1990, San Francisco; June 26, 1991, Washington; and October 8, 1991, Cambridge, Massachusetts); another member of the National Security Council staff; Bowman Miller, director, Office of Analysis for Western Europe and Canada, Intelligence and Research, State Department (September 5, 1990; May 13, 1991; June 23, 1992, Washington); Marten van Heuven of the National Intelligence Council, (December 8, 1989; March 1 and November 27, 1990, Washington, New York, and Boston); Colonel Karl Lowe, chief, Conventional Arms Control Division, Office of the Deputy Chief of Staff for Operations and Plans, Department of the Army (May 13, 1991, Washington); John P. Hardt, associate director for research coordination, Congressional Research Service (December 10, 1989; March 28, 1990, Washington); and Helmut Sonnenfeldt, guest scholar, Brookings Institution (February 28, 1990; June 24, 1992, Washington).

Others

General John R. Galvin, NATO supreme allied commander, Europe (April 4, 1990, Heidelberg); members of the NATO secretary-general's staff (Brussels); Sir David Gillmore, permanent under secretary of state and head of Diplomatic Service designate in the British Foreign Office (November 1990, Cambridge, Massachusetts); Sir Christopher Mallaby, British ambassador to Bonn (November 27, 1989; January 8, March 21, May 14, and December 19, 1990; January 10, 1992, Bonn); Pauline Neville-Jones, British minister to Bonn (February 19, May 3, and June 28, 1990, Bonn); Jan G. van derTas, ambassador of the Netherlands (March 12, 1990, Bonn); Dominique Chassard, French minister (January 18, February 21, and May 3, 1990; January 15, 1991, Bonn); Dominique Moïsi, executive director of the French Institute for International Relations (January 23, 1990, Bonn; and July 17, 1991, telephone); General Wojtiech Jaruzelski, former president of the Polish People's Republic (May 7, 1992, Warsaw); Mieczyslaw F. Rakowski, former first secretary of the Polish United Workers Party (November 1, 1991, Warsaw); and a senior allied military officer in West Berlin.

Names of interviewees who requested anonymity have been omitted.

A Further Word

Since interviews are often treated as second-class evidence in academia, a further word in defense of this heavy reliance on interviews is probably necessary. As witness, I call on Robert Zoellick, a history buff as well as the key American formulator of policy toward Germany in 1989–90. When he was asked how accurately he thought documents reflected the extraordinary course of events in this period, he expressed some reservations. In this instance, he suggested, the documentary evidence is probably better than it usually is; the two "treasure troves" are the series of "talking points" for Secretary of State James A. Baker III's conversations and the "mem cons" (notes) of these conversations with the Soviet foreign minister, all of which Dennis Ross, head of Policy Planning at the State Department, preserved. (I did not have access to these, a fact that no doubt strengthens my bias toward interviews.) Yet Zoellick noted that much government business is done orally, without records. He and Ross reached many decisions in conversation with each other, he said, and they were so much in tune that "one of us would start a sentence and the other finish it." Those who then wrote the implementing memos did not necessarily realize precisely what went into a decision, and they might have put their own gloss on it.

It is this less tangible pulse of decisions and reactions I have tried to capture in interviews. Many of the interviews were conducted in the heat of events; many came at a distance of months or even (at most) three years. My evaluation here develops, and sometimes revises, judgments I first formed in Bonn in reporting about East-West and West-West diplomacy for *The Christian Science Monitor* throughout the 1980s. Summaries of my contemporary interpretations, apart from my contributions to the *Monitor,* may be found in "Andropov, Kohl, and the East-West Issues," *Problems of Communism,* vol. 32 (July–August 1983), pp. 35–45; "The Security Debate in West Germany," *Survival,* vol. 28 (July–August 1986), pp. 322-36; "Federal Republic of Germany: *Westpolitik, Ostpolitik,* and Security," in Catherine M. Kelleher and Gale A. Mattox, eds., *Evolving European Defense Policies* (Lexington, Mass.; Lexington Books, 1987), pp. 223–43; "Impact on the Two German States and Their Alliances," in Walther Stützle and others, *The ABM Treaty: To Defend or Not to Defend?* (Oxford: Oxford University Press for the Stockholm International Peace Research Institute, 1987), pp. 174–86; "Sie gehören alle geprügelt," *Die Zeit,* May 12, 1989, p. 15; "Ohne Schobsen keine Schritte," *Die Zeit,* September 22, 1989, p. 6; "Aufbruch mit neuer Identität," *Die Zeit,* August 3, 1990, p. 31; "Germany: This Time It Really Will Work," *Washington Post,* February 25, 1990, p. B2; "The New German Pride," *Michigan Alumnus,* March–April 1990, pp. 31–34; "A Wall Destroyed: The Dynamics of German Unification in the GDR," *International Security,* vol. 15 (Fall 1990), pp. 35–36; "Deutsch-deutsche Medienkultur von aussen gesehen," *Bertelsmann Briefe,* vol. 127 (April 1992), pp. 60–65; and "Germany in the New Europe," *Foreign Affairs,* vol. 71 (Spring 1992), pp. 114-30. This book, of course, fleshes out my earlier monograph *After the Wall* (New York: Priority Press for the Twentieth Century Fund) published on unification day, October 3, 1990.

For the most recent period I have tried to indicate my sources for specific points in some detail in the chapter notes, given the multiple versions extant of the happenings of 1989–90. For the period before the revolutions of 1989, by contrast, I document sources or interviews only sparingly, since events in that decade are already well known and this book is intended for the general rather than the specialist reader. For the background material I confine myself to giving some broad idea in this note of where my analysis or interpretation of events draws on or differs from previous perceptions.

I have been working in Germany, of course, but it is should be recorded that the best single collection of documents on the East German revolution in the United States is at the Hoover Institution, Stanford University.

Note to Chapter 4

On NATO and other transatlantic issues, I am a maverick. I never shared the conventional wisdom of the 1980s that alliances are unnatural, that their strains are cumulative—and that as Germany matured, it must necessarily kick off the encumbering American traces.

A few examples illustrate the conventional wisdom. Gregory F. Treverton, Europeanist at the Council on Foreign Relations, took a much more somber view of alliance relations in the 1980s than he had earlier. Originally he had defined the problem of intramural quarrels as one of "alliance management;" in the 1980s he concluded instead that the alliance was facing real crisis. (Treverton 1992a, p. vii.) Similarly, Josef Joffe saw in the disputes of the 1980s "not the familiar tremor of clashing interests but the rumble of shifting foundations." (Joffe 1987, p. xviii.) Historians Dennis L. Bark and David R. Gress also viewed the Euromissile issue in the 1980s not as a discrete tactical tussle, but as a fundamental "battle for or against Atlanticism" in the Federal Republic, especially within the Social Democratic party. Bark and Gress (1989, vol. 2, p. 316). Retired diplomat and old German hand William R. Smyser pessimistically flagged warnings about a U.S.-German "systemic crisis" and entitled one of his chapters "Present at the Dissolution?" Smyser (1990, pp. 151, 159). More circumspectly, political scientist Wolfram F. Hanrieder, in his magisterial history of German foreign policy, saw in 1989 a risk of collision between American and European "unilateralism." Citing Claude Cheysson, he foresaw transatlantic "progressive divorce" if the Western alliance continued with "the increasingly outmoded function of containing the Federal Republic while containing the Soviet Union." Hanrieder (1989, pp. 130 and 377ff.)

Other books that described a NATO in crisis included David Calleo (1987), and, from the point of view that Europe should in fact break away from American hegemony, John Palmer (1987), and, from the point of view that the United States should break away from Europe, Melvyn Krauss, *How NATO Weakens the West* (Simon and Shuster, 1986). Further breakup scenarios included, for example, Robert S. Dudney, "New Fissures in NATO," *Air Force Magazine*, vol. 71 (October 1988), pp. 34–40; David M. Keithly, "The German Fatherland—of the Left," *Orbis*, vol. 34 (Winter 1990), pp. 67–82; and Walter F. Hahn, "NATO and Germany," *Strategic Review*, vol. 5 (Winter 1990), pp. 1–18.

For the contrary, classic assessment of stability in NATO, see A. W. DePorte (1986), and Stanley Sloan (1989). For an early vote of confidence in German democracy, see Swiss journalist Fritz-René Allemann, *Bonn ist nicht Weimar* (Cologne: Kiepenheuer und Witsch, 1956). For a restatement of Germany's enduring Western ties, see Richard Löwenthal (1986).

In military specifics, it is beyond the scope of this book to rehearse the fierce arguments of the 1980s over the real significance of the conventional imbalance in

Europe. Basically, peace activists either gave no credence to Western military statistics or else dismissed "bean counting" as irrelevant, since the quality of Soviet weapons was inferior to that of the West. The Western government officials rebutted this by saying that quantity matters a great deal, especially in the case of tanks, and especially when the initiative of attack, concentration, and surprise lies with the numerically superior force; and that in a number of cases (such as multiple-launch rocket systems) the Soviet Union actually preceded the West in fielding new technology. Sober studies of the conventional balance include Joerg F. Baldauf (1987), and, for the 1990s, Wolfgang Schlör, "Force without a Cause? The Paradox of Means and Missions and Conventional Defense Planning for Western Europe," University of Pittsburgh.

Also outside the scope of this book is any evaluation of the Soviet Union's own war scares. The premise underlying the analysis here is that Soviet fears were probably fed less by NATO's Euromissiles as such than by the anti-Soviet rhetoric of Ronald Reagan during his first years in office—and by such anomalies as full tank loading in a regular NATO military exercise code-named Able Archer in 1983. The relevant Soviet alert period—when the order went out to KGB stations in the West to note such anomalies as late-burning lights in the Pentagon in order to identify any Western plans to invade the Soviet Union—began in 1981 and ended in 1983 before NATO's INF deployments actually began.

Domestic Soviet concern first came to Western attention through Oleg Gordievsky, the KGB chief in Britain in the early 1980s and a long-time double agent for the British. The British took his information about the KGB alert very seriously, and thought that a KGB conclusion that the West was not plotting an attack may have influenced Gorbachev's "new thinking" about international interdependence. The West Germans did not accord much importance to the episode; American analysts were mixed in their evaluation. See Oleg Gordievsky, *KGB: The Inside Story of Its Foreign Operations from Lenin to Gorbachev* (Harper Collins, 1990).

On INF, the left, most Germans (and perhaps even most Americans) took for granted the gloss that the United States was forcing INF down the throats of the Germans. A decade later the left would consider it a great revelation to discover that INF actually fit Bonn's preference of early use of nuclear weapons on Soviet territory much better than Washington's interpretation of flexible response to mean nuclear resort as late as possible. See Susanne Peters (1990).

On INF negotiations, the best account of the early talks is Strobe Talbott (1984). A retrospective account of the INF negotiations in the broader context of strategic talks and the whole US-Soviet relationship is given in Don Oberdorfer (1991). For political analysis of the INF debate in the Federal Republic, see Barry M. Blechman and Cathleen S. Fisher (1988), Jeffrey Boutwell (1990), Jeffrey D. Boutwell, Paul Doty, and Gregory F. Treverton (1985), Joseph Lepgold (1990), Thomas Risse-Kappen (1988), Diane Rosolowsky (1987), Leon V. Sigal (1984), David N. Schwartz (1983), and Stanley R. Sloan (1985).

For nuclear history preceding the INF controversy, see Catherine McArdle Kelleher (1975), and Gregory F. Treverton, *The Dollar Drain and American Forces in Germany: Managing the Political Economics of Alliance* (Ohio University Press, 1978). For analysis of the Soviet approach to the controversy, see Jonathan Haslam (1990).

For a discussion of Reagan's nuclear abolition, see John Newhouse, *War and Peace in the Nuclear Age* (Knopf, 1989). The various twists and turns of the administration are also well charted in Strobe Talbott, *The Master of the Game: Paul Nitze and the Nuclear Peace* (Knopf, 1988). An opposing point of view is presented in Richard Perle, "Strobe Lite," *National Interest*, no. 15 (Spring 1989), pp. 87–91. McGeorge Bundy, *Danger and Survival: Choices about the Bomb in the First Fifty Years* (Random House, 1988) gives a magisterial overview of the evolution of American nuclear thinking. Lawrence Freedman (1989) remains the classic.

Technical evaluations of the various SDI projects are outside the scope of this book. The technological premises for the political discussion here, however, are essentially drawn from the mainstream post-Reagan assessment of SDI, as presented most coherently in lay language in the studies by the U.S. Office of Technology Assessment: *SDI: Technology, Survivability, and Software*, OTA-ISC-353 (May 1988); *Ballistic Missile Defense Technologies*, OTA-ISC-254 (September 1985); and *Anti-Satellite Weapons, Countermeasures, and Arms Control*, OTA-ISC-281 (September 1985).

Note to Chapter 5

On the rejuvenation of the EC in the mid-1980s, I draw on besides William Wallace (1990), Nicholas Colchester and David Buchan (1990), Michael Calingaert (1990), Alfred Grosser (1980), and Simon Serfaty, "Defining 'Europe': Purpose without Commitment?" in Michael T. Clark and Simon Serfaty (1991), pp. 127–59.

Note to Chapters 6 and 7

On Soviet-East European relations, Mark Kramer (1989–90) offers one of the best explorations of the situation just before the explosions of fall 1989. His article is indicative of the unexpectedness of the events of that autumn. It seemed daring in its conclusions at the time it was written, but far too timid—as illustrated by the question mark in the headline—within weeks of its publication. Other good analysis is to be found in the running Radio Free Europe analysis; in Allen Lynch, "The Changing Contours of Soviet-East European Relations," *Journal of International Affairs*, vol. 42 (Spring 1989), pp. 423–34; and in Hannes Adomeit (1990). A later summary of the evolution is Alvin Z. Rubenstein, "Soviet Client-States: From Empire to Commonwealth," *Orbis*, vol. 35 (Winter 1991), pp. 69–78.

Veteran Swiss-Sudeten German journalist Ernst Kux (1991) adds several other factors to the explanations of why Eastern Europe pulled away from the Soviet Union in the late 1980s and not earlier. He includes the fright that all countries in the region got as fallout from the nuclear Chernobyl accident hit them; a " 'modernization crisis' brought on by the information revolution"; and, specifically, the impact on East European viewers of television images of the West and of instant Western broadcast information about the latest demonstrations in their own countries. He takes as his framework Jacob Burckhardt's prescient thesis of two decades after the failed 1848 revolutions that crises develop over a long period, then explode suddenly. "But when the time is ripe, the contagion spreads with electrical speed over hundreds of miles and among populations that otherwise are hardly conscious of one another," Burckhardt noted. By contrast, Kux strongly opposes the popular thesis that Gorbachev gave "his colonies freedom like some enlightened and benevolent Kremlin tsar. Gorbachev's *perestroyka* first inspired and then accelerated the developments in Eastern Europe. Ultimately, however, it was the *failure* of perestroyka as a 'revolution from above' in Eastern Europe and the Soviet Union that brought on the 'revolution from below' in Poland, Hungary, Leipzig, Prague, Sofia, and Bucharest."

A thoughtful summary of the pre-1989 era in the GDR is presented in the interview with Hans-Otto Bräutigam after his six years as permanent representative of Bonn in East Berlin, "Die deutsche Geschichte ist voller Spaltung," *Die Zeit*, January 13, 1989. For running reports on the political role of the Protestant church in this period, see the bimonthly issues of *Kirche im Sozialismus* (renamed *Übergänge* in April 1990), published in West Berlin. See also Gert-Joachim Glaessner (1988); Inner-German Ministry (Bonn), *DDR Handbuch*, vols. 1 and 2 (Cologne: Verlag Wissenschaft und Politik, rev. ed., 1985); Peter Bender (1989); Bärbel Bohley and others, *40 Jahre DDR . . . und die Bürger melden sich zu Wort* (Frankfurt, Munich: Büchergilde Gutenberg und Carl Hanser, 1989); and Wolfgang-Uwe Friedrich, ed., *DDR-Deutschland zwischen Elbe und Oder*, 2d ed. (Stuttgart: Kohlhammer, 1989). For virtually the only admissions in the official East German media that things were deteriorating badly, see two reprints of Polish articles: Jerzy Weber, "Umgestaltung in den Farben der DDR—Kontinuität and Erneuerung," *Neues Deutschland*, February 20, 1989, p. 5; and Ryszard Wonja, "Eine Frucht des Sieges," *Neues Deutschland*, May 8, 1989, p. 5. For official documents on East-West German relations from the Basic Treaty of December 21, 1972, through the West Berlin land adjustments of March 31, 1988, see Inner-German Ministry (Bonn), *Dokumentation zu den innerdeutschen Beziehungen*, 12th ed. (Bonn: Leck, 1989).

In English, see Daniel Hamilton, "Dateline East Germany: The Wall behind the Wall," *Foreign Policy*, no. 76 (Fall 1989), pp. 176–97; A. James McAdams (1985, 1986); Henry Krisch (1985); David Childs (1985); and Henry Ashby Turner, Jr. (1987).

Note to Chapters 8–11

On the ouster of Erich Honecker in October 1989, Günter Schabowski is the only Politburo member from that time who has been willing, in interviews and in his own writing, to provide details. Egon Krenz was the first of the SED politicians to publish his version of the drama. Krenz (1990). Although his book appeared early in 1990, it still fit the old vague and bland paradigm of communist political writing. Honecker's subsequent book—a compilation of interviews with the deposed party chief that Honecker's lawyers tried to block from publication—is even less illuminating. Andert and Herzberg (1991). Honecker, remembering his glory days in getting the Soviet nod to supplant Ulbricht in 1971, cannot conceive that his German colleagues might have deposed him on their own; he blames his overthrow entirely on (undocumented) betrayal by the Russians.

It was therefore left to Schabowski to write the first book that made any attempt to describe the actual sequence of events within the Politburo. Schabowski (1990). This book too was a compilation of interviews by the first journalists Schabowski was willing to talk to after he was dropped from his party posts in December 1989. In *Das Politbüro* and in his later *Der Absturz* (1991), Schabowski did break away from the old communist style to adopt the more Western promotion of one's own case by a flood of chosen facts rather more than by sheer obfuscation.

On the GDR Ministry for State Security, unless otherwise noted, this book's description of the *Stasi*, with supporting facts, is drawn primarily from the interview and later telephone conversation with Karl Wilhelm Fricke and from his prolific writings about the *Stasi*. Fricke was himself the victim of a *Stasi* kidnapping from West to East Berlin in 1955 and was sentenced to four years in prison. He is the author of the standard study of the *Stasi* (1989), and the wealth of new information that has come to light since the GDR democratized itself (1991b). His running analysis in *Deutschland Archiv* (December 1989, January 1990, February 1990, December 1990, January 1991, February 1991, May 1991, July 1991, September 1991, February 1992, and November 1992) is supplemented by essays in *German Comments* (October 1990, July 1991), *Aussenpolitik* (4th quarter 1990), a speech at the Tutzing Protestant Academy (Heft 8, November 1990), and other publications.

Besides noted references, other sources include Dietrich Fischer, "Die 'Juristische Hochschule Potsdam,'" *Deutschland Archiv*, no. 12 (December 1990), pp. 1891–94; and Richard Schröder, "Keine Amnestie für die Stasi," *Die Zeit*, April 12, 1991, p. 12.

West German government sources, while crediting most of Schabowski's version of Politburo intrigue, do not believe that he could have been as innocent as he claims of police and *Stasi* plans in his own city—or that Krenz, the Politburo member responsible for security, could have been equally ignorant. Fricke's sense is that Krenz would not have been informed about the specifics of individual operations, since these were held very tightly by the *Stasi*, but that he would have known much more than he now claims about the basic political decisions—and that Schabowski and Modrow, as city secretaries, would have had similar, if less full, knowledge in Berlin and Dresden respectively.

Note to Chapters 12–15

My portrayal of American policy and of the American-German-Soviet-allied interaction is a composite based on interviews with Richard Barkley, Reginald Bartholomew, J. D. Bindenagel, Dominique Chassard, Klaus J. Citron, Claus J. Duisberg, Frank Elbe, Hans-Dietrich Genscher, David Gillmore, Peter Hartmann, Marten van Heuven, Karl-Heinz Hornhues, Robert Hutchings, Uwe Kästner, Dieter Kastrup, Helmut Kohl, John Kornblum, Christopher Mallaby, Andreas Meyer-Landrut, Bowman Miller, Dominique Moïsi, Pauline Neville-Jones, Hans-Friedrich von Ploetz, Rozanne Ridgway, Konrad Seitz, Jan G. van der Tas, Horst Teltschik, Vernon Walters, Philip Zelikow, Robert Zoellick, and others. The interviews were generally on background, except where permission for specific attribution was given; therefore, few notes indicating the source of individual points are provided.

Most points of difference in analysis between the National Security Council, State Department, Chancellery, and Foreign Ministry are explored in the text of this book. A few more points might be made here, however, on the question of who was more forthcoming on the Soviet side, Shevardnadze or Gorbachev. The State Department and Foreign Ministry stressed Shevardnadze's role; the NSC and Chancellery thought Gorbachev the key.

Kohl himself gives both men credit, but says it was clearly Gorbachev who was in charge. He relates as one sign of Gorbachev's flexibility a conversation he and the Soviet leader had sitting on a retaining wall overlooking the Rhine during Gorbachev's visit to Bonn in June 1989. Kohl recounts, "I then said, 'Mr. President, the Rhine flows down to the sea. You may be amazed by what I say. But that's the way German unity will come. You can't stop German unity. And you can't stop European unification either.' He didn't contradict me." (Kohl interview.)

For the NSC's Philip Zelikow, "Gorbachev's role in all this is crucial." He asserted, "Gorbachev is making the key decisions, not Shevardnadze. The widespread perception in the West that on most issues Shevardnadze was the Olof Palme, the advocate of new thinking, and Gorbachev either backed Shevardnadze or didn't, [depending on] the tactical political situation, is basically accurate, but not [in respect to] Germany. Shevardnadze was a hardliner on Germany from the beginning. He had a consistently harder line on Germany, pretty much reflecting the views of his bureaucracy. The key decisionmaker—this was evident at Malta— was always Gorbachev." Teltschik seconded this view.

This view was not shared by those in the State Department or the Bonn Foreign Ministry who dealt most intensively with Shevardnadze; in the half year to come they would find the Soviet foreign minister most helpful in dissolving the Soviet adamancy on Germany. One factor in these surprisingly divergent evaluations may have been the crucial role played by Shevardnadze's personal assistant, Sergei Tarasenko. Both the State Department and the German Foreign Ministry realized early on that Shevardnadze was taking enormous political risks at home in his German policy and that he had to cover himself with tough public statements and even some private ambiguity. To an unusual degree he left the real probes for flexibility—and the explanation of domestic Soviet political needs on the issue—to Tarasenko's contacts with Zoellick and Elbe. The NSC and the Chancellery, while they knew of this byplay, did not experience it directly, and therefore accorded it less weight.

Certainly the NSC/Chancellery view of Shevardnadze's secondary importance was not shared by virulent Soviet hardliners, who accused the Soviet foreign minister of scandalous softness on Germany. When their personal attacks on Shevardnadze came to a head in July 1990—the sluggish reactions of the hardliners were again evident in this delay—Gorbachev mounted no robust defense of his political ally. At that point Shevardnadze felt deserted by Gorbachev, according to Genscher. (Genscher interview.)

One of the most striking aspects of U.S. policy toward Germany in early 1990 was the contrast between the serenity about German unity at the top—and the hunch that it could be achieved with full NATO membership—and the alarm in the media. Former CIA director Richard Helms wrote, "German unification has become a kind of runaway freight train that nobody—East or West—seems able to contain. . . . One would have thought that the countries of Europe that suffered such enormous human losses in World War II would be profoundly uneasy about these developments." ("Hold On, Helmut—Let's Slow Reunification," *Washington Post*, February 25, 1990, pp. B1–2.) See also Christopher Hitchens, "Washington's Kohl Front: Embracing a Chancellor, Eschewing Debate," *Harper's*, October 1990, pp. 74–82. *The Nation* countered this view editorially, arguing, "It's bigoted to believe that the Germans, because of some *völkisch* character quirk, are more prone to the abuse of super power than anyone else. History holds too many nightmares all around." ("The Newest Superpower," March 12, 1990, p. 1). For a different concern—that the "real danger" of a united Germany lay in arresting "Europe's great confederational project"—see Charles Krauthammer, "The German Revival," *New Republic*, March 26, 1990, pp. 18–21.

Fears that Germany might turn nationalist had been fed especially a few years earlier by the "historians' debate," which was widely seen as an attempt by conservative German historians to get rid of the burden of the Holocaust by "relativizing" it. There are several good overviews of the dispute, including Peter Baldwin (1990); Richard J. Evans (1989); Ian Kershaw (1989); Charles Maier (1988); and Thomas Nipperdey (1990). For an expression of Jewish concern, see David A. Jodice, "United Germany and Jewish Concerns: Attitudes toward Jews, Israel, and the Holocaust," Working Paper of the American Jewish Committee, New York, February 1991; and Thomas Rietzschel, "Droht eine Verniedlichung des Holocaust?" *Frankfurter Allgemeine Zeitung* (hereafter *FAZ*) June 14, 1991. See also such contrasting treatments of the subject as Art Levine and Sheila Kaplan, "Finally, a Solution to the Fatherland's Image Problem," *Spy*, December 1990, pp. 38–39; and David Rieff, "United States," *Times Literary Supplement*, November 2–8, 1990, pp. 1178, 1189.

Only a few voices questioned the conventional wisdom that the debate shows how much present-day German views are shaped by the past; one such wry voice from the State Department, Bowman H. Miller, inverted the judgment and argued that what the dispute really showed is the German proclivity to "instrumentalize" history. ("German Unity and the Politics of German History," in Joseph J. Lee and Walter Korter, eds., *Europe in Transition* (Austin: University of Texas Press, 1991), pp. 89–114).

Raw mistrust of the Germans among the American elite never reached British or French proportions; but the specific elite conviction that Moscow would never grant a united Germany full membership in NATO certainly did match British forebodings. For a range of views in the American and British debate in this period, see Ronald Asmus, "A United Germany," *Foreign Affairs*, vol. 69 (Spring 1990), pp. 63–76; Richard Barnet, "Defining the Moment," *New Yorker*, July 16, 1990, pp. 46–53; Coral Bell, "Why Russia Should Join NATO," *National Interest*, no. 22 (Winter 1990–91), pp. 37–47; Christoph Bertram, "The German Question," *Foreign Affairs*, vol. 69 (Spring 1990), pp. 45–62; Klaus von Beyone, "Transition to Democracy—or Anschluss? The Two Germanies and Europe," *Government and Opposition*, vol. 25 (Spring 1990), pp. 170–90; Marshall Brement, "Reaching Out to Moscow," *Foreign Policy*, vol. 80 (Fall 1990), pp. 56–76; Leigh Bruce, "Europe's Locomotive," *Foreign Policy*, vol. 78 (Spring 1990), pp. 68–90, Zbigniew Brzezinski, "Beyond Chaos: A Policy for the West," *National Interest*, no. 19 (Spring 1990), pp. 3–12; James Chace, "Answering 'the German Question,' " *New Republic*, December 11, 1989, pp. 19–23; Alexander Cockburn, "Beating the Devil," *Nation*, April 9, 1990, pp. 478–79; Christopher Coker, "At the Birth of the Fourth Reich," *Political Quarterly*, vol. 61 (July–September 1990), pp. 278–84; Karl Cordell, "Soviet Attitudes to the GDR," *Political Quarterly*, vol. 61 (July–September 1990), pp. 285–88; Peter Corterier, "Quo Vadis NATO?" *Survival*, vol. 32 (March–April 1990), pp. 141–56; Marta Dassu, "The Future of Europe: The View from Rome," *International Affairs*, vol. 66 (April 1990), pp. 299–311; Ian Davidson, "The Search for a New Order in Europe," *International Affairs*, vol. 66 (April 1990), pp. 275–84; Lynn E. Davis, "Beyond German Unification: Defining the West Strategic and Arms Control Policies" (Washington: Woodrow Wilson Center, August 1990); Jonathan Dean, "After the Bloc Party" (Washington: Woodrow Wilson Center, August 1990); Jonathan Dean, "Building a Post-Cold War European Security System," *Arms Control Today*, vol. 20 (June 1990), pp. 8–12; Jonathan Dean, "Components of a Post-Cold War Security System for Europe," Working Paper at Ninth Workshop of the Pugwash Study Group on Conventional Forces in Europe, April 17–21, 1990, Vienna; Jacques Delors, "Europe's Ambitions," *Foreign Policy*, vol. 14 (Spring 1990), pp. 48–58; Milovan Djilas, "A Revolutionary Democratic Vision in Europe?" *International Affairs*, vol. 66 (April 1990), pp. 265–73; David French, "Britain and NATO: Past, Present and Future" (Washington: Woodrow Wilson Center, August 1990); John Lewis Gaddis, "Toward the Post-Cold War World," *Foreign Affairs*, vol. 70 (Spring 1991), pp. 102–22; Jean-Marie Guehenno, "America's Role in New Security Architectures," Adelphi Papers 256–57 (London: International Institute for Strategic Studies, 1990–91); Jim Hoagland, "Europe's Destiny," *Foreign Affairs*, vol. 69 (1989–90), pp. 33–50; Michael Howard, "The Remaking of Europe," *Survival*, vol. 32 (March–April 1990), pp. 99–106; Robert Hunter, "The Future of European Security," *Washington Quarterly*, vol. 13 (Autumn 1990), pp. 55–68; Josef Joffe, "One-and-a-Half Cheers for German Unification," *Commentary*, vol. 89 (June 1990), pp. 28–32; Josef Joffe, "The 'Revisionists': Germany and Russia in a Post-Bipolar World," in Clark and Serfaty (1991), pp. 95–125; Karl Kaiser, "From Nuclear Deterrence to Graduated Conflict Control," *Survival*, vol. 32 (November–December 1990), pp. 483–96; Lawrence Kaplan, " 'The End of the Alliance': Lessons of the 1960s" (Washington: Woodrow Wilson Center, August 1990); Robert D. Kaplan, "The Character Issue: Can the Germans Get It Right This Time?" *Atlantic*, May 1990, pp. 24–34; Sergei A. Karaganov, "The Year of Europe: A Soviet View," *Survival*, vol. 32 (March–April 1990), pp. 121–28; Catherine Kelleher, "The Changing Currency of Power: The Future Nature of U.S. Influence in Western Europe and North-East Asia," Adelphi Papers 256–57 (London: International Institute for Strategic Studies, 1990–91); Catherine Kelleher, "Classical Arms Control in a Revolutionary Future: Europe," paper prepared for presentation at the Daedalus Conference, Harvard University, January 19, 1990; Thomas Kielinger, "The Future of Europe: A Debate," *International Affairs*, vol. 66 (April 1990), pp. 249–63; William H. Kincade, "The Politics (and Future) of Deterrence," *Arms Control Today*, vol. 20 (April 1990), p. 34; Jane Kramer, "Letter from Germany," *New Yorker*, June 18, 1990, pp. 36–66; Charles Krauthammer, "The German Revolution: The Berlin Wall Came Down too Soon," *New Republic*, March 26, 1990, pp. 18–21; Irving Kristol, "Why Not Neutralize Eastern Europe?"

International Herald Tribune, September 13, 1989; Marcin Krol, "A Europe of Nations or a Universalistic Europe?" *International Affairs*, vol. 66 (April 1990), pp. 285–89; Christopher Layne, "Superpower Disengagement," *Foreign Policy*, vol. 78 (Spring 1990), pp. 3–25; Pierre Lellouche, "Kohls Apart: Schemes of Reunification," *New Republic*, March 19, 1990, pp. 12–14; Eckhard Lubkemeier, "NATO's Identity Crisis," *Bulletin of Atomic Scientists*, vol. 46 (October 1990), pp. 30–33; A. James McAdams, "Germany and the World," *World Policy Journal*, vol. 7 (Spring 1990), pp. 357–75; A. James McAdams, "Towards a New Germany? Problems of Unification," *Government and Opposition*, vol. 25 (Summer 1990), pp. 304–16; William H. McNeill, "Winds of Change," *Foreign Affairs*, vol. 69 (Fall 1990), pp. 152–75; Michael Mandelbaum, "Reconstructing the European Security Order," Critical Issues 1990 (New York: Council on Foreign Relations, March 1990); Charles Maynes, "The New Decade," *Foreign Policy*, vol. 80 (Fall 1990), pp. 3–13; Walter Russell Mead, "The Once and Future Reich," *World Policy Journal*, vol. 7 (Fall 1990), pp. 593–98; Roger Morgan, "Germany in Europe," *Washington Quarterly*, vol. 13 (Autumn 1990), pp. 147–57; John Mueller, "A New Concert of Europe," *Foreign Policy*, vol. 7 (Winter 1989–90), pp. 3–16; "The Newest Superpower," *Nation*, March 12, 1990, p. 329; John Newhouse, "The Diplomatic Round: Sweeping Change," *New Yorker*, August 27, 1990, pp. 78–89; Paul Nitze, "America: An Honest Broker," *Foreign Affairs*, vol. 69 (Fall 1990), pp. 1–14; Sam Nunn, "Challenges to NATO in the 1990s," *Survival*, vol. 32 (January–February 1990), pp. 3–13; Joseph Nye, Jr., "Soft Power," *Foreign Policy*, vol. 80 (Fall 1990), pp. 153–71; William E. Odom, "Only Ties to America Provide the Answer," *Orbis*, vol. 34 (Fall 1990), pp. 483–504; Keith B. Payne and Michael Ruehle, "The Future of the Alliance: Emerging German Views," *Strategic Review*, vol. 19 (Winter 1991), pp. 37–45; William Pfaff, "Redefining World Power," *Foreign Affairs*, vol. 70, no. 1 (1991), pp. 34–48; Thomas Risse-Kappen, "Predicting the New Europe," *Bulletin of Atomic Scientists,* vol. 46 (October 1990), pp. 25–29; John Roper, "Europe and the Future of Germany—A British View," *The World Today*, vol. 46 (March 1990), pp. 46–49; John Roper, "Shaping Strategy without the Threat," Adelphi Papers 256–57 (London: International Institute for Strategic Studies, 1990–91); Hélène Seppain, "The Divided West: Contrasting German and U.S. Attitudes in Soviet Trade," *Political Quarterly*, vol. 61 (March 1990), pp. 51–65; Stanley R. Sloan, "NATO's Future in a New Europe: An American Perspective," *International Affairs*, vol. 66 (July 1990), pp. 495–511; Stanley Sloan, "The United States and a New Europe: Strategy for the Future," speech at NATO Defense College, Rome, October 25, 1990; Ronald Steel, "NATO's Last Mission," *Foreign Policy*, vol. 76 (Fall 1989), pp. 83–95; Angela Stent, "The One Germany," *Foreign Policy*, vol. 81 (Winter 1990–91), pp. 53–70; Stephen F. Szabo, "The German Answer," *SAIS Review*, vol. 10 (Summer–Fall 1990), pp. 41–56; Stephen F. Szabo, "The New Germany and European Security" (Washington: Woodrow Wilson Center, August 1990); Peter Tarnoff, "America's New Special Relationships," *Foreign Affairs*, vol. 69 (Summer 1990), pp. 67–80; John Templeman and Aimery Dunlap Smith, "German Unity: A Threat to Europe 1992?" *Business Week*, January 22, 1990, pp. 40–41; Gregory F. Treverton, "America's European Engagement" (Washington: Woodrow Wilson Center, November 1990); Robert Tucker, "1989 and All That," *Foreign Affairs*, vol. 69 (Fall 1990), pp. 93–114; Stephen Van Evera, "Why Europe Matters, Why the Third World Doesn't: American Grand Strategy after the Cold War," *Journal of*

Strategic Studies, vol. 13 (June 1990), pp. 1–51; William Wallace and Martin Spät, "Coming to Terms with Germany," *The World Today*, vol. 46 (April 1990), pp. 56–56; Jenonne Walker, "Keeping America in Europe," *Foreign Policy*, vol. 83 (Summer 1991), pp. 128–42; and Jenonne Walker, "Security in Post-Confrontation Europe" (Washington: Woodrow Wilson Center, August 1990).

For a range of European continental views, see Ernst-Otto Czempiel, "Die Modernisierung der Atlantischen Gemeinschaft," *Europa Archiv*, April 25, 1990, pp. 275–86; Stanley Hoffmann, "Abschied von der Vergangenheit: Politik und Sicherheit in Europa der neunziger Jahre," *Europa Archiv*, October 25, 1990, pp. 595–606; Jürgen Nötzold and Reinhardt Rummel, "On the Way to a New European Order," *Aussenpolitik*, vol. 41 (3d Quarter 1990), pp. 212–24; Berndt von Staden, "Nothing Less than the Whole of Europe Will Do," *Aussenpolitik*, vol. 41 (3d Quarter 1990) pp. 24–37; and Berndt von Staden, "Das vereinigte Deutschland in Europa," *Europa Archiv*, December 10, 1990, pp. 685–90.

For background on German-Polish relations, see Marlies Jansen, "Der Grenzvertrag mit Polen," *Deutschland Archiv*, no. 12 (December 1990), pp. 1820–21; Marlies Jansen, "Nachbarschaft mit Polen," *Deutschland Archiv*, no. 8 (August 1991), pp. 787–89; Michael Ludwig, "The Foreign Policy of the New Polish Government and the German Question," *Politics and Society in Germany, Austria and Switzerland*, vol. 3, no. 2 (1991), pp. 1–18; Krzysztof Skubiszewski, "Change versus Stability in Europe: A Polish View," *The World Today*, vol. 46 (August–September 1990), pp. 148–51; Horst Teltschik, "The Federal Republic and Poland—A Difficult Partnership in the Heart of Europe," *Aussenpolitik*, vol. 41 (1st Quarter 1990), pp. 3–14; and Jozef-Janusz Wec, "Die polnische Haltung zum deutschen Einigungsprozess," *Deutschland Archiv*, no. 5 (May 1991), pp. 519–29.

Note to Chapter 14

Very little about the dramatic crisis of the left following German unification has been written in English. Two English-language essays on the narrower literary dispute appeared in *German Studies Review*, vol. 14 (May 1991): David Bathrick, "The End of the Wall before the End of the Wall," pp. 297–311, and Patricia Herminghouse, "Confronting the 'Blank Spots of History': GDR Culture and the Legacy of 'Stalinism,' " pp. 345–65. They are twinned with two German-language essays: Frank Hörnigk, "Verlust von Illusionen—Gewinn an Realismus," pp. 313–24, and Wolfgang Emmerich, "*Affirmation—Utopie—Melancholie* Versuch einer Bilanz," pp. 325–44. An earlier look at the Greens and security issues in English is Hans-Georg Betz, "Strange Love? How the Greens Began to Love NATO," *German Studies Review*, vol. 12 (October 1989), pp. 487–505. Essays by Judith Ryan, Ulrich Greiner, Martin Jay, David Bathrick, and Jens Reich on postmodernism, the Christa Wolf controversy, and the diminished role of the intellectual in united Germany also appear in *German Politics and Society*, vol. 27 (Fall 1992), pp. 12–24, 61–92. Since I wrote this manuscript, my attention has also been drawn to *New German Critique*, vol. 52 (Winter 1991), with essays there by Karl Heinz Bohrer, Jürgen Habermas, Stefan Heym, and Andreas Huyssen; and to Helmut Dubiel's essay in *Praxis International*, vol. 10 (October 1990–January 1991).

The plethora of German newspaper and magazine articles on the post-Wall polemics precludes citing more than a few of them here: Interview with Daniel Cohn-Bendit, "Die Linke darf den Begriff Sozialismus nicht mehr blauäugig gebrauchen," *Süddeutsche Zeitung*, October 31, 1989; Stefan Heym, Christa Wolf, and others, "Für unser Land," *Neues Deutschland*, November 28, 1989; "Linksradikal contra deutschnational," *Tageszeitung*, January 23, 1990; Günter Kunert interview, "Die ausgeträumte DDR-Traum von Antifaschismus and Solidarität," *Deutschland Archiv*, no. 2 (February 1990), pp. 207–11; "Die schweigende Mehrheit meldet sich," *FAZ*, March 28, 1990; "Tabus darf es nicht geben," *Tageszeitung*, April 18, 1990, p. 10; Daniel Cohn-Bendit, "Die postsozialistische Linke," *Tageszeitung*, April 30, 1990, p. 4; *German Quarterly* special edition on literature of the 1980s, vol. 63 (Summer–Fall 1990); Lothar Probst, "Die Revolution entlässt ihre Schriftsteller," *Deutschland Archiv*, no. 6 (June 1990), pp. 921–25; Bernd Schick, "Preussisches Interregnum? Anmerkungen zum kleindeutschen Patriotismus der Reformbewegung in der DDR," *Deutschland Archiv*, no. 6 (June 1990), pp. 936–44; Detlef Pollack, "Aussenseiter oder Repräsentanten?" *Deutschland Archiv*, no. 8 (August 1990), pp. 1216–23; Günter Kunert, "Der Sturz vom Sockel: Zum Streit der deutschen Autoren," *FAZ*, September 3, 1990; Antonia Grunenberg, "Antifaschismus—ein deutscher Mythos," *Die Zeit*, May 3, 1991; Karl Corino, "Es ist unglaublich viel gelogen worden: Ein Gespräch mit Reiner Kunze," *Deutschland Archiv*, no. 2 (February 1991), pp. 130–38; Erich Loest, "Augen zu und durch? Ein offenes Brief an Dietmar Keller," *Deutschland Archiv*, no. 2 (February 1991), pp. 199–200; Peter Glotz, "Gefärliche Demokratie? Eine Antwort auf Klaus Hartung," *Die Zeit*, May 24, 1991; Rolf Henrich, "Wir sind nicht die Opfer der Geschichte," *FAZ*, June 6, 1991; Lutz Rathenow, "Offener Brief," *Deutschland Archiv*, no. 7 (August 1991), pp. 743–46; Eckhard Lübkemeier, "Wie bricht der Frieden aus?" *Die Zeit*, November 22, 1991, p. 56; Frank Schirrmacher, "Der grosse Verdacht," *FAZ*, November 23, 1991; Durs Grünbein, "Im Namen der Füchse," *FAZ*, November 26, 1991; Lutz Rathenow, " 'Schreiben Sie doch für uns!' " *FAZ*, November 27, 1991, p. 36; Hajo Steinert, "Die Szene und die Stasi," *Die Zeit*, November 29, 1991; Fritz J. Raddatz, "Ich kann doch nicht mein Leben wegwerfen: Ein ZEIT-Gespräch mit Stefan Heym," *Die Zeit*, December 6, 1991, pp. 65–66; Günter Kunert, "Homunculus kehrt zurück," *FAZ*, December 11, 1991, p. 31; Frank Schirrmacher, "Literatur und Lüge," *FAZ*, December 16, 1991, p. 10; Wolf Lepenies, "Ressentiment und Überheblichkeit," *FAZ*, March 7, 1992; Henryk M. Broder, "Beschwerden über den Abbruch der Vorstellung," *FAZ*, March 30, 1992, p. 36; and Rainer Zittelman, "Wiedervereinigung und deutscher Selbsthass," *Deutschland Archiv*, no. 8 (August 1992), pp. 811–20.

Beyond noted references, books on various aspects of the subject, or that have had some impact on the debate, include: Hannes Bahrmann and Peter Michael Fritsch, *Sumpf: Privilegien, Amtsmissbrauch, Schiebergeschäfte* (Berlin: LinksDruck, 1991); Bernd Biesen and Claus Leggewie, eds., *Experiment Vereinigung* (Berlin: Rotbuch, 1991); Frank Blohm and Wolfgang Herzberg, eds., *"Nichts wird mehr so sein, wie es war": Zur Zukunft der beiden Republiken* (Frankfurt and Leipzig: Reklam, 1990); Peter Bordihn, *Bittere Jahre am Polarkreis: Als Sozialdemokrat in Stalins Lagern* (Berlin: LinksDruck, 1991); Herbert Crüger, *Verschwiegene Zeiten: Vom geheimen Apparat der KPD ins Gefängnis der Staatssicherheit* (Berlin: LinksDruck, 1991); Peter Glotz, *Die deutsche Rechte* (Stuttgart: Deutsche Verlags-Anstalt, 1989); Peter Glotz,

Manifest für eine neue Europäische Linke (Berlin: Siedler, 1985); Horst Heimann, *Die Voraussetzungen des Demokratischen Sozialismus und die Aufgaben der Sozialdemokratie* (Bonn: Dietz-Verlag, 1991); Hubertus Knabe, ed., *Aufbruch in eine andere DDR* (Reinbek: Rowohlt-aktuell, 1990); Wolfgang Kowalsky, *Rechtsaussen . . . und die verfehlten Strategien der deutschen Linken* (Frankfurt: Ullstein, 1992); and Reinhard Müller, ed., *Die Säuberung* (Reinbek: Rowohlt, 1992).

Note to Chapter 15

The discussion in this section draws on interviews and also on Ingo Kolboom, "Die Vertreibung der Dämonen: Frankreich und das vereinte Deutschland," *Europa Archiv*, August 25, 1991, pp. 470–75; Jolyon Howorth, "France since the Berlin Wall: Defence and Diplomacy," *The World Today*, vol. 46 (July 1990), pp. 126–30; Renata Fritsch-Bournazel, "German Unification: A Durability Test for the Franco-German Tandem," *German Studies Review*, vol. 14 (October 1991), pp. 575–86; Roger Morgan, "French Perspectives of the New Germany," *Government and Opposition*, vol. 26 (Winter 1991), pp. 108–14; Diego A. Ruiz Palmer, "French Strategic Options in the 1990s," Adelphi Papers 260 (London: International Institute for Strategic Studies, 1991); Jochen Thies, "Communication Breakdown," *European Affairs*, vol. 1 (February–March 1991), pp. 63–64; David Yost, "France in the New Europe," *Foreign Affairs*, vol. 69 (Winter 1990–91), pp. 107–28; and David Yost, "France and West European Defence Identity," *Survival*, vol. 33 (July–August 1991), pp. 327–51.

Note to Chapter 16

For some of the debate about the poisonous *Stasi* role in GDR society and how to handle it, see, for example, Erich Loest, "Das Jahr der Täter," *FAZ*, October 13, 1990, unpaginated; interview with Richard Schröder, " 'Ein Tanz auf dem Vulkan,' " *Der Spiegel*, January 21, 1991, pp. 41–48; speech in the Saxon Landtag by Karl-Heinz Kunckel on October 24, 1991 (available from Kunckel's office, Dresden); Jürgen Fuchs, "Landschaften der Lüge," *Der Spiegel*, November 18, 1991, and four succeeding issues through December 16, 1991; Lutz Rathenow, " 'Schreiben Sie doch für uns?' " *FAZ*, November 27, 1991, p. 36; Hajo Steinert, "Die Szene und die Stasi," *Die Zeit*, November 29, 1991; Vera Wollenberger, "Diese Entdeckung," *Tageszeitung,* December 19, 1991, p. 12; Benjamin Korn, "Bald Schwein, bald Schmetterling," *Die Zeit,* December 20, 1991. pp. 47–48; Rainer Schedlinski, "Dem Druck, immer mehr sagen zu sollen, hielt ich nicht stand," *FAZ,* January 14, 1992, p. 25; Klaus Hartung, "Deutsche Akten," *Die Zeit*, February 2, 1992; "Geht es am Ende nur um Mielkes Hut?" *FAZ*, February 29, 1992; Wolf Biermann, "Das Kaninchen frisst die Schlange," *Der Spiegel*, March 2, 1992, pp. 40–51; Bärbel Bohley, Katja Havemann, and others, "Thesen zur Aufklärung der Vergangenheit," *Deutschland Archiv*, no. 4 (April 1992), pp. 446–47; Richard Schröder, "Stasi-Akten als Zerrspiegel," *Bertelsmann Briefe*, vol. 127 (April 1992), pp. 30–36; Jürgen Habermas, "Bemerkungen zu einer verworrenen Diskussion,"

Die Zeit, April 3, 1992, pp. 81–84; Karl Wilhelm Fricke, "Das Stasi-Spitzelunwesen in Dokumenten," *Deutschland Archiv,* no. 5 (May 1992), p. 546; letter from Ludwig Mehlhorn, "Dimensionen der Schuld/Zur Kontinuität deutscher Tätergeschichte," *Deutschland Archiv,* no. 6 (June 1992), pp. 620–24; Jens Reich, "Waren wir alle gelähmt?" *FAZ,* July 11, 1992, unpaginated; Joachim-Rüdiger Groth, "Tödliche Berührung," *FAZ,* July 18, 1992, unpaginated; Herbert Obenaus, "Stasi kommt—Nazi geht?" *Die Zeit,* July 31, 1992; Wolf Biermann, " 'à la lanterne! à la lanterne!' " *Der Spiegel,* September 21, 1992, pp. 81–92; "Destasifying Germany," *Economist,* December 1, 1990, pp. 19–21; Stephen Kinzer, "East Germans Face Their Accusers," *New York Times Magazine,* April 12, 1992, pp. 24–52; Melvin J. Lasky, "Protest, Scandal, Guilt," *The National Interest* (Spring 1992), pp. 61–67; and Amos Elon, "East Germany: Crime and Punishment," *New York Review of Books,* May 14, 1992, pp. 6–11.

On church-*Stasi* relations see, for example, Ernst-Michael Brandt, "So war Kirche wahrhaftig," *Die Zeit,* March 6, 1992; Christof Ehrler, "Es gibt Mittel, die selbst den besten Zweck entheiligen," *FAZ,* March 14, 1992; interview with Rainer Eppelman on Deutschlandfunk, May 3, 1992, reprinted in *Deutschland Archiv,* no. 6 (June 1992), pp. 668–72; Joachim Nawrocki, "Wenn aus Vieldeutigem Eindeutiges wird," *Die Zeit,* April 24, 1992; Robert Leicht, "Auswüchse des Verdachts," and Ilka Piepgras, "Tribunal am Altar," *Die Zeit,* May 1, 1992; Richard Schröder, "Blick auf die Hinterbühne," *FAZ,* May 5, 1992; Richard Schröder, " 'Der Mann für grobe Fälle,' " *Der Spiegel,* May 11, 1992, pp. 38 ff.; Richard Schröder, "Zu Tisch mit dem Teufel," *FAZ,* June 12, 1992, p. 37; Helmut Müller-Enbergs, "Schwierigkeiten mit der Vergangenheit," *FAZ,* July 24, 1992, p. 8; Wolf Krötke, "Musste die Kirche mit der Stasi reden?" *Die Zeit,* September 4, 1992; and Richard Schröder, "Am Schnittpunkt von Macht und Ohnmacht," *Die Zeit,* October 9, 1992, pp. 11–12.

This book is not concerned with theories of collective security as such. It assumes that CSCE will supplement but not supplant the old collective-defense alliance of NATO (or its junior WEU). It takes elements of collective defense as relevant to post–cold war Europe, however. Useful discussions of collective security include Gregory Flynn and David J. Scheffer, "Limited Collective Security," *Foreign Policy,* vol. 80 (Fall 1990), pp. 77–101; Daniel Nelson, "Europe's Unstable East," *Foreign Policy,* vol. 82 (Spring 1991), pp. 137–58; Charles A. Kupchan and Clifford A. Kupchan, "Concerts, Collective Security, and the Future of Europe," *International Security,* vol. 16 (Summer 1991), pp. 114–61; Josef Joffe, "Collective Security and the Future of Europe: Failed Dreams and Dead Ends," *Survival,* vol. 34 (Spring 1992), pp. 36–50; and Richard K. Betts, "Systems for Peace or Causes of War?" *International Security,* vol. 17 (Summer 1992), pp. 5–43.

Notes

Chapter 1: November 1989

1. Gaddis (1987). For full entries see References.

2. Interview with Karl-Heinz Arnold, private secretary to Hans Modrow during Modrow's term as the GDR's prime minister, November 1989–March 1990. For a listing of interviews see the Bibliographical Essay.

3. Conversation, West Berlin, June 7, 1990.

4. Schabowski (1991, pp. 309–10) says that he learned later from an unspecified source that secret police chief Erich Mielke telephoned party general secretary Krenz at about 9 P.M., saying that "several hundred" wanted to cross to West Berlin, and asking what he should do. According to Schabowski, Krenz replied, "Let them go." Krenz (1990) did not make any reference to such a phone call, however, nor has Mielke ever mentioned it. Schabowski's inclusion of this third-hand report in his book therefore looks less like hard information than like an attempt to keep up with the latest rumor in case it should turn out to be true.

5. Interviews with Arnold and GDR Foreign Ministry press spokesman Denis Ruh, East Berlin, June 6, 1990.

6. Interviews with Ruh, Arnold, and others.

7. This and other Brandt speeches are available in Brandt (1990).

8. Both Helmut Kohl himself and Horst Teltschik, Kohl's foreign policy adviser during this period, elaborated on this reasoning in interviews.

9. The original Gorbachev message came through the Soviet ambassador to the Federal Republic's Juli Kvitzinsky, who reached Teltschik by phone in West Berlin just before Kohl spoke at the rally (Teltschik interview). Besides contacting Kohl, Gorbachev also got in touch with Bush, instructed his ambassador in East Berlin to talk to the American, British, and French ambassadors there, and urged the East German communist leadership to assure a "peaceful passage." On the night of November 9, Kohl had already specified that the Germans would reject any four-power dealings over their heads (Teltschik 1991, p. 23).

10. Kohl interview.

11. Teltschik (1991, pp. 21–22, 28). Senior Foreign Ministry officials did not share Kohl's concern about provocations. They believed that the security organs' pullback from violence in Leipzig a month earlier had set the peaceful pattern. Their one worry—Shevardnadze had personally warned them of this danger—was that some East Germans might provoke Soviet soldiers, the Soviet military might react rashly, and events might careen out of control (Foreign Ministry interview). On the other hand, some danger was signaled in the order on November 11 to the East German First Motorized Division in Potsdam to move in the direction of Berlin at full battle strength and with live ammunition to close the border again. The order was rescinded before the troops left their base; it is still unclear who gave either command (Wolle 1992). A West German general involved in the Bundeswehr's dissolution of the National People's Army confirmed the existence of the alert, but noted that the Bundeswehr, with other priorities in 1990–91, never verified the degree of seriousness of the incident (telephone conversation, December 1, 1992).

12. See, for example, Ammer and Kruppe (1989); Fricke (1990e); and Wielgohs and Schulz (1990).

13. See, for example, "Der Ring wird zur Dauerschleife," *Tageszeitung,* November 15, 1989.

14. Rein (1990, pp. 291–92).

15. De Maizière interview; de Maizière's acceptance speech on November 10, 1989, reprinted in Rein (1990, pp. 287–90). See also Lapp (1990).

16. "Chronik," *Deutschland Archiv,* no. 12 (December 1989), pp. 1473–88; "Drei SED Funktionäre töteten sich selbst," *Tagesspiegel,* November 12, 1989; and "Erneut Selbstmord," *Die Welt,* November 13, 1989, p. 6. The total number of suicides is not known, but it included the minister for housing construction, *Stasi* generals, and trade union and other officials appointed by the party, according to Karl Wilhelm Fricke, chief of the East-West Section at Deutschlandfunk (telephone conversation).

17. Number given by Gregor Gysi at a campaign rally in Schwerin, February 15, 1990.

18. Estimate by new Economics Minister Christa Luft to the roundtable on January 3, 1990. A month later, on February 5, the chairman of the roundtable Economics Committee, Karl Grünheld, reduced the figure to $18.5 billion.

19. Excerpts of Mielke transcript reprinted in "Erich Mielke über den Staatssicherheitsdienst," *Deutschland Archiv,* no. 1 (January 1990), p. 121.

20. Janka (1989). See also Janka (1991b); and Knoth (1991). There was a bizarre coda to the Janka saga in 1992, when Mielke, then under indictment in a Berlin court for manslaughter of East Germans at the GDR border, secured a court injunction (before it was reversed on appeal) barring sale of Janka's memoirs, *Spuren eines Lebens.* Mielke, who, according to Janka, had been Janka's secret police interrogator in Spain when the communists temporarily jailed Janka for insubordination during the Spanish Civil War, took offense at Janka's portrayal of Mielke as having been a NKVD agent and having assiduously avoided the front lines in Spain. Mielke persuaded a judge to agree with him that Janka had no proof, and therefore had no right to publish the claim. "Mielkes Sieg: Walter Janka soll schweigen," *Frankfurter Allgemeine Zeitung* (hereafter *FAZ*), November 12, 1992, p. 33.

21. Czechoslovak Ambassador to the United States Rita Klimova noted the critical impact of the large, peaceful Leipzig demonstration and the opening of the Berlin Wall in suddenly convincing her compatriots after twenty-one years of passivity that now a revolution in Czechoslovakia might succeed too (talk to Women in Security Studies, Washington, May 6, 1991).

22. For an exploration of the failure of realists, behaviorists, structuralists, and various other theorists of international relations to predict the end of the cold war, see Gaddis (1992–93).

Chapter 2: Prologue West

1. Dönhoff interview, Hamburg, July 4, 1985.

2. Baudissin interview, Hamburg, July 4, 1985.

3. On macro stability and micro change see especially Katzenstein (1987). For a comprehensive history of the Federal Republic, see the six volumes edited by Bracher (1983–87). For the only comprehensive history of the Federal Republic in English, written from the point of view of the West German right, see Bark and Gress (1989).

4. In his rise to power, Hitler played on the myth that the German army was stabbed in the back by the civilian politicians who ended World War I unfavorably.

5. Mitscherlich and Mitscherlich (1991).

6. The classic analysis of a postmaterialist attitude change is Inglehart (1977).

7. For a useful discussion (and partial debunking) of the thesis of *Sonderweg* from the retrospective of the historians' debate of the 1980s, see Kocka (1988). In particular, Kocka contests the categorization of Britain and France's industrialization as the normal standard. See also Baldwin (1990, pp. 12–13, 279–93, and the rest of the volume). See also Blackbourn and Eley (1984).

8. Mitchell and Gee (1985). For other presentations of the NATO in crisis view, see the Bibliographical Essay.

Chapter 3: Prologue East

1. *Macropaedia* (1988).

2. For an account of this incident by an East German historian using newly declassified information from GDR archives, see Diedrich (1991). New revelations include the extent of the unrest, with almost half a million on strike in 373 cities and towns, and the numbers of victims. Thirty-three demonstrators were shot dead in East Berlin, Leipzig, Dresden, Halle, and Magdeburg, and another eighteen also died. In the following week more than 6,000 were imprisoned, almost two-thirds of them workers.

3. Internal GDR National People's Army (NVA) documents now in possession of the German Bundeswehr confirm this participation, according to a German Defense Ministry source who has worked with the documents (telephone conversation, Bonn, August 18, 1992). Some 2,000 NVA logistics, communications, and

other support troops entered northern Czechoslovakia, but did not go as far as Prague. No East German combat troops were involved, and the support units were withdrawn within a few weeks. At the time, Western commentary widely condemned this first instance since Hitler of the invasion of a neighboring country by German troops.

In the 1980s, when the GDR was seeking to project a more peace-loving image, it officially denied—even to the NVA's own junior officers—that it had joined the 1968 aggression. As late as 1992 Honecker's old Polish ally and sometime sparring partner General Wojtiech Jaruzelski still maintained this fiction in an interview (Warsaw, May 7, 1992). The last high-level East German allegation to this effect was made by former parliamentary president Horst Sindermann in an interview, Sindermann (1990).

4. Schabowski interview.

5. For an account of this event based on newly accessible GDR archives, see Möbius and Trotnow (1991).

6. Schabowski interview. See also Schabowski (1991, pp. 203–06), and Mayer (1991a).

7. For a description of this division of life and abdication from politics among intellectuals, see Reich (1991).

8. As late as October 1989 Gorbachev would still think the GDR economy was functioning well. See " 'Das habt ihr verbrochen,' " Der Spiegel, September 14, 1992, pp. 87–104, in particular Günter Schabowski's comments on p. 91.

9. The banks, backed by government guarantees, extended credits of DM 1 billion in 1983 and another DM 950 million in 1984. Official public-sector payments throughout the 1980s ran at about DM 1 billion per year, according to Lipschitz and McDonald (1990, p. 67). Overall payments, including nonofficial infusions of cash and commodities, averaged DM 2.0 billion annually, giving a total of DM 24.5 billion between 1975 and 1988, according to a Bundesbank study issued in 1990. These calculations include West German transfers of DM 15.0 billion for transit, road, and entry fees, transport improvement, and water protection; DM 2.6 billion for gifts purchased by West Germans for East Germans through the Genex firm; and spending by West German travelers in East Germany of DM 16.0 billion, as against spending by East German travelers in West Germany of DM 2.5 billion. Interest-free credits were increased from DM 600,000 to DM 850,000 in 1985. The GDR paid an amount equivalent to what the interest would have been in miscellaneous hard currency transfers owed to former GDR citizens living in the Federal Republic. See also Lisiecki (1990).

10. Aslund (1985).

11. One of the best summaries of the two Germanys' policies on unification before 1989 is Nawrocki (1988).

12. See " 'Wir Brüderländer stehen fest,' " Der Spiegel, October 12, 1992, pp. 95–99.

13. See "Honecker in Gera," Deutschland Archiv, no. 11 (November 1980), pp. 1220ff. Honecker appeared to have listed his demands as a kind of thermostat. When East-West German relations were improving, his demands were played down. When contacts were deteriorating for embarrassing reasons (such as Soviet intransigence), he restated the demands more urgently, as if they were the main obstacle to better relations.

14. For East German treatment of historical figures, see Brinks (1992); Eckert, Küttler, and Seeber (1992); and, in English, Dorpalen (1985).

15. One infamous French cartoon from the early 1980s showed Schmidt groveling and polishing Brezhnev's boots. For a milder version of this mistrust, see "German 'Togetherness' Could Cause Trouble for East and West," *Business Week,* April 20, 1987, p. 41.

16. Genscher interview.

17. Herf (1991) develops this theme thoroughly in his dissection of the West German left's response to the INF debate. For other treatments of the issue, see the Bibliographical Essay.

18. See, for example, Bender (1981).

19. Honecker and Kohl grew up within forty miles of each other, and despite their age difference, they had some mutual acquaintances (Kohl interview).

20. See Adomeit (1984); Jens Kaiser (1991); Wettig (1991); and Spanger (1989).

21. Bezyminsky (1984). In rebuttal, the SED authorized an editorial in *Neues Deutschland* that pointedly restated the goal of damage limitation in East-West relations on the basis of both East and West German independence in domestic and foreign affairs. "Zum 9. Jahrestag der Unterzeichnung der Schlussakte von Helsinki," August 1, 1984, p. 2.

22. The Soviets did finally, at Honecker's request, change their ambassador from the abrasive Pyotr Abrasimov to the much more civil Vyacheslav Kochemasov in 1983. The then Soviet General Secretary Yuri Andropov instructed Kochemasov that the Soviet ambassador was no longer supposed to exercise command in East Berlin, but to cooperate with the leaders there. "We no longer need a governor, but a new ambassador in the GDR," Kochemasov (1992) quotes Andropov as telling him. Yet even Kochemasov exercised the right to enter the GDR Foreign Ministry at will until the elected government took office in 1990, according to Markus Meckel, foreign minister in that government (Meckel group interview).

In a retrospective interview with *Izvestia* in summer 1992, Abrasimov portrayed a stiff relationship between Moscow and East Berlin even at the best of times. KGB officers kept a beady eye on their *Stasi* colleagues, Soviet Army officers and other agents placed throughout the National People's Army did the same in the East German armed forces, and the suspicious Russians long proscribed private meetings between East and West Germans. In policy issues, however (by the 1980s, Abrasimov implies), the GDR's leadership became skilled at nodding politely to Moscow and then doing as it pleased. "When Honecker and his entourage did not want to do something, no one could bring them to do it." Excerpts from the *Izvestia* interview were carried in German in Abrasimov (1992).

23. Chancellery interview, mid-1980s. In his book, Rehlinger (1991), the state secretary who managed Bonn's purchase of East German political prisoners in the 1980s, says the normal price was DM 40,000 per person. When the GDR demanded DM 2 million for a particular count, he relates, Bonn asked rhetorically whether a nobleman "was worth fifty times as much as a worker in the worker and peasant state of the GDR." (In this case the count's father did top off the government's DM 40,000 with an additional DM 410,000, he adds.) Rehlinger lists a total value of DM 3.5 billion as having been spent by the Federal Republic to attain the release

of 33,755 political prisoners, or more than DM 100,000 per person (pp. 65–66, 247). See also Kleine-Brockhoff and Schröm (1992).

24. Schabowski interview. See also Kochemasov (1992).

25. See, for example, Asmus (1986); Glaessner (1988); and McAdams (1985, 1986).

Chapter 4: Nuclear Angst and Reassurance

1. Genscher interview. For the contrary view that the U.S. military buildup of the early 1980s was not responsible for the major Soviet concessions of the late 1980s—as measured in American and Soviet defense budgets—see Chernoff (1991).

2. For a summary of this conclusion, see Kaysen (1990). Kaysen rebuts the thesis that nuclear weapons had nothing to do with creating peace in Europe, as argued in Mueller (1989).

3. See discussion of this chapter in Bibliographical Essay.

4. Genscher interview.

5. For a discussion of Schmidt's intent, see Peters (1990, pp. 146–49ff).

6. Schmidt speech at the Free University, Berlin, honoring Richard Löwenthal, December 8, 1991.

7. Karber (1983).

8. Genscher interview.

9. Interviews with West German generals and civilian defense analysts, NATO officials, and General Rogers.

10. The abundant Soviet propaganda in Western Europe stressed the dangers as the INF deployment date approached. Foreign Minister Andrei Gromyko even warned Europeans that they risked following Pompeii's example.

11. Howard (1982–83).

12. Cited in Adomeit (1982, p. 208); Roberts (1991).

13. For one report of opinion against nuclear weapons in the late 1980s, see Noelle-Neumann (1988).

14. The characterization of the Reagan administration's approach in this section is based on interviews with U.S., British, and West German officials and nongovernmental observers in Washington, Geneva, Bonn, and London in the early 1980s.

15. Teltschik interview, Bonn, March 8, 1985.

16. With the assent of the Europeans this had, of course, been the American negotiators' formal goal at the beginning. In response to the firm Soviet rejection, however, the West had moved to a compromise interim proposal in 1983 that would have had the Soviets build down and NATO build up to a few hundred INF warheads in Europe. The interim solution was actually the outcome the Europeans preferred. It was in returning to the original zero option that the United States failed to consult its European allies.

17. Interviews with Paul Nitze, Rozanne Ridgway, Edward L. Rowny, and others, Washington, week of October 13, 1986; and Oberdorfer (1991, pp. 183–209). In somewhat more premeditated fashion, American negotiators at Reykjavik floated an alternate offer to scrap all superpower nuclear missiles, but not bombs.

This notion was only slightly less repugnant to Europeans dependent on these missiles for their ultimate guarantee.

18. Genscher interview.

19. Interviews with West German generals and civilians working in defense.

20. Genscher (1987).

21. For the best single analysis of conventional arms control, see the numerous articles and books by Jonathan Dean, including *Watershed in Europe* (1987) and *Meeting Gorbachev's Challenge* (1989).

Chapter 5: Meanwhile, Europe

1. Katzenstein (1991) and Schwarz (1985).

2. Ullman (1989).

3. This insight comes from Michael Naumann of the Rowohlt Publishing House.

4. See, for example, Tranholm-Mikkelsen (1991) and Moravcsik (1991).

5. Kohl interview.

6. "Britain Backs Europe by Telephone Vote," *Financial Times,* September 26, 1991, p. 22.

7. Interviews with German generals and with NATO supreme allied commanders for Europe Bernard W. Rogers and John Galvin, as well as with French military and civilian sources, 1983 through 1989.

8. See, for example, Laird (1991b).

9. Wallace (1990, p. 96). Much of the interpretation in this chapter draws on this book.

Chapter 6: Meanwhile, Eastern Europe

1. The term *East Central Europe* excludes the Balkans and comprises Poland, Czechoslovakia, and Hungary, as well as the GDR before German unification. In terms of identification with mainstream Europe, a case could be made for including Slovenia, but as Slovenia was still locked into the Yugoslav federation and unable to join the initial wave of self-determination in 1989, it is excluded here for the sake of simplicity. The term *Eastern Europe* is used here to signify, before 1989, all the client states to the west of the Soviet Union.

2. The notion of civil society became the uniting theme of dissidents in Poland, Czechoslovakia, and Hungary in the 1980s. Vladimir Tismaneanu (1992) defines civil society as "the ensemble of grassroots, spontaneous, nongovernmental (although not necessarily anti-governmental) initiatives from below that emerge in the post-totalitarian order as a result of a loosening of state controls and the decline of the ideological constraints imposed by the ruling parties" (pp. 170–71 and chaps. 4 and 5). Descriptively, the term *civil society* was used to identify the historical difference between the East Central European countries and the far more mono-

lithic and regimented Russia and Soviet Union. Normatively, dissidents advocated a vigorous civil society as the proper goal of reforms. See also Geremek (1992).

3. Although the Soviets objected to this phrase as a Western concoction, Gorbachev had no compunction about using it in its full negative connotation. See the interview with Gorbachev (1992).

4. Kramer (1989–90). For other discussions of Soviet-East European relations, see the Bibliographical Essay.

5. For an indication of this perception by Polish workers, see Laba (1991, p. 87). Communist officials, including one-time party First Secretary Mieczyslaw Rakowski, never did acknowledge this point (Rakowski interview).

6. Interview (Pragel and Völklein 1987).

7. Kochemasov (1992).

8. Peter Przybylski, at the time the spokesman for the state prosecutor in East Berlin, describes this tactic from the point of view of GDR enforcement agencies (1992, pp. 90–95).

9. Western economists calculated that there was an absolute decline in goods and services available in the GDR in the 1980s (Glaessner 1988). My and other reporters' street interviews in major East German cities in the late 1980s suggested, however, that in popular concerns economic grievances ranked well below the indignity of restrictions on travel, education, and speech.

10. Blumenwitz (1992).

11. Ammer (1992). Much later, Mielke (1992) complained about the propensity of other ministries to dump all their problems on the *Stasi* by telling interviewers how he would have improved things: "I would not have given others the chance to leave all the responsibility to us. State security, state security! You wouldn't believe what trivialities we had to tend to! When something in supplies didn't work; when, for example, it rained through the roof of a hospital."

12. Fricke (1990c) and Fricke (1990a).

13. *Junge Welt,* June 18, 1990, cited in Fricke (1990c).

14. A personal anecdote might illustrate the *Stasi's* pervasiveness. After publishing an utterly apolitical feature about the famous Bach Boys' Choir in Leipzig's Thomas Church in the early 1980s, I received a letter from an American reader of German background with the same surname as one of the boys I had interviewed. He asked me to forward the letter to the boy. As I had caught the East German caution by then and thought a personal letter from America might cause trouble for the youth, I simply took the letter with me the next time I went to Leipzig and gave it to the choir conductor, Hans Joachim Rotzsch, to deliver. A decade later Rotzsch, a professed Christian and a musician who was clearly devoted to his young charges, had to resign his post of nineteen years after an investigation identified him as a *Stasi* informer.

15. An official report on the Ministry of State Security given to the roundtable January 8, 1990; roundtable hearings on January 15 and 22, 1990; Fricke (1990b); telephone conversation with Fricke; Ammer (1992). On January 15, 1990, the Modrow government gave the roundtable the figure of 109,000 unofficial collaborators; former MfS General Heinz Engelhardt (who remained in office until mid-1990 as an adviser to the MfS dissolution committee) gave the figure in May 1991 as 180,000 (Ammer 1992, p. 548).

16. The Gestapo employed 32,000 people in 1944. Richard Bessel (1991) pointed out this contrast.

17. "Modrow wegen Falschaussage angezeigt," *FAZ,* June 3, 1992, p. 1.

18. "Der Prediger als politischer Tribun," *Die Zeit,* September 18, 1992, p. 2. Excerpts from secret 1967 and 1986 *Stasi* directives about the preventive detention of those with negative attitudes are reprinted in Przybylski (1991, pp. 398–411).

19. Quoted in Fricke (1990d).

20. Schabowski interview.

21. Politburo member Werner Krolikowski states this in notes he wrote on January 16, 1990 (Przybylski 1991, p. 336). See also Schabowski (1991, pp. 211–15); and in various Politburo members' testimony in the secret party postmortem in January 1990 (" 'Ich hab' an den geglaubt,' " *Der Spiegel,* September 14, 1992, pp. 86–104).

22. Wolfgang Vogel interviews. See also Schell and Kalinka (1991a). The article in *Die Welt* relates that as late as July 1989, *Stasi* chief Mielke told his top officers that Honecker, after his latest visit to Moscow, was convinced that the economic collapse of the Soviet Union was imminent, while Gorbachev was bullheadedly proceeding with glasnost and perestroika.

23. For a contemporary assessment of the visit, see Winters (1987).

24. See the discussion of this chapter in Bibliographical Essay.

25. Emigration figures from West German Interior Ministry; travel estimates commissioned by the West German Inner-German Ministry.

26. For the text of the original statement, "Streit der Ideologien und die gemeinsame Sicherheit," see *Neues Deutschland,* August 28, 1987, p. 3, or *Frankfurter Allgemeine Zeitung,* August 28, 1987, p. 7. See also Phillips (1989); Spittmann (1988); and Japs (1992). Hager (1987) presents a rejection of the paper. A late defense of the paper against conservative attacks is presented in, for example, Carl-Christian Kaiser (1992). For a brief description of the unsettling effect the paper had on the Stasi, see Knauer (1992, especially p. 722f.).

27. Telephone conversation with the chief East German author of the paper, Rolf Reissig.

28. See, for example, contributions by Fricke, Spittmann, Kleinschmid, and Helwig ("Kommentare und aktuelle Beiträge," *Deutschland Archiv,* no. 3 [March 1988], pp. 225–38); and Przybylski (1992, pp. 90–95). For a portrait of the last would-be escapee killed at the wall, on February 6, 1989, see Serke (1990).

29. See "Eine klammheimliche Kungelei," *Der Spiegel,* August 24, 1992, pp. 44–50; and "Angst vor den Akten," *Der Spiegel,* August 24, 1992, pp. 50–63.

30. The charge that a steady program of buying political prisoners' freedom might act as an incentive to the East German regime to jail more people was corroborated after unification. In 1992 prosecutors in Magdeburg indicted six former jurists for such practices in twenty-two cases. The per capita price was listed as DM 96,000. " 'DDR produzierte bewusst politische Gefangene,' " *Süddeutsche Zeitung,* September 4, 1992, p. 6; and " 'Bewusst politische Häftlinge produziert,' " *FAZ,* September 4, 1992, p. 4.

31. See Kusin (1989) and Kux (1991). Radical Gorbachev kibbitzers like Oleg Bogomolov and Vyacheslav Dashichev of Moscow's Institute of the Economics of the World Socialist System went even further. They suggested that there were few

Soviet taboos left on experimentation in Hungary and Poland, and they even seemed to spur their East European colleagues to greater daring in virtual pilot projects for the more unwieldy Soviet Union. Sensationally, in an internal paper at his institute in spring 1988, Dashichev blamed Soviet hegemonic aspirations and stagnant neo-Stalinism for the political crisis in Eastern Europe (Dashichev 1988).

32. Genscher interview.

33. See Kramer (1989–90) and Adomeit (1990).

Chapter 7: Annus Mirabilis

1. The most notable public expression of this Soviet attitude was coined by Soviet Foreign Ministry spokesman Gennady Gerasimov in October 1989, when he formulated the "Sinatra doctrine" toward Eastern Europe, borrowing from Frank Sinatra's song, "I Did It My Way" (Keller 1989).

2. Przybylski (1992, pp. 101–02). For East German developments from January to October 1989, see also Wolle (1992).

3. Przybylski (1992, pp. 101–02).

4. For secret police reports on the elections and protests—gleaned later by citizens' committees that took over secret police offices—see Mitter and Wolle (1990, pp. 34–39, 42–45, 72–78, 93–94, 97–110, 139–40).

5. Enough voters crossed out the candidates' names that they did not receive the margin of more than 50 percent required for election on the first ballot.

6. Pravda, July 7, 1989. For a brief discussion of the evolving Soviet usage of the term *common European house*, see Waever (1990, especially p. 482).

7. Schabowski interview. At the risk of tedium, I have footnoted each segment of information from Schabowski to make clear what comes from his books and what from my interviews. For further discussion of sources on the palace coup, see the Bibliographical Essay.

8. Schabowski interview.

9. Schabowski (1990, pp. 24–25). Other Politburo members confirmed this iron discipline and ban on faction building in the party's secret postmortem of January 1990. See " 'Ich hab' an den geglaubt,' " *Der Spiegel*, September 14, 1992, pp. 86–104, especially pp. 97–99.

10. Schabowski (1990, p. 47). Politburo member Erich Mückenberger also testified to the coldness of personal relations in Wandlitz when he testified in the secret party postmortem in January 1990 (" 'Ich hab' an den geglaubt,' " especially p. 91).

11. Schabowski (1990, p. 37).

12. Schabowski (1990, p. 64, and elsewhere); and Schabowski (1991, pp. 226–30).

13. Schabowski interview.

14. For an exploration of the church's postwar turn to social activism in the Federal Republic, see Spotts (1973).

15. For a discussion of communist manipulation and coercion of church officials in this decision, see Schmoll (1992).

16. Estimates from Pollack (1990b). This is probably the best single summary of the role of the Protestant church in the 1980s. The figure of 23 percent is specifically dated as 1988. See also Henkys (1990), and Cordell (1990). For a detailed chronicle of the social and political function of the church in Honecker's last years, see Rein (1990).

17. For a discussion of this tension by a theologian, see Neubert (1992). See discussion of this chapter in Bibliographical Essay.

18. Schröder, a Protestant professor of philosophy who became Social Democratic floor leader in the free East German parliament, was one of the unsung heroes of the GDR's half-year experiment with democracy. He wrote the most nuanced portrayal of the netherworld of betrayal and ambiguity that prevailed in the decades after outright Stalinist terror ceased (Schröder 1991b, p. 23).

19. For a discussion of how these two rival groups decided to work together, see Hirschman (1992a, p. 1 and 1992b).

20. Rein (1990, pp. 215–19).

21. The appeal to others to join may be found in an excellent compilation of quotes and documents on the citizens' movements and unification (Gransow and Jarausch 1991, pp. 60–61).

22. Neues Forum Leipzig (1989, p. 289). This book, a sober documentation of events in Leipzig, eschews the broad brush to bring together instead raw chronologies, eyewitness interviews, and summaries of contemporary GDR newspaper coverage. It was published with incredible speed, appearing on the street by the end of 1989, yet it is the most reliable single source for disentangling sparse fact from the abundant rumors in Leipzig in fall 1989.

23. Vogel interviews. The precise figures come from the book by the main West German partner in these deals, Inner-German Ministry State Secretary Ludwig A. Rehlinger (1991, p. 247). Vogel's connections with the *Stasi* were widely assumed for decades, but allegations about the specific nature of the relationship surfaced only as the sifting through of *Stasi* documents proceeded after unification. See, for example "Eva und Georg," *Der Spiegel,* August 24, 1992, pp. 96–97; and "Vogel gesteht seine Stasi-Kontakte," *FAZ,* August 24, 1992, p. 2.

24. Interviews with officials in Washington.

25. Genscher interview.

26. This statement, made on August 19, 1989, can be found in Gransow and Jarausch (1991, p. 57).

Chapter 8: The October Revolution: Dresden and Berlin

1. Interview in Rein (1990, especially p. 345). A contrary view widely held in the United States is that the passive East Germans did nothing but collect what fell into their lap. Jane Kramer (1992, especially pp. 42–43) asserts, for example, "There was never a revolution in East Germany . . . East Germany fell because the state was bankrupt, industry was bankrupt, agriculture was bankrupt, and there was no money, and thus there was no way short of a massacre to stop East Germans from leaving."

2. October 1, 1989, as quoted in *Neues Deutschland,* October 1, 1989. Information about Honecker's authorship from Schabowski interview. See also Schabowski (1990, p. 81, and 1991, pp. 235–56); Krenz (1990, p. 30).

3. Neues Forum Leipzig (1989); Mitter and Wolle (1990, pp. 190–91).

4. The description of events in Dresden is drawn from Rein (1990); Modrow (1991, pp. 13–16); Süss (1991a); and Mitter and Wolle (1990, pp. 192–99).

5. The observer most qualified to judge, Rolf Reissig, would also list Chairman of the Council of Ministers Willi Stoph in the inner core. Stoph and Mielke worked together, he believes. Reissig resists drawing final conclusions at this stage about who did what to whom, however. He himself started to interview the old Politburo members about the events, but before he could finish this pursuit he got diverted to more urgent, future-oriented research (telephone conversation). In 1989 Reissig was a political scientist at the Central Committee research institute who kept writing liberal-inclining drafts for the 1990 SED congress that were regularly rejected.

6. Krenz (1990, p. 123), and Przybylski (1991, p. 200), citing testimony of Honecker's secretary in the GDR prosecution's pre-indictment investigation of Honecker in early 1990. Honecker, maintaining that collective leadership reigned in the Politburo, denies that there was any such inner circle (Andert and Herzberg 1991, pp. 361, 367–68). He promoted the rise of Mielke, however, getting him named as a candidate member of the Politburo as soon as Ulbricht was dumped in 1971, then as a full member in 1976. By this measure Mielke clearly outranked all others in security matters. Defense Minister Heinz Kessler, by contrast, did not take on his portfolio until 1985 and did not become a Politburo member until 1986. For Honecker's interviews, see Andert and Herzberg (1991).

7. Notes of a secret Mielke-Stoph conversation on November 13, 1980, about the "even more dangerous" course of Honecker read: "It is apparent, especially in relations with the FRG [Federal Republic of Germany], that he [Honecker] is obviously acting provocatively." The two men also blamed Honecker for not admitting the growing economic problems the country was facing. The notetaker for the two was Politburo member Werner Krolikowski, a lightweight with a reputation of simply following others' bidding. The text of the minutes appears in Przybylski (1991, pp. 345–48). It is discussed further in Przybylski (1992, pp. 58–61). Soviet Ambassador to the GDR Vyacheslav Kochemasov also reports that in 1986 Krolikowski, in effect, asked him to get the Russians to dump Honecker, this time, however, from obverse unhappiness with Honecker's "dogmatism" and "centralization to absurd lengths." Kochemasov (1992) rebuffed the plea, reminding Krolikowski that "Moscow was no longer responsible for naming the (GDR) general secretary. You must solve your own internal problems by yourselves."

Mielke (1992) is probably correct in denying that he, Stoph, Krolikowski, and soulmate Defense Minister Heinz Hoffmann ever formed a secret faction, as Przybylski calls it. Krolikowski regularly sent secret reports to Moscow—apparently directly to Brezhnev—about internal GDR politics and, implicitly, Honecker's ideological laxness, but there is no evidence so far that these men translated their misgivings into any active plotting against Honecker. Honecker's sanction on Mielke of not inviting him to hunts to which he invited Günter Mittag seems to have been sufficient discipline to prevent any real faction building.

Mielke also denies Przybylski's allegation that he planted listening devices to eavesdrop on Honecker.

8. See Schabowski (1990, pp. 85-91, 102, and 105-06, and 1991, pp. 269–70); and Krenz (1990, p. 31). No confirmation of his stance—whatever it was—can be expected from Mielke, who would hardly drop his clandestine habits in his eighties and confess to the victorious class enemy about his role, even if inadvertent, in killing off the GDR. In the only extensive interview Mielke has given since the GDR's collapse (Mielke 1992), the journalists did not ask about his participation in the palace coup, and Mielke volunteered no information. In this interview Mielke claimed to have urged dialogue with dissidents all along, but to have been overruled by Honecker.

9. See Andert and Herzberg (1991, especially pp. 374–76).

10. Fricke interview. See also Fricke (1991b); Markus Wolf (1990), cited in Fricke's article; and Schell and Kalinka (1991b, especially pp. 76–88, 253–265, 297–300, and 317).

11. Mitter and Wolle (1990, p. 113–38), from transcript of taped meeting with senior *Stasi* officers on August 31, 1989. I am indebted to Fricke for pointing out the central importance of this concern.

One journalist's report, without identifying any source, maintains that Mielke hinted to his top officers as early as this August 31 meeting that things might change in the near future, since there were finally "critical forces in the party leadership" that were ready to act (Schell and Kalinka 1991a, p. 4). These words do not appear in the extensive Mielke excerpts from August 31 in Mitter and Wolle (1990), however, and Fricke doubts the authenticity of the quote. Mielke would not have diverged from party solidarity so early, he believes. At that time the SED was still expecting the fortieth anniversary to set things right. Nor—even if Mielke had decided to drop Honecker that early—would the cagey minister have revealed his thinking in a group in which one or two would have been sure to warn Honecker of the danger, Fricke contends (Fricke interview and telephone conversation).

12. Hahn (1990), cited in Fricke (1991a).

13. Mielke's words (1992, especially p. 39) imply just such a consideration: "When 10,000 or 100,000 men are there [demonstrating], you certainly can't shoot."

14. Schell and Kalinka (1991a). Caution is appropriate here, too, however. Again, no source was cited.

15. Abrasimov, until 1983 the virtual proconsul in the GDR in both the Ulbricht and Honecker incumbencies, made this observation in an interview with *Izvestia* in summer 1992. Excerpts were carried in German in Abrasimov (1992).

16. Wolle (1992, especially pp. 86–88).

17. Schabowski (1991, pp. 245–47).

18. Schabowski (1990, pp. 105–06); Schabowski (1991, p. 269).

19. There seems to be no doubt that General Mielke was the commander-in-chief of all the security forces. Testimony heard by the mixed government-citizens' commission looking into the Berlin violence of October 7 and 8, 1989, would identify Mielke as the person that both Police Colonel Dietze (first name not given) and *Stasi* Lieutenant General Wolfgang Schwanitz constantly telephoned for operational orders during the fast-changing situation. See Dahn and Kopka (1991,

especially pp. 15–16, 206–27). Here Schwanitz is identified as a colonel general, but by Fricke as a lieutenant general.

20. Schabowski (1990, p. 76). Egon Krenz declares—without offering any substantiating detail—that he already began rethinking the party's hard line in 1985 (Dahn and Kopka 1991, p. 151), and initiated a group of like-minded "renewers" as early as 1988 (Krenz 1990, pp. 24–25). Schabowski doubts Krenz's claim, pointing out that he and Krenz would hardly have had to conduct their delicate last-minute probes to solicit their colleagues' support in October 1989 if Krenz had already started building a clique more than a year before. Circumstantial support for Schabowski's skepticism is to be found in Krenz's failure to provide any details that might corroborate his assertion. After making it he skips lightly over the dramatic session of the Politburo that toppled Honecker on October 17 and leaps to the Central Committee plenum of October 18 that simply ratified the Politburo's action (Krenz 1990, pp. 16–17, 207–08). Krenz was somewhat less bland in his testimony of January 1990 before the independent special investigating commission looking into police brutality the previous October (Dahn and Kopka 1991, pp. 147–78).

Krenz does seem to have begun keeping his options open by at least spring 1988 in listening to economic planners' tales of woe without reporting such heresies to Honecker. He continued to advocate a hard line toward dissidents well into fall 1989, however (Przybylski 1992, p. 69ff., pp. 98–100).

21. Schabowski (1991, pp. 231–33).

22. From the stenographic transcript of the Gorbachev–East German Politburo session in Mittag (1991, pp. 359–84). Curiously, although minutes from Politburo meetings are stored in the central party archives at the Institute for the History of the Workers' Movement in Berlin, librarians could find no minutes of this session there. The version of Gorbachev's quote that obtained instant notoriety in Germany was slightly different: "He who comes too late is punished by life." See, for example, "Gorbatschow wies Honecker auf notwendige Reformen in der DDR hin," *Tagesspiegel,* October 10, 1992, p. 6; and Krenz (1990, p. 87).

23. Schabowski interview; Schabowski (1990, p. 74–75); Schabowski (1991, pp. 238–42). As a plotter against Honecker who was unsure of success, Schabowski would have been acutely attuned to any hint of active Soviet assistance in ousting the East German boss. His judgment that such help was not offered is therefore significant. The Soviet leak to journalists of Gorbachev's catchphrase about latecomers being punished by life certified Soviet interest in publicizing Gorbachev's distaste for Honecker, of course, but there is no evidence of any active Soviet role in the East Berlin coup.

For a rather different account of the Politburo meeting with Gorbachev, see Krenz (1990, pp. 86–88). Modrow, without first-hand knowledge of the Politburo meeting, but with considerable direct experience with the Soviets, interprets Gorbachev's proverb as no more than an expression of the Soviet leader's well-known desire to see perestroika in Eastern Europe. East German communists who wanted change in fact regretted the Soviet hands-off attitude, he says (Modrow interview). For an expression of Gorbachev's disappointment that none of the East German leaders spoke up at the meeting, see Kochemasov (1992).

24. Krenz (1990, p. 88); Schabowski (1991, pp. 241–42).

25. For excerpts from Honecker's public address on October 6, see Gransow and Jarausch (1991, pp. 70–71).

26. Przybylski (1992, p. 87).

27. Schabowski (1990, pp. 76–77).

28. The Protestant church and the semi-independent investigative commission in Berlin that the church insisted on instituting made a concerted effort to collect testimony from those detained, to identify the individual police officers responsible for maltreatment, and to bring them to court. The examples cited here appeared, with names of testifiers, in Rein (1990, pp. 244–64); Mitter and Wolle (1990, pp. 200–15); or Dahn and Kopka (1991, throughout). For a report that states that East German soldiers were issued live ammunition over the anniversary weekend and ordered to shoot any East Berlin demonstrators who tried to break through the border barriers to West Berlin, see " 'Wir machen alles gründlich,' " Der Spiegel, June 24, 1991, pp. 58–83.

29. Schabowski interview; Schabowski (1991, pp. 243–50; and 1990, pp. 78–79). See also Krenz (1990, pp. 95–96).

30. Krenz (1990, p. 96).

31. Schabowski interview; Schabowski (1991, p. 242; and 1990, pp. 77–78). Modrow was equally skeptical. Krenz would know what Gorbachev said to him directly, but was hardly credible on the basis of such hearsay evidence, Modrow suggested (Modrow interview).

32. Schabowski (1990, pp. 80–83; and 1991, pp. 245–55).

33. Modrow, despite maintaining that he had no authority over the security forces, says he telephoned the police to ask them to let the pastors through their cordons (Modrow interview).

34. A later fill-in for one of the twenty went on to become the mayor of Dresden in Berghofer's stead in the first free city election in 1990.

35. Rein (1990, pp. 229–37).

36. Wolfgang Bergsdorf, head of the domestic division of the Bonn government's press office, analyzing the "catalytic" effect of the few participants in alternative political groups in the GDR, estimates their number before fall 1989 as no more than 10,000, or at most 15,000. ("Von der Vorhut zur Nachhut," Deutschland Archiv, no. 2 [February 1991], pp. 113–15.) The Stasi put the relevant number still lower as of June 1989, with a hard core of 60 persons, 600 in leading circles, and 2,500 activists spread among 170 small groups (Mitter and Wolle 1990, pp. 47f).

37. Both quotes from Modrow (1991, pp. 13–16).

38. Modrow phrased his initial denial very carefully. After contact with the committee investigating the Dresden clashes he said that the "repeatedly warmed-over reproach that I had ordered the operations of state security and police in Dresden is off the agenda" (Modrow 1990).

39. Modrow specified that the unarmed army units, under the command of an army general seconded to the police staff, were used in crowd control (Modrow interview).

40. Modrow (1991, pp. 13–16); Süss (1991a); Rein (1990, pp. 228–37).

Chapter 9: The October Revolution: Leipzig and Berlin

1. See, for example, Neues Forum Leipzig (1989, pp. 313-19). For an indication that "China" was a conscious code word to the Protestant churches as well as to the Socialist Unity party, see "Disturbed over China" (1990, p. 180). For Honecker's protestation that the Tienanmen model never played a role in planning for Leipzig—despite the evidence of a concerted campaign to communicate just such a threat beforehand—see Andert and Herzberg (1991, pp. 94-99).

2. Church source.

3. These actions were taken under NVA order no. 105/89, "Measures on the Transition to a Higher Level of Battle Alert." The order carried the instruction that all copies of the order were to be destroyed by October 30 (Schell and Kalinka 1991b, pp. 312–14). No border troops were redeployed to the Leipzig region, according to informed West German sources. Nor were any Soviet forces in the GDR put on alert, despite numerous rumors and a statement to this effect by East German Protestant Consistory President Manfred Stolpe in his address to the combined East and West German parliaments on June 17, 1990. Modrow asserts that Soviet armed forces in Saxony were never put on any special status. The Soviet commander of the First Guards Tank Division in Dresden, Lieutenant General A. K. Chernyshev, told him at the time, Modrow said, that Soviet forces were noting the various incidents, but were not disturbed by them (Modrow interview). Informed West German sources confirmed that Soviet troops were "totally quiet" throughout the period of East German turmoil.

4. The mobile police were paramilitary units under the Interior Ministry. Service in them fulfilled military draft requirements and entailed living in barracks and being on call twenty-four hours a day.

5. Neues Forum Leipzig (1989, p. 69, 92–93).

6. Neues Forum Leipzig (1989, p. 90).

7. This detail comes from Hans de With, (West) German member of the Bundestag, who came from Gera originally and maintained close ties with the city.

8. Similarities of content and style suggest that ZDF's officer and Die Welt's officer were probably the same person.

9. Nor were the East German military units that were brought to the Leipzig area ever deployed in the city, apparently because of disappointment over the military's performance in Dresden the preceding week, according to informed West German sources. The extra troops stayed in the Leipzig region for a month and received some training from the regular police, then returned to their original posts on November 14.

10. Concurring with this judgment, Karl Wilhelm Fricke notes that copies of Stasi orders in this period are the most complete of any of the various security agencies and should have revealed an order to shoot if any existed. He adds that however banal the observation might sound, the best evidence that no such order was issued is the fact that nobody actually fired a shot (Fricke interview).

11. Mitter and Wolle (1990, pp. 199–202); Dahn and Kopka (1991, pp. 240, 317–20). Fricke interprets this phraseology as including leave to shoot, depending on the circumstances (telephone conversation).

12. Dahn and Kopka (1991, pp. 240-41); Neues Forum Leipzig (1989, pp. 88, 92).

13. Mielke suggested as much when he told interviewers, "When 10,000 or 100,000 men are there, you can't shoot." Mielke (1992, especially p. 39). This was a less sweeping and probably more accurate explanation than his earlier claim, "I deliberately ruled out the Chinese solution" ("Mielke bricht sein Schweigen/Kritik an Honecker und Krenz," *FAZ*, March 2, 1992, p. 4).

14. Neues Forum Leipzig (1989, pp. 288–93).

15. Neues Forum Leipzig (1989, p. 86).

16. Neues Forum Leipzig (1989, pp. 84–85).

17. Neues Forum Leipzig, (1989, pp. 83–84). For the internal *Stasi* report on October 9 labeled "strictly secret," see Mitter and Wolle (1990, pp. 216–19).

18. Neues Forum Leipzig (1989, pp. 273–77).

19. Bonn Foreign Ministry interview.

20. Interview with Roland Wötzel. See also Kuhn (1992).

21. Schabowski (1991, pp. 250–52); Przybylski (1992, p. 125).

22. Neues Forum Leipzig (1989, pp. 82–83, 273–93); Schabowski (1991, pp. 250–52).

23. Neues Forum Leipzig (1989, pp. 292 and 289).

24. Neues Forum Leipzig (1989, p. 301).

25. Neues Forum Leipzig (1989, p. 91–92).

26. The experience of Dresden police Lieutenant Colonel (his rank in 1991) Horst Zimmermann would support this thesis indirectly. Before joining the city police under the elected government, he served for twenty years in the old police force. In October 1989 he was in a unit outside the city in one of the GDR's most sensitive areas, running from Dresden east to the Czech border, and therefore the gathering point for all the East Germans trying to get to Prague and the West German embassy there. What struck Zimmermann most about the whole period was the total muteness (*Sprachlosigkeit*) at all levels of command from mid-1989 on (group interview, Dresden, September 6, 1991). Modrow confirmed the existence of this muteness at a political level as well from the time Hungary opened the Austrian border to East Germans (Modrow interview).

27. Biedenkopf group interview. Stefan Wolle, East German historian of the *Stasi*, similarly inclines to the view that "the commanders in Leipzig, however, were sufficiently unsettled by the huge mass of people that no one was found to give the order [to attack the demonstrators]." (Wolle 1992, especially p. 107). Without going into the same nuances, Gransow and Jarausch (1991, p. 76) share this general evaluation in *Die deutsche Vereinigung*. So, in effect, does Opp (1991), though he downplays the civil courage exhibited in the turnout on October 9 and stresses the reverse impact of the nonuse of state sanctions on October 9 in shifting popular values and expectations thereafter and transforming the East Germans into revolutionaries.

28. Neues Forum Leipzig (1989, p. 286–87).

29. And as Berlin commission investigators highlighted the discrepancy between Krenz's professed lack of authority in his hometown of Berlin on October 7 and 8, but decisive influence in faraway Leipzig on October 9 (Dahn and Kopka 1991, p. 152). For a sampling of contradictory popular apportioning of praise and

blame, see " 'Von den Arbeitern verlassen,' " *Der Spiegel,* November 27, 1989, pp. 19–27; " 'Chinesische Lösung': Wollten Stasi-Leute ein Blutbad unter Demonstranten provozieren?" *Der Spiegel,* December 18, 1989, pp. 42–44; Hermann (1990); and "Krenz und Mielke vereinbarten auf Geheimkonferenz chinesische Lösung," *Die Welt,* May 21, 1990.

30. Andert and Herzberg (1991, p. 94–99). See also, for example, Krenz (1990, pp. 138–40); Przybylski (1992, pp. 129–30). Przybylski says Krenz told him that Honecker still wanted to let a tank regiment roll through Leipzig on October 16, when the next regular demonstration would take place.

31. "Brandt: Sowjet-offiziere verhinderten Blutbad in Leipzig," *Süddeutsche Zeitung,* December 14, 1989, p. 1; and "Warten bis irgendwann nach dem Jahr 2000?" *Süddeutsche Zeitung,* December 14, 1989, p. 14. Brandt said initially, "On this day Soviet, high Soviet officers prevented a bloodbath in Leipzig." When pressed by his interviewer, he indicated no source for this view and watered it down to the common wisdom that "several dozen high Soviet officers sit on the higher floors in the higher staffs" of the NVA. "And when a clever general there says, said, you can do what you want, but our troops and our tanks will remain in the barracks, that is a date to remember." To a further question whether that was what happened, Brandt replied delphic-like, "I did not think that up myself."

32. Meckel group interview. See also Josef Joffe's (1990) implicit acceptance of this claim.

33. Schabowski interview; Schabowski (1990, pp. 77–80).

34. Modrow interview.

35. Group interview with West German Major General Hubert Marquitan, deputy commander of the Eastern Corps and Territorial Command, Potsdam, September 4, 1991. Such claims are self-serving, of course, but if there had been a Soviet army order to the NVA, some hint of it should have emerged in the intensive East-West German military contact that followed unification and absorption of the NVA into the Bundeswehr.

36. Teltschik (1991, p. 43).

37. For a broad East German analysis of the bloodless nature of the East German revolution, see Hanf (1992).

38. Schabowski (1991, pp. 250–51).

39. Schabowski (1991, pp. 253–57); Schabowski (1990, pp. 87–97).

40. "Erklärung des Politbüros des Zentralkomitees der Sozialistischen Einheitspartei Deutschlands," *Neues Deutschland,* October 12, 1989, p. 1.

41. For a contemporary SED evaluation of New Forum and other fledgling groups, see "Wer Sympathie bekundet, muss wissen, worauf er sich einlässt," *Frankfurter Rundschau,* November 1, 1989, giving the text of an internal party document of October 11.

42. Schabowski interview; Schabowski (1991, pp. 259–64); Schabowski (1990, pp. 100–02).

43. Mielke indirectly confirmed this presumption in his August 31, 1992, interview (1992, especially pp. 41–44) when he denied ever having blackmailed Honecker with documents about his prison record, but said he had guarded this information, with Honecker's knowledge, to prevent blackmail by others.

44. Schabowski (1990, pp. 104–06); Schabowski (1991, pp. 267–71). The official minutes of this Politburo session, available at the central party archives at the

Institute for History of the Workers' Movement in Berlin, offer no insights about the confrontation. Two sentences say laconically that Comrade Erich Honecker was released from his duties for reasons of health, and that comrades Herrmann and Mittag were released from their functions, with no reasons given. The remainder of the ninety pages of minutes and appendixes are devoted to such issues as the coming five-year economic plan and awarding GDR orders to third world leaders.

45.   The one book (Gedmin 1992) that hints at doing so in its title does not do so in the text. It presents the various rumors, abundantly qualified by such phrases as "reportedly," "or so it appeared," "exceedingly unlikely that [X] would not have had contact with [Y]," and "alluded to reports that high ranking army officers stationed in the GDR may have been directly or indirectly involved." It further relies heavily on American press articles about possible Soviet influence that were written under tremendous time pressures during that turbulent period, but the author never actually commits himself to believing the various reports. His own bottom line is the unexceptionable, "It was the folly of Soviet reformers, who, believing that East Germany could be transformed into a legitimate and viable Socialist state, took steps that led to the dissolution of an empire" (p. 117).

46.   For example, Andert and Herzberg (1991, pp. 19–21). Mittag (1991, p. 181) by contrast, accuses Krenz and Schabowski of just the opposite sin, of trying to hide behind the Russians to disguise their own regicide.

47.   Genscher interview.

48.   See also notes 31–36 and 50 in this chapter, and notes 30 and 31 in chapter 8.

49.   Schabowski interview.

50.   Modrow interview. Modrow also dismisses speculation that Valentin Falin, on his secret visit to East Berlin the week after the Berlin Wall fell, ordered Krenz to cede power to Modrow. He exhibits some pleasure at having been included in Krenz's conversation with Falin, but says no promotion of him was involved. Modrow had in any case already been named to the Politburo and prime minister's office the week before.

The anonymous *Stasi* officer interviewed on ZDF television on April 11, 1990, first launched the allegation about Falin's intervention. It was never advanced by Krenz himself. Even Schabowski, who harbors reservations about Modrow as the Russians' fair-haired boy, gives no credence to this interpretation (Schabowski interview).

At the time, one Western ambassador to the GDR surmised that Falin, the SED contact on the Soviet Central Committee staff, blew into town "to find out what the hell was going on, like everybody else."

Falin, a former Soviet ambassador to West Germany and then head of the International Department of the party Central Committee, liked to cultivate his aura among West German contacts as a power behind the scenes. In summer 1989 he had written an internal memo that found its way to West German intelligence and then to *Die Welt*. In the memo he predicted that with the failure of the GDR government to respond to the exodus, mass demonstrations would break out by the following spring at the latest. He did not think the opposition would be strong enough to force reform, however. Adomeit (1990).

51.   Including in private to West German leaders. Had Moscow pulled strings in overthrowing Honecker, Gorbachev and Shevardnadze would presumably have wanted to get credit for this act with Kohl and Genscher. Yet Genscher notes that

Shevardnadze never claimed this. The view of the Russians was instead that the GDR regime had simply outlived itself and did not need an outside push to fall (Genscher interview).

52. According to testimony in the GDR prosecutors' investigation of Honecker (Przybylski 1992, p. 74).

53. An indirect quote given in Oberdorfer (1991, p. 364).

54. Abrasimov (1992).

55. Broder (1992). Inclining in the same direction are the early books, Wawrzyn (1990); and Wilkening (1990).

56. Wolle gave this judgment at the Society of Independent Historians workshop in Berlin in January 1992. Pannen (1992).

57. Wolle (1992, pp. 103–05).

58. The *Stasi* was overwhelmingly male.

59. Knauer (1992). The one reform circle Knauer found—a group of *Stasi* majors who met in Brandenburg in December 1988—fell into inactivity in 1989.

60. Ammer (1992); Schlomann (1992).

61. Andert and Herzberg (1991, pp. 374–75).

62. Fricke interview.

63. According to Ernst Wollweber, head of the *Stasi* until 1957, cited in Fricke (1990a, especially p. 1882).

64. Ambassador Pyotr Abrasimov, calling the GDR a "humanoid out of the Soviet test tube," confirmed to *Izvestia* in 1992 that KGB agents watched their East German colleagues closely. He also described the comparable Soviet penetration of the East German army. Soviet advisers were distributed liberally throughout the National People's Army, he declared. Formally these officers had no authority, but in practice the Germans had to follow their advice. Abrasimov (1992). On the military side, see also Macgregor (1989).

65. West German intelligence sources, discussing the debriefing of financial czar and *Stasi* Major General Alexander Schalck-Golodkowski and others. See also the interview with Mielke (1992, especially p. 53). Public reminiscences by *Stasi* agents—which mushroomed from 1990 on—also displayed a conspicuous reverence for KGB mentors, mixed with anger and incomprehension at the Soviet failure to rescue the ancien regime in East Berlin.

66. For three early concurring assessments, see Oldenburg (1990); Dawydow and Trenin (1990); and Adomeit (1990).

67. Krenz's reform government program announced the same day, October 24, may be found in Gransow and Jarausch (1991, pp. 83–84).

68. And with live ammunition, according to Richard Schröder (interview). For contemporary reports on the gathering, see, for example, "Berlin Alexanderplatz: Geschichte wird gemacht," *Tageszeitung*, November 6, 1989, p. 1; and "Massenflucht-Reformzusagen-Forderungen," *FAZ*, November 6, 1989, pp. 1–2. For the text of speeches given at Alexanderplatz by Christoph Hein, Stefan Heym, Christa Wolf, and Markus Wolf, see *Tageszeitung*, November 9, 1989. The countercultural Berlin daily *Tageszeitung* also published two compilations of its selected reportage: "DDR Journal zur Novemberrevolution: August bis Dezember 1989" and "DDR Journal Nr. 2 Die Wende der Wende: Januar bis März 1990" (no listed dates of publication).

69. Author's interviews with demonstrators, East Berlin, November 4, 1989.

Chapter 10: The Wall Falls

1. Greifswald Untersuchungsausschuss (1990, p. 3).
2. According to a Chancellery source.
3. Schabowski interview.
4. Schabowski interview.
5. Schabowski (1990, pp. 138–39).
6. Krenz (1990, pp. 176–82, 229–30) repeated this explanation.
7. Modrow (1991, p. 25). Modrow repeated this assessment orally (Modrow interview). West German officials, including Wolfgang Schäuble, then interior minister, also read the East German failure to give any advance warning to the Soviets as an indication that the opening of the wall resulted from unpremeditated, panicked actions by East Berlin (interview, Schäuble). Shevardnadze's assistant Sergei Tarasenko and the Soviet Foreign Ministry's top specialist on the United States, Aleksandr Bessmertnykh, both indicated to Stephen F. Szabo, author of *The Diplomacy of German Unification* (1992), that the Soviets knew in advance of the opening of the Berlin Wall. They spoke only in generalities, however, and did not specify any details (telephone conversation with Szabo, November 8, 1992). The West German interpretation of such assertions is that the Soviets, like the East Germans, understood that the GDR would have to take a major step soon toward freeing travel for its citizens, but that the Soviets were as surprised as everyone else by the timing and the impact of the spontaneous westward surge by millions of East Germans. Foreign Minister Genscher confirms that so far as he knows, the Russians did not know beforehand that the East Germans would open the wall on November 9 (information from Genscher's office in response to a telephone query, November 19, 1992).
8. Teltschik interview.
9. Schabowski interview. Schabowski denies not only Krenz's version, but also the multiple alternatives that cropped up afterward, including the one suggesting that some mid-level communist slyly slipped a more liberal regulation into the draft provision than the Politburo actually intended. See, for example, Schnibben (1990). One other claim of credit for opening the wall came much later from Alexander Schalck-Golodkowski, the GDR's hard currency accumulator and secret *Stasi* major general. In an interview with the *Frankfurter Allgemeine Zeitung* (Weimer 1991), Schalck said that he was in Krenz's office on the night of November 8 and personally gave the instructions to open the borders. Evaluating the veracity of this claim is hard, not only because the date is wrong, but also because there is no full direct quote and because it is mixed with an otherwise unexplained assertion of possible intervention by the Soviet Army. The key passage reads: "In the critical Wende days Schalck allegedly warned the federal [West German] government about a possible forthcoming operation by Soviet troops. On the night of November 8/ 9 he [allegedly] sat in the office of Egon Krenz and in the chaotic confusion personally gave the instructions to open the border 'for mass travel.' "
10. For the text of the more considered New Forum statement, see "Die Mauer ist gefallen," *Tageszeitung*, November 12, 1989.
11. See Gransow and Jarausch (1991, pp. 97–98).
12. That same day *Die Zeit* editor Theo Sommer expressed the standard view among analysts that neither East nor West Germans were interested in a merger

(1989a). Genscher, by contrast, instantly heard the Leipzig chant as a harbinger. The foreign minister flew to Washington on November 21, and his assistant gave Baker's assistant the new message that stability might now be endangered if unification did not come fast. The Americans responded that they concurred totally with this estimate (Foreign Ministry interview).

13. The West German polling firms of Emnid Institute and the Mannheim Group, consultants to the sociologists from the GDR Academy of Sciences who conducted the survey, pointed out that the cross-section was biased toward SED members, who constituted only 13 percent of the population but 23 percent of those interviewed. See "Ein Staat, Zwei Staaten?" *Der Spiegel*, December 18, 1989, p. 89. Another East German survey taken at approximately the same time by the Leipzig Zentralinstitut für Jugendforschung classified 48 percent of East German women as favoring unification at the end of November 1989, shooting up to 76 percent at the beginning of February 1990.

14. Author's street interview. For impressions in English from this stage of development, see Garton Ash (1989).

15. Teltschik (1991, p. 37); Zelikow interviews.

16. Teltschik (1991, pp. 42–44). The Soviets were certainly not confiding such thoughts to the East Germans at the time. Modrow wrote that when talk of confederation first surfaced in the Volkskammer, the Soviets were irritated by it (Modrow 1991, p. 119).

17. Marsh and others (1989).

18. "Chronik," *Deutschland Archiv*, no. 12 (December 1989), pp. 1473–88.

19. Gransow and Jarausch (1991, pp. 100–01).

20. For a contemporary report, see Wirsing (1989). For evaluation soon afterward, see Spittmann (1990b).

21. Kohl interview. The text of the speech is available in Bundesregeirung (1989); and in Gransow and Jarausch (1991, pp. 101–04). In his press briefings at the time, Teltschik put more stress on Kohl's reassurance about the intended international framework for German growing together. In retrospect, Kohl puts much more emphasis on not getting locked into confederation. See Teltschik (1991, pp. 54–58).

22. Modrow (1991, p. 96).

23. Teltschik and Kohl interviews and Teltschik (1991, p. 63).

24. Teltschik interviews and Teltschik (1991, p. 63).

25. Interview, Foreign Mnistry.

26. Interviews with Genscher, State Department, and Foreign Ministry officials. See also Teltschik (1991, pp. 47–48).

Chapter 11: Taming the *Stasi*

1. According to law professor Dieter Blumenwitz of the University of Würzburg, GDR courts over the years convicted 78,000 people for "asocial behavior hurting security," 23,000 for "fleeing the republic," and 10,000 for "resistance to state measures." "Zur strafrechtlichen Verfolgung Erich Honeckers: Staats- und völkerrechtliche Fragen," *Deutschland Archiv*, no. 6 (June 1992), pp. 567–79.

2. Some West German sources found Schalck's picture exaggerated. Their analysis was that the East German economy performed acceptably until the global economic crisis of the 1970s reached the GDR in 1982–83.

3. See Blutke (1991).

4. Schabowski (1991, pp. 322–23).

5. Greifswald Untersuchungsausschuss (1990, pp. 3–5).

6. Author's interviews, including with police Lieutnenant Colonel Klaus Pinkau in Leipzig, December 18, 1990, and Hubertus Haufe, member of the committee that occupied *Stasi* headquarters in Dresden, December 19, 1990.

7. First name for Jonas not given.

8. The etymology of the phrase *security partnership* is instructive. It originated in the Western and East German antinuclear movements in the early 1980s and was especially associated with Egon Bahr and the left wing of the Social Democrats. Initially it stood for a policy of East-West cooperation, as opposed to Reagan's heightening of East-West tension. Its implication, which raised Washington's hackles, was either equidistant moral disdain for the American and Soviet superpowers that were seen as holding their respective German clients in thrall, or else, after 1985, a particular reproach to the Americans for continuing the cold war while Gorbachev kept producing one peace proposal after another.

In fall 1989 the term underwent a shift of meaning among East German activists and became the standard phrase designating an unwritten pact between demonstrators and security forces in any locality to refrain from violence. When activists in Greifswald said, referring to the first demonstration there on October 18, "We didn't have a security partnership here then," that meant that police and *Stasi* security forces were still roughing up protesters and were armed with pistols at the demonstration.

9. Greifswald Untersuchungsausschuss (1990), third (unnumbered) introductory page; interview in Greifswald with Thomas Meyer, physicist, member of New Forum, leader of the investigating committee's section on Greifswald University, and, after the 1990 free city elections, president of the city council, elected by votes from Christian Democratic and Social Democratic councilors.

10. Interviews. See also "MfS hörte Weizsäcker und Kohl ab: Modrow überlässt Agenten Moskau," *Die Welt*, April 6, 1990, p. 1; and "Auf Jahre andauerndes Sicherheitsrisiko," *Die Welt*, April 6, 1990, p. 5.

11. Modrow (1990). Gorbachev's purpose at the Moscow meeting was to inform the East Europeans about the Malta superpower summit. Modrow thought it would have been better had the Soviet leader paid more attention to Eastern Europe, and, by implication, been less fixated on the West (Modrow interview).

12. For an inside account of the party congress, see Falkner (1990 and 1991).

13. For a summary of the party congress, see Kuppe (1990).

14. Modrow (1991, p. 65); interviews with West German intelligence sources; ADN reports of civilians forcing their way into Soviet garrisons in German newspapers on December 7, 1989.

15. So did others. West German President Richard von Weizsäcker gave a long TV interview urging common sense on both East and West German viewers ("Weizsäcker mahnt Deutsche zu Besonnenheit," *Frankfurter Rundschau*, November 1, 1989.)

16. Apart from interviews, the material in this section is drawn primarily from Thaysen (1990); Herles and Rose (1990b); and Süss (1991b). The Herles and Rose book is the stenographic record of the roundtable's resolutions and most important statements compiled by the just-retired chief stenographer of the Bundestag as a service donated by West Germans to the infant East German democracy.

17. See Fricke (1990a, 1990b); and Süss (1991b); Thaysen (1990, especially pp. 55–70); Herles and Rose (1990b, especially pp. 25–26, 30–31, 35–36, 43–58, 60–62, 67–70, 78–79, 83–87, 104–05); and Greifswald Untersuchungsausschus (1990).

18. Schäuble interview.

19. Kohl interview. See also Fink (1990); excerpts from joint statement in Gransow and Jarausch (1991, p. 112).

20. Teltschik (1991, pp. 87–92). This was consistent with the caution Kohl had also urged on East German "firebrands" in the run-up to his Dresden visit. See Colitt (1989).

21. Kohl interview.

22. The *Neues Deutschland* report on it is carried in Gransow and Jarausch (1991, pp. 113–14).

23. Modrow was not yet ready to admit that his attempt to prolong the *Stasi* was a mistake at the time he published his book *Aufbruch und Ende* in early 1991. By fall 1991 he conceded, however, that "everything looks different in retrospect" (Modrow interview).

24. See Fricke (1991b). Debunking of the original image of the incident was considered sufficiently newsworthy to appear in the German papers for a good year and a half after the event. See, for example, "Stürmte die Stasi die eigene Zentrale?" *FAZ*, August 5, 1991, p. 5.

25. *Stasi* generals Heinz Engelhardt and Edgar Braun continued in active posts in the ministry until summer 1990, and a total of 337 ministry employees remained active as late as August 1990. Their main accomplishment was the destruction of the *Stasi* electronic database in March 1990; the roundtable agreed to this destruction on February 26, 1990, primarily to keep information about spies from getting to West German intelligence. This presumably did no more than delay identification of former agents, however, since the ministry's mania for records assured that most or all could eventually be tracked down in other files. Ammer (1992, pp. 547–50).

Even under the elected government of Lothar de Maizière, his shadowy Interior Minister Peter-Michael Diestel would want to obliterate all *Stasi* records, and would be backed not only by the old *Stasi* officers still working in the ministry, but also by East German idealists who wanted to keep the data out of the hands of West German intelligence. That comprehensive operation would not be carried out, however.

26. The last practice continued through 1989, with 326 cases recorded in that year ("326 Zwangsadoptionen 1989 in der früheren DDR," *Tagesspiegel*, August 14, 1991, p. 2).

Chapter 12: Acceleration

1. Deibel (1991).
2. Moens (1991).

3. Kohl interview.

4. Adomeit (1990, p. 5). Adomeit points out that this phraseology was not inadvertent. It had been used in West Germany for four decades in reference to free elections in the GDR, and this was the first time the Soviets had accepted it. In the Russian text the Soviets also called the Federal Republic *Federativnaya Respublika Germaniya* rather than the previous genitive *Germanii*, thus implying the existence of a single Germany with a federal structure.

5. In *Perestroika: New Thinking for Our Country and the World* (Gorbachev 1987) and again in his remarks during Kohl's maiden visit to Gorbachev's Moscow in October of 1988. See Adomeit (1990, especially p. 7), and Oldenburg (1990, pp. 73–74). Academic advisers Vyacheslav Dashichev and Oleg Bogomolov offered the most relaxed views about possible German unification. Some Western evaluators saw their comments as probes for Gorbachev, while others discounted them as little more than personal ruminations in a period when Russian opinion was no longer a monolith. For a late view that Gorbachev's real aim was still to woo the Federal Republic away from NATO, see Wettig (1990).

6. Shevardnadze did this most conspicuously in his speech at the United Nations on September 26, 1989. (See "Genscher bekräftigt die Unverletzlichkeit der Grenzen in Europa," *FAZ*, September 27, 1989, pp. 1–2.) He repeated this concern in Rome on November 30 (see Küppers 1989, p. 1).

7. See Fein (1989).

8. See Peel and Goodhart (1989).

9. Oldenburg (1990, p. 75), citing *Pravda* of November 15 and 18.

10. Teltschik (1991, p. 68). Shevardnadze's private comments to West German diplomats were sometimes more forthcoming. As early as November 17 the Soviet foreign minister told Bonn's ambassador in Moscow that although he excluded one-sided changes in the status quo, he did not exclude agreed, peaceful changes in a pan-European consensus (Teltschik 1991, p. 45). In this light, some of Shevardnadze's later promotion of a demilitarized and neutral status for Germany might be seen less as a categorical rejection of unification—as it was widely interpreted at the time—and more as probing about terms of union that might separate a united Germany from the West. See for example, Shevardnadze's speech to the European Parliament's foreign affairs committee in Brussels on December 19, 1989. (Shevardnadze 1989.) For Bonn's reading of these remarks as contradictory, but not threatening, see Teltschik (1991, p. 93).

In this period the Foreign Ministry consistently had the most charitable reading of Soviet officials'—and especially of Shevardnadze's—remarks. Senior diplomats repeatedly interpreted Soviet criticisms of the West Germans in light of the fierce ongoing feud between the chancellery and the Foreign Ministry, and viewed them as aimed not at West Germans in general, but only at the conservatives. Shevardnadze's September 26, 1989, speech at the United Nations reviving the specter of revanchism, they interpreted, for example, as a reaction to injudicious comments at the Christian Democratic Union party convention a few days earlier. They took Gorbachev's very friendly visit to Bonn in June 1989 as the standard and believed that this forthcoming standard applied even to the very new issue of unification.

In retrospect, Shevardnadze (1992, especially p. 198) said he had begun thinking about a unified Germany as early as 1986 (though he clearly was thinking then of some amalgam of the Federal Republic and a vigorous reformed GDR).

11. The Soviet leader's first mention of possible unification after the opening of the Berlin Wall came in a speech to Moscow students on November 15. In it Gorbachev dropped his previous references to a hundred years and said only that unification was "today no issue of current policy" (Teltschik 1991, p. 37). See also Adomeit (1990, especially p. 8); Oldenburg (1990, especially pp. 74–75); "Gorbatschow warnt vor 'Geschrei über den Sieg im kalten Krieg,' " FAZ, November 16, 1989, p. 3; and Dalziel (1989).

12. Kohl interview.

13. "Thatcher Sees East European Progess As More Urgent Than Germans' Unity," Wall Street Journal, January 26, 1990, p. A12.

14. Teltschik (1991, pp. 115–16).

15. Teltschik still identified this as her position on February 9, well after the American-German two plus four plan was in the works, and only four days before it was announced (Teltschik 1991, p. 134).

16. Teltschik (1991, pp. 148, 171).

17. Gransow and Jarausch (1991, pp. 160–62).

18. Interview published in the Spectator, July 12, 1990. Ridley's forced resignation two days after his interview appeared was yet another example of a latecomer being punished by life. His opinions reflected Thatcher's views of February and March, but did not keep up with the prime minister's shift of April to align Britain with the United States. See also Garton Ash (1990a, p. 65); Lawson (1990, pp. 505–07); and Scruton (1989).

19. Surveys commissioned by the U.S. Information Agency in France showed 71 percent in October 1989 and 59 percent in December 1989 in favor of German unity in a ratio about equal to Britons' 70 percent and 52 percent respectively. Notably, French support was much higher than the West German 56 percent support for unification in October, but marginally lower than the German 57 percent support in December (U.S. Information Agency 1990, pp. 1 and 3). The first polls in which a French majority saw no danger in German unification were taken in 1983–84 (Kolboom 1991b, p. 30).

20. At a talk at Harvard's Center for European Studies, September 24, 1990. Moïsi was the executive director of the French Institute of International Relations.

21. Or at least it imitated the Chancellery. Various Foreign Ministry officials tended to see the French snub as a justified tit-for-tat after Kohl sprang his ten points on the French without consulting them first.

22. For an expression of Bonn's annoyance—and Mitterrand's later claim that he was only trying to help German unification—see Teltschik (1991, pp. 60–61 and 372).

23. Soviet publicist Fyodor Burlatsky, among others, credits this version (conversation, Cambridge, Massachusetts, February 6, 1991). So does Karl Kaiser (1990–91, especially p. 191). Adomeit strongly doubts that Gorbachev, even had he already believed this, would have tipped his hand to Mitterrand two months before publicly accepting unification (conversation, Cambridge, February 1991).

24. Moïsi identifies three stages of the French reaction: first, before the GDR election, ambiguity; second, from March 18 until unification day on October 3, concern; third, thereafter, indifference. The striking disappearance of the German issue from the French media after fall 1990 Moïsi attributes to the discovery that

Bonn's digestion of East Germany was going to be much tougher than originally thought, and to the Gulf War diversion that again put traditional French military power almost back on stage center. See also Thies (1991); and Yost (1991).

25. See Feldman (1992).

26. See discussion of this chapter in the Bibliographical Essay.

27. Kohl interview.

28. Zoellick interview.

29. Retired *New York Times* editor A. M. Rosenthal (1990), for example, wrote, "Did not the two earlier German unifications lead to war? Is there not a terror in millions of human minds and hearts that the nightmare visage of the past may be the face of the future?" A later presentation of the same views by Rosenthal (1992) appeared. For other discussions of this issue, see the Bibliographical Essay.

30. Genscher's (1990) laying out of this opinion at the Davos World Economic Forum on February 1, 1987, had renewed the Reagan administration's suspicions of the West Germans in general, and their foreign minister in particular.

31. Apple (1989). The opinion page of the *New York Times* clearly did not believe Bush's expression of support for unification in the paper's news pages. An editorial ("One Germany: Not Likely Now," November 19, 1989, News of the Week in Review, p. 22) a month later said flatly (and with poor predictive accuracy), "Washington doesn't want reunification, because that would end the U.S. military presence in West Germany and dissolve NATO without an adequate substitute." The writer was perhaps misled by Scowcroft's reserve—or by Washington's rebuke of Ambassador Vernon Walters in Bonn over his public partisanship on behalf of German unity.

32. For one late expression of a widespread conviction among American commentators that these troops still allowed the Soviets to dictate terms to the Germans, see Harsch (1990, p. 1).

33. Interviews. See also Oberdorfer (1991, pp. 370–74).

34. Genscher vigorously contests this characterization of him. He told Baker early on that the Germans would stay in NATO, he says. "I always fought in Germany against a German neutralization, because I considered it the most dangerous course," he adds (Genscher interview).

35. Statement in the concluding press conference. See Adomeit (1990, especially p. 8).

36. The NSC and the Chancellery staff went so far as to believe that Gorbachev's flexibility exceeded that of Shevardnadze's. See the Bibliographical Essay.

37. Baker had first set forth essentially the same four principles at a press conference the day after Kohl's November 28 speech. See U.S. State Department (1989).

38. "Jetzt Wissen Wir, Wer unsere Freunde Sind," *Bild Zeitung*, December 13, 1989, p. 1.

39. Sommer (1989b, p. 3).

40. Augstein (1989, p. 26).

41. Dederichs (1989). Curiously, the public in the Federal Republic had a much more accurate view of American policy than did the media. In a survey commissioned by the U.S. Information Agency a week after the four-power ambassadorial meeting, 45 percent of West Germans thought Washington supported German

unity, while 35 percent thought it opposed unity (U.S. Information Agency 1990, p. 5).

42. Baker (1989). For German press coverage of the speech, see, for example, "Die USA halten am Ziel der Wiedervereinigung fest," *Süddeutsche Zeitung*, December 13, 1989.

43. When asked about this, one senior Foreign Ministry source was baffled by the question. He asserted that Bonn had "not the slightest" feeling that Baker was "treading on our corns." An American diplomat closely involved in the debate about Baker's visit seconded this judgment. Ambassador Richard Barkley's arguments, which won the day, were that Baker should use a visit to throw American weight on the side of the East German demonstrators who were then pressing a still noncommittal Modrow to set free elections, and that this prospect would help stabilize the situation and avoid irrational eruptions. U.S. Embassy analysts acknowledged the risk that Modrow might try to capitalize on the visit to prolong his own longevity, but calculated they could offset this with Baker's companion visit with Protestant church leaders.

44. The description of the Kohl government's decision to accelerate the process of unification in January is drawn from interviews with Kohl, Schäuble, Teltschik, and other officials.

45. This point was much clearer in interviews than in the contemporary German media coverage, which tended to lose the forest for the trees of endless detail. The Bonn government was distressed by the Marxist orthodoxy that Modrow displayed, and it was also dissatisfied with his eventual offer to grant majority shares in joint ventures to small and medium-sized Western firms only on a generous administrative (rather than legal) basis, since the lengthy red tape would deter many investors. For one of the first official admissions of the catastrophic economic situation, see the report in the January 11 *Neues Deutschland* excerpted in Gransow and Jarausch (1991, pp. 114–18).

46. Through the end of 1989 the rule of thumb among economists in the Federal Republic had been that East German productivity was about 60 percent of West German levels. As more accurate information became available, this estimate was decreased, to about 36 percent. See, for example, Becker (1992); and Hertle (1992). Hertle revealed that GDR economic planners alarmed about the economy finally managed to get the Politburo to listen to a report on the catastrophic state of affairs on October 30, 1989, though without getting Politburo approval for the radical economic reform they recommended. Two days later Krenz carried to a shocked Gorbachev the bad news that a bankrupt GDR, if deprived of Western credits and squeezed in raw materials deliveries from the Soviet Union, would face an immediate 30 percent drop in the standard of living. "Comrade Gorbachev, astounded, asked if these figures were exact. He hadn't imagined the situation to be so precarious," read the East German notes of the meeting in Moscow (Hertle 1992, p. 1027).

47. Interviews with East and West German sources. The issue of the GDR's financial straits entered the public debate with a background briefing that Kohl's foreign policy adviser, Horst Teltschik, gave to reporters on the eve of the chancellor's departure for a visit to Moscow in February. Teltschik was named in print as the source, and he was described as wanting to leak this viewpoint to convince

Gorbachev that the only salvation for the disintegrating GDR lay in union with the Federal Republic.

48. "Chronik," *Deutschland Archiv*, no. 1 (January 1990), p. 176, and no. 2 (February 1990), p. 336.

49. Teltschik interviews.

50. See, for example, "Eine 'Regierung der nationalen Verantwortung' bis zur vorgezogenen Wahl am 18. März in der DDR," *FAZ*, January 30, 1990, p. 1.

51. ADN wire service, January 30, 1990. For key excerpts from the most important public statements on German unification in the next few weeks, see "Dokumentation," *Deutschland Archiv*, no. 3 (March 1990), pp. 466–80. Included are Modrow's speech in the Volkskammer on January 29, 1990; Gorbachev's remarks at the press conference in Moscow on January 30; a Tass report on Modrow's visit from January 30; Modrow's statement on German unity of February 1; and the official declaration and Kohl's statement on his visit to Moscow on February 10.

52. ADN wire service, February 1, 1990.

53. Modrow was surprised by Gorbachev's silence, since he had understood the bid for neutrality as a joint position, intended to smoke out a compromise from the West (Modrow interview).

54. "Chronik," *Deutschland Archiv*, no. 2 (February 1990), p. 335, and no. 3 (March 1990), pp. 484–86; and "Bonner Pläne im Blick auf die Einheit: Verhandlungen über eine Währungsunion," *FAZ*, February 8, 1990, p. 1.

55. "First engage [the enemy], and then look around."

Chapter 13: Two Plus Four Equals One Germany

1. An exception was a survey commissioned by the U.S. Information Agency conducted in October and again in December 1989. In October the results showed 56 percent support for German unity in the abstract in the Federal Republic, dropping to only 40 percent if a unified Germany would have to leave NATO, and 57 percent and 34 percent, respectively, in December (U.S. Information Agency 1990, p. 1). The West German political class did not share this perception, however, and acted, across the spectrum, as if the public did not draw this distinction.

2. RAND analyst Ronald D. Asmus (1991, especially p. 549) cited polls showing 68 percent of East Germans favoring neutrality and 79 percent favoring total American withdrawal from Germany.

3. In a prepared speech at the Wehrkunde Conference in Munich, February 2–4, 1990, Voigt said, "Unity in a federal state cannot be achieved through accession of the GDR to NATO. This would be neither realistic nor desirable. The SPD considers the alliances to be still necessary for the foreseeable future, but we are striving to transcend them in a European order of peace." The text of the speech was available at the conference. Bahr expressed the same view more forcefully in his interventions at the conference, and saw a continuing role for Soviet and American troops in Germany only "for a transitional period" ("Zwischen die Blöcke geraten: Die deutsch-deutsche Frage," *Tageszeitung*, February 5, 1990, p. 2).

4. Genscher's thinking evolved quickly in January. On January 6, at the Liberal Party convention in Stuttgart, he spoke of a "special political steering function" for both NATO and the Warsaw Pact in "cooperative security structures." (Text of speech distributed by the Free Democratic party press service.) On January 14 he stressed the "important stabilizing function" of both alliances in a speech carried on Deutschlandfunk radio. (Genscher 1990). (On the same day his sister Liberal party in East Germany was calling for a demilitarized Europe from the Atlantic to the Urals.) In mid-January Genscher floated with a group of private American citizens the idea of offering the Soviet Union, as his visitors understood it, a neutralized east Germany that would not be part of NATO at all. On January 31, at the Protestant Academy in Tutzing, the foreign minister stressed that a united Germany would remain in NATO, but warned that "notions that the part of Germany that today constitutes the GDR should be drawn into the military structures of NATO, would block German-German growing closer." See Gennrich (1990b), and key excerpts from the Tutzing speech in Karl Kaiser (1991, pp. 190–01). On February 2, in a joint press conference with Baker in Washington, Genscher edged back, in the interpretation of some of his NSC listeners, to the idea of a neutral East Germany. The top levels of the State Department did not share this worry. For one report of the Genscher press conference, see Friedman (1990, p. 8).

5. Despite the compliment the British paid to the success of two plus four in claiming a share in its paternity, the American and German versions of its origins seem to be the most specific and trustworthy. Foreign Secretary Douglas Hurd did discuss two plus four in one session with Zoellick and Blackwill at the British embassy in Washington at the end of January, but as late as February 9 Thatcher was still lobbying for a four plus two conference (Teltschik 1991, p. 134.) The interest of British diplomats in claiming some authorship seemed to be primarily a means of wending their way back into the diplomatic game after Thatcher had almost written them out. What was true was that in the end the British did not fight the two plus four formula as the Soviets and French did. Because of this controversy the phrase *two plus four* would never appear in any official document.

6. As seen by Zoellick, this was the clearest description of the policy need, and not just, as commentators sometimes interpreted it, a need to get Gorbachev's signature on a disarmament treaty in Vienna and the Soviet leader's approval in order to counter German doubts about NATO. For the latter view see, for example, "Defence Survey," *Economist*, September 1, 1990, p. 1.

7. For a description of the four-power rights, see Stares (1990).

8. In the perception in Washington, the American decision to aim for full German sovereignty was reached very early, when Bonn itself was still toying with the idea of continuing four-power rights as a lever to get Soviet agreement on final terms of unification. This view astounded West German diplomats, who surmised in interviews that their tactical caution on speed in the early stages may have been misread by the Americans as vacillation about full sovereignty.

9. "Balky" according to an American official.

10. According to Zoellick, the American side was acutely aware of the German sensitivities on this score and had already used the phrase *two plus four* in an internal paper. If this was not clear in the discussion with Elbe, he said, it was only a slip in the shorthand reference to it in conversation.

11. Zoellick interview.

12. Zelikow described the Soviet gap: "They never could get their act together effectively. They were always coming up with positions about a month too late that we had already anticipated and walled off. If they had [made the same proposals] six weeks earlier, they could have been dangerous. So by the time the two plus four [ministers] met in early May Shevardnadze's hardline views were already out of date. If he had hit the West harder with them in February or March they could have been dangerous. But by then we had already rallied a solid Western consensus."

13. Teltschik (1990, pp. 134–35) does not treat the letter as anything special, however. Nor did Kohl in retrospect.

14. For texts, including the various explanatory statements by Kohl, see Bundesregierung (1990) and "Dokumentation," *Deutschland Archiv*, no. 3 (March 1990), pp. 466–80. For press reports see, for example, "Kohl erzielt Durchbruch in Moskau: Der Weg zur Einheit ist jetzt frei," *Die Welt*, February 12, 1990, p. 1.

15. Focusing on one aspect of that telephone call—the NSC's wish to be sure that Kohl also backed the two plus four notion—the German Foreign Ministry interpreted the tug of war less in terms of Washington's than of Bonn's bureaucratic politics. In this framework, ministry officials thought the NSC would not have had misgivings if Teltschik had not put a bee of doubt into its bonnet.

16. Karl Kaiser (1991, pp. 199–200, emphasis added). See Teltschik (1991, p. 152) for his laconic description of the tiff.

17. "Vogel schliesst Neutralität eines deutschen Gesamtstaates aus," *FAZ*, February 7, 1990, p. 4. In early February SPD centrists mounted a concerted counterattack against the left's dreams of opting out of a messy world by means of neutrality. See, for example, Seebacher-Brandt (1990a).

18. "It is no accident that withdrawal from NATO and a wish for neutrality belong to the standard repertoire of foreign policy conceptions of the extreme right" ("Neutralität als Ausweg? Zum Perspektive zukünftiger europäischer Sicherheit gibt es mehr Fragen als Antworten," *Tageszeitung*, February 5, 1990, p. 10.

19. Kohl contends that he cited the need for Germany to stay in NATO in a hundred speeches before the Camp David meeting, but that these pledges went unnoticed (Kohl interview). Teltschik (1991, pp. 139, 158–63) also describes previous occasions—such as the chancellor's visit to Moscow on February 10—on which Kohl expressed the view that German neutrality would be a "historical stupidity." He does not seem to regard the Camp David statement as having pinned Kohl down especially on NATO. The NSC felt before Camp David, however, that Germany's rhetorical commitment to NATO had not yet ruled out a French-type status for Germany in NATO, or linkage of the future of American and Soviet troops in Germany.

20. Genscher interview.

21. Curiously, Soviet officials and senior advisers seemed readier to accept the virtue of American forces in Europe than of the NATO organization. One of the bits of Soviet conditioning that American diplomats had to undertake was to convey the understanding that if NATO vanished, so would American troops in Europe.

22. Shevardnadze's first bid for a neutral Germany, or, barring that, at least some kind of simultaneous German membership in both alliances, came at the Ottawa conference in mid-February. The Soviet foreign minister already softened

this in an interview with *Izvestia* on his flight home to Moscow, however, in saying he had nothing against German membership in NATO if the Soviet Union were given guarantees about fundamental changes in NATO. The toughest Soviet rejection of German membership in NATO came on March 6, when Gorbachev told West German TV interviewers flatly, "We will not agree to that. That is absolutely excluded." Even as late as June 12 Gorbachev was still fishing for at least associate German membership in a Warsaw Pact that was already disintegrating (Teltschik 1991, pp. 151, 153, 168).

23. *Pravda*, February 21, 1990. Excerpts carried in *New York Times*, February 21, 1990, p. 11.

24. "Vereinigung vielleicht schon bis Anfang nächsten Jahres," *Die Welt*, March 20, 1990, p. 9.

25. For analysis even before the opening of the Berlin Wall suggesting Soviet appreciation of NATO and the U.S. presence in Europe as a check on the Germans, see Rumer (1989). For dismissal of Rumer's thesis and contention that German and Soviet interests coincided in wanting both U.S. and Soviet troops out of Germany, see Habakkuk (1990). This article was written in March 1990.

26. Kennan (1989).

27. Brzezinski (1989–90).

28. Gaddis (1990).

29. Hoffmann (1990a, 1990b, 1990c, 1990d, 1990–91).

30. Huntington (1990–91).

31. Mearsheimer (1990a, 1990b). As late as fall 1992 columnist Charles Krauthammer (1992) still expected Germany and Japan to want to acquire nuclear weapons of their own as the United States "becomes more isolationist."

32. Snyder (1990).

33. For other comment, see discussion of this chapter in the Bibliographical Essay.

34. Habsburg (1990). For a statement of the new SPD adoption of the Genscher plan (and dropping of the idea of abandoning NATO) after the SPD loss in the March East German election, see Voigt (1990). For other views in the continental European debate in this period, see the Bibliographical Essay.

35. Genscher interview. An exception to Genscher's stance would occur in early May, when Shevardnadze would propose separating settlement of internal and external aspects of German developments. Kohl and the Americans would categorically refuse such a split, not wanting to give Moscow the leverage of unregulated troops still stationed in eastern Germany. After a one-day flurry, Genscher too would return to the standard line. For rather different treatments of the issue, see "Erstes 2+4 Gespräch in Bonn öffnet den Weg zur Vereinigung Deutschlands," *Süddeutsche Zeitung*, May 7, 1990, pp. 1–2; Gennrich (1990b); and Forudastan (1990).

Chapter 14: Meanwhile, Domestic Politics

1. The best portrayal of this is Feldman (1984).

2. See discussion of this chapter in the Bibliographical Essay.

3. The member of parliament was Volker Rühe, in the mid-1980s, before he became more circumspect as Christian Democratic Union general secretary.

4. Key excerpts from Kohl's talk are carried in Karl Kaiser (1991, pp. 187–89).

5. Harden (1990, pp. 1 and 4). See also Ludwig (1990, pp. 51–91).

6. The Poles' public protests subsided only after Bush spoke directly to Mazowiecki on the issue in Washington on March 21 and in effect placed America's word behind Kohl's assurances. Bush spoke to Kohl on the telephone both before and after his meeting with Mazowiecki. Teltschik (1991, p. 181) notes Blackwill's call to him.

7. For the key exchanges at the press conference and Kohl's follow-up interview with GDR television on February 28, see Ludwig (1990, pp. 208–12).

8. On March 8. Text of the declaration in Ludwig (1990, p. 219).

9. AFP translation of a Walesa interview with the Dutch weekly *Elsevier*. Cited in Ludwig (1990, p. 76, fn. 176).

10. Key excerpts in Ludwig (1990, pp. 227-30). For an expression of Germany's annoyance, see Teltschik (1991, p. 171).

11. " 'Alle gegen Deutschland—Nein!" (1990). Kohl was so angry that he refused to ride in the same car with Thatcher on his arrival in England for a conference later that week (Teltschik 1991, pp. 188–89).

12. Polls conducted by Leipzig's Zentralinstitut für Jugendforschung and Institut für Marktforschung in early February, for example, projected an absolute majority for the SPD at 53 percent, with the CDU getting only 13 percent, hardly better than the communists' 12 percent (*Das Parlament*, March 9, 1990, p. 3). One element of distortion in the surveys, beyond the residual East German wariness of strangers asking questions, was the high percentage of citizens who could not decide how to vote until the last moment in such a fateful election. Most of the voters I spoke with after the election said that they had made their final selection only the night before, or even the morning of, the election.

13. The signal was the Dresden Declaration of the executive committee of the Bundestag conservative caucus of March 9. This statement endorsed Article 23 as the best way "to secure for all Germans the freest and most democratic constitution that ever existed in a German state." See "CDU und CSU verabschieden 'Dresdner Erklärung,' " *FAZ*, March 10, 1990, p. 1.

14. Even so, the conservatives' projected pace was not as fast as some East German conservatives would have liked. Kohl had to restrain members of the Alliance who—not sharing de Maizière's wish to preserve as much of the GDR's identity as possible—wanted the first Volkskammer session after the election to vote immediately to join the Federal Republic. Kohl's counterargument was that at this point the domestic aspects of unification had to wait for external agreement to catch up.

15. West German philosopher Habermas (1990a) coined the pejorative term.

16. Schröder interview.

17. For contemporary analysis of the election, see Rudolph (1990); Berger and others (1990); and Mantzke (1990, pp. 287–92). For analysis in English, see Hamilton (1990); and Garton Ash (1990b).

18. Quoted in Nawrocki (1990).

19. Street interviews in East Berlin.

20. For the definitive account of the West German side of the talks on economic union and the ones on political union that opened immediately thereafter, see Schäuble (1991). The basic treaty on economic and social union of May 18, 1990, though not its hundreds of pages of supplementary specifications, can be found in "Dokumentation," *Deutschland Archiv*, no. 6 (June 1990), pp. 970–83. The text of the August 31, 1990, final treaty on union, which was not required under Article 23, but was concluded at the wish of the East Germans, can be found in "Dokumentation," *Deutschland Archiv*, no. 10 (October 1990), pp. 1637–56.

21. See, for example, Kilian (1992); "Vergangenheitsbewältigung," *Deutschland Archiv*, no. 5 (May 1990), pp. 656–57; "Gelbe Kuchen aus Sachsen," *Der Spiegel*, August 19, 1991, pp. 58–64; " 'Schwarz heisst Gefahr,' " *Der Spiegel*, August 19, 1991, pp. 64–68; and "Massengräber im früheren Lager Sachsenhausen entdeckt," *FAZ*, August 3, 1992, p. 4.

22. Controversy about whether Stalin was serious in his offer raged over the years. The issue lost relevance after unification, but did not altogether die. For one late discussion of it, see Baring (1991b, p. 35).

23. Baring (1988) in particular takes a scalpel to this mentality.

24. See, for example, Berg (1990, pp. 897–906); and Petschow and others (1990).

25. Schneider (1989). See also Schneider (1990a, 1990b, 1990c, 1991a).

26. Seebacher-Brandt (1989). See also Seebacher-Brandt (1990b and 1991).

27. See, for example, Grass (1990a, 1990b); Grass interview carried in Gransow and Jarausch (1991, pp. 125–28); Sloterdijk (1990); Enzensberger (1990); Biermann (1990, pp. 43–44); and Hartung (1990).

28. Asked whether he agreed with his wife's criticism of the left, Brandt first parried that his wife had her own independent opinions. When pressed, he acknowledged agreement, however (Brandt interview).

29. See the Bibliographical Essay.

30. Cited by Buruma (1990). The forum was a discussion in Berlin in October 1990 of Hans-Jürgen Syberberg's *Hitler—A Film from Germany*.

31. See contributions by Greiner, Hage, and Königsdorf (1990); and Greiner (1990).

32. See, for example, Süskind (1990b); and Rolf Schneider (1991).

33. See, for instance, Schröder (1990a, 1990b, 1991a).

34. Wolf (1990a). See also Wolf (1990b).

35. Wolf said this at a roundtable on the history and literature of the GDR at the East Berlin Academy of Artists in early summer 1990. Cited in Mohr (1990, especially p. 1370).

36. See, for example, Schirrmacher (1990a, 1990c).

37. This discussion draws on Wagner (1991). See also Hoesterey (1991).

Chapter 15: Denouement

1. See discussion of this chapter in Bibliographical Essay.

2. See, for example, Lowe and Young (1991).

3. Stanley Hoffman used the phrase *post-Gaullist Gaullists* in a lecture at Harvard's Center for European Studies on October 17, 1990.

4. According to a chancellery source, who expressed relief that Teltschik left this particular episode out of his published diary.

5. Teltschik (1991, pp. 226f., 230–35).

6. The American team made its first enumeration of the nine points during Baker's visit to Moscow in mid-May, then refined them after getting the initial Soviet response. Zoellick summarized their significance for the Russians: "What they read into those nine points . . . was that the U.S. was not leaving the Soviet Union out of the game."

7. For one description of the discussion about Germany at the summit, see Beschloss and Talbott (1993, pp. 216–27).

8. For a discussion of the Bundeswehr's rethinking of its structure in the new era and absorption of the NVA, see Orden (1991).

9. There seems to be a discrepancy here between Washington's and Kohl's perceptions. Teltschik, in his diary, saw both the superpower summit and the Copenhagen message—and the subsequent Genscher-Shevardnadze meetings in Brest and Münster—as inconclusive, and would be all the more surprised by the full success of Kohl's visit to the Soviet Union in mid-July (Teltschik 1991, pp. 255ff., 267–68, 276–78, and 319ff.).

10. Grunenberg (1991). De Maizière would go on to be elected to the Bundestag and become deputy Christian Democratic Union leader in December, then make a bitter exit from politics less than a year later under suspicion of having been a *Stasi* informer. De Maizière would charge that the Christian Democratic Union hierarchy, wanting to get rid of him, had passed ambiguous documents to *Der Spiegel* to allege *Stasi* connections, but to the distress of his friends he would never really rebut the accusation. Some thought he was too proud to do so; others speculated that he despaired of bringing West Germans to understand the murky *Stasi* world he had had to operate in. Everyone considered de Maizière a tragic figure. See, for example, Hans-Joachim Meyer (1991, p. 3).

11. Karl Kaiser (1991, pp. 224–25).

12. Statement and other excerpts in Karl Kaiser (1991, pp. 219–26).

13. Bonn Foreign Ministry sources.

14. Teltschik (1991, pp. 276–77).

15. Genscher interview.

16. See, for instance, Teltschik (1991, pp. 297–98).

17. Text and excerpts from Kohl's Bundestag speech in Jacobsen and Tomala (1991, pp. 533–38).

18. Major excerpts from the Soviet foreign minister's statement at the two plus four conference appear in Karl Kaiser (1991, pp. 233–38).

19. Interviews, Washington.

20. *Pravda*, June 26, 1990.

21. *Literaturnaya Gazeta* (1991), cited in Kux (1991, p. 4, n. 25).

22. Collier (1992).

23. Meckel group interview. Meckel, along with the other Social Democratic party ministers, would leave de Maizière's government after final Soviet agreement

to German membership in NATO and before the conclusion of the final East-West German treaty on political union.

24. Ligachev confirmed his hard line on Germany in conversations with Princeton professors in fall 1991, according to one faculty member. Asked about claims that Shevardnadze and other Soviet officials had been contemplating some form of German unity as early as 1987, Ligachev responded that he certainly did not know of any such ruminations at the time. If Shevardnadze had been known to entertain such thoughts, he added, he would have been sacked immediately.

25. Interviews, Bonn, and Teltschik (1991, pp. 319–42). In retrospect, Shevardnadze explained the Soviet reasoning in reaching this agreement as "We no longer saw any other possibility, it was a question or either-or: go to war, or take part in the world process and have some influence on it. Any other position could have led to the Third World War" (Shevardnadze 1992).

26. According to a Chancellery source, Kohl personally jacked the number back up to 370,000 at Zheleznovodsk. The argument that convinced Gorbachev was Kohl's contention that he wanted to maintain a conscript army (and, by implication, avoid creating a new German military caste), but that any figure below 370,000 would require him to resort to a professional army. In his interview Kohl confirmed that the conscript army was his clinching argument.

Bonn and its allies were chary of any troop ceilings that would "singularize" Germany (that is, set limitations on Germany that would apply to no other country). Kohl's promise to limit the armed forces was therefore conceived of as an interim political pledge, valid until the final conventional forces in Europe agreement would set ceilings for all European participants.

27. The vehement National Security Council (NSC) contention is that Stoltenberg's concept eventually prevailed. The equally vehement German Foreign Ministry contention is that the original Genscher plan prevailed. Either way, in both interpretations Gorbachev's final important concession was to let the NVA be treated immediately as German territorial forces, without any restriction other than that it must not come under NATO command until 1994.

28. Company level down, plus half of the battalions, could be led by former NVA officers, according to a briefing at the Brookings Institution in May 1991 by members of the German Defense Ministry Armed Forces Staff. Cited in Stares (1992). See also Orden (1991).

29. Teltschik (1991, pp. 313–42).

30. Major excerpts of Kohl's address on August 5 at the fortieth anniversary celebration of the founding of the Charter of Germans Expelled from their Homelands in Jacobsen and Tomala (1990, pp. 539–43); and Ludwig (1990, pp. 255–59).

31. For a warier American view of risks in the Soviet-German relationship, see Smyser (1991).

32. A last-minute hitch occurred when the British in the political directors' meeting the night before indicated they could not sign unless the Soviet Union explicitly agreed to allow NATO maneuvers in eastern Germany after the withdrawal of Soviet forces. Genscher's aides began a salvage operation by routing the German foreign minister out of bed at about midnight, while Genscher routed Baker out of bed, enlisted Dumas's help at breakfast the next morning, and appealed personally to Hurd, who assured the Germans of British signature. Follow-

ing the British intervention, the final text did leave the possibility somewhat more open than the original text had (interview, German Foreign Ministry).

33. See Karl Kaiser (1991, pp. 260–70).

34. For a historical comparison with earlier German unifications, see Craig (1991).

35. Dean and Forsberg (1992, esp. p. 93). For analysis of the CFE Treaty, see also Dunay (1991); Dean (1989, 1990); and Walker (1991).

36. For full or partial texts of these agreements, see Karl Kaiser (1991, pp. 334–75).

Chapter 16: Hangover

1. In the negotiations, Schäuble had advocated leaving the GDR's much simpler legal system in place initially, with exceptions from West German law introduced as needed. He failed to win that argument. West German law became the norm, with transitional East German exceptions.

The other main element Schäuble would have changed in regularizing East-West German unity was the priority of restitution over indemnity in property claims. This preference was specified in the June 15, 1990, bilateral statement preceding economic union, at the insistence of the Free Democratic party, the Christian Social Union, and one section of the Christian Democratic Union, in part to minimize the government's financial burden. The principle led to time-consuming legal contests that became a major barrier to investment. It was subsequently modified twice in legislation in the direction of indemnity.

Given the pressures of writing the legal framework for the total disappearance of a country within weeks, however—and of writing one that would command the two-thirds parliamentary majority needed to change the West German constitution—Schäuble thinks overall that the negotiators can be proud of their work (Schäuble interview).

2. See Schönbohm (1992); Koop and Schössler (1992); Reeb (1992); and Kirchbach (1992).

3. Rückerl (1979).

4. Conversations with prosecutors in Berlin. For representative discussions of the legal considerations, see Altenhof (1992); Blumenwitz (1992); Winters (1992); Frenkel (1992); Schueler (1992); and Augstein (1992).

5. By contrast, there was apparently extensive destruction or tampering with secret police files in the more leisurely transition to full noncommunist rule in Poland, and even in Czechoslovakia. After two years in office, Commissioner Joachim Gauck notes that although some Stasi files were missing—including the electronic organizer and index—his commission has found no Stasi files that were actively falsified. Bundesbeauftragte für die Unterlagen des Staatssicherheitsdienstes der ehemaligen Deutschen Demokratischen Republik (1992, p. 2).

6. On the advisers see Ammer (1992).

7. See, for example, Reich-Ranicki (1991); Peter Schneider (1991b); Biermann (1991); and Hartung (1991).

8. Gauck (1991); and Lapp (1992).

9   For some of the debate about the poisonous *Stasi* role in GDR society and how to handle it, see discussion of this chapter in the Bibliographical Essay.

10. Stolpe (1992).

11. For discussion about these issues see the Bibliographical Essay.

12. For one discussion of the specific East German disappointments, see Schorlemmer (1992a). For one opinion poll showing loss of confidence in the market economy among easterners, see Köcher (1992).

13. Kohl interview.

14. Calculated the other way, from the ground up, one Family Ministry poll in late fall 1991 showed that 46 percent of households thought their standard of living had risen since unification, while 15 percent thought it had dropped. Only a third of households had telephones, but three-quarters had freezers, 50 percent had video recorders, and almost 20 percent had computers ("Umfrage über Lebensstandard ostdeutscher Familien," *FAZ*, August 29, 1992).

15. The preceding description draws especially on Collier (1992); and on the OECD country report, *Germany* (1992). For two discussions of the impact of economic difficulties and the east-west cleft on Germany's domestic and foreign policies, see Hamilton (1992); and Livingston (1992). For interpretation of opinion polls about security issues and American troops in Germany, and their implications for German foreign policy, see Asmus (1992).

16. Significantly, they did not rebel against footing two-thirds of the EC's bills; they rebelled only against giving up the deutsche mark.

17. A survey sponsored by CNN International and the *International Herald Tribune* just after the French referendum showed massive 80 percent-plus support for EC membership in France, Germany, the Benelux countries, Italy, Portugal, Spain, and Greece, and creditable 56 percent support in the United Kingdom, Denmark, and Ireland. An overall 60 percent said they would vote for the Maastricht treaty; 70 percent favored a single European currency ("Europeans Favor EC but Want to Vote on the Treaty," *International Herald Tribune*, September 28, 1992, pp. 1, 6).

18. Campbell and others (1991); Miller (1992).

19. These are virtually all ex-Warsaw Treaty Organization weapons. Their destruction will, by the Treaty on Conventional Armed Forces in Europe completion date of 1995, lead to parity between 76,000 tanks, armored personnel vehicles, artillery, aircraft, and helicopters in NATO territory and 79,000 in the territory of the former Warsaw Pact. Dean and Forsberg (1992) actually calculate the total number of Warsaw Pact heavy weapons that will have been destroyed or otherwise removed between 1988 and 1995 (counting Gorbachev's initial unilateral cuts) at 131,000. See also Daalder (1991).

20. Simultaneously, Soviet forces completed their withdrawal from Czechoslovakia and Hungary in 1991 and pledged withdrawal from Poland by 1993.

21. Klaus Naumann, "Sicherheitspolitik im Umbruch—Neue Herausforderungen an die Bundeswehr," talk at the Friedrich-Ebert-Stiftung, September 24, 1991.

22. See Kaiser and Becher (1992).

23. See the exchange of letters between Andrei Markovits and Jürgen Hoff-mann (1991); Erd (1991); Markovits (1991a); Markovits (1991b); "An der deutschen Heimatfront," *Der Spiegel*, March 4, 1991, pp. 238–45; Pond (1991); and Broder (1991). For a late restatement of the more classical left position of the 1970s and 1980s that "there is no just war," see Koch (1992).

24. Schirrmacher (1991).

25. Augstein (1991).

26. Germany's previous gingerly participation in UN operations—in a sleight of hand to circumvent the standard interpretation that a constitutional ban pre-vented German soldiers from being sent outside the NATO area—had involved border troops rather than Bundeswehr soldiers.

27. For a summary of the discussions, see Menon and others (1992); Fassbender (1991); Wyle (1991); Broer and Diehl (1991); and Buchan (1991).

28. Genscher interview.

29. Schäuble interview.

30. In one representative survey by the polling firm IPOS in spring 1992, only 2 percent thought the general economy was good, but 32 percent said their own economic position was good; 57 percent thought the economy was bad, but only 15 percent thought their own situation was bad. These evaluations would corre-spond roughly to the macroeconomic figures showing an actual rise in the standard of living in the east since unification. The remarkably similar values and upbeat expectations of young people in east and west Germany, as shown in the 1992 study of youth in Germany by IBM Germany, also augur a lessening of east-west tensions fairly soon, even if 80 percent of easterners still felt themselves to be second-class Germans (Institut für Empirische Psychologie 1992). See also Jugendwerk der Deutschen Shell, *Jugend '92* (1992). One final—literally—measure of content or discontent is the suicide rate for East Germans. This went down after unification, according to Helga Schubert, an east German writer and former psychologist at the Berlin Charity Hospital. This figure was kept secret in the GDR days ("Xeno-phobie, Rachsucht, wenig Freude," *FAZ*, May 25, 1992, p. 35).

31. Maron (1992) and Maron (1991).

32. Lippett (1992).

33. Greiner (1992). Other contributions to the late polemics on the left include Reich (1992); and Loest (1992).

34. Konrad-Adenauer-Stiftung sponsored the surveys; the results are available from the foundation.

35. Weizsäcker (1992). See also responses to Weizsäcker's criticism in Hofmann and Perger (1992).

Chapter 17: Agenda for America

1. See Rielly (1991a, 1991b). This survey, conducted in fall 1990, showed Amer-icans to be "more attuned than ever to global events," with an increasing 53 percent reading news about American foreign relations. Support for NATO, the report

said, "remains strong, but is shifting, most dramatically among the leaders, in favor of cutting back the number of troops stationed [in Europe]." Some 62 percent (and 97 percent of leaders) wanted the United States to take an active part in world affairs; a plurality of 48 percent favored West European economic unification. A year after the poll, Rielly said that support for American intervention abroad had decreased somewhat since the poll, but that of all foreign regions, Americans felt closest to Europe. He did not expect any significant popular drive to bring the remaining GIs home from Germany (conversation, Harriman, New York, November 17, 1991.)

2. For the best discussion of this, see Gunlicks (1989).

3. For discussion of the earlier American shift, see Buckley (1991). Huntington (1991) implicitly raises similar questions.

4. For the argument that peace is now divisible and that any fighting in Eastern Europe no longer risks sucking in Russia or Germany, see Ullman (1991). See also Ullman (1990).

5. For an exploration of this residual nuclear reinsurance, see Slocombe (1990); and Bajusz and Shaw (1990). For a discussion of NATO nuclear issues before November 1989 see Binnendijk (1989); and May, Herman, and Francis (1989).

6. For a passionate plea for such a mature relationship, see Zbigniew Brzezinski's lead address (1991–92) and Brzezinski (1991).

7. See, for example, "U.S. Alliance Management toward the Year 2000," *Journal of International Affairs*, vol. 43 (Summer-Fall 1989). In different ways Stephen M. Walt, David P. Calleo, Josef Joffe, Friedrich Kratochwil, and Stephen D. Krasner all represent these views. See also the section on chapters 12–15 in the Bibliographical Essay.

8. See, for instance, Davidson (1990); Bluth (1990).

9. O'Brien (1989), reprinted in James and Stone (1992).

10. See, for example, Mearsheimer (1990a, 1990b), and Joffe (1987).

11. See, for example, Bertram (1992).

12. See, for instance, Mortimer (1992); Van Evera (1990–91); and the eighteen-page "Defence Survey," *Economist*, September 1, 1990. The *Economist* assumed that a Euro-Atlantic community of perceived interests already exists, and that the new psychological balance between the two sides of the ocean should make their alliance easier. For another upbeat view of the alliance based largely on German domestic evolution, see Markovits and Reich (1991).

13. Still to be resolved is the question of how non-nuclear Germany can shoulder its equitable portion of NATO's residual risk sharing and, concomitantly, maintain its voice in NATO's remaining nuclear decisions. The United Kingdom and France already share the nuclear risk by virtue of their own deterrents, and Paris would be quite happy, as Mitterrand's repeated proposals advertise, to exclude the Germans altogether from the continent's nuclear management by turning this job over to a forum of nuclear powers. The United States should not play along with such exclusion of Germany. Presumably Germany will share its part of the nuclear risk by continuing to host dual-capable aircraft, and thus earn the voice it should have in administering the risk.

14. For a contrary view, see Asmus (1991). For a revisionist view that even in the past the NATO allies in general handled out-of-area crises with considerable

skill, see Sherwood (1990). Sherwood, who finished writing her book before the Gulf War, argues that the allies avoided "overburdening their collective agenda" and "overextending NATO's commitments." Instead, they developed an effective "shadow alliance" of informal consultations among those allies interested in any particular out-of-area issue, and made this consultation "one of the unrecognized strengths of the Atlantic partnership" (p. 184).

15. For the case for promoting nonproliferation by radical elimination of all ballistic missiles, including those of the United States and Russia, see Frye (1992). See also Wander and Arnett (1992). On Germany's recent passage of model laws blocking exports of technology of mass destruction, see Harald Müller (1992).

16. So far the United States, the world's largest arms exporter, has shown little inclination even to clean up its own house. According to the *SIPRI Yearbook 1991: World Armaments and Disarmament* (1991), the United States held a 40 percent share of world arms exports in 1990, followed by the Soviet Union (29 percent) and EC countries (21 percent). The 1990 totals were sharply down, by a third, from the peak year of 1987. The reduction cannot be attributed to policy, however, but only the drop in demand with the end of the Iran-Iraq war.

17. For articles exploring collective security, see the Bibliographical Essay.

18. See Weisenfeld (1991).

19. These statements are tracked by Taylor (1991).

20. See "EC Says 57% of Aid to Soviets Is German," *International Herald Tribune,* January 22, 1992, p. 2; and Reinicke (1992).

References

Abenheim, Donald. 1988. *Reforging the Iron Cross*. Princeton University Press.

Abrasimov, Pyotr. 1992. " 'Wir wechselten zum Du.' " *Der Spiegel*, August 17, pp. 20–22.

Adelman, Jonathan R., and Deborah Anne Palmiere. 1989. *The Dynamics of Soviet Foreign Policy*. Harper & Row.

Adomeit, Hannes. 1982. *Soviet Risk-Taking and Crisis Behavior: A Theoretical and Empirical Analysis*. London: Allen & Unwin.

———. 1984. "Capitalist Contradictions and Soviet Policy." *Problems of Communism* 33 (May–June), pp. 1–18.

———. 1989. "Moskau befürchtet Aufstand in der DDR, Kaum Gemeinsamkeiten mit SED." *Die Welt*, September 15, p. 1.

———. 1990. "Gorbachev and German Unification: Revision of Thinking, Realignment of Power." *Problems of Communism* 39 (July–August), pp. 1–23.

Albers, Detlev, Frank Deppe, and Michael Stamm. 1989. *Fernaufklärung: Glasnost und die bundesdeutsche Linke*. Cologne: Kiepenheuer & Witsch.

Altenhof, Ralf. 1992. "Die Toten an Mauer und Stacheldraht." *Deutschland Archiv* 4 (April), pp. 430–32.

Ammer, Thomas. 1992. "Struktur, Arbeitsweise und Auflösung des MfS." *Deutschland Archiv* 5 (May), pp. 547–50.

Ammer, Thomas, and Hans-Joachim Memmler, eds. 1991. *Staatssicherheit in Rostock: Zielgruppen, Methoden, Auflösung*. Cologne: Wissenschaft und Politik.

Ammer, Thomas, and Johannes L. Kruppe. 1989. "Ein langer Abschied: Die SED nach dem Sturz Honeckers." *Deutschland Archiv* 12 (December), pp. 1393–1401.

Andert, Reinhold, and Wolfgang Herzberg. 1991. *Der Sturz: Honecker im Kreuzverhör*. Berlin: Aufbau.

Apple, R. W., Jr. 1989. "Possibility of a Reunited Germany Is No Cause for Alarm, Bush Says." *New York Times*, October 25.

Arnold, Karl-Heinz. 1990. *Die ersten hundert Tage des Hans Modrow*. East Berlin: Dietz.

Aslund, Anders. 1985. *Private Enterprise in Eastern Europe*. St. Martin's.

Asmus, Ronald D. 1986. "Bonn and East Berlin: The 'New' German Question?" *Washington Quarterly* 9 (Winter), pp. 47–66.

———. 1991. "Germany and America: Partners in Leadership?" *Survival* 33 (November–December), pp. 546–66.

———. 1992. "Germany in Transition: National Self-Confidence and International Reticence." RAND Note N-3522-AF. Santa Monica, Calif.: RAND.

Augstein, Rudolf. 1989. "An den Kanzleien Vorbei." *Der Spiegel* 49, December 4, p. 26.

———. 1991. ". . . und die Deutschen?" *Der Spiegel*, June 3, p. 22.

———. 1992. "Ein politischer Prozess." *Der Spiegel*, August 3, p. 22.

Bahr, Egon. 1991. *Sicherheit für und vor Deutschland: Vom Wandel durch Annäherung zur Europäischen Sicherheitsgemeinshaft.* Munich: C. Hanser.

Bajusz, William D., and Lisa D. Shaw. 1990. "The Forthcoming 'SNF Negotiations,'" *Survival* 32 (July–August), pp. 333–47.

Baker, James A., III. 1989. "A New Europe, A New Atlanticism: Architecture for a New Era." State Department press release, December 12.

Baldauf, Joerg F. 1987. "Implementing Flexible Response: The US, Germany, and NATO's Conventional Forces." Ph.D. thesis, Massachusetts Institute of Technology.

Baldwin, Peter, ed. 1990. *Reworking the Past: Hitler, the Holocaust, and the Historians' Debate.* Boston: Beacon Press.

Baring, Arnulf. 1988. *Unser neuer Grössenwahn: Deutschland zwischen Ost und West.* Berlin: Siedler.

———. 1991a. *Deutschland, was nun? Ein Gespräch mit Dirk Rumberg und Wolf Jobst Siedler.* Berlin: Siedler.

———. 1991b. "Volksarmee schaffen—ohne Geschrei." *Franfurter Allgemeine Zeitung*, September 25, p. 35.

Bark, Dennis L., and David Gress. 1989. *A History of West Germany.* 2 vols. Cambridge: Basil Blackwell.

Baumann, Eleonore, and others. 1990. *Der Fischer Weltalmanach, Sonderband DDR.* Frankfurt: Fischer Taschenbuch.

Beck, Ulrich. 1992. *Jenseits von Rechts und Links.* Frankfurt: Suhrkamp.

Becker, Harald. 1992. "Wirtschaft in den neuen Bundesländern." *Deutschland Archiv* 5 (May), pp. 461–75.

Becker, Ulrich, Horst Becker, and Walter Ruhland. 1992. *Zwischen Angst und Aufbruch: Das Lebensgefühl der Deutschen in Ost und West nach der Wiedervereinigung.* Dusseldorf: Econ.

Bender, Peter. 1981. *Das Ende des ideologischen Zeitalters: Die Europäisierung Europas.* Berlin: Severin und Siedler.

———. 1989. *Deutsche Parallelen.* Berlin: Siedler.

———. 1992. *Unsere Erbschaft: Was war die DDR—was bleibt von ihr?* Hamburg: Luchterhand.

Berendonk, Brigitte. 1991. *Doping-Dokumente—Von der Forschung zum Betrug.* Berlin: Springer.

Berg, Michael von. 1990. "Umweltschutz in Deutschland." *Deutschland Archiv* 6 (June), pp. 897–906.

Berger, Manfred, and others. 1990. "Ein votum für die Einheit." *Die Zeit*, March 23.

Bergmann-Pohl, Sabine. 1991. *Abschied ohne Tränen*. Berlin/Frankfurt: Ullstein.

Bertram, Christoph. 1992. "Visions of Leadership: Germany," in Muller and Schweigler (1992).

Beschloss, Michael R., and Strobe Talbott. 1993. *At the Highest Levels: The Inside Story of the End of the Cold War*. Little, Brown.

Besier, Gerhard, and Stephan Wolf, eds., 1992. *"Pfarrer, Christen und Katholiken." Das Ministerium für Staatssicherheit und die Kirchen*. Neukirchen: Neukirchener Verlag des Erziehungsvereins.

Bessel, Richard. 1991. "How the Gestapo Policed the Third Reich." *Times Literary Supplement*, March 8.

Bezyminsky, L. 1984. "In the Shadow of American Missiles." *Pravda*, July 27.

Biermann, Wolf. 1990. "Nur wer sich ändert, bleibt sich treu." *Die Zeit*, August 24, pp. 43–44.

———. 1991. "Lass, O Welt, O lass mich sein!" *Die Zeit*, November 2.

———. 1992. *Der Sturz des Dädalus oder Eizes für die Eingeborenen der Fidschi-Inseln über den IM Judas Ischariot und den Kuddelmuddel in Deutschland seit dem Golfkrieg*. Colonge: Kiepenheuer & Witsch.

Binnendijk, Hans. 1989. "NATO's Nuclear Modernization Dilemma." *Survival* 31 (March–April), pp. 137–55.

Blackbourn, David, and Geoff Eley. 1984. *The Peculiarities of German History: Bourgeois Society and Politics in Nineteenth-Century Germany*. Oxford University Press.

Blackwill, Robert D., and Stephen Larrabee, eds. 1989. *Conventional Arms Control and East-West Security*. Duke University Press.

Blanke, Thomas, and Rainer Erd, eds. 1990. *DDR—Ein Staat vergeht*. Frankfurt: Fischer Taschenbuch.

Blechman, Barry M., Cathleen Fisher, and others. 1988. *The Silent Partner: West Germany and Arms Control*. Cambridge: Ballinger.

Blumenwitz, Dieter. 1992. "Zur strafrechtlichen Verfolgung Erich Honeckers: Staats- und völkerrechtliche Fragen." *Deutschland Archiv* 6 (June), pp. 567–79.

Bluth, Christoph. 1990. "Germany and the Soviet Union: Towards a New Rapallo?" *The World Today* 46 (November), pp. 199–200.

Blutke, Günter. 1991. *Obskure Geschäfte mit Kunst und Antiquitäten: Ein Kriminalreport*. Berlin: LinksDruck.

Bornstein, Morris, Zvi Gitelman, and William Zimmerman, eds. 1981. *East-West Relations and the Future of Eastern Europe*. London: Allen & Unwin.

Boutwell, Jeffrey. 1990. *The German Nuclear Dilemma*. Cornell University Press.

Boutwell, Jeffrey D., Paul Doty, and Gregory F. Treverton, eds. 1985. *The Nuclear Confrontation in Europe*. London: Croom Helm.

Bracher, Karl Dietrich, and others, eds. 1983–87. *Geschichte der Bundesrepublik Deutschland*. 6 vols. Stuttgart and Wiesbaden: Deutsche Verlags-Anstalt and Brockhaus.

Brandon, Henry, ed., 1992. *In Search of a New World Order: The Future of U.S.-European Relations*. Brookings.

Brandt, Willy. 1990. ". . . was zusammengehört," Reden zu Deutschland. Bonn: J. H. W. Deitz Nachf.

Brinks, Jan Herman. 1992. Die DDR-Geschichtswissenschaft auf dem Weg zur deutschen Einheit: Luther, Friedrich II. und Bismarck als Paradigmen politischen Wandels. Frankfurt: Campus.

Broder, Henryk M. 1991. "Unser Kampf." Der Spiegel, April 29, pp. 255–67.

———. 1992. "Eine schöne Revolution." Die Zeit, January 10, p. 41.

Broer, Michael, and Ole Diehl. 1991. "Die Sicherheit der neuen Demokratien in Europa und die NATO." Europa Archiv 46 (June 25), pp. 367–76.

Brown, J. F. 1988. Eastern Europe and Communist Rule. Duke University Press.

Bruns, Wilhelm. 1989. Von der Deutschland-Politik zur DDR-Politik? Prämissen—Probleme—Perspektiven. Opladen: Leske + Budrich.

Brzezinski, Zbigniew. 1989–90. "Post-Communist Nationalism." Foreign Affairs 68 (Winter), pp. 1–25.

———. 1991. "Selective Global Commitment." Foreign Affairs 70 (Fall), pp. 1–20.

———. 1991–92. "The Consequences of the End of the Cold War for International Security." Adelphi paper 265. New Dimensions in International Security, pt. 1, pp. 3–17. London: International Institute for Strategic Studies.

Buchan, David. 1991. "Whither WEU?" European Affairs (February–March), pp. 69–71.

Buckley, William F., Jr. 1991. "Who Says Americans Want Out?" International Herald Tribune, October 19, p. 8.

Bulmer, Simon, and William Paterson. 1987. The Federal Republic of Germany and the European Community. London: Allen & Unwin.

Bundesbeauftragte für die Unterlagen des Staatssicherheitsdienstes der ehemaligen Deutschen Demokratischen Republik. 1992. "Presseinformation." October 6, p. 2.

Bundesregierung. Presse- und Informationsamt. 1989. "Zehn-Punkte-Programm zur Überwindung der Teilung Deutschlands und Europas." Bulletin no. 134. Bonn, November 29.

———. 1990. Bulletin no. 24. Bonn, February 10.

Bundeszentrale für politische Bildung, Westeuropa und die USA. 1988. Gemeinsamkeiten, Unterschiede, Perspectiven. Bonn: Bundeszentrale.

Bürgerkomitee Leipzig, Stasi intern. 1991. Macht und Banalität. Leipzig: Forum Verlag.

Buruma, Ian. 1990. "There's No Place Like Heimat." New York Review of Books, December 20, p. 34.

Calingaert, Michael. 1989. The 1992 Challenge from Europe. Washington: National Planning Association.

Calleo, David P. 1987. Beyond American Hegemony: The Future of the Western Alliance. Basic Books.

Campbell, Edwina S. 1989. Germany's Past and Europe's Future. Washington: Pergamon-Brassey's.

Campbell, Kurt, and others. 1991. Soviet Nuclear Fission: Control of the Nuclear Arsenal in a Disintegrating Soviet Union. CSIA Studies in International Security, no. 1. Cambridge: Harvard Center for Science and International Affairs.

Carnegie Endowment National Commission. 1992. *Changing Our Ways*. Brookings.

Chace, James. 1991. *The Consequences of the Peace: The New Internationalism and American Foreign Policy*. Oxford University Press.

Chernoff, Fred. 1991. "Ending the Cold War: The Soviet Retreat and the U.S. Military Buildup." *International Affairs* 67 (January), pp. 111–26.

Childs, David. 1983. *The GDR: Moscow's German Ally*. London: Allen & Unwin.

———. 1985. *Honecker's Germany*. London: Allen & Unwin.

Childs, David, and others. 1988. *East Germany in Comparative Perspective*. London: Routledge.

Cimbala, Stephen J. 1989. *NATO Strategies and Nuclear Weapons*. St. Martin's.

Clark, Michael T., and Simon Serfaty, eds. 1991. *New Thinking and Old Realities*. Washington: Seven Locks for Johns Hopkins Foreign Policy Institute.

Clawson, Robert W., and Lawrence S. Kaplan, eds. 1982. *The Warsaw Pact: Political Purpose and Military Means*. Wilmington: Scholarly Resources.

Clemens, Clay. 1989. *Reluctant Realists: The Christian Democrats and West German Ostpolitik*. Duke University Press.

Cline, Ray. 1987. *Western Europe in Soviet Global Strategy*. Boulder: Westview.

Colchester, Nicholas, and David Buchan. 1990. *Europower: The Essential Guide to Europe's Economic Transformation in 1992*. New York: Economist/Times Books.

Colitt, Leslie. 1989. "Kohl Warns E. German 'Firebrands' over Unity." *Financial Times*, December 16.

Collier, Irwin L., Jr. 1992. "German Economic Integration: The Case for Optimism." University of Houston, May.

Conradt, David P. 1986. *The German Polity*. 3d ed. New York: Longman.

Cooney, James A., Wolfgang-Uwe Friedrich, and Gerald R. Kleinfeld. 1989. *Deutsch-Amerikanische Beziehungen, Jahrbuch 1*. Frankfurt: Campus.

Cordell, Karl. 1990. "The Role of the Evangelical Church in the GDR." *Government and Opposition* 25 (Winter), pp. 48–59.

Craig, Gordon A. 1982. *The Germans*. Putnam's.

———. 1991. "German Unification in Historical Perspective." *Proceedings of the American Philosophical Society* 135, no. 1, pp. 49–60.

Cuthbertson, Ian M., and David Robertson. 1990. *Enhancing European Security: Living in a Less Nuclear World*. St. Martin's.

Cuthbertson, Ian M., and Peter Volten, eds. 1990. *The Guns Fall Silent: The End of the Cold War and the Future of Conventional Disarmament*. New York: Institute for East-West Security Studies.

Cyr, Arthur. 1987. *U.S. Foreign Policy and European Security*. St. Martin's.

Daalder, Ivo H. 1991. *The CFE Treaty: An Overview and an Assessment*. Washington: Johns Hopkins Policy Institute.

Dahn, Daniela, and Fritz-Jochen Kopka, eds. 1991. "Und diese verdammte Ohnmacht." *Report der unabhängigen Untersuchungskommission zu den Ereignissen vom 7./8. Oktober 1989 in Berlin*. Berlin: BasisDruck.

Dahrendorf, Ralf. 1969. *Society and Democracy in Germany*. Anchor.

———. 1990. *Reflections on the Revolution in Europe*. Random House, Times Books.

Dalziel, Stephen. 1989. "Soviets Say No to German Reunification." BBC Central Talks and Features, November 30.

Darnton, Robert. 1991. *Berlin Journal 1989–1990*. Norton.

Dashichev, Vyacheslav. 1988. "The Soviet Perspective." *Problems of Communism* 37 (May–August), pp. 60–67.

Davidson, Ian. 1990. "Atlantic Alliance Fails to Read the Writing on the Wall." *Financial Times*, July 12, p. 2.

Dawisha, Karen. 1988. *Eastern Europe, Gorbachev and Reform: The Great Challenge*. Cambridge University Press.

Dawisha, Karen, and Philip Hanson, eds. 1981. *Soviet-East European Dilemmas: Coercion, Competition, and Consent*. London: Heinemann.

Dawydow, Jurij P., and Dmitrij W. Trenin. 1990. "Die Haltung der Sowjetunion gegenüber der Deutschen Frage." *Europa Archiv*, April 25, pp. 251–63.

de Bruyn, Günter. 1991. *Juberschreie, Trauergesänge: Deutsche Befindlichkeiten*. Frankfurt: S. Fischer.

Dean, Jonathan. 1987. *Watershed in Europe: Dismantling the East-West Military Confrontation*. Lexington Books.

———. 1989. *Meeting Gorbachev's Challenge: How to Build Down the NATO-Warsaw Pact Confrontation*. St. Martin's.

———. 1990. "The CFE Negotiations, Present and Future." *Survival* 32 (July–August), pp. 313–24.

Dean, Jonathan, and Randall Watson Forsberg. 1992. "CFE and Beyond: The Future of Conventional Arms Control." *International Security* 17 (Summer), pp. 76–121.

Dedcrichs, Mario R. 1989. "Von Malta zurück nach Jalta." *Stern*, December 21, pp. 130–32.

Deibel, Terry. 1991 "Bush's Foreign Policy: Mastery and Inaction." *Foreign Policy* 84 (Fall), pp. 3–23.

DePorte, A. W. 1986. *Europe between the Superpowers: The Enduring Balance*. Yale University Press.

deZayas, Alfred M. 1988. *Nemesis at Potsdam: The Expulsion of the Germans from the East*. University of Nebraska Press.

Diedrich, Torsten. 1991. *Der 17. Juni 1953 in der DDR: Bewaffnete Gewalt gegen das Volk*. Berlin: Dietz.

Di Palma, Giuseppe. 1990. *To Craft Democracies: An Essay on Democratic Transitions*. University of California Press.

"Disturbed over China: Declaration of the Synod of the Protestant Church of Saxony." 1990. In Rein (1990).

Ditfurth, Christian von. 1991. *Blockflöten: Wie die CDU ihre realsozialistische Vergangenheit verdrängt*. Cologne: Kiepenheuer & Witsch.

Dohnanyi, Klaus von. 1991. *Das deutsche Wagnis: Über die wirtschaftlichen und sozialen Folgen der Einheit*. Munich: Droemer-Knaur.

Dorpalen, Andreas. 1985. *German History in Marxist Perspective: The East German Approach*. Wayne State University Press.

Drachkovitch, Milorad M., ed. 1992. *East Central Europe: Yesterday, Today, Tomorrow*. Hoover Institution Press.

Duke, Simon. 1989. *United States Military Forces and Installations in Europe*. Oxford University Press for SIPRI.

Dunay, Pal. 1991. "The CFE Treaty: History, Achievements and Shortcomings." PRIF Reports no. 24. Frankfurt: Peace Research Institute, October.

Eckert, Rainer, Wolfgang Küttler, and Gustav Seeber, eds. 1992. *Krise—Umbruch—Neubeginn: Eine Kritische und selbstkritische Dokumentation der DDR-Geschichtswissenschaft 1989/90.* Stuttgart: Klett-Cotta.

Enzensberger, Hans Magnus. 1990. "Gangarten. Ein Nachtrag zur Utopie." *Frankfurter Allgemeine Zeitung,* May 19, "Bilder und Zeiten" section.

Eppelmann, Rainer. 1992. *Wendewege: Briefe an meine Familie.* Bonn: Bouvier.

Erd, Rainer. 1991. "Deutsche Linke an die Front?" *Frankfurter Rundschau,* February 20, p. 4.

European Strategy Group. 1988. *The Gorbachev Challenge and European Security.* Baden-Baden: Nomos.

Evans, Richard J. 1989. *In Hitler's Shadow.* Pantheon.

Falcke, Heino. 1991. *Die unvollendete Befreiung: Die Kirchen, die Umwälzung in der DDR und die Vereinigung Deutschlands.* Munich: Chr. Kaiser.

Falkner, Thomas. 1990. "Die letzten Tage der SED." *Deutschland Archiv* 11 (November), pp. 1750–62.

———. 1991. "Von der SED zur PDS." *Deutschland Archiv* 1 (January), pp. 30–51.

Fassbender, Bardo. 1991. "Zur staatlichen Ordnung Europas nach der deutschen Einigung." *Europa Archiv,* July 10, pp. 395–404.

Federal Republic of Germany. Foreign Ministry. 1989. *40 Jahre Aussenpolitik der Bundesrepublik Deutschland: Eine Dokumentation.* Bonn.

———. 1990. *Umbruch in Europa: Die Ereignisse im 2: Halbjahr 1989: Eine Dokumentation.* Bonn.

———. 1991. *Deutsche Aussenpolitik 1990/91: Auf dem Weg zu einer europäischen Friedensordnung: Eine Dokumentation.* Bonn.

Fein, Esther B. 1989. "The Kremlin Reacts Calmly, But Says Border Must Stay." *New York Times,* November 11, p. 3.

Feldman, Lily Gardner. 1984. *The Special Relationship between West Germany and Israel.* Boston: Allen & Unwin.

———. 1992. "The European Community and German Unification." In Hurwitz and Lequesne (1992).

Filmer, Werner, and Heribert Schwan. 1991. *Die Opfer der Mauer. Die geheime Protokolle des Todes.* Munich: Bertelsmann.

Fink, Hans-Jürgen. 1990. "Deutscher Gipfel an der Elbe." *Deutschland Archiv* 1 (January), pp. 1–6.

Fischer, Joschka. 1992. *Die Linke nach dem Sozialismus.* Hamburg: Hoffmann und Campe.

Flanagan, Stephen J., and Fen Osler Hampson, eds. 1986. *Securing Europe's Future.* London: Croom Helm.

Flynn, Gregory, ed. 1990. *The West and the Soviet Union: Politics and Policy.* St. Martin's.

Förster, Peter, and Günter Roski. 1990. *DDR zwischen Wende und Wahl: Meinungsforscher analysieren den Umbruch.* Berlin: LinksDruck.

Forudastan, Ferdos. 1990. "Moskau vertagt sein Njet." *Tageszeitung,* May 7, p. 1.

Frankland, E. Gene, and Donald Schoonmaker. 1992. *Between Protest and Power: The Green Party in Germany.* Boulder: Westview.

Frankland, Mark. 1991. *The Patriots' Revolution: How Eastern Europe Toppled Communism and Won Its Freedom*. London: Sinclair Stevenson.

Freedman, Lawrence. 1989. *The Evolution of Nuclear Strategy*. St. Martin's.

———. 1990. *Europe Transformed: Documents at the End of the Cold War*. St. Martin's.

Freney, Michael A., and Rebecca S. Hartley. 1991. *United Germany and the United States*. Washington: National Planning Association.

Frenkel, Rainer. 1992. ". . . getötet zu haben, ohne Mörder zu sein?" *Die Zeit*, July 31, p. 3.

Fricke, Karl Wilhelm. 1989. *Die DDR-Staatssicherheit: Entwicklung, Strukturen, Aktionsfelder*. 3d ed. Cologne: Wissenschaft und Politik.

———. 1990a. "Entmachtung und Erblast des MfS." *Deutschland Archiv* 12 (December), pp. 1881–90.

———. 1990b. "Das Instrument des Überwachungsstaates—Der Staatssicherheitsdienst in der DDR." Speech at the Tutzing Protestant Academy, reprinted as Heft 8 (November).

———. 1990c. "Die Liquidierung des MfS/AfNS." *Deutschland Archiv* 2 (February), pp. 242–46.

———. 1990d. "The Power of the *Stasi*." *German Comments* (October), pp. 16–23.

———. 1990e. "Symptome eines Verfalls: Impressionen vom Ausserordentlichen Parteitag der SED." *Deutschland Archiv* 1 (January), pp. 7–9.

———. 1990f. "Zur Abschaffung des Amtes für Nationale Sicherheit." *Deutschland Archiv* 1 (January), pp. 59–62.

———. 1991a. "Honeckers Sturz mit Mielkes Hilfe." *Deutschland Archiv* 1 (January), pp. 5–7.

———. 1991b. *MfS intern: Macht, Strukturen, Auflösung der DDR-Staatssicherheit: Analyse und Dokumentation*. Cologne: Wissenschaft und Politik.

———. 1991c. "'Das sogenannte Volk,' Ex-Stasi-Offiziere zu ihrer Vergangenheit." *Deutschland Archiv* 5 (May), pp. 540–42.

Friedman, Thomas. 1990. "Baker and West German Envoy Discuss Reunification Issues." *New York Times*, February 3, p. 8.

Friedrich, Wolfgang-Uwe, ed. 1991. *Die USA und die deutsche Frage 1945–1990*. Frankfurt: Campus.

Friend, Julius W. 1991. *The Linchpin: French-German Relations, 1950–1990*. Praeger.

Fritsch-Bournazel, Renata. 1988. *Confronting the German Question*. Oxford: Berg.

———. *Europe and German Unification*. New York: Berg.

Frye, Alton. 1992. "Zero Ballistic Missiles." *Foreign Policy* 88 (Fall), pp. 3–20.

Gaddis, John Lewis. 1982. *Strategies of Containment*. Oxford University Press.

———. 1987. *The Long Peace: Inquiries into the History of the Cold War*. Oxford University Press.

———. 1990. "Coping with Victory." *Atlantic*, May, pp. 49–60.

———. 1992. *The United States and the End of the Cold War: Implications, Reconsiderations, Provocations*. Oxford University Press.

———. 1992–93. "International Relations Theory and the End of the Cold War." *International Security* 17 (Winter), pp. 5–58.

Garten, Jeffrey E. 1992. *A Cold Peace: America, Japan, Germany, and the Struggle for Supremacy*. New York Times Books.

Garton Ash, Timothy. 1989. "The German Revolution." *New York Review of Books,* December 21, pp. 14–19.

———. 1990a. "The Chequers Affair." *New York Review of Books,* September 27, p. 65.

———. 1990b. "East Germany: The Solution." *New York Review of Books,* April 26, pp. 14–20.

———. 1990c. *The Magic Lantern.* Random House.

———. 1990d. *The Uses of Adversity.* Vintage.

Gati, Charles. 1990. *The Bloc That Failed: Soviet-East German Relations in Transition.* Indiana University Press.

Gauck, Joachim. 1991. *Die Stasi-Akten: Das unheimliche Erbe der DDR.* Reinbek: Rororo.

Gaus, Günter. 1983. *Wo Deutschland Liegt: Eine Ortsbestimmung.* Munich: DTV Zeitgeschichte.

———. 1990. *Deutscher Lastenausgleich.* Frankfurt: Luchterhand.

Gedmin, Jeffrey. 1992. *The Hidden Hand: Gorbachev and the Collapse of East Germany.* Washington: AEI Press.

Geipel, Gary, ed. 1990. *The Future of Germany.* Indianapolis: Hudson Institute.

Gennrich, Claus. 1990a. "Genscher bescheinigt Gorbatschow Realismus und Weitblick." *Frankfurter Allgemeine Zeitung,* February 1, pp. 1–2.

———. 1990b. "Moskau will die deustche Einheit bald." *Frankfurter Allgemeine Zeitung,* May 7, pp. 1–2.

Genscher, Hans-Dietrich. 1987. "Gorbatschow ernst nehmen—Gorbatschow beim Wort nehmen." February 1, 1987, reprinted in Genscher (1990), pp. 7–20.

———. 1990. *Zukunftsverantwortung: Reden.* Berlin: Der Morgen.

Geremek, Bronislaw. 1992. "Civil Society and the Present Age." In "The Idea of a Civil Society," conference report from the National Humanities Center, Research Triangle Park, N.C.

Gerlach, Manfred. 1991. *Mitverantwortlich: Als Liberaler im SED-Staat.* Berlin: Morgenbuch.

Geron, Leonard. 1990. *Soviet Foreign Economic Policy under Perestroika.* New York: Council on Foreign Relations Press for RIIA.

Gerster, Florian, and Dietrich Stobbe. 1990. *Die linke Mitte heute.* Bonn: Dietz Nachf.

Giesen, Bernhard, ed. 1991. *Nationale und kulturelle Identität: Studien zur Entwicklung des Kollektiven Bewusstseins in der Neuzeit.* Frankfurt: Suhrkamp.

Giesen, Bernard, and Claus Leggewie, eds. 1991. *Experiment Vereinigung: Ein Sozialer Grossversuch.* Berlin: Rotbuch.

Gill, David, and Ulrich Schröter. 1991. *Das Ministerium für Staatssicherheit: Anatomie des Mielke-Imperiums.* Berlin: Rowohlt.

Glaessner, Gert-Joachim, ed. 1988. *Die DDR in der Ära Honecker.* West Berlin: Westdeutscher.

———. 1991. *Der schwierige Weg zur Demokratie: Vom Ende der DDR zur deutschen Einheit.* Wiesbaden: Westdeutscher.

Goeckel, Robert F. 1990. *The Lutheran Church and the East German State: Political Conflict and Change under Ulbricht and Honecker.* Cornell University Press.

Gorbachev, Mikhail. 1987. *Perestroika: New Thinking for Our Country and the World.* Harper and Row.

———. 1992. Interview. "'Honecker è colpevole/non può accusare l'URSS.'" *Il Giornale,* August 22.

Gordon, Lincoln, and others. 1987. *Eroding Empire: Western Relations with Eastern Europe.* Brookings.

Gorholt, Martin, and Norbert W. Kunz, eds. 1990. *Deutsche Einheit, deutsche Linke: Reflexionen der politischen und gesellschaftlichen Entwicklung.* Cologne: Bund.

Grabner, Wolf-Jürgen, ed. 1990. *Leipzig im Oktober: Kirchen und alternative Gruppen in Umbruch der DDR: Analysen zur Wende.* Berlin: Wichern.

Grafe, Peter. 1991. *Tradition und Confusion.* Frankfurt: Eichborn.

Gransow, Volker, and Konrad H. Jarausch, eds. 1991. *Die deutsche Vereinigung: Dokumente zu Büregerbewegung, Annäherung und Beitritt.* Cologne: Wissenschaft und Politik.

Grass, Günter. 1990a. *Deutscher Lastenausgleich: Wider das dumpfe Einheitsgebot: Reden und Gespräche.* Frankfurt: Luchterhand.

———. 1990b. *Two States—One Nation?* San Diego: A Helen and Kurt Wolff Book/ Harcourt Brace Jovanovich.

———. 1990c. "Was rede ich: wer hört noch zu." *Die Zeit,* May 11.

Greifswald Untersuchungsausschuss. 1990. *Abschlussbericht.* Greifswald: Unter-suchungsausschuss der Stadt Greifswald.

Greiner, Ulrich, Volker Hage, and Helga Königsdorf. 1990. In "Was bleibt. Bleibt was?: Pro und Contra: eine Zeit-Kontroverse über Christa Wolf und ihre neue Ezrählung," *Die Zeit,* June 1.

Greiner, Ulrich. 1990. "Die deutsche Gesinnungsästhetik," *Die Zeit,* November 9.

———. 1992. "Flucht in die Trauer," *Die Zeit,* September 18, p. 69.

Gremliza, Hermann L. 1990. *Krautland einig Vaterland.* Hamburg: Konkret.

Griffith, William E., ed. 1989. *Central and Eastern Europe: The Opening Curtain?* Boulder: Westview.

Groh, Dieter, and Peter Brandt. 1992. *Vaterlandslose Gesellen: Sozialdemokratie und Nation 1860–1990.* Munich: C. H. Beck.

Grosser, Alfred. 1980. *The Western Alliance: European-American Relations since 1945.* New York: Continuum.

Grunenberg, Nina. 1991. "Der kurze Weg zum langen Abschied." *Die Zeit,* Sep-tember 26, pp. 12–13.

Gunlicks, Arthur, ed. 1989. "Federalism and Intergovernmental Relations in West Germany: A Fortieth Year Appraisal." *Publius* 19 (Fall).

Habakkuk, David. 1990. "NATO and Soviet Decline." *Political Quarterly* 61 (July–September), pp. 252–62.

Habermas, Jürgen. 1990a. "Der DM-Nationalismus." *Die Zeit,* March 30, pp. 61–62.

———. 1990b. *Die nachholende Revolution.* Frankfurt: Suhrkamp.

———. 1992. *Faktizität und Geltung.* Frankfurt: Suhrkamp.

Habsburg, Otto von. 1990. Interview. "A Tale of Two Empires." *The World Today* (May), pp. 94–inside back cover.

Hacker, Jens. 1992. *Deutsche Irrtümer: Schönfärberei und Helfershelfer der SED-Diktatur im Westen.* Berlin: Ullstein.

Hager, Kurt. 1987. "Friedenssicherung und ideologischer Streit." *Neues Deutschland,* October 28, p. 3.

Haglund, David G. 1991. *Alliance within the Alliance: Franco-German Military Cooperation and the European Pillar of Defense.* Boulder: Westview.

Hahn, Reinhardt O. 1990. *Ein Stasi-Major erzählt.* Halle: Mitteldeutscher, 1990.

Hamilton, Daniel. 1990. *After the Revolution: The New Political Landscape in East Germany.* German Issues no. 7. Washington: American Institute for Contemporary German Studies.

———. 1992. "Unified Germany." *Problems of Communism* 41 (May–June), pp. 1–18.

Hanf, Thomas. 1992. "Gewalt und Ohnmacht: Zum friedlichen Charakter der Herstellung der staatlichen Einheit Deutschlands." *BISS Public,* vol. 6, pp. 23–47.

Hanrieder, Wolfram R., ed. 1987. *Arms Control, the FRG, and the Future of East-West Relations.* Boulder: Westview.

———. 1989. *Germany, America, Europe: Forty Years of German Foreign Policy.* Yale University Press.

Harden, Blaine. 1990. "Poland Toughens on Unity." *International Herald Tribune,* February 22, pp. 1, 4.

Harsch, Joseph. 1990. "Gorbachev's Ace in the Game for Europe's Future." *Christian Science Monitor,* December 7, p. 1.

Hartung, Klaus. 1990. *Neunzehnhundertneunundachtzig: Ortsbesichtigung nach einer Epochenwende.* Frankfurt: Luchterhand.

———. 1991. "Den Stein umgedreht." *Die Zeit,* November 8, p. 6.

Haslam, Jonathan. 1990. *The Soviet Union and the Politics of Nuclear Weapons in Europe, 1969–87.* Cornell University Press.

Hein, Christoph. 1990. *Die fünfte Grundrechenart: Aufsätze und Reden 1986–1989.* Frankfurt: Luchterhand.

Heisenberg, Wolfgang. 1991. *German Unification in European Perspective.* London: Brassey's.

Helwig, Gisela. 1987. *Frau und Familie: Bundesrepublik Deutschland DDR.* Cologne: Wissenschaft und Politik.

———. 1990. *Die letzten Jahre der DDR: Texte zum Alltagsleben.* Cologne: Wissenschaft und Politik.

Henkys, Reinhard. 1990. "Die Kirchen im Umbruch der DDR." *Deutschland Archiv* 2 (February), pp. 177–80.

Herf, Jeffrey. 1991. *War by Other Means: Soviet Power, West German Resistance, and the Battle of the Euromissiles.* Free Press.

Herles, Helmut, and Ewald Rose, eds. 1990a. *Parlaments-Szenen einer deutschen Revolution: Bundestag und Volkskammer im November 1989.* Bonn: Bouvier.

———. 1990b. *Vom runden Tisch zum Parlament.* Bonn: Bouvier.

Hermann, Kai. 1990. "Das Stundenbuch einer deutschen Revolution." *Stern,* January 25, pp. 20–25; February 1, pp. 34–38; and February 8, pp. 160–64.

Hertle, Hans-Hermann. 1992 "Staatsbankrott." *Deutschland Archiv* 10 (October), pp. 1019–30.

Heym, Stefan. 1990. *Einmischung: Gespräche, Reden, Essays.* Munich: Bertelsmann.

Hill, Christopher, ed. 1983. *National Foreign Policies and European Political Cooperation*. London: Allen & Unwin.

Hillenbrand, Martin. 1983. *Germany in an Era of Transition*. Paris: Atlantic Institute for International Affairs.

Hirschman, Albert O. 1992a. "Wir weinen ihnen keine Träne nach." *Frankfurter Allgemeine Zeitung*, August 22, "Bilder und Zeiten" section, p. 23.

———. 1992b. "Exit, Voice, and the Fate of the German Democratic Republic." Princeton: Institute for Advanced Study.

Hodge, Carl C., and Cathal J. Nolan. 1992. *Shepherd of Democracy?* Westport, Conn.: Greenwood.

Hoesterey, Ingeborg. 1991. "Postmodern Bricoleurs: The New Syncretism in German Studies." *German Studies Review* 14 (October), pp. 587–96.

Hoffmann, Christa. 1992. *Die Stunde Null? Vergangenheitsbewältigung in Deutschland 1945 und 1989*. Bonn: Bouvier.

Hoffmann, Stanley. 1990a. "A New World and Its Troubles." *Foreign Affairs* 69 (Fall), pp. 115–22.

———. 1990b. "A Plan for the New Europe." *New York Review of Books*, January 18, pp. 18–21.

———. 1990c. "Reflections on the 'German Question.' " *Survival* 32 (July–August), pp. 291–98.

———. 1990d. "Today's NATO and Tomorrow's." *New York Times*, May 27, p. E13.

———. 1990–91. "The Case for Leadership." *Foreign Policy* 81 (Winter), pp. 20–38.

Hofmann, Gunter, and Werner A. Perger, eds. 1992. *Die Kontroverse: Weizsäckers Parteienkritik in der Diskussion*. 1992. Frankfurt: Eichborn.

Hogan, Michael J., ed. 1992. *The End of the Cold War: Its Meaning and Implications*. Cambridge University Press.

Holloway, David, and Jane M. O. Sharp. 1984. *The Warsaw Pact: Alliance in Transition?* London: Macmillan.

Holmes, Kim R. 1984. *The West German Peace Movement and the National Question*. Cambridge: Institute for Foreign Policy Analysis.

Honecker, Erich. 1991. *Der Sturz*. See Andert and Herzberg (1991).

Hosking, Geoffrey. 1990. *The Awakening of the Soviet Union*. Harvard University Press.

Howard, Michael. 1982–83. "Reassurance and Deterrence: Western Defense in the 1980s." *Foreign Affairs* 61 (Winter), pp. 309–24.

Huntington, Samuel P. 1990–91. "American's Role in a Changing World." Adelphi Papers 256–57 (Winter). London: International Institute for Strategic Studies.

———. 1991. "America's Changing Strategic Interests." *Survival* 33 (January–February), pp. 3–17.

Hurwitz, Leon, and Christian Lequesne, eds. 1992. *The State of the European Community, 1989–90*. Boulder: Lynne Rienner.

Hyde-Price, Adrian. 1991. *European Security beyond the Cold War*. London: Sage.

Inglehart, Ronald. 1977. *The Silent Revolution: Changing Values and Political Styles among Western Publics*. Princeton University Press.

Institut für Empirische Psychologie, ed. 1992. *Die selbstbewusste Jugend: Orientierungen und Perspektiven zwei Jahre nach der Wiedervereinigung: Die IBM-Jugendstudie '92*. Cologne: Bund.

Jacobsen, Hans-Adolf, and Mieczyslaw Tomala, eds. 1991. *Warschau-Bonn: Die deutsch-polnischen Beziehungen 1945–1990: Analyse und Dokumentation*. Cologne: Wissenschaft und Politik.

James, Harold A. 1990. *A German Identity 1770–1990*. New York: Routledge.

James, Harold, and Marla Stone. 1992. *When the Wall Came Down: Reactions to German Unification*. New York: Routledge.

Janka, Walter. 1989. *Schwierigkeiten mit der Wahrheit*. Reinbek: Rowohlt.

———. 1991a. *Spuren eines Lebens*. Berlin: Rohwohlt.

———. 1991b. Interview. "Ich habe es abgelehnt, Dissident zu sein." *Süddeutsche Zeitung*, May 25, p. 16.

Japs, Goda. 1992. "Riskanter Dialog: Das gemeinsame Ideologie-Papier von SPD und SED." *Deutschland Archiv* 10 (October), pp. 1011–14.

Jesse, Eckhard, and Armin Mitter, eds. 1992. *Die Gestaltung der deutschen Einheit: Geschichte, Politik, Gesellschaft*. Bonn: Bouvier.

Joffe, Josef. 1987. *The Limited Partnership: Europe, the United States, and the Burdens of Alliance*. Cambridge: Ballinger.

———. 1990. "Once More: The German Question." *Survival* 32 (March–April), pp. 129–40, n. 2.

Johnson, A. Ross, Robert W. Dean, and Alexander Alexiev. 1982. *East European Military Establishments: The Warsaw Pact Northern Tier*. New York: Crane Russak.

Jones, Christopher D. 1981. *Soviet Influence in Eastern Europe*. Praeger.

Jugendwerk der Deutschen Shell. 1992. *Jugend '92*. Opladen: Leske und Budrich.

Kaiser, Carl-Christian. 1992. "Der General ging unter die Decke." *Die Zeit*, August 28, p. 74.

Kaiser, Jens. 1991. "Zwischen angestrebter Eigenständigkeit und traditioneller Unterordnung: Zur Ambivalenz des Verhältnisses von sowjetischer und DDR-Aussenpolitik in den achtziger Jahren." *Deutschland Archiv* 5 (May), pp. 478–95.

Kaiser, Karl. 1990–91. "Germany's Unification." *Foreign Affairs* 70 (America and the World), pp. 179–205.

———. 1991. *Deutschlands Vereinigung: Die internationale Aspekte, mit den wichtigen Dokumenten*. Bergisch-Gladbach: Bastei Lübbe.

Kaiser, Karl, and Klaus Becher. 1992. *Deutschland und der Irak-Konflikt: Internationale Sicherheitsverantwortung Deutschlands und Europas nach der deutschen Vereinigung*. Bonn: Forschungsinstitut der Deutschen Gesellschaft für Auswärtige Politik.

Kaiser, Karl, and Pierre Lellouche, eds. 1986. *Deutsch-Französische Sicherheitspolitik*. Bonn: Europa Union.

Kaiser, Karl, and John Roper, eds. 1988. *British-German Defence Cooperation*. London: Jane's.

Kandler, Karl-Hermann. 1991. *Die Kirchen und das Ende des Sozialismus: Betrachtungen eines Betroffenen*. Asendorf: MUT-Verlag.

Kant, Hermann. 1991. *Abspann: Erinnerungen*. Berlin: Aufbau.

Karber, Phillip. 1983. "To Lose an Arms Race: The Competition in Conventional Forces Deployed in Central Europe 1965–1980." In Uwe Nerlich, ed. *Soviet Power and Western Negotiating Policies*, vol. 1, *The Soviet Asset: Military Power in the Competition over Europe*. Cambridge, Mass.: Ballinger, pp. 31–88.

Katzenstein, Peter. 1987. *Policy and Politics in West Germany: The Growth of a Semisovereign State*. Temple University Press.

———. 1989. *Industry and Politics in West Germany: Toward the Third Republic*. Cornell University Press.

———. 1991. "The Taming of German Power: Unification 1989–90." Paper presented as part of a workshop held at Northwestern University, April 20–21.

Kaysen, Carl. 1990. "Is War Obsolete? A Review Essay." *International Security*, 14 (Spring), pp. 42–64.

Kegley, Charles W., Jr., ed. 1991. *The Long Postwar Peace: Contending Explanations and Projections*. Harper Collins.

Kelleher, Catherine McArdle. 1975. *Germany and the Politics of Nuclear Weapons*. Columbia University Press.

Kelleher, Catherine M., and Gale A. Mattox, eds. 1987. *Evolving European Defense Policies*. Lexington, Mass.: Lexington Books.

Keller, Bill. 1989. "Gorbachev, in Finland, Disavows Any Right of Regional Intervention." *New York Times*, October 26, p. A1.

Kennan, George F. 1989. "This Is No Time To Talk of German Reunification." *Washington Post*, November 12, p. D1.

Kennedy, Ellen. 1991. *The Bundesbank*. New York: Council on Foreign Relations Press.

Kershaw, Ian. 1989. *The Nazi Dictatorship: Problems and Perspectives of Interpretation*. 2d ed. London: Edward Arnold.

Kilian, Achim. 1992. *Einzuweisen zur völligen Isolierung: NKWD-Speziallager Mühlberg/Elbe 1945–1948*. Leipzig: Forum.

Kirchbach, Hans-Peter von. 1992. "Reflections on the Growing Together of the German Armed Forces." Special Report of the Strategic Studies Institute, U.S. Army War College, February 14.

Kirchner, Emil J., and James Sperling, eds. 1992. *The Federal Republic of Germany and NATO: 40 Years After*. London: Macmillan.

Kittrie, Nicholas N., and Ivan Volgyes. 1990. *Eastern Europe between the Superpowers: The Quest for a New Balance*. Washington: Washington Institute Press.

Kleine-Brockhoff, Thomas, and Oliver Schröm. 1992. "Das Kirchengeschäft B." *Die Zeit*, August 28, pp. 11–14.

Knauer, Gerd. 1992. "Innere Opposition im Ministerium für Staatssicherheit?" *Deutschland Archiv* 7 (July), pp. 718–27.

Knoth, Nikola. 1991. "Johannes R. Becher 1956/57—eine DDR-Misere?: Dokumentarischer Bericht." *Deutschland Archiv* 5 (May), pp. 502–11.

Koch, Dirk. 1992. "Nur nicht drängeln." *Der Spiegel*, October 5, p. 25.

Kochemasov, Vyacheslav. 1992. Interview. " 'Schmeichelei und Unterwürflichkeit.' " *Der Spiegel*, November 16, pp. 148–49.

Köcher, Renate. 1992. "Die Ostdeutschen frösteln in der Freiheit." *Frankfurter Allgemeine Zeitung*, September 9, p. 5.

Kocka, Jürgen. 1988. "German History before Hitler: The Debate about the German *Sonderweg*." *Journal of Comparative History*, vol. 23, pp. 3–16.

Koelbe, Thomas A. 1991. *The Left Unraveled: Social Democracy and the New Left Challenge in Britain and West Germany*. Duke University Press.

Kolboom, Ingo, ed. 1991a. *XIV. Deutsch-Französische Konferenz: Deutschland und Frankreich im neuen Europa*. Bonn: Europa.

———. 1991b. *Vom geteilten zum Vereinten Deutschland: Deutschland-Bilder in Frankreich*. Bonn: Europa.

Kommers, Donald P. 1989. *The Constitutional Jurisprudence of the Federal Republic of Germany*. Duke University Press.

Koop, Volker, and Dietmar Schössler. 1992. *Erbe NVA—Eindrücke aus ihrer Geschichte und den Tagen der Wende*. Waldbröl: Akademie der Bundeswehr für Information und Kommunikation.

Korte, Karl-Rudolf. 1990. *Der Standort der Deutschen: Akzentlagerungen der deutschen Frage in der Bundesrepublik Deutschland seit den siebziger Jahren*. Cologne: Wissenschaft und Politik.

Kovrig, Bennett. 1991. *Of Walls and Bridges: The United States and Eastern Europe*. New York University Press.

Kramer, Mark. 1989–90. "Beyond the Brezhnev Doctrine: A New Era in Soviet-East European Relations?" *International Security* 13 (Winter), pp. 25–67.

Kramer, Jane. 1992. "Letter from Europe." *New Yorker*, May 25, pp. 40–64.

Krause, Axel. 1991. *Inside the New Europe*. Harper Collins.

Krauthammer, Charles. 1992. "The Fragile Peace: 1989–93." *Washington Post*, October 30, p. A27.

Krenz, Egon. 1990. *Wenn Mauern fallen: Die friedliche Revolution: Vorgeschichte—Ablauf—Auswirkungen*. Vienna: Paul Neff.

Krisch, Henry. 1985. *The German Democratic Republic: The Search for Identity*. Boulder: Westview.

Kuby, Erich. 1990. *Der Preis der Einheit: Ein deutsches Europa formt sein Gesicht*. Hamburg: Konkret.

Kuhn, Ekkehard. 1992. *Der Tag der Entscheidung: Leipzig, 9 Oktober 1989*. Berlin: Ullstein.

Kunze, Reiner. 1990. *Deckname "Lyrik": Eine Dokumentation von Rainer Kunze*. Frankfurt: Fischer Taschenbuch.

Kuppe, Johannes L. 1990. "Der Ausserordentliche Parteitag der SED." *Deutschland Archiv* 1 (January), pp. 52–58.

Küppers, Bernard. 1989. "Moskau bekräftigt Warnung vor deutschem Revanchismus." *Süddeutsche Zeitung*, December 1, p. 1.

Kusin, Vladimir. 1989. "Gorbachev's Evolving Attitude towards Eastern Europe." Radio Free Europe Research Background Report 128, July 20.

Kux, Ernst. 1991. "Revolution in Eastern Europe—Revolution in the West?" *Problems of Communism* 40 (May–June), pp. 1–13.

Laba, Roman. 1991. *The Roots of Solidarity: A Political Sociology of Poland's Working-Class Democratization*. Princeton University Press.

Lahann, Birgit. 1992. *Genosse Judas: Die zwei Leben des Ibrahim Böhme*. Berlin: Rowohlt.

Laird, Robbin. 1991a. *The Europeanization of the Alliance*. Boulder: Westview.

———. 1991b. "France, Germany, and the Future of the Alliance." In Wessell (1991), pp. 50–59.

———. 1991c. *The Soviets, Germany, and the New Europe*. Boulder: Westview.

Lang, Rainer, ed. 1990. *Das Umbaupapier (DDR): Argumente gegen die Wiedervereinigung*. Berlin: Rotbuch.

Langguth, Gerd, ed. 1990. *Berlin vom Brennpunkt der Teilung zur Brücke der Einheit*. Cologne: Wissenschaft und Politik.

Lapp, Peter Joachim. 1990. "Ehemalige DDR-Blockparteien auf der Suche nach Profil und Glaubwürdigkeit." *Deutschland Archiv* 1 (January), pp. 62–68.

———. 1992. "Probleme des Zusammenwachsens." *Deutschland Archiv* 6 (June), pp. 643–45.

Larrabee, F. Stephen, ed. 1989. *The Two German States and European Security*. St. Martin's.

Lawson, Dominic. 1990. "Saying the Unsayable." *Orbis* 34 (Fall), pp. 505–07.

Le Gloannec, Anne-Marie. 1991. *Die deutsch-deutsche Nation: Anmerkungen zu einer revolutionären Entwicklung*. Munich: Printul.

Lemke, Christiane. 1991. *Die Ursachen des Umbruchs 1989: Politische Sozialisation in der ehemaligen DDR*. Opladen: Westdeutscher.

Leonhard, Elke. 1991. *Wo sind Schmidts Erben? Die SPD auf dem Weg zur Macht*. Stuttgart: DVA.

Leonhard, Wolfgang. 1990. *Das kurze Leben der DDR: Berichte und Kommentare aus vier Jahrzehnten*. Stuttgart: Deutsche Verlags-Anstalt.

Lepenies, Wolf. 1992. *Folgen einer unerhörten Begebenheit: Die Deutschen nach der Vereinigung*. Berlin: Corso bei Siedler.

Lepgold, Joseph. 1990. *The Declining Hegemon: The United States and European Defense, 1960–1990*. Praeger.

Liebert, Ulrike, and Wolfgang Merkel, eds. 1991. *Die Politik zur deutschen Einheit: Probleme—Strategien—Kontroversen*. Opladen: Leske + Budrich.

Lippelt, Helmut. 1992. Interview. "'Die Lager müssen befreit werden.'" *Der Spiegel*, August 24, pp. 136–41.

Lipschitz, Leslie, and Donogh McDonald. 1990. *German Unification: Economic Issues*. Occasional Paper 75. Washington: International Monetary Fund.

Lisiecki, Jerzy. 1990. "Financial and Material Transfers between East and West Germany." *Soviet Studies* 42 (July), pp. 513–34.

Livingston, Robert Gerald, ed. 1983. *The Federal Republic of Germany in the 1980s: Foreign Policies and Domestic Changes*. New York: German Information Center.

———. 1992. "United Germany: Bigger and Better." *Foreign Policy* 87 (Summer), pp. 157–74.

Lochner, Axel, ed. 1990. *Linke Politik in Deutschland: Beiträge aus DDR und BRD*. Hamburg: Galgenberg.

Loest, Erich. 1990. *Der Zorn des Schafes: Aus meinem Tagewerk*. Leipzig: Lindenverlag.

———. 1991. *Die Stasi war mein Eckermann: Oder: Mein Leben mit der Wanze*. Göttingen: Steidl.

———. 1992. "Mao in Bitterfeld." *Deutschland Archiv* 7 (July), pp. 740–41ff.

Lösche, Peter, and Franz Walter. 1992. *Die SPD: Klassenpartei–Volkspartei—Quotenpartei: Zur Entwicklung der Sozialdemokratie von Weimar bis zur deutschen Vereinigung.* Darmstadt Wissenschaftliche Buchgesellschaft.

Lovenduski, Joni, and Jean Woodall. 1987. *Politics and Society in Eastern Europe.* Indiana University Press.

Lowe, Karl, and Thomas-Durell Young. 1991. "Multinational Corps in NATO." *Survival* 33 (January–February), pp. 66–77.

Löwenthal, Richard. 1986. *The Federal Republic: An Integral Part of the Western World.* German Issues 2. Washington: American Institute for Contemporary German Studies (June).

Lucas, Michael R. 1990. *The Western Alliance after INF: Redefining U.S. Policy toward Europe and the Soviet Union.* Boulder: Lynne Rienner.

Ludwig, Michael. 1990. *Polen und die deutsche Frage, Mit einer Dokumentation zum deutsch-polnischen Vertrag vom 17. Juni 1991.* Bonn: Europa.

Maaz, Hans-Joachim. 1990. *Der Gefühlsstau: Ein Psychogramm der DDR.* Berlin: Argon.

———. 1991. *Das gestürzte Volk: Die verunglückte Einheit.* Berlin: Argon.

McAdams, A. James. 1985. *East Germany and Detente: Building Authority after the Wall.* Cambridge University Press.

———. 1986. "Inter-German Detente: A New Balance." *Foreign Affairs* 65 (Fall), pp. 136–53.

McCauley, Martin. 1979. *Marxism-Leninism in the German Democratic Republic.* London: Macmillan.

Macgregor, Douglas A. 1989. *The Soviet-East German Military Alliance.* Cambridge University Press.

McNamara, Robert S. 1989. *Out of the Cold: New Thinking for American Foreign and Defense Policy in the 21st Century.* Simon & Schuster.

Macropaedia. 1988. 15th ed., vol. 20. Chicago: Encyclopaedia Britannica, p. 123.

Maier, Charles S. 1988. *The Unmasterable Past: History, Holocaust, and German National Identity.* Harvard University Press.

Malcolm, Neil. 1989. *Soviet Policy Perspectives on Western Europe.* New York: Council on Foreign Relations Press.

Malek, Bernhard. 1991. *Wolfgang Ullmann: "Ich werde nicht schweigen."* Berlin: Dietz.

Mantzke, Martin. 1990. "Eine Republik auf Abruf: Die DDR nach der Wahl vom 18. März 1990." *Europa-Archiv,* April 25, pp. 287–92.

Markovits, Andrei S. 1991a. "Eine ernüchternde Erfahrung." *Die Zeit,* February 22.

———. 1991b. " 'Die Linke gibt es nicht—und es gibt sie doch.' " *Frankfurter Rundschau,* March 7, p. 6.

Markovits, Andrei, and Jürgen Hoffman. 1991. "Ein amerikanischer Jude und eine deutsche Friedensrede." *Frankfurter Rundschau,* February 16, p. 6.

Markovits, Andrei S., and Simon Reich. 1991. "Should Europe Fear the Germans?" *German Politics and Society* (Summer), pp. 1–20.

Maron, Monika. 1991. *Stille Zeile Sechs.* Frankfurt/Main: S. Fischer.

———. 1992. " 'Peinlich, blamabel, lächerlich,' " *Der Spiegel,* August 24, pp. 136–41.

Marsh, David. 1989. *The Germans: Rich, Bothered and Divided.* London: Century.

———. 1992. *The Bundesbank: The Bank that Rules Europe.* London: Heinemann.

Marsh, David, and others. 1989. "Krenz Declares Socialist Loyalty." *Financial Times,* November 25, pp. 1, 22.

Mastny, Vojtech. 1992. *The Helsinki Process and the Reintegration of Europe 1986–1991.* New York University Press.

May, Michael M., Paul T. Herman, and Sybil Francis. 1989. "Dealing with Nuclear Weapons in Europe." *Survival* 31 (March–April), pp. 157–70.

Mayer, Hans. 1991a. "Der Fall einer Grösse: Die zwei Seelen in der Brust des Erich Honecker." *Süddeutsche Zeitung,* February 16–17, weekend supplement, p. II.

———. 1991b. *Der Turm von Babel: Erinnerung an eine Deutsche Demokratische Republic.* Frankfurt: Suhrkamp.

Mearsheimer, John. 1990a. "Back to the Future: Instability in Europe after the Cold War." *International Security* 15 (Summer), pp. 5–56.

———. 1990b. "Why We Will Soon Miss the Cold War." *Atlantic,* August, pp. 35–50.

Meissner, Boris. 1991. *Das Verhältnis von Partei und Staat in der UdSSR und DDR.* Cologne: Wissenschaft und Politik.

Menges, Constantine. 1991. *The Future of Germany and the Atlantic Alliance.* Washington: AEI Press.

Menon, Anand, Anthony Forster, and William Wallace. 1992. "A Common European Defence?" *Survival* 34 (Autumn), pp. 98–118.

Merkl, Peter H., ed. 1989. *The Federal Republic of Germany at Forty.* New York University Press.

Meyer, Thomas. 1991. *Was bleibt vom Sozialismus? Essay.* Reinbek: Rowohlt.

Meyer, Hans-Joachim. 1991. "Mit Augenmass und Festigkeit." *Frankfurter Allgemeine Zeitung,* May 25, "Bilder und Zeiten" section, p. 3.

Mielke, Erich. 1992. Interview. "Ich sterbe in diesem Kasten." *Der Spiegel,* August 31, pp. 38–53.

Miller, Steven E. 1992. "Western Diplomacy and the Soviet Nuclear Legacy." *Survival* 34 (Autumn), pp. 3–27.

Mitchell, R. Judson, and Teresa Gee. 1985. "The Soviet Succession Crisis and Its Aftermath." *Orbis* 28 (Summer), pp. 293–317.

Mitscherlich, Alexander, and Margarete Mitscherlich. 1991. *Die Unfähigkeit zu trauern: Grundlagen kollectiven Verhaltens.* Munich: Piper.

Mittag, Günter. 1991. *Um jeden Preis: Im Spannungsfeld zweier Systeme.* Berlin/Weimar: Aufbau.

Mitter, Armin, and Stefan Wolle, eds. 1990. *"Ich liebe euch doch alle . . . ," Befehle und Lageberichte des MfS, January–November 1989.* East Berlin: BasisDruck.

Möbius, Peter, and Helmut Trotnow. 1991. "Das Mauer-Komplott: Honecker verschärfte die Teilung Berlins von Tag zu Tag." *Die Zeit,* August 9, pp. 33–34.

Modrow, Hans. 1990. "Bilanz nach 150 Tagen." *Die Zeit,* April 13, p. 5; "Abschied von der zweiten Heimat." *Die Zeit,* April 20, pp. 5, 7; "Viele Fragen ohne Antworten." *Die Zeit,* April 27, pp. 6–7.

———. 1991. *Aufbruch und Ende.* Hamburg: Konkret.

Moeller, Michael Lukas, and Hans-Joachim Maaz. 1991. *Die Einheit beginnt zu zweit: Ein deutsch-deutsches Zwiegespräch.* Berlin: Rowohlt.

Moens, Alexander. 1991. "American Diplomacy and German Unification." *Survival* 33 (November–December), pp. 531–45.

Mohr, Heinrich. 1990. "'Trauer, Reue, Scham.'" *Deutschland Archiv* 9 (September), pp. 1367–71.

Moravcsik, Andrew. 1991. "Negotiating the Single European Act: National Interests and Conventional Statecraft in the European Community." *International Organization* 45 (Winter), pp. 19–56.

Moreton, N. Edwina. 1978. *East Germany and the Warsaw Alliance: The Politics of Detente*. Boulder: Westview.

———. 1987. *Germany between East and West*. Cambridge University Press.

Moreton, Edwina, and Gerald Segal, eds. 1984. *Soviet Strategy toward Western Europe*. London: Allen & Unwin.

Mortimer, Edward. 1992. "European Security after the Cold War." Adelphi Paper 271 (Summer). London: International Institute for Strategic Studies.

Mueller, John. 1989. *Retreat from Doomsday: The Obsolescence of Major War*. Basic Books.

Müller-Enbergs, Helmut, Marianne Schulz, and Jan Wielgohls, eds. 1991. *Von der Illegalität ins Parlament: Werdegang und konzept der neuen Bürgerbewegung*. Berlin: LinksDruck.

Müller, Harald. 1992. "German Foreign Policy after Unification." In Stares (1992), pp. 142–46.

Müller, Heiner. 1990. *Zur Lage der Nation: Heiner Müller im Interview mit Frank M. Raddatz*. Berlin: Rotbuch.

Muller, Steven, and Gebhard L. Schweigler, eds. 1992. *From Occupation to Co-operation: The United States and United Germany in a Changing World Order*. Norton.

National Academy of Sciences. 1991. *The Future of the U.S.-Soviet Nuclear Relationship*. Washington: National Academy Press.

Naumann, Klaus. 1991. "Sicherheitspolitik im Umbruch—Neue Herausforderungen an die Bundeswehr." Talk at the Friederich-Ebert-Stiftung, September 24.

Nawrocki, Joachim. 1988. *Relations between the Two States in Germany*. Bonn: Press and Information Office.

———. 1990. "Anwürfe aus dem Untergrund." *Die Zeit*, March 30, p. 11.

Nelson, Daniel. 1986. *Alliance Behavior in the Warsaw Pact*. Boulder: Westview.

———. 1987. *Defenders or Intruders? The Dilemmas of U.S. Forces in Germany*. Boulder: Westview.

Neubert, Ehrhart. 1992. "Das MfS und die Kirchenpolitik der SED: Schäden, Gefahren und Bewährung." *Deutschland Archiv* 4 (April), pp. 346–58.

Neues Forum Leipzig. 1989. *Jetzt oder nie-Demokratie: Leipziger Herbst '89*. Leipzig: Forum.

Nipperdey, Thomas. 1990. *Nachdenken über die deutsche Geschichte: Essays*. Munich: dtv Geschichte.

Noack, Paul. 1991. *"Deutschland, deine Intellektuellen": Die Kunst, sich ins Abseits zu stellen*. Stuttgart: Bonn Aktuell.

Noelle-Neumann, Elisabeth. 1988. "Wenn das Gefühl der Bedrohung schwindet: Die Verteidigungspolitik vor einem Wachsenden Akzeptanz-Problem." *Frankfurter Allgemeine Zeitung*, July 22, p. 6.

Nye, Joseph S. 1990. *Bound to Lead: The Changing Nature of American Power.* Basic Books.

O'Brien, Conor Cruise. 1989. "Beware, the Reich is Reviving." *Times* (London), October 31.

Oberdorfer, Don. 1991. *The Turn: From the Cold War to a New Era, 1983–1990: The United States and the Soviet Union.* New York: Poseidon.

OECD. 1992. *Germany.* Paris: Organization for Economic Cooperation and Development, July.

Oldenburg, Fred. 1990. "Sowjetische Deutschland-Politik nach der Oktober-Revolution in der DDR." *Deutschland Archiv* 1 (January), pp. 68–76.

Opp, Dieter. 1991. "DDR '89. Zu den Ursachen einer spontanen Revolution." *Kölner Zeitschrift für Soziologie* 43.

Orden, Geoffrey Van. 1991. "The Bundeswehr in Transition." *Survival* 33 (July–August), pp. 352–70.

Palmer, John. 1987. *Europe without America? The Crisis in Atlantic Relations.* Oxford University Press.

Pannen, Stefan. 1992. "'Geheimdienste und politische Polizei in der modernen Gesellschaft.'" *Deutschland Archiv* 4 (April), pp. 413–15.

Peel, Quentin, and David Goodhart. 1989. "Moscow Calls on Bonn to Renounce Pre-War Frontiers." *Financial Times*, November 30, pp. 1, 16.

Perle, Richard N. 1991. *Reshaping Western Security: The United States Faces a United Europe.* Washington: AEI Press.

Peters, Susanne. 1990. *The Germans and the INF Missiles: Getting Their Way in NATO's Strategy of Flexible Response.* Baden-Baden: Nomos.

Petschow, Ulrich, Jürgen Meyerhoff, and Claus Thomasberger. 1990. *Umweltreport DDR.* Frankfurt: S. Fischer.

Pfaltzgraff, Robert L., Jr., and others. 1983. *The Greens of West Germany: Origins, Strategies, and Transatlantic Implications.* Cambridge: Institute for Foreign Policy Analysis.

Phillips, Ann L. 1986. *Soviet Policy toward East Germany Reconsidered: The Postwar Decade.* New York: Greenwood Press.

———. 1989. "Seeds of Change in the German Democratic Republic: The SPD–SED Dialogue." Research Reports no. 1. Washington: American Institute for Contemporary German Studies.

Pierre, Andrew J., ed. 1986a. *The Conventional Defense of Europe: New Technologies and New Strategies.* New York: Council on Foreign Relations.

———. 1986b. *A Widening Atlantic? Domestic Change and Foreign Policy.* New York: Council on Foreign Relations.

Pinder, John. 1991. *The European Community and Eastern Europe.* New York: Council on Foreign Relations Press.

Pollack, Detlef, ed. 1990a. *Die Legitimität der Freiheit: Politisch alternative Gruppen in der DDR unter dem Dach der Kirche: Forschungen zur Praktischen Theologie 8.* Frankfurt on Main: Peter Lang.

———. 1990b. "Religion und Gesellschaftlicher Wandel." *Übergänge* 6 (December), pp. 236–43.

Pond, Elizabeth. 1991. "After Gulf War, a Drive Toward European Unity." *Boston Globe*, March 31.

Pragel, Peter, and Ulrich Völklein. 1987. "Jedes Land wählt seine Lösung." *Stern*, April 9, pp. 140–44.

Przybylski, Peter. 1991, 1992. *Tatort Politbüro: Die Akte Honecker.* vol. 1. *Tatort Politbüro: Honecker, Mittag und Schalck-Golodkowski.* vol. 2. Berlin: Rowohlt.

Rabla, Kurt, Christoph Stoll, and Manfred Vasold. 1988. *From the U.S. Constitution to the Basic Law of the Federal Republic of Germany.* Gräfelfing: Moos & Partner.

Reeb, Hans-Joachim. 1992. "Eingliederung ehemaliger NVA-Berufssoldaten in die Bundeswehr." *Deutschland Archiv* 8 (August), pp. 845–57.

Rehlinger, Ludwig A. 1991. *Freikauf: Die Geschäfte der DDR mit politisch Verfolgten 1963–1989.* Berlin: Ullstein.

Reich, Jens. 1991. *Rückkehr nach Europa: Bericht zur neuen Lage der deutschen Nation.* Munich: Carl Hanser.

———. 1992. *Abschied von den Lebenslügen: Die Intelligenz und die Macht.* Berlin: Rowohlt.

Reich-Ranicki, Marcel. 1991. "Der leidende Liedermacher." *Frankfurter Allgemeine Zeitung*, October 26, "Bilder und Zeiten" section, p. 4.

Rein, Gerhard, ed. 1990. *Die Protestantische Revolution 1987–1990: Ein deutsches Lesebuch.* Berlin: Wichern.

Reinicke, Wolfgang H. 1992. "Toward a New European Political Economy." In Stares (1992), p. 192.

Reissig, Rolf, and Gert-Joachim Glaessner, eds. 1991. *Das Ende eines Experiments: Umbruch in der DDR und deutsche Einheit.* Berlin: Dietz.

Reshetar, John S., Jr. 1989. *The Soviet Polity: Government and Politics in the USSR.* 3d ed. Harper & Row.

Richter, Edelbert. 1991. *Christentum und Demokratie in Deutschland: Beiträge zur geistigen Vorbereitung der Wende in der DDR.* Leipzig and Weimar: Gustav Kiepenheuer.

Rielly, John E., ed. 1991a. *American Public Opinion and U.S. Foreign Policy, 1991.* Chicago Council on Foreign Relations.

———. 1991b. "Public Opinion: The Pulse of the '90s." *Foreign Policy* 82 (Spring), pp. 79–96.

Risse-Kappen, Thomas. 1988. *Die Krise der Sicherheitspolitik: Neuorientierungen und Entscheidungsprozesse im politischen System der Bundesrepublik Deutschland 1977–1984.* Mainz: Matthias-Grünewald and Munich: Kaiser.

Rizopoulos, Nicholas X., ed. 1990. *Sea-Changes: American Foreign Policy in a World Transformed.* New York: Council on Foreign Relations Press.

Roberts, Brad, ed. 1992. *U.S. Foreign Policy after the Cold War.* MIT Press.

Roberts, Frank. 1991. "In the Heat of the Cold War." *Financial Times*, August 24.

Rollo, J. M. C. 1990. *The New European Europe: Western Responses.* New York: Council on Foreign Relations Press.

Rosenthal, A. M. 1990. "Let's Keep Hearing About the German Yesterday." *International Herald Tribune*, February 5, p. 8.

———. 1992. "Germany Is Everyone's Business." *International Herald Tribune*, September 23, p. 8.

Rosolowsky, Diane. 1987. *West Germany's Foreign Policy: The Impact of the Social Democrats and the Greens.* New York: Greenwood Press.

Rotfeld, Adam Daniel, and Walther Stützle, eds. 1991. *Germany and Europe in Transition*. Oxford University Press.

Rubinstein, Alvin Z. 1989. *Soviet Foreign Policy since World War II: Imperial and Global*. Scott, Foresman.

Rückerl, Adalbert. 1979. *The Investigation of Nazi Crimes 1945–1978*. Heidelberg: C. F. Müller.

Rudolph, Hermann. 1990. "Abgerechnet—mit der DDR überhaupt." *Süddeutsche Zeitung*, March 20, p. 4.

Rueschemeyer, Marilyn, and Christiane Lemke. 1989. *The Quality of Life in the German Democratic Republic*. Armonk, N.Y.: M. E. Sharpe.

Rühle, Jürgen, and Günter Holzweissig. 1981. *13. August 1961: Die Mauer von Berlin*. Cologne: Edition Deutschland Archiv.

Rumer, Eugene B. 1989. "The German Question in Moscow's 'Common European Home': A Background to the Revolutions of 1989." RAND Note N-3220-USDP. Santa Monica, Calif.: RAND.

Rusi, Alpo M. 1991. *After the Cold War: Europe's New Political Architecture*. St. Martin's.

Sandford, John. 1983. *The Sword and the Ploughshare: Autonomous Peace Initiatives in East Germany*. London: Merlin for END.

Sauer, Heiner, and Hans-Otto Plumeyer. 1991. *Der Salzgitter Report: Die zentrale Erfassungsstelle bericht über Verbrechen im SED-Staat*. Esslingen-Munich: Bechtle.

Sbragia, Alberta M., ed. 1992. *Euro-Politics: Institutions and Policymaking in the "New" European Community*. Brookings.

Schädlich, Hans Joachim, ed. 1992. *Aktenkundig*. Berlin: Rowohlt.

Schabowski, Günter. 1990. *Das Politbüro: Ende eines Mythos* (from interviews with Frank Sieren and Ludwig Koehne). Reinbek: Rororo.

———. 1991. *Der Absturz*. Berlin: Rowohlt.

Schäuble, Wolfgang. 1991. *Der Vertrag: Wie ich über die deutsche Einheit verhandelte*. Stuttgart: Deutsche Verlags-Anstalt.

Schell, Manfred, and Werner Kalinka. 1991a. "Mielke leitete den Sturz Honeckers ein." *Die Welt*, July 11, p. 4.

———. 1991b. *Stasi und kein Ende: Die Personen und Fakten*. Frankfurt/Main: Die Welt/Ullstein.

Schirrmacher, Frank. 1990a. "Dem Druck des härteren, strengeren Lebens standhalten." *Frankfurter Allgemeine Zeitung*, June 2.

———. 1990b. *Im Osten erwacht die Geschichte: Essays zur Revolution in Mittel- und Ost Europa*. Stuttgart: Deutsche Verlags-Anstalt.

———. 1990c. "Jeder ist mit seiner Wahrheit allein." *Frankfurter Allgemeine Zeitung*, April 10, pp. L1–L2.

———. 1991. "Eilige Wortführer: Stefan Heym dankt Helmut Kohl." *Frankfurter Allgemeine Zeitung*, September 11, p. 33.

Schlomann, Friedrich-Wilhelm. 1992. "Strukturen und Methoden des MfS in Rostock." *Deutschland Archiv* 5 (May), pp. 550–52.

Schmidt, Helmut. 1990a. *Die Deutschen und ihre Nachbarn*. Berlin: Siedler.

———. 1990b. *Men and Powers: A Political Retrospective*. Random House.

Schmoll, Heike. 1992. "War die Kirchenbundgründung von der SED geplant?" *Frankfurter Allgemeine Zeitung*, October 9, p. 3.

Schneider, Michael. 1991. *Die abgetriebene Revolution: Von der Staatsfirma in die DM-Kolonie*. Berlin: Elefantenpress.

Schneider, Peter. 1989. "Was wäre, wenn die Mauer fällt." *Tageszeitung*, November 14, pp. 13–14.

———. 1990a. *Extreme Mittelage: Eine Reise durch das deutsche Nationalgefühl*. Reinbek: Rowohlt.

———. 1990b. "Mann kann ein Erdbeben auch verpassen." *Die Zeit*, April 27, pp. 57–58. Also printed in *German Politics and Society* 20 (Summer 1990), pp. 1–21.

———. 1990c. "'Wir haben uns bei den Mächtigen wohl gefühlt.'" *Die Zeit*, May 4, p. 80.

———. 1991a. *The German Comedy*. Farrar, Straus & Giroux.

———. 1991b. "Weil er keinen Anwalt hatte, blendete sich Ödipus." *Frankfurter Allgemeine Zeitung*, October 26, p. 29.

Schneider, Rolf. 1991. "Von linker Melancholie." *Der Spiegel*, August 19, pp. 46–47.

Schnibben, Cordt. 1990. " 'Diesmal sterbe ich, Schwester.' " *Der Speigel*, October 8, pp. 102–09.

Schönbohm, Jörg. 1992. *Zwei Armeen und ein Vaterland: Das Ende der nationalen Volksarmee*. Berlin: Siedler.

Schorlemmer, Friedrich. 1992a. "Die Früchte der Freiheit ernten." *Die Zeit*, July 31, p. 6.

———. 1992b. *Worte öffnen Fäuste: Die Rückkehr in ein schwieriges Vaterland*. Munich: Kindler.

Schröder, Richard. 1990a. "Erblast der Gespensterfurcht." *Frankfurter Allgemeine Zeitung*, September 29.

———. 1990b. "'Naturschutzpark für 'DDR-Identität.'" *Neue Zürcher Zeitung*, April 22.

———. 1991a. "Es ist doch nicht alles schlecht." *Die Zeit*, May 31.

———. 1991b. "Soll die Zersetzungsarbeit endlos weitergehen?" *Frankfurter Allgemeine Zeitung*, January 2, p. 23.

Schueler, Hans. 1992. "Die Schuld des Gesellen." *Die Zeit*, July 31, p. 3.

Schulz, Eberhard. 1982. *Die deutsche Nation in Europa: Internationale und historische Dimensionen*. Bonn: Europa Union.

———. 1989. *Die deutsche Frage und die Nachbarn im Osten*. Munich: R. Oldenbourg.

Schürer, Gerhard. 1992. Interview. "Das reale Bild War eben Katastrophal!" *Deutschland Archiv* 10 (October), pp. 1031–39.

Schwartz, David N. 1983. *NATO's Nuclear Dilemmas*. Brookings.

Schwarz, Hans-Peter. 1985. *Die gezähmten Deutschen: Von der Machtbesessenheit zur Machtvergessenheit*. Stuttgart: Deutsche Verlags-Anstalt.

Schweigler, Gebhard. 1985. *Grundlagen der aussenpolitischen Orientierung der Bundesrepublik Deutschland: Rahmenbedingungen, Motive Einstellungen*. Baden-Baden: Nomos.

Scruton, Roger. 1989. "Don't Trust the Germans." *Sunday Telegraph*, May 21, 1989.

Seebacher-Brandt, Brigitte. 1989. "Die Linke und die Einheit." *Frankfurter Allgemeine Zeitung*, November 21.

———. 1990a. "Moskaus Spiel mit kleiner Münze." *Rheinische Merkur*, February 9.

———. 1990b. "Warum Totgesagtes lange lebt: Was bleibt von der DDR?" *Frankfurter Allgemeine Zeitung Magazine*, April 20, pp. 50–62.

———. 1991. *Die Linke und die Einheit.* Berlin: Corso bei Siedler.

Serfaty, Simon. 1992. *Taking Europe Seriously.* St. Martin's.

Serke, Jürgen. 1990. "Das ausgestrichene Leben des Chris Gueffroy." *Die Welt*, June 2.

Sherwood, Elizabeth D. 1990. *Allies in Crisis: Meeting Global Challenges to Western Security.* Yale University Press.

Shevardnadze, Eduard. 1989. Speech to European Parliament's Foreign Affairs Committee, Brussels, December 19, translated in FBIS, December 20, pp. 25–28.

———. 1991. *The Future Belongs to Freedom.* Free Press.

———. 1992. Interview. " 'Unser Gewissen ist rein.' " *Der Spiegel*, April 13, pp. 193–98.

Sigal, Leon V. 1984. *Nuclear Forces in Europe: Enduring Dilemmas, Present Prospects.* Brookings.

Simons, Thomas W., Jr. 1990. *The End of the Cold War?* St. Martin's.

———. 1991. *Eastern Europe in the Postwar World.* St. Martin's.

Sindermann, Horst. 1990. Interview. "'Wir sind keine Helden gewesen': Der frühere Volkskammer-Präsident Horst Sindermann über Macht und Ende der SED." *Der Spiegel*, May 7, pp. 53–66.

SIPRI Yearbook 1991: Armaments and Disarmament. 1991. Stockholm International Peace Research Institute.

Sloan, Stanley R. 1985. *NATO's Future: Toward a New Transatlantic Bargain.* Washington: National Defense University Press.

———. 1989. *NATO in the 1990s.* Washington: Pergamon-Brassey's.

Slocombe, Walter B. 1990. "Strategic Stability in a Restructured World." *Survival* 32 (July–August), pp. 299–312.

Sloterdijk, Peter. 1990. *Versprechen auf Deutsch: Rede über das eigene Land.* Frankfurt: Suhrkamp.

Smyser, William R. 1990. *Restive Partners—Washington and Bonn Diverge.* Boulder: Westview.

———. 1991. "U.S.S.R.-Germany: A Link Restored." *Foreign Policy* 84 (Fall 1991), pp. 125–41.

Snyder, Jack. 1990. "Averting Anarchy in the New Europe." *International Security* 15 (Spring), pp. 5–41.

Social Democratic Party. 1985. "Konzept für die Selbstbehauptung Europas." April 11. Bonn.

Sodaro, Michael J. 1990. *Moscow, Germany, and the West from Khrushchev to Gorbachev.* Cornell University Press.

Sommer, Theo. 1989a. "A Dog That Doesn't Bark." *Newsweek,* November 20, p. 39.

————. 1989b. "Wem gehört die deutsche Frage?" *Die Zeit*, December 15, p. 3.

Souchon, Lennart. 1991. *Neue deutsche Sicherheitspolitik*. Herford: Mittler & Sohn.

Spangenberg, Dietrich, ed. 1987. *Die blockierte Vergangenheit: Nachdenken über Mitteleuropa*. Berlin: Argon.

Spanger, Hans-Joachim. 1989. *The GDR in East-West Relations*. International Institute for Strategic Studies Adelphi Paper 240, pp. 1–88.

Spittmann, Ilse. 1988. "Irritationen zur Jahreswende." *Deutschland Archiv* 1 (January), pp. 1–4.

————. 1990a. *Die DDR unter Honecker*. Cologne: Wissenschaft und Politik.

————. 1990b. "Deutschland einig Vaterland," *Deutschland Archiv* 2 (February), pp. 187–90.

Spotts, Frederic. 1973. *The Churches and Politics in Germany*. Wesleyan University Press.

Stares, Paul. 1990. *Allied Rights and Legal Constraints on German Military Power*. Brookings.

————, ed. 1992. *The New Germany and the New Europe*. Brookings.

Stolpe, Manfred. 1992. *Schwieriger Aufbruch*. Berlin: Siedler.

Stolz, Rolf. 1990. *Der deutsche Komplex: Alternativen zur Selbstverleugnung*. Bonn: Straube.

Stromseth, Jane E. 1988. *The Origins of Flexible Response: NATO's Debate over Strategy in the 1960s*. St. Martin's.

Stürmer, Michael. 1992. *Die Grenzen der Macht: Begegnung der Deutschen mit der Geschichte*. Berlin: Siedler.

Süskind, Patrick. 1990a. *Angst vor Deutschland*. Hamburg: Hoffmann und Campe.

————. 1990b. "Deutschland, eine Midlife-crisis." *Der Spiegel*, September 17, pp. 116–25.

Süss, Walter. 1991a. "Bilanz einer Gratwanderung—Die kurze Amtszeit des Hans Modrow." *Deutschland Archiv* 6 (June), pp. 596–608.

————. 1991b. "Mit Unwillen zur Macht: Der runde Tisch in der DDR der Übergangszeit." *Deutschland Archiv* 5 (May), pp. 470–78.

Süssmuth, Hans, ed. 1990. *Wie geht es weiter mit Deutschland? Politisches Gespräch am 24./25. Januar 1990*. Baden-Baden: Nomos.

Szabo, Stephen F., ed. 1990. *The Bundeswehr and Western Security*. St. Martin's.

————. 1992. *The Diplomacy of German Unification*. St. Martin's.

Talbott, Strobe. 1984. *Deadly Gambits: The Reagan Administration and the Stalemate in Nuclear Arms Control*. Knopf.

Taylor, Trevor. 1991. "NATO and Central Europe." *NATO Review* 39 (October), pp. 17–22.

Teltschik, Horst. 1991. *329 Tage: Innenansichten der Einigung*. Berlin: Siedler.

Terry, Sarah Meiklejohn, ed. 1984. *Soviet Policy in Eastern Europe*. Yale University Press.

Thatcher, Margaret. 1990. Interview. "Alle gegen Deutschland—Nein!" *Der Spiegel*, March 26, pp. 182–87.

Thaysen, Uwe. 1990. *Der runde Tisch: Oder: Wo blieb das Volk? Der Weg der DDR in die Demokratie*. Opladen: Westdeutscher.

Thierse, Wolfgang. 1992. *Mit eigener Stimme sprechen*. Munich: Piper.

Thies, Jochen, and Wolfgang Wagner, eds. 1990. *Das Ende der Teilung: Der Wandel in Deutschland und Osteuropa*. Bonn: Verlag für internationale Politik.

Thies, Jochen. 1991. "German Unification—Opportunity or Setback for Europe?" *The World Today* 47 (January), pp. 8–11.

Thurow, Lester. 1992. *Head to Head: The Coming Economic Battle among Japan, Europe and America*. William Morrow.

Tismaneanu, Vladimir. 1992. *Reinventing Politics: Eastern Europe from Stalin to Havel*. Free Press.

Tranholm-Mikkelsen, Jeppe. 1991. "Neofunctionalism: Obstinate or Obsolete? A Reappraisal in the Light of the New Dynamism of the EC." *Millennium* 20 (no. 1), pp. 1–22.

Treverton, Gregory F. 1992a. *America, Germany, and the Future of Europe*. Princeton University Press.

———. 1992b. *The Shape of the New Europe*. New York: Council on Foreign Relations.

Tsoukalis, Loukas. 1992. *The New European Community: The Politics and Economics of Integration*. Oxford University Press.

Turner, Henry Ashby, Jr. 1987. *The Two Germanies since 1945*. Yale University Press.

U.S. Information Agency. 1990. Research Memorandum, February 14.

U.S. State Department. 1989. *Policy Information and Texts*. No. 148, December 1.

Ullman, Richard H. 1989. "The Covert French Connection." *Foreign Policy* 75 (Summer), pp. 3–33.

———. 1990. "Enlarging the Zone of Peace." *Foreign Policy* 80 (Fall), pp. 102–20.

———. 1991. *Securing Europe*. Princeton University Press.

Ullmann, Wolfgang. 1992. *Verfassung und Parlament: Ein Beitrag zur Verfassungsdiskussion*. Berlin: Dietz.

Van Evera, Stephen. 1990–91. "Primed for Peace: Europe after the Cold War." *International Security* 15 (Winter), pp. 7–57.

Vine, Richard D., ed. 1987. *Soviet-East European Relations as a Problem for the West*. London: Croom Helm.

Voigt, Karsten D. 1990. "Deutsche Einheit und gesamteuropäische Ordnung des Friedens und der Freiheit." *Deutschland Archiv* 4 (April), pp. 562–68.

Waever, Ole. 1990. "Three Competing Europes: German, French, Russian." *International Affairs* 66 (July), pp. 477–93.

Wagner, Irmgard. 1991. "Divided Literature in a United Germany?—A Western Perspective." Paper prepared for Pacific Workshop on German Affairs, April.

Walker, Jenonne. 1991. "New Thinking about Conventional Arms Control." *Survival* 33 (January–February), pp. 53–65.

Wallace, William. 1990. *The Transformation of Western Europe*. New York: Council on Foreign Relations Press.

Wallach, H. G. Peter, and Ronald A. Francisco. 1992. *United Germany: The Past, Politics, Prospects*. Westport, Conn.: Greenwood.

Walser, Martin. 1989. *Über Deutschland reden*. Frankfurt: Suhrkamp.

Walther, Joachim, and others. 1991. *Protokoll eines Tribunals: Die Ausschüsse aus dem DDR-Schriftstellerverband 1979*. Reinbek: Rororo.

Wander, W. Thomas, and Eric H. Arnett. 1992. *The Proliferation of Advanced Weaponry: Technology, Motivations, and Responses.* Washington: American Association for the Advancment of Science.

Watson, Alan. 1992. *The Germans: Who Are They Now?* London: Methuen.

Wawrzyn, Lienhard. 1990. *Der Blaue: Das Spitzelsystem der DDR.* Berlin: Klaus Wagenbach.

Weber, Hermann. 1985. *Geschichte der DDR.* Munich: Deutscher Taschenbuch Verlag.

Weidenfeld, Werner, and others. 1989. *Geschichtsbewusstsein der Deutschen: Materialien zur Spurensuchen einer Nation.* Cologne: Wissenschaft und Politik.

Weidenfeld, Werner, and Hartmut Zimmermann. 1989. *Deutschland-Handbuch: Eine doppelte Bilanz 1949–1989.* vol. 275. Bonn: Bundeszentrale für politische Bildung.

Weidenfeld, Werner, ed. 1990. *Die Deutschen und die Architektur des Europäischen Hauses: Materialen zu den Perspektiven Deutschlands.* Cologne: Wissenschaft und Politik.

Weidenfeld, Werner, and Karl-Rudolf Korte. 1991. *Die Deutschen: Profil einer Nation.* Stuttgart: Klett-Cotta.

Weidenfeld, Werner, and Josef Janning, eds. 1991. *Global Responsibilities: Europe in Tomorrow's World.* Gütersloh: Bertelsmann Foundation.

Weidenfeld, Werner. 1992. *Deutschland: Eine Nation—doppelte Geschichte: Materialien zum deutschen Selbstvertändnis.* Cologne: Wissenschaft und Politik.

Weimer, Wolfram. 1991. "Vom Kassenwart der Diktatur zum Informanten der Bonner Regierung." *Frankfurter Allgemeine Zeitung,* August 10, p. 3.

Weisenfeld, Ernst. 1991. "Mitterands Europäische Konföderation: Eine Idee im Spannungsfeld der Realitäten." *Europa Archiv,* September 10, pp. 513–18.

Weizsäcker, Richard von. 1992. *Richard von Weizsäcker: Im Gespräch mit Gunter Hofmann und Werner A. Perger.* Frankfurt: Eichborn.

Wellershoff, Dieter, ed. 1991. *Frieden ohne Macht? Sicherheitspolitik in konfliktarmer Zeit und Streitkräfte.* Bonn: Bouvier.

Wells, Samuel, Jr., ed. 1991. *The Helsinki Process and the Future of Europe.* Washington: Wilson Center Press.

Wessell, Nils H., ed. 1991. *The New Europe: Revolution in East-West Relations.* New York: Proceedings of the Academy of Political Science 38 (no. 1).

Wettig, Gerhard. 1990. "The German Problem in Soviet Policy." *Aussenpolitik* 41 (First Quarter), pp. 38–51.

———. 1991. "Betrifft: Jens Kaiser, Sowjetische Aussenpolitik in den achtziger Jahren." *Deutschland Archiv* 8 (August), pp. 846–47.

Wiedemann, Erich. 1990. *Die deutschen Ängste: Ein Volk in Moll.* Frankfurt: Ullstein.

Wielgohs, Jan, and Marianne Schulz. 1990. "Reformbewegung und Volksbewegung: Politische und soziale Aspekte in Umbruch der DDR-Gesellschaft." *Aus Politik und Zeitgeschichte: Beilage zur Wochenzeitung Das Parlament,* B16–17/90, April 13, pp. 15–24.

Wilke, Manfred, and Hans-Hermann Hertle. 1992. *Das Genossenkartell: Die SED und die IG-Druck und Papier/IG Medien.* Berlin: Ullstein.

Wilkening, Christina. 1990. *Staat im Staate: Auskünfte ehemaliger Stasi-Mitarbeiter.* Berlin/Weimar: Aufbau.

Winckler, Lutz, and Françoise Barthelemy. 1990. *Mein Deutschland findet sich in keinem Atlas: Schriftsteller aus beiden deutschen Staaten über ihr nationales Selbstverständnis.* Frankfurt: Luchterhand.

Winters, Peter Jochen. 1987. "Erich Honecker in der Bundesrepublik." *Deutschland Archiv* 10 (October), pp. 1009–16.

————. 1992. "Was Erich Honecker den Deutschen politisch angetan hat, kann kein Strafgericht sühnen." *Frankfurter Allgemeine Zeitung*, July 31, p. 3.

Wirsing, Sibylle. 1989. "Deutschland einig Vaterland." *Frankfurter Allgemeine Zeitung*, November 29, p. 3.

Wolf, Christa. 1990a. *Im Dialog: Aktuelle Texte.* Frankfurt: Luchterhand.

————. 1990b. *Was bleibt: Eine Erzählung.* Frankfurt: Luchterhand.

Wolf, Markus. 1990. "In eigenem Auftrag," *Stern*, November 29, p. 110.

————. 1991. *In eigenem Auftrag: Bekenntnisse und Einsichten.* Munich: Franz Schneekluth.

Wolle, Stefan. 1992. "Der Weg in den Zusammenbruch: Die DDR vom Januar bis zum Oktober 1989." In Jesse and Mitter (1992), pp. 73–110.

Worst, Anne, and others. 1991. *Das Ende eines Geheimdienstes: Oder: Wie lebendig ist die Stasi?* Berlin: LinksDruck.

Wyle, Frederick S. 1991. "Europhantasien und die Feinabstimmung der europäischen Sicherheit." *Europa Archiv*, July 10, pp. 389–94.

Yost, David S. 1988. *Soviet Ballistic Missile Defense and the Western Alliance.* Harvard University Press.

Zimmermann, Hartmut, ed. 1985. *DDR Handbuch.* vols. I, II. 3d ed. Cologne: Wissenschaft und Politik.

Index

Abrasimov, Pyotr, 104, 124
Acheson, Dean, 249
Adenauer, Konrad, 5,19; France, relations with, 58–59; GDR, relations with, 24, 25; incorporation of right into political system by, 14–15
AfNS. *See* Office for National Security (AfNS)
Alliance for Germany coalition, 197–98
Alliance 90 party (GDR), 199
Allied Control Council, 168
Anderson, Sascha, 227, 229
Andriessen, Frans, 160
Antiballistic missile (ABM) treaty, U.S.-Soviet, 47, 50
Antinuclear movement. *See* Peace movement
Arms control: effect of German unification and collapse of Soviet Union on, 237–38; effect of INF on, 39–41, 44–48, 50–54; NATO summit negotiations, 54–55
Arms sales, control of, 261
Aslund, Anders, 23
Association for Mutual Farmers (GDR), 145
Augstein, Rudolf, 168, 207, 241
Axen, Hermann, 108, 111

Baader-Meinhof gang, 16
Bahr, Egon, 174, 204, 205
Baker, James, 97, 138, 169; on Conventional Forces in Europe Treaty, 262; on German membership in NATO, 179; on German

unification, 162, 163, 164, 169, 178, 179; Soviets' relations with, 165–66
Baltic states, 89
Bartholomew, Reginald, 213
Baudissin, Wolf von, 13
Berger, Götz, 11
Berghofer, Wolfgang, 108
Beria, Lavrenti, 25
Berlin Wall, 21, 58, 79; fall of, 1–6, 132–34
Bernstein, Leonard, 5
Beuys, Joseph, 17
Biedenkopf, Kurt, 119, 244
Biermann, Wolf, 11, 22, 229
Biological weapons, 238
Bismarck, Otto von, 27
Blackwill, Robert, 162, 164, 213
Bohley, Bärbel, 96, 134, 200
Böhme, Ibrahim, 198, 201
Border crossings, opening of, 1–6, 10, 130–32, 169
Brandt, Willy, 4–5, 16, 119, 137, 206; *Ostpolitik* of, 4, 24, 203
Braun, Edgar, 229
Brecht, Bertolt, 15, 200
Brezhnev, Leonid, 20, 21, 71, 123; nuclear missile policy of, 39
Brezhnev doctrine, 74, 88, 188
Broder, Henryk M., 124
Britain. *See* Great Britain
Brzezinski, Zbigniew, 53, 188
Bulgaria, 11
Bush, George, administration of: arms con-

trol negotiations, 54–55; position on German-Polish boundary dispute, 194–95; position on German unification, 153–54, 162–64, 167–69, 173, 215; refusal to scrap NATO, 189

Carter, Jimmy, administration of, 38, 60, 162
Catholic church, 75, 95
Center for Democracy, 263
Central Office for Political Education, 226
Chemical weapons, 238
Chernenko, Konstantin, 21
China, 10, 88, 111–12
Christian Democratic Union party (GDR), 8, 144, 145, 247; on boundary dispute, 193; in elections of *1990*, 197–201; on unification, 136
Church. *See* Catholic church; Protestant church (GDR)
Clinton, Bill, administration of, 260
Collaborators, purges of, 227–30
Colombo, Emilio, 60–62
Common market. *See* European Community (EC)
Communist leadership: delegitimation of, in Eastern Europe, 70–71; disintegration of, in GDR, 6–8
Conference on Security and Cooperation in Europe (CSCE), 85, 87, 95, 169, 178, 189–91, 193, 213–19, 221, 228, 241, 243, 252, 255; future role of, 261–63, 267–68
Conflict Prevention Center, 262–63
Conventional Armed Forces in Europe, Treaty on, 53, 224, 238, 262
Convention on Refugees, 88
Coordinating Committee (Ko-Ko), 141
Council of Europe, 263
Cruise missiles, 29–30, 39
CSCE. *See* Conference on Security and Cooperation in Europe (CSCE)
Cuba, 58
Cultural revolution of *1968*, 15, 17, 206
Czechoslovakia, 11, 59, 69, 116; communist rule in, 71, 76; emigration of GDR citizens through, 96–99, 100–02; Warsaw Pact invasion of, 74

Dashichev, Vyacheslav, 188

De Gaulle, Charles, 35; FRG's relations with, 58, 59
Delors, Jacques, 160, 212, 234
de Maizière, Lothar, 8, 197, 198; as GDR prime minister, 200, 216
Democracy Now party (GDR), 96, 145
Democratic Awakening (GDR), 96, 145, 197, 198
Democratic Farmers party (GDR), 8, 144, 145
Détente: between eastern and western Germany, 23–26, 29; between eastern and western nations, 72–73
Dickel, Friedrich, 3
Diehn, Ewald, 115
Dönhoff, Marion, 13
Dregger, Alfred, 160
Dresden, political demonstrations in, 101–02, 108–10
Dumas, Roland, 178

Eastern Europe, 69–99, 250; delegitimation of communist leadership in, 70–71; détente as stabilizing force in, 72–73; economic and humanitarian aid for, 264–67; GDR's resistance to democratic change in, 76–81, 90–93; Gorbachev's permissive policies toward, 69, 73–76, 83–84; managing contemporary transition in, 261–63; reforms in Hungary and Poland, 74–76, 85–90; Soviet troop cuts in, 53, 84. *See also* Czechoslovakia; Hungary; Poland
East Germany. *See* German Democratic Republic (GDR)
Economic conditions: in Federal Republic of Germany, 25; in German Democratic Republic, 11, 20, 22–23, 79, 170–72; in unified Germany, 225, 230–33, 243–44
Egypt, 58
Eichmann, Adolf, 16
Elbe, Frank, 138, 163, 176, 178
Emigration from German Democratic Republic, 32, 78, 82, 88, 100, 130, 171; through Czechoslovakia, 96–99, 100–02; through Hungary, 92–93, 96; Protestant church's stance against, 95, 102
Engelhardt, Heinz, 229
England. *See* Great Britain
Enzensberger, Hans Magnus, 206, 207

Eppelmann, Rainer, 216
Erhard, Ludwig, 25
Eureka program, 65
Euromissiles, 18, 29, 30, 46
European Act, 61
European bank, 154, 159, 211, 212
European Coal and Steel Community, 57
European Commission, 160–61, 221, 234
European Community (EC), 250; in con-
    temporary Europe, 255–58; German uni-
    fication and, 159–61, 211–12, 221;
    rejuvenation of, in 1980s, 60–64, 68, 154;
    as security institution, 255; as single
    market, 236; stagnation of, in 1970s,
    59–60; tacit integration of GDR into, 23;
    trade disputes with United States,
    257–58
European Defense Community, 58
European Economic Community (EEC),
    57, 58, 59. See also European Commu-
    nity (EC)
European Free Trade Association (EFTA),
    233, 256
European integration, 56–68, 233–36;
    French–German relations and, 65–68;
    German unification, relationship to, 154,
    210–13, 233; Maastricht treaty on,
    233–36, 245; post–World War II steps
    toward, 56–60; rejuvenation of EC in
    1980s, 60–64; U.S. role in, 56–57,
    64–65, 251–53
European Monetary System, 60, 61, 154,
    159, 211, 234
European Parliament, 63, 221, 234
European Strategic Program for Research
    and Development in Information Technol-
    ogies, 64
European Strategy Steering Group, 213

Falin, Valentin, 218
Fassbinder, Rainer Werner, 17
Federal Republic of Germany (FRG),
    13–19; Adenauer's incorporation of right
    wing in, 14–15; channeling of left-wing
    energies in, 15–16; economic conditions
    in, 25; economic strains between United
    States and, 60; foreign policy of, 24, 25,
    26, 29; France, relations with, 58–59, 61,
    65–68; GDR, relations with, 24, 25–26,
    29, 83; nuclear angst of, 35–37, 52; nucle-
    ar restraint of, 47–48; political system of,

16–18; Sonderweg (special path) of, 18–19;
    tensions in, before unification, 170–72.
    See also German Democratic Republic
    (GDR); German unification; Germany,
    postunification; Kohl, Helmut
Fischer, Gudrun, 115
Fischer, Oskar, 97, 135, 144
France: European integration and, 234–35;
    FRG, relations with, 58–59, 61, 65–68;
    on German unification, 153, 154, 156–61,
    211–13; in NATO, 59, 65–66, 220; nucle-
    ar policy, 65–67; treatment of terrorists,
    16. See also Mitterand, François; Two
    plus four plan
Frederick the Great, 27
Free Democratic party (FRG), 202, 247
FRG. See Federal Republic of Germany
    (FRG)
Fricke, Karl Wilhelm, 103
Friedmann, Bernhard, 52

Gaddis, John Lewis, 188
Gates, Robert, 165–66, 167, 213
Gauck, Joachim, 230
GDR. See German Democratic Republic
    (GDR)
General Agreement on Tariff and Trade,
    257
General Political Guidelines of 1986
    (NATO), 40, 52
Genscher, Hans-Dietrich, 28, 137; confer-
    ences with Soviets on unification,
    217–18; emigration of GDR citizens wit-
    nessed by, 97–98; on nuclear missile
    deployments, 33–35, 38, 52, 162; plan for
    German unification by, 173–76, 189, 223;
    predictions of social disruption in GDR
    by, 84; role of, in European Community
    rejuvenation, 60–64; two plus four nego-
    tiations and, 178, 181, 182–83, 185
Gerasimov, Gennady, 156
German character, 13, 15, 17, 18–19, 202
German Democratic Republic (GDR),
    20–32; abuses of power in, 140–42, 201,
    227–30; costs of postwar communist rule
    in, 70–71; democratic reforms initiated
    in, 8–12, 127–29, 130–32; disintegration
    of SED party control in, 6–8, 170–72;
    dissidents in, 82–83, 96; economic condi-
    tions in, 11, 20, 23, 79, 170–72; emigra-
    tion from (see Emigration from German

Democratic Republic); FRG, relations with, 24, 25–26, 29, 83; Honecker era in, 20, 21–32, 77–84, 90–93; national identity of, 26–28; nuclear angst of, 28–32; Protestant church, 22, 87, 93–99, 108–09, 114–19; resistance to Eastern European reforms, 76–81; rigged elections in, 87; Soviet Union, relations with, 20, 30–32, 81–84; travel restrictions, 82, 96–97, 101, 127, 130–32. See also Federal Republic of Germany (FRG); German unification; Germany, postunification; Socialist Unity (SED) party (GDR); Stasi security agency

German unification, 5, 12, 134–39, 153–224; British response to, 153, 154, 156–61, 210–11; Conference on Security and Cooperation in Europe and, 190–91; European Community and, 159–61; European integration and, 154, 210–13, 233–36; French response to, 153, 154, 156–61, 211–13; FRG's initial stance on, 23–26; FRG's internal politics and, 182–83; GDR citizens' attitudes toward, 135–37; GDR election upset and, 197–201, 212; GDR's initial stance on, 23–26; Genscher plan for role of NATO and, 173–76, 189, 223; Kohl's position on, 137–38, 148, 154–56, 171–72, 182–83, 214–15; left-wing resistance to, 134, 201–09; NATO membership following, 168, 173–75, 179, 182–83, 186–90, 195, 203, 204, 215–16, 222; Polish boundary and, 192–96, 212, 218, 223; Soviet position on, 135–36, 153, 155–56, 171, 184–88, 215–24; tensions before, 170–72; timing of, 183–84; two plus four plan for, 176–82; U.S. position and role in, 138–39, 153, 154, 161–69. See also Two plus four plan

Germany, postunification, 225–48; consensus creation in, 248; east-west gaps in, 243–46; economic problems of, 225, 231–33, 243–44; election agreements, 223–24; European integration and, 233–36; governance of, 226–27; problem of collaborators with GDR regime, 227–30; right-wing and left-wing alienation in, 245–46; security and foreign policy in, 236–43; violence in, 225–26, 245; voter-political elite division in, 246–47;

U.S. partnership with, 253–54, 268–69
Giscard d'Estaing, Valery, 61
Globke, Hans–Maria, 14
Gorbachev, Mikhail, 19, 250; arms control negotiations, 46–50; on Eastern Europe's economic crisis, 72; effect of German unification on, 176–77, 214, 230; GDR Politburo's meeting with, 106–08; on German unification, 135, 155–56, 159–60, 167, 171, 178, 214–15, 221–22; Honecker, relationship with, 81–84, 122–24; on opening of Berlin border, 5; permissive policies of, in Eastern Europe, 69, 73–76, 83–84. See also Soviet Union
Götting, Gerald, 8
Grass, Günter, 205, 208, 229
Great Britain, 4; European integration and, 61, 62, 234–35; response to German unification, 153, 154, 156–61, 210–11. See also Thatcher, Margaret; Two plus four plan
Green party (FRG), 17, 44, 62, 203, 205
Green party (GDR), 145, 199
Greiner, Ulrich, 207, 246
Grosz, Karoly, 75
Group of Seven, 220–21
Gulf War, 238–41
Gysi, Gregor, 81, 144

Habsburg, Otto von, 189
Hackenburg, Helmut, 117
Hager, Kurt, 78, 82
Hahn, Reinhardt O., 104
Haig, Alexander, 64
Halbritter, Walter, 149
Hallstein Doctrine, 25, 26
Harmel report, 59
Hattenhauer, Katrin, 118
Havel, Vaclav, 76, 78
Havemann, Robert, 11, 22
Helsinki Final Act of 1975, 60, 72, 77, 190, 262
Hempel, Johannes, 102
Herger, Wolfgang, 104
Hermlin, Stephan, 208
Heym, Stefan, 11, 241
Hitler, Adolf, 13, 42
Hoffmann, Stanley, 188
Höfner, Ernst, 9
Honecker, Erich, 20–32, 76–84, 90–93; fall from political power, 9, 11, 102–08,

120–22, 163; foreign policy of, 23–26, 31–32; on German unification, 163; Gorbachev, relationship with, 81–84, 122–24; on nuclear threat to GDR, 26, 28, 31; political, social, and economic policies of, 20–23, 27; resistance to reforms in Eastern Europe, 76–81; support for China, 10, 111; on travel and emigration, 96–98; trial of, 228
Honecker, Margot, 9, 127
Howard, Michael, 41
Human rights, 72, 77, 190, 262; violations of under GDR regime, 227–30
Hungary: cost of communist rule in, 71; democratic and economic reforms in, 74–75, 76, 85, 87–90; economic problems in, 72, 73; emigration of GDR citizens through, 92–93, 190
Huntington, Samuel, 189

IMES firm, weapons sales by, 140–42
Independent Women's Association, 145, 199
INF. See Intermediate-range nuclear forces (INF)
INF Treaty, 34, 39, 50, 53
Initiative Peace and Human Rights, 145
Intermediate-range nuclear forces (INF), 28, 31, 38–39, 50–54; arms control negotations, 39–41, 44–48; effect on East-West relations, 33–35; French support for deployment of, 65
Iraq, 140, 239, 240, 246
Israel, 200, 218–19, 240
Italy, 159, 181

Jakes, Milos, 131
Janka, Walter, 9–10, 11
Jaruzelski, Wojciech, 85, 87, 196
Jaspers, Karl, 15
Jonas, First Deputy Mayor, 142–43

Kadar, Janos, 74
Kähler, Christoph, 7
Keller, Dietmar, 11
Kennan, George, 188
Kessler, Heinz, 109
KGB security agency: fall of Berlin Wall and, 3, 5; role of, in Honecker's downfall, 126
Khrushchev, Nikita, 58, 71, 82
Kiefer, Anselm, 17

Kissinger, Henry, 35, 53
Kleiber, Erich, 111
Knauer, Gerd, 125
Koch, Peter, 149
Kochemasov, Vyacheslav, 78, 121, 124
Kohl, Helmut, 5, 29–30, 131; European Community rejuvenation and, 60–64; on European integration and Maastricht treaty, 233–36; on GDR elections, 197–98; on nuclear missiles and arms control, 28–30, 44, 49–50, 52, 65; on Polish boundary dispute, 193–95; on unification, 137–38, 148, 154–56, 171–72, 182–83, 214–15, 221–22; unification, political effect on, 202–03
Kovacs, Maria, 85–87
Krenz, Egon, 91, 144, 159; on border openings, 131, 133; overthrow of Honecker and, 102–08, 120–22; reform policies of, 2, 6–7, 127–28, 131–32; response to political demonstrations, 111, 113, 117, 119, 120; support for China, 10, 111; on unification, 135, 136
Krolikowski, Werner, 92, 123
Kryuchkov, Vladimir, 126
Kühirt, Theo, 118

Lafontaine, Oskar, 196, 198, 204, 206, 212
Lance missiles, 52, 55, 162, 237
Lange, Bernd-Lutz, 116
Left-wing politics: in FRG, 15–16; gap between right and, in unified Germany, 245–46; resistance to unification, 134, 201–09
Legal system, postunification, 226
Leipzig, political demonstrations in, 7–8, 85, 108, 114–20
Leuze, Ruth, 16
Lévy, Bernard-Henri, 211
Liberal party (FRG), 59, 202
Liberal party (GDR), 8, 144, 145, 199
Ligachev, Egor, 221
Lippelt, Helmut, 246
Löffler, Kurt, 111–12
Lorenz, Siegfried, 102–08
Lukacs, György, 9
Luther, Martin, 27

Maastricht treaty, 233–36, 245
McNamara, Robert, 35
Maron, Monika, 244

Marshall Plan, 57, 249–50
Masur, Kurt, 116–17
Mauriac, François, 57
Mazowiecki, Tadeusz, 89, 194, 196
Mearsheimer, John, 189
Meckel, Markus, 119, 218, 220
Meyer, Kurt, 117, 119
Michelis, Gianni de, 181
Mielke, Erich, 91–92; authorization of counterrevolutionary violence by, 113; imprisoning of, 143; investigation of, by parliament, 9, 11, 131; overthrow of Honecker and, 102–08, 122, 126; trial of, 228
Military: postunification German, 227; response of four-power, to opening of Berlin border, 2–3; response of Soviet, to GDR political demonstrations, 119–20; Soviet troop cuts in Eastern Europe, 53, 84, 181, 218, 222; troops in postunification Europe, 181, 216, 218, 220, 222–23, 242–43; U.S. troops in Europe, 175, 218, 223, 242
Mitscherlich, Alexander, 15
Mitscherlich, Margarete, 15
Mittag, Günter, 11, 92, 103, 106, 108, 111, 122
Mitterrand, François: on European integration, 154, 235; FRG, relations with, 65; on German-Polish boundary dispute, 196, 212; on German unification, 154, 158–60, 211–12; rejuvenation of European Community and, 60–64
Modrow, Hans, 6, 10, 106, 123, 144; on border openings, 133; dialog with demonstrators, 108–10; meeting with James Baker, 169; naming of, as GDR prime minister, 131; obstruction of attempts to control Stasi, 147–49; strains on, in final days of GDR, 170–72; on unification, 135, 137; visit to FRG, 192
Moens, Alexander, 153
Moïsi, Dominique, 158
Momper, Walter, 4
Monnet, Jean, 57
Müller, Heiner, 208
Mutual and Balanced Force Reduction talks, 53

National Democratic party (FRG), 15, 202
National Democratic party (GDR), 145

National People's Army (NVA), 3, 112, 216, 227
National Security Council, U.S., on German unification, 164–67, 177, 181, 182–83, 184
NATO, 188–90, 258–61; Brussels summit, 54–55; and Eastern European nations, 261–62; France's status in, 59, 65–66, 220; General Political Guidelines of 1986, 40, 52; Genscher plan, 175–76, 189, 223; German postunification membership in, 168, 173–75, 179, 182–83, 186–87, 195, 203, 204, 215–19, 222; German unification and, 180–81, 213, 216–18; missile deployments, 18, 29, 30, 39, 45, 52; nuclear deterrence policy and role of, 36, 37, 38–39, 51; postunification role of, 242, 255, 258–60
Naumann, Klaus, 238
Neo–Nazism, 149
New Forum party (GDR), 8, 10, 96, 97, 101, 114, 145; resistance to unification by, 134
Nikolai Church, Leipzig, 7, 8, 87, 97, 111, 114
Nixon, Richard, administration of, 60
North Atlantic Cooperation Council, 267
Nuclear deterrence concept, 35–36
Nuclear missiles, 29–30, 33–55; antinuclear movement, 17, 28, 41–43, 203–04; arms control agreements and, 39–41, 44–46, 50–54, 237–38; French policy on, 65–67; German angst over, 28–30, 35–37, 41–43, 52; NATO deployment of, 18, 29, 30, 39; public opinion on deployment of, 41–43; short–range, 50–54; Soviet deployment of, 37–39, 43–44; Strategic Defense Initiative, 46–48; superpower summits on, 48–50, 54–55; as superpower threat, 28–30, 50–54; unification agreement on, 224. See also Intermediate-range nuclear forces (INF)
Nuclear Planning Group, 59

Oberdorfer, Don, 124
O'Brien, Conor Cruise, 258
Office for National Security (AfNS), 142, 147–52. See also Stasi security agency
Ohnesorg, Benno, 15
Organization for Economic Cooperation and Development, 57

Parliament (GDR), 8–12, 199
Party of Democratic Socialism (GDR), 144, 199, 244
Peace movement, 17, 28, 41–43, 203–04; German versus American, 42–43
Perle, Richard, 44, 45
Pershing missiles, 29–30, 39, 41
Poland: boundary dispute with West Germany, 192–96, 212, 218, 223; costs of communist rule in, 70–71; democratic and economic reforms in, 75–76, 85, 87–90, 190; economic problems of, 72, 73
Politburo, Socialist Unity party, 2, 7, 91–93; plot in, to overthrow Honecker, 102–08, 120–22, 123; resignation and reformation of, 131, 142
Pommert, Jochen, 117
Popieluszko, Jerzy, 76
Portugal, 256
Portugalov, Nikolai, 135
Pozsgay, Imre, 85, 87
Protestant church (GDR): democratic reform process, 07, 93–99, Honecker's relations with, 22; role in nonviolent demonstrations, 108–09, 114–19; stance on emigration from GDR, 95

Quadripartite Agreement of 1971, 23–24

Rauch, Christian, 27
Reagan, Ronald, administration of, 162; INF nuclear missile controversy and, 34, 40, 41, 44–46; rejuvenation of European Community and, 60, 64–65; Strategic Defense Initiative (SDI) of, 46–50, 53
Reinhold, Otto, 98
Republican party (FRG), 202–03
Reykjavik summit, 48–50, 51
Ridgway, Rozanne, 162
Ridley, Nicholas, 157
Right-wing politics: gap between left and, in unified Germany, 245–46; incorporation into FRG politics, 14–15; violence, 225–26, 245
Rogers, Bernard W., 40
Romania, 11
Ross, Dennis, 162, 176, 178
Rostropovich, Mstislav, 5
Roundtable (GDR), 109, 171; confrontation with Stasi, 146–52; establishment and role of, 145–46

Rummel, Susanne, 116

Safire, William, 53
Sakharov, Andrei, 49, 78
Schabowski, Günter, 10, 127, 128; border crossings opened by, 1, 2, 131–33; on GDR's relations with Soviets, 81; on period before Honecker's fall, 90–91, 93; overthrow of Honecker and, 102–08, 120–21
Schalck-Golodkowski, Alexander, 141–42
Schäuble, Wolfgang, 226, 244
Schily, Otto, 246
Schirrmacher, Frank, 208–09
Schmidt, Helmut, 28, 246; on nuclear missile deployments, 38–39; support for European Monetary System, 61
Schmidt, Max, 136
Schneider, Peter, 205, 207
Schnitzler, Karl Eduard von, 134
Schnur, Wolfgang, 201
Schorlemmer, Friedrich, 100
Schröder, Richard, 94, 207, 230
Schuman, Robert, 57
Schwanitz, Wolfgang, 142, 144
Scowcroft, Brent, 162, 163, 164
SED. See Socialist Unity (SED) party (GDR)
Seebacher–Brandt, Brigitte, 205
Seiters, Rudolf, 133
Seitz, Raymond, 213
Shevardnadze, Eduard, 84, 123, 138, 165; on German unification, 155–56, 178, 187, 213–14, 217–20
Shultz, George, 64
Sindermann, Horst, 8, 9
Single European Act of 1985, 62
Skubiszewski, Krzysztof, 196
Sloterdijk, Peter, 206
Snyder, Jack, 189
Social Democratic (SPD) party (FRG), 16, 174, 202; GDR elections of 1990 and, 198; on NATO membership and German rearmament, 203; nuclear policy of, 29, 65; Socialist Unity party, relations with, 25–26, 205; on unification, 83, 137, 183, 203–06
Social Democratic (SPD) party (GDR), 96, 145, 247; in elections of 1990, 197–201; on unification, 137
Socialist party (France), 62, 65

Socialist Unity (SED) party (GDR), 90–93; challenges to leadership of, by church, 127; disintegration and reform of, 6–8, 144–46; entrenched rule of, 76–81; Politburo (see Politburo, Socialist Unity party); Social Democrat party, relations with, 25–26

Socialist Workers party (Hungary), 75, 85

Solidarity trade union (Poland), 71, 75–76, 87, 88, 190

Sonderweg (special path), 18–19

Soviet Union: arms control negotiations of, 48–49, 53, 54–55; collapse of, 237; democratic reforms in, 87, 88; economic and humanitarian aid for former, 264–67; effect of German unification in, 176–77; failed coup in, 11, 236–37; GDR, relations with, 20, 30–32, 81–84; on German unification, 135–36, 153, 155–56, 215–24; Honecker's downfall and, 122–26; missile deployment, 31, 37–39, 43–44; nuclear deterrence concept and, 35–37; permissive policies in Eastern Europe, 69, 73–76, 83–84; response to fall of Berlin Wall, 5; response to political demonstrations in GDR, 119–20; U.S.-European dispute over Europe's trade with, 64–65; U.S. policy toward, 165–66. See also Gorbachev, Mikhail; Two plus four plan

Spain, 159, 256

SPD. See Social Democratic (SPD) party (FRG); Social Democratic (SPD) party (GDR)

Stalin, Joseph, 23, 25

Stalinism, in GDR, 23

Stasi security agency, 79–81; abuses by, 201; collaborators with, 228–30; concern of, over disintegration of GDR, 103–05; plans to suppress counterrevolution, 112–13; destruction of sensitive files by, 131, 142; fall of Berlin Wall and, 3, 5; investigations of, 9, 131, 228–30; offices occupied by citizens, 142–44; overthrow of Honecker and, 103–05, 124–26; repression of demonstrators by, 107; roundtable confrontation and taming of, 146–52; terrorism by, 151, 152

State Department, U.S., on German unification, 164–67, 176–78, 180, 218

Status of Forces Agreement, U.S.–Germany, 242

Sterzinsky, Georg, 95

Stockholm Agreement, 74

Stolpe, Manfred, 169, 227, 230

Stoltenberg, Gerhard, 182, 216, 223

Stoph, Willi, 9, 103, 121, 133

Strategic Arms Limitation Treaty (SALT I), 37, 40

Strategic Arms Limitation Treaty (SALT II), 38, 40, 215

Strategic Arms Reduction Treaty of 1991, 237

Strategic Defense Initiative (SDI), 46–50, 53

Strauss, Franz Josef, 15, 52, 141, 174

Summits, superpower: NATO, in Brussels, 54–55; NATO, in London and Houston, 220–21; U.S.-Soviet, in Malta, 167; U.S.-Soviet, in Reykjavik, 48–50, 51; U.S.-Soviet, in Washington, 215–21

Süskind, Patrick, 207, 209

Tarasenko, Sergei, 217, 218

Teltschik, Horst, 135–36, 163, 179, 214, 222

Terrorism, 16; Stasi-sponsored, 151, 152

Thatcher, Margaret: on arms control and nuclear missile deployment, 49; on European integration and trade, 61, 62, 64, 154; on German–Polish boundary dispute, 196; on German unification, 154, 156–57. See also Great Britain

Tisch, Harry, 121, 127, 228

Tito, Josip Broz, 71

Treaty of Cooperation (France-Germany), 58–59

Treaty of Rome, 62

Tsipko, Aleksandr, 124

Two plus four plan, 176–82, 213–18, 223–24; Conference on Security and Cooperation in Europe and, 178, 190–91; German membership in NATO and, 179, 182–83, 186–87, 195; NATO–Warsaw Pact relations and, 180–81, 216–18; Poland and, 195–96; Soviet–German declarations on, 179–80, 217–18; Soviet internal politics and, 176–77; Soviet policy toward, 184–88, 215–24; U.S. State Department's and National Security

Council's positions on, 176–77, 180, 181, 182–83, 184, 218

Ulbricht, Walter, 21, 22, 25, 123
Ullman, Wolfgang, 146
Unification. *See* German unification
United Left party (GDR), 96, 145
United States: CSCE and, 169, 190–91, 261–63; economic strains between FRG and, 60; European integration and, 56–57, 64–65, 255–58; Europe's postunification security and, 251–53, 254–55, 258–63; INF controversy and, 34, 41–46, 48, 51–55; management of new European order and, 251–53, 263–68; nuclear deterrence concept and, 35–37, 38; peace movement in, 42–43; policy toward Soviet Union, 165–66, 185–86; post–World War II role of, 249–50; Strategic Defense Initiative (SDI) of, 46–50, 53; unified Germany, relations with, 253–54, 268–69
United States, German unification and, 138–39, 153, 154, 161–69; Bush administration policy, 153–54, 162–64, 167–69, 173, 215; in Gulf War, 239–41; National Security Council's and State Department's positions, 164–67, 176–78, 180, 181, 182–83, 184, 218; two plus four plan, 176–82. *See also* Two plus four plan
United Workers' party (Poland), 89

Vietnam War, 59
Vogel, Hans-Jochen, 183
Vogel, Wolfgang, 97, 227
Voigt, Karsten, 174
Volkskammer (GDR), 8–12, 199

Walesa, Lech, 75, 85, 89, 195
Wallace, William, 68
Walser, Martin, 207
Walters, Vernon, 163
Warsaw Treaty Organization, 39, 71, 177: German unification and NATO relationship to, 180–81, 216–17; invasion of Czechoslovakia by, 74
Wehner, Herbert, 246
Weimar Republic, 13
Weinberger, Caspar, 45
Weizsäcker, Richard von, 214, 247
Wenders, Wim, 17
Western European Union (WEU), 57, 58, 66, 67
West Germany. *See* Federal Republic of Germany (FRG)
Wolf, Christa, 207, 208
Wolf, Markus, 103, 126, 227
Wolfowitz, Paul, 262
Wolle, Stefan, 124–25
Wollenberger, Vera, 230
Wörner, Manfred, 182, 221
Wötzel, Roland, 117
Writers' Union (GDR), 11, 95

Yeltsin, Boris, 238
Yilin, Yao, 111
Yugoslavia, 11, 71; war in, 238, 241–42, 246, 259–60, 262, 263

Zelikow, Philip, 165, 213
Ziemer, Christof, 102, 108
Zimmermann, Peter, 114, 116, 117, 118
Zoellick, Robert, 138; on German unification, 161–62, 163, 164, 166–67, 176, 178